FAIRY TAIL

フェアリーテイル

22

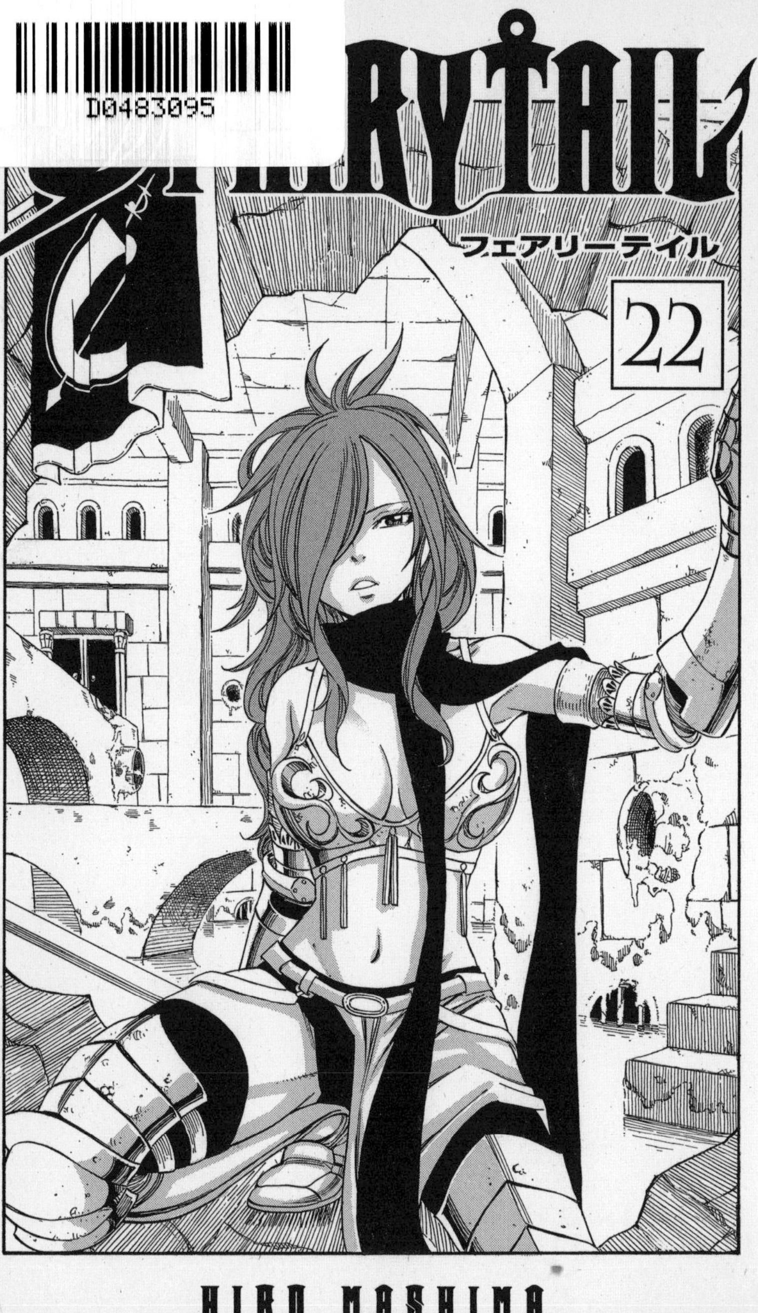

HIRO MASHIMA

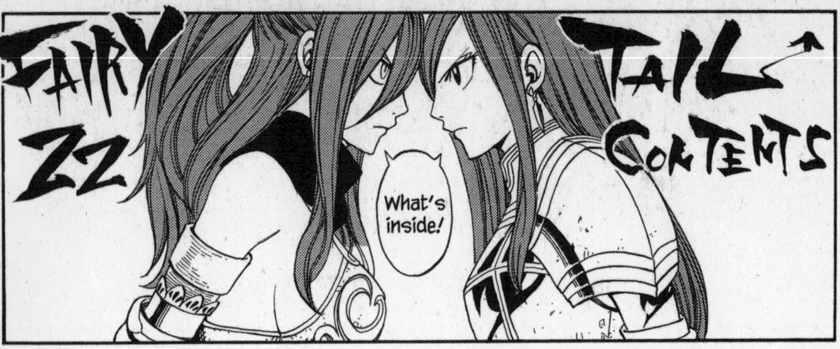
FAIRY TAIL
22
CONTENTS
What's inside!

Published in serial form in Weekly Shônen Magazine 2010 Volumes 19 - 28

FAIRY TAIL

フェアリーテイル

Chapter 179, Code ETD

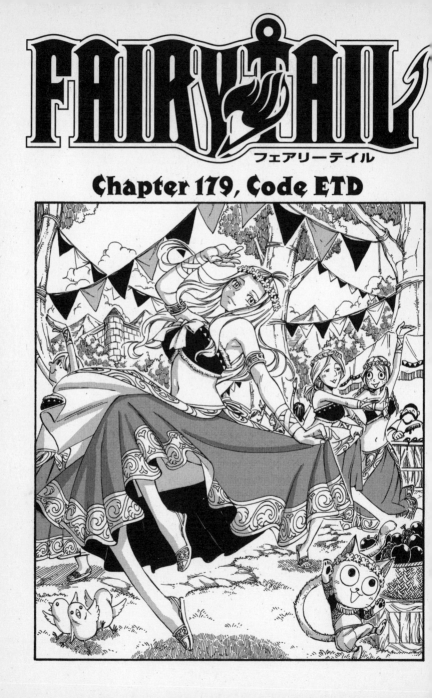

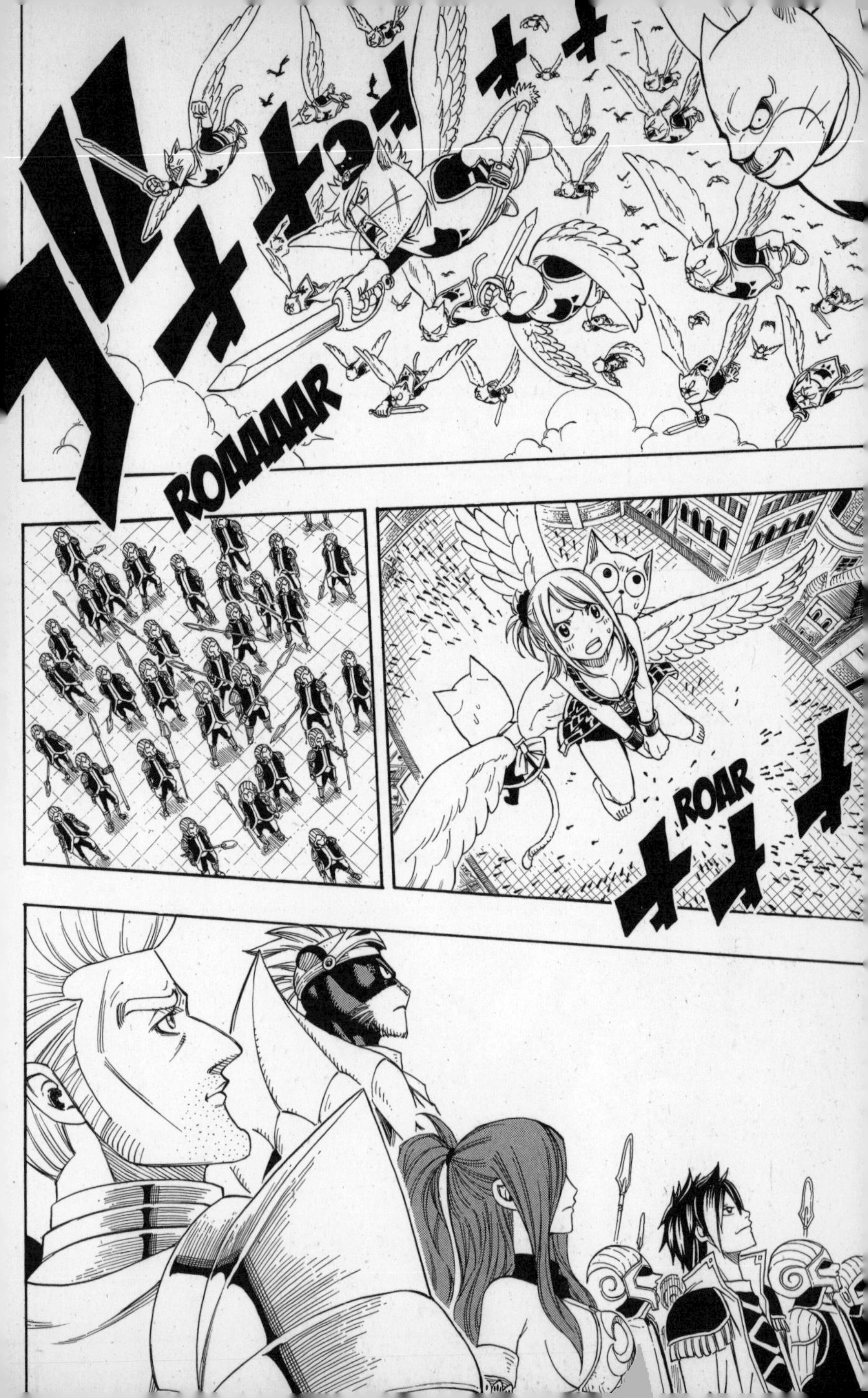
ROAAAAR
ROAR

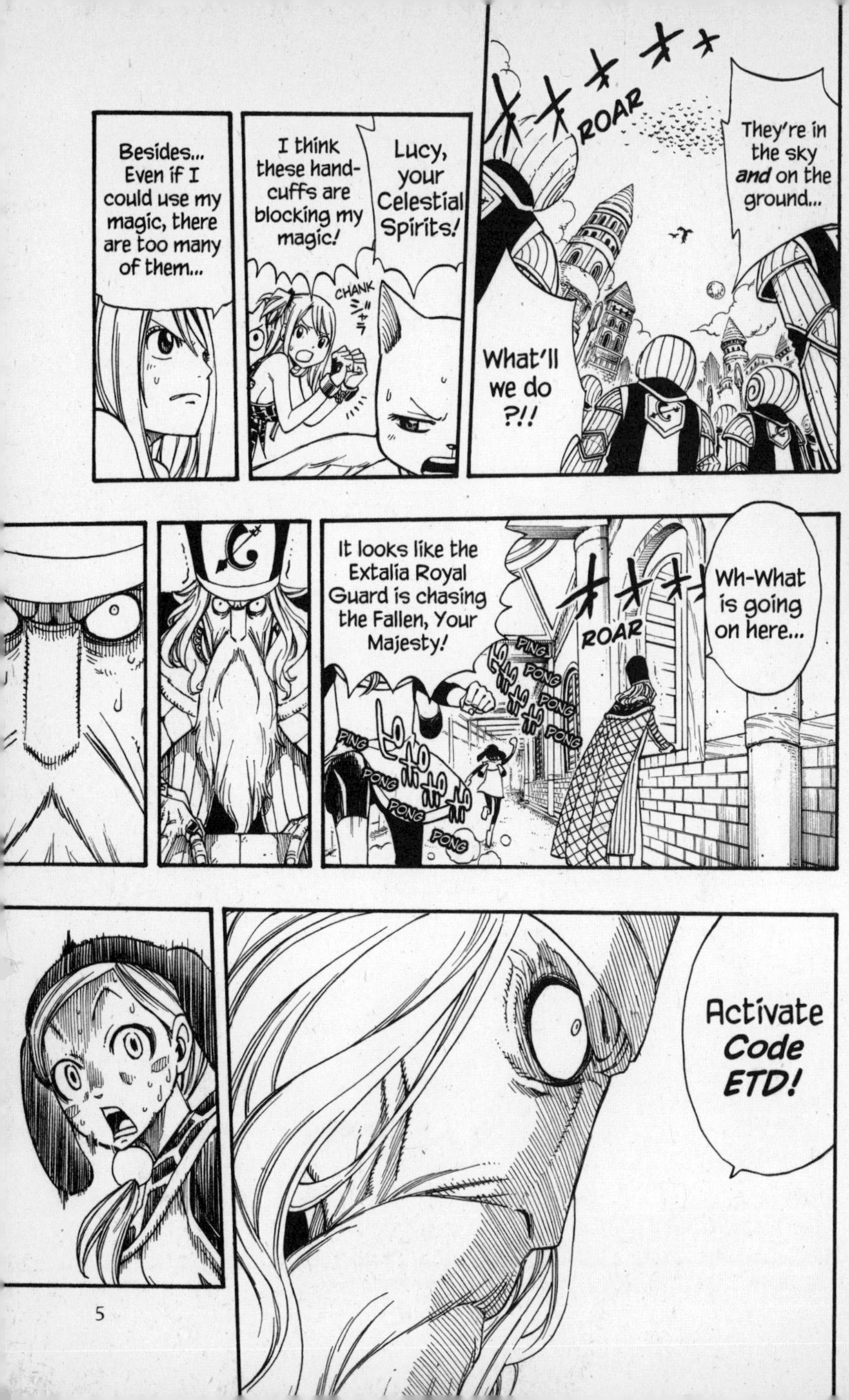
ROAR
They're in the sky *and* on the ground...
What'll we do ?!!
Lucy, your Celestial Spirits!
I think these hand-cuffs are blocking my magic!
CHANK
Besides... Even if I could use my magic, there are too many of them...
Wh-What is going on here...
ROAR
It looks like the Extalia Royal Guard is chasing the Fallen, Your Majesty!
PING PONG PONG PONG
PING PONG PONG PONG
Activate *Code ETD!*

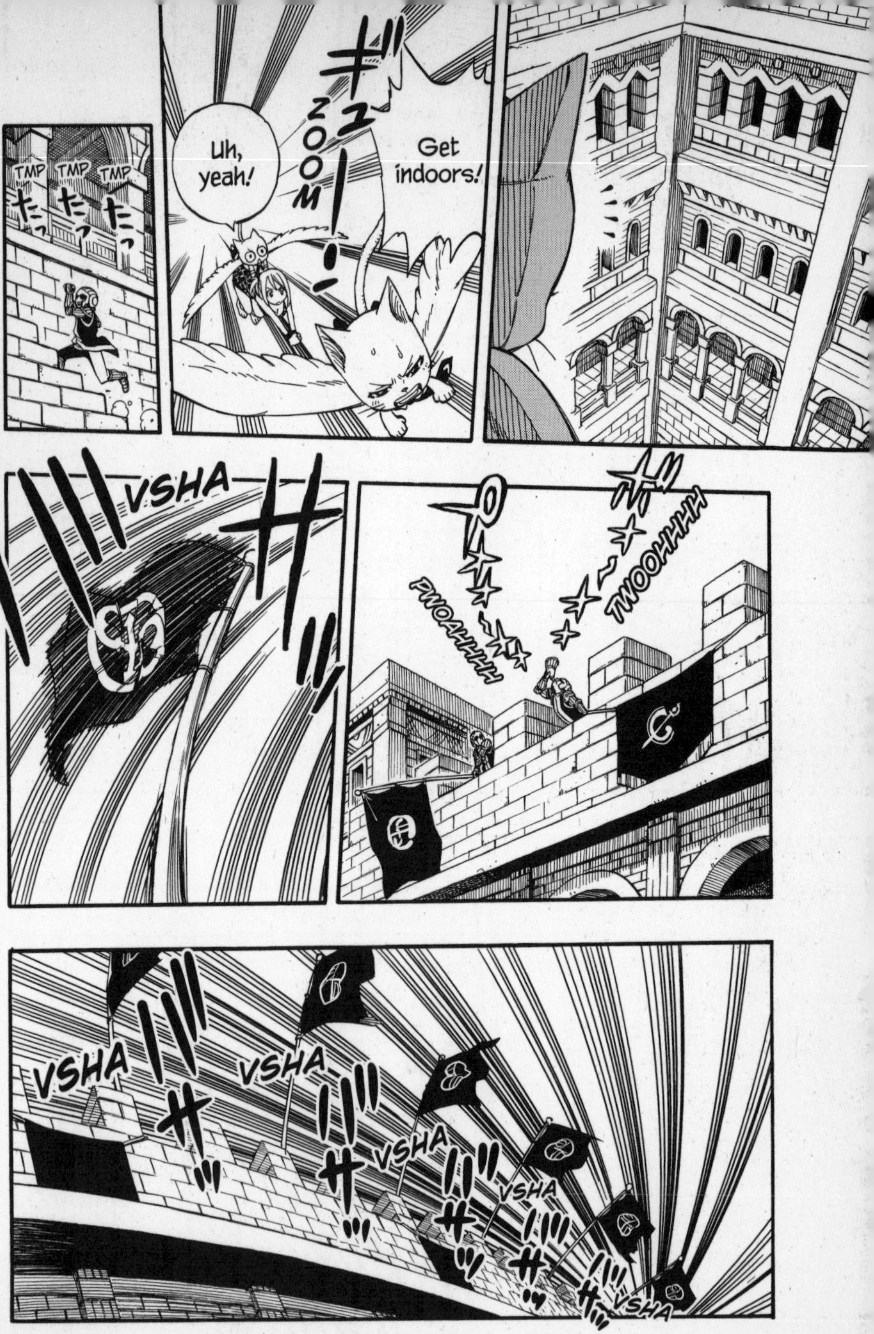
Get indoors!
ZOOOM
Uh, yeah!
TMP TMP TMP
TWOOHHHH
PWOAHHHH
VSHA
VSHA
VSHA
VSHA
VSHA
VSHA

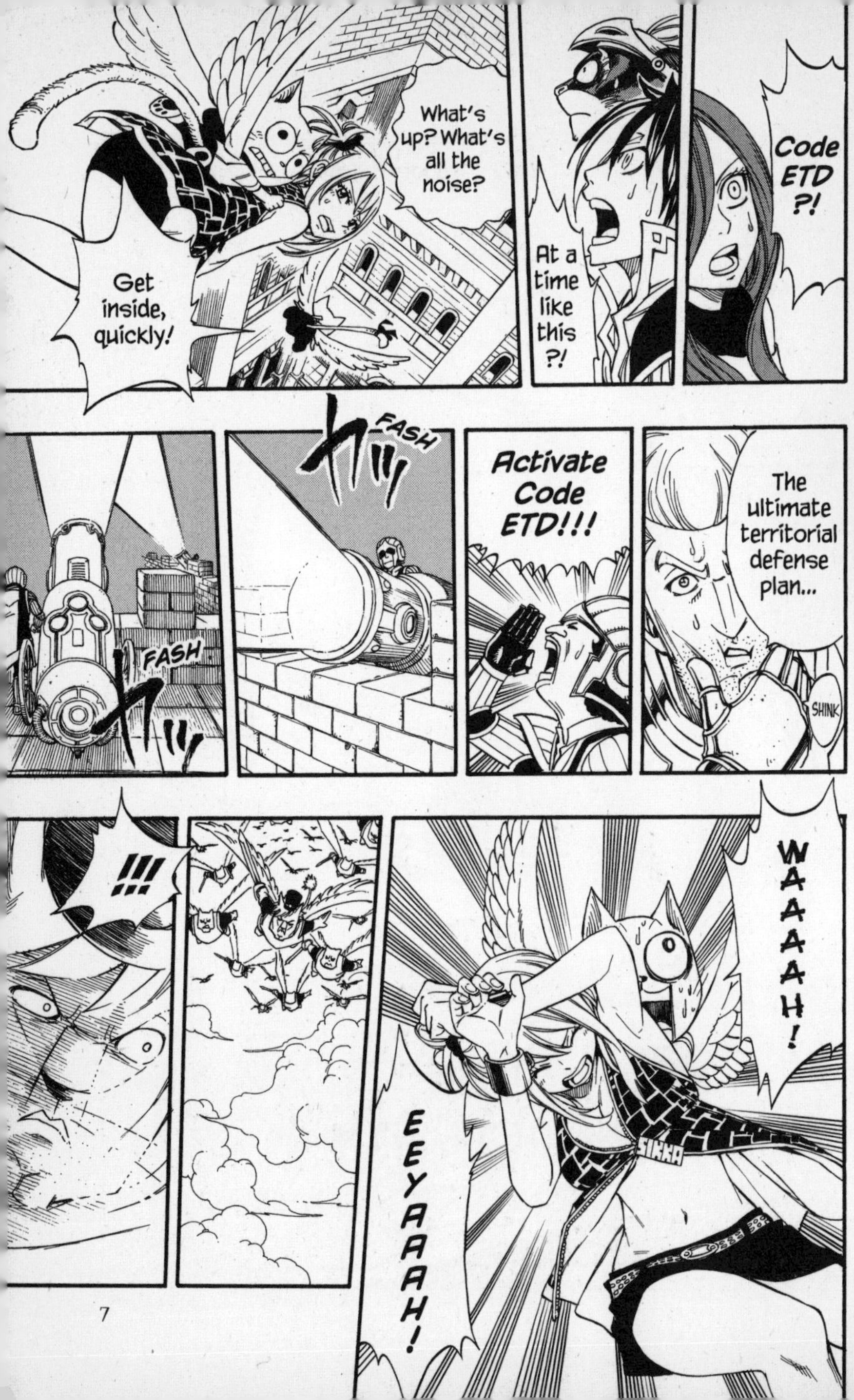
Code ETD ?!
At a time like this ?!
What's up? What's all the noise?
Get inside, quickly!
The ultimate territorial defense plan...
SHINK
Activate Code ETD!!!
FASH
FASH
WAAAAAH!
EEYAAAAAH!
!!!

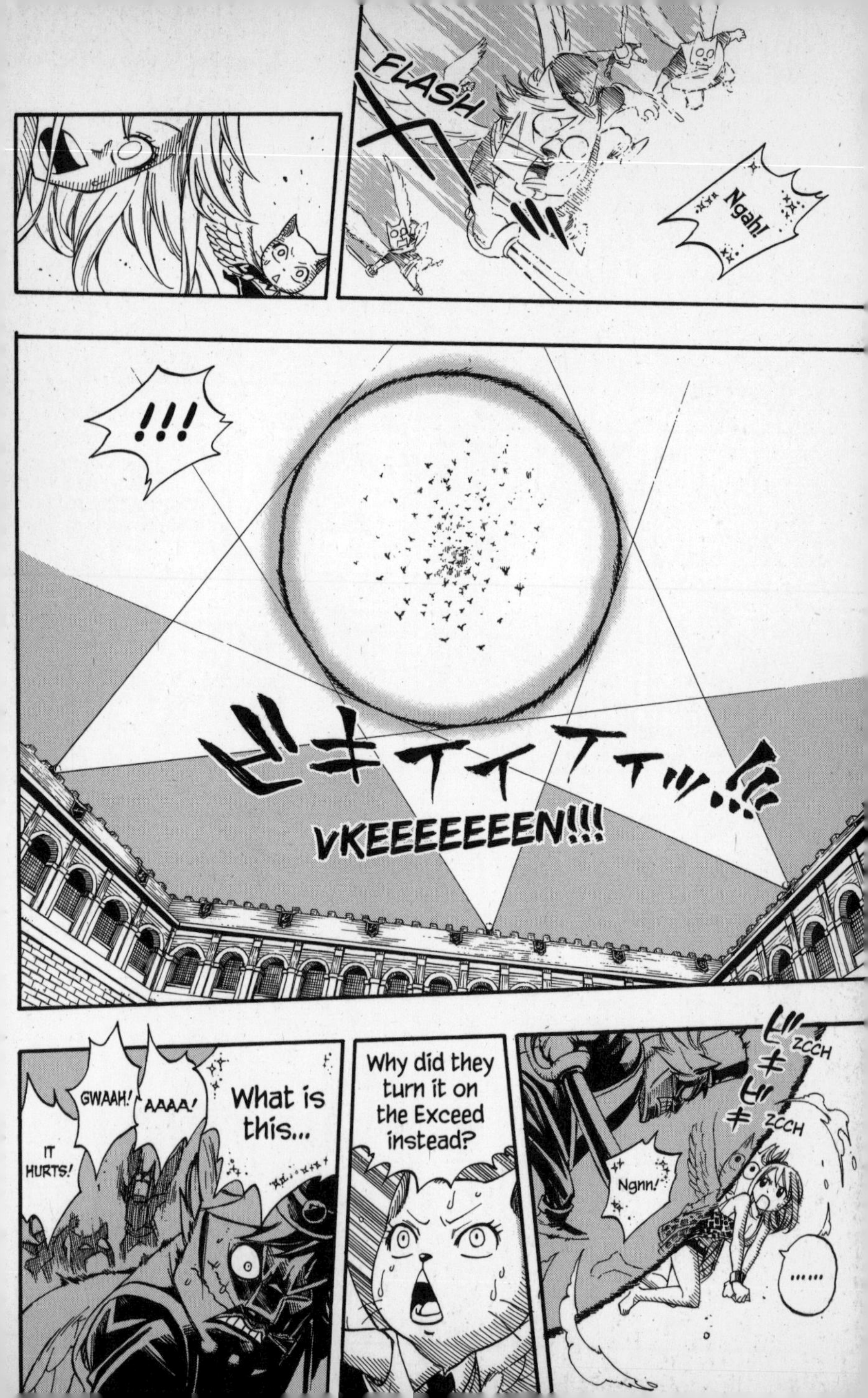
FLASH
Ngah!
!!!
VKEEEEEEEEN!!!
ZCCH
ZCCH
Ngnn!
......
Why did they turn it on the Exceed instead?
What is this...
AAAA!
GWAAH!
IT HURTS!

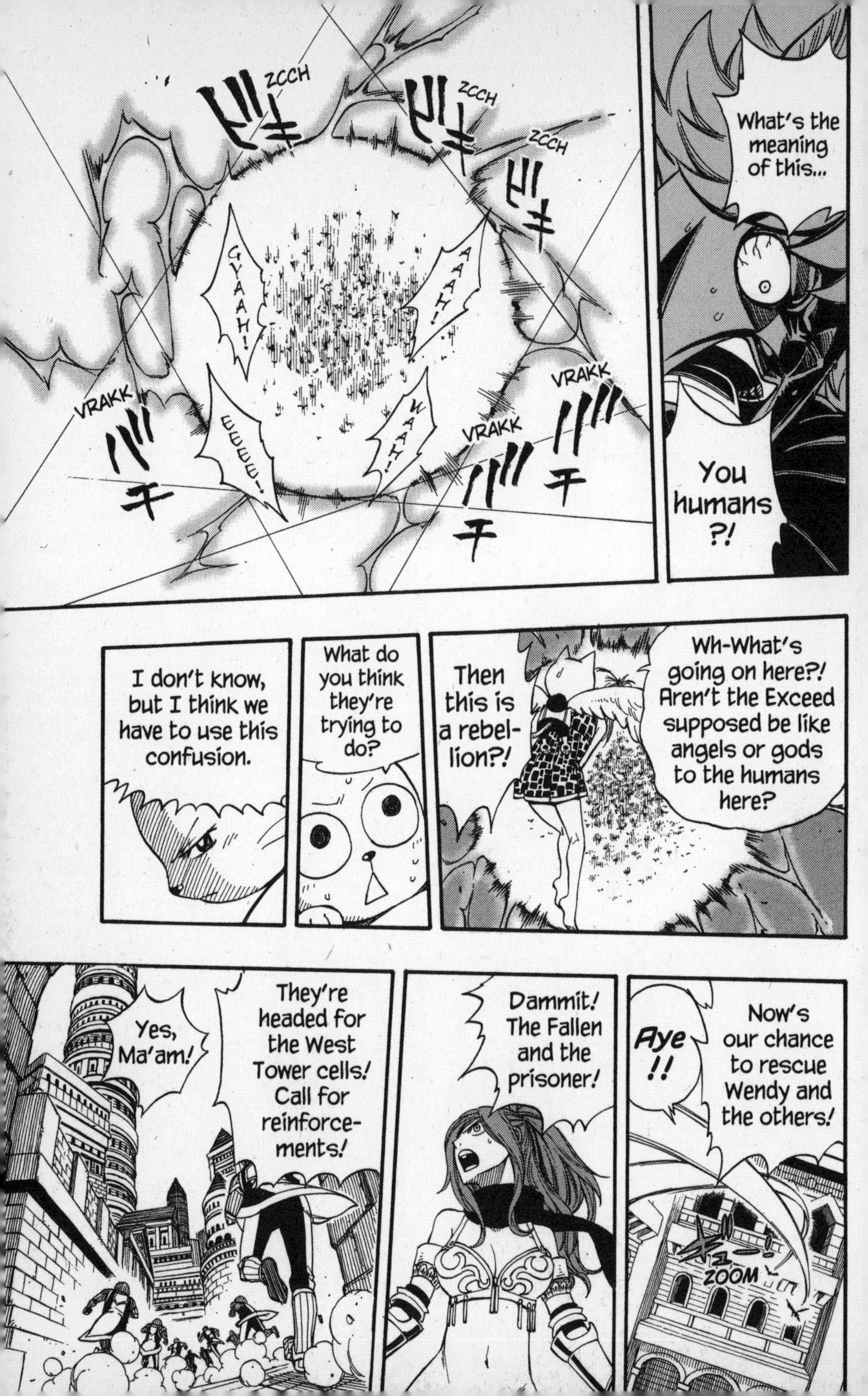
What's the meaning of this...
You humans ?!
ZCCH
ZCCH
ZCCH
AAAH!
GYAAH!
VRAKK
WAAH!
VRAKK
EEEEE!
VRAKK
Wh-What's going on here?! Aren't the Exceed supposed be like angels or gods to the humans here?
Then this is a rebellion?!
What do you think they're trying to do?
I don't know, but I think we have to use this confusion.
Now's our chance to rescue Wendy and the others!
Aye !!
ZOOM
Dammit! The Fallen and the prisoner!
They're headed for the West Tower cells! Call for reinforcements!
Yes, Ma'am!

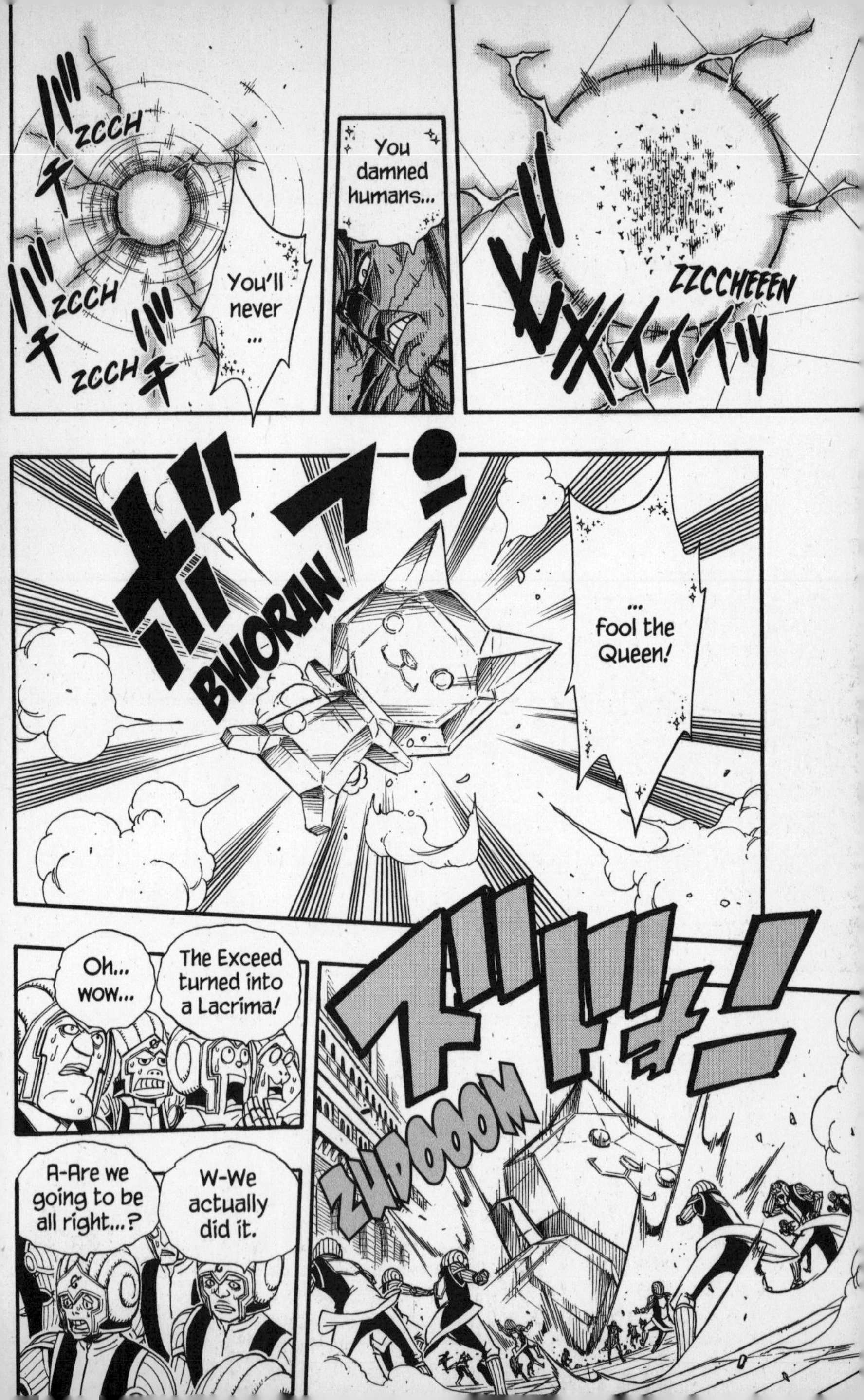
ZZCCHEEEN
You damned humans...
ZCCH
ZCCH
ZCCH
You'll never ...
... fool the Queen!
BWORAN
ZUDOOOM
The Exceed turned into a Lacrima!
Oh... wow...
W-We actually did it.
A-Are we going to be all right...?

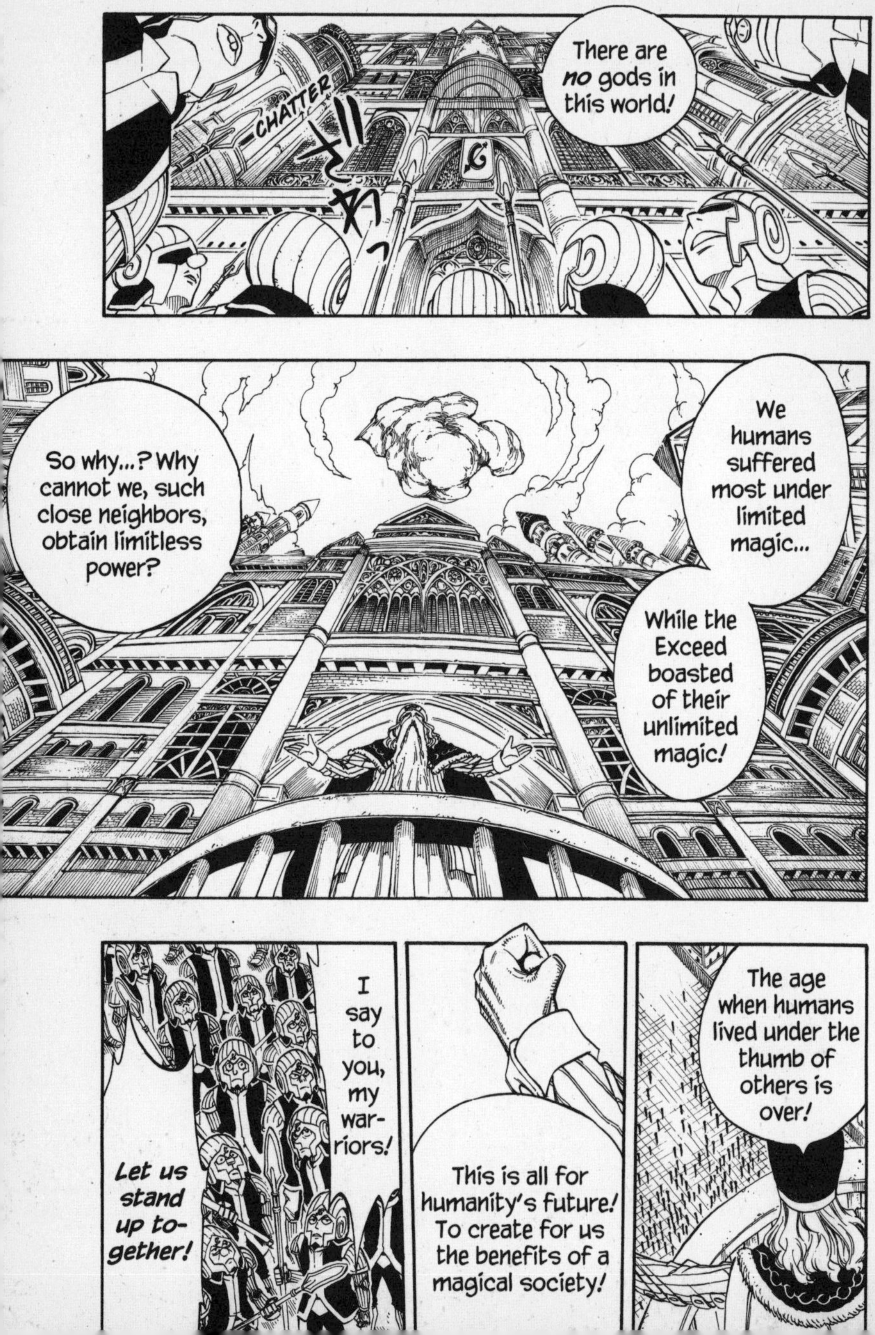

There are *no* gods in this world!
CHATTER
We humans suffered most under limited magic...
While the Exceed boasted of their unlimited magic!
So why...? Why cannot we, such close neighbors, obtain limitless power?
The age when humans lived under the thumb of others is over!
This is all for humanity's future! To create for us the benefits of a magical society!
I say to you, my warriors!
Let us stand up together!

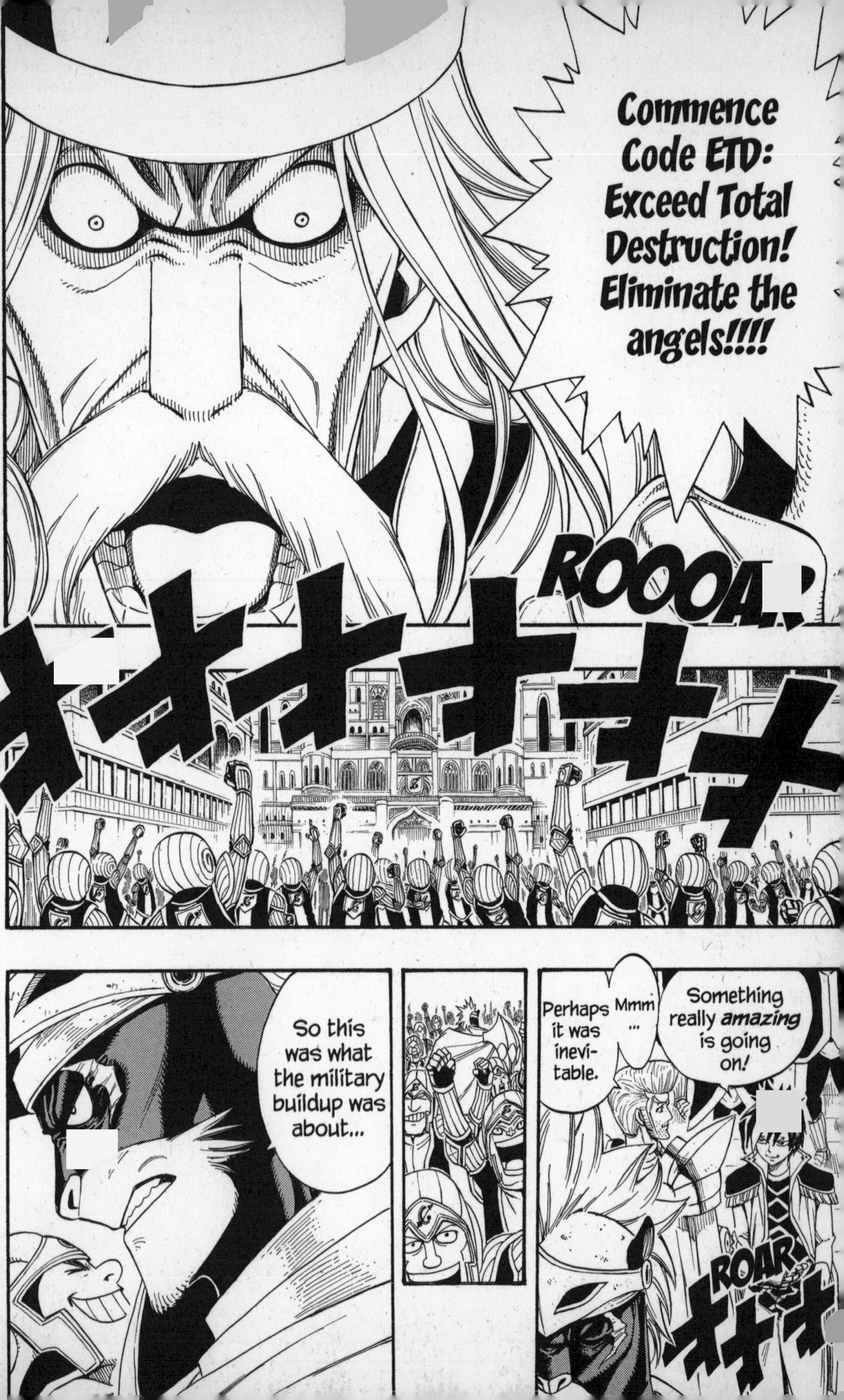
Commence Code ETD: Exceed Total Destruction! Eliminate the angels!!!!
ROOOAR
Something really *amazing* is going on!
Mmm...
Perhaps it was inevitable.
ROAR
So this was what the military buildup was about...

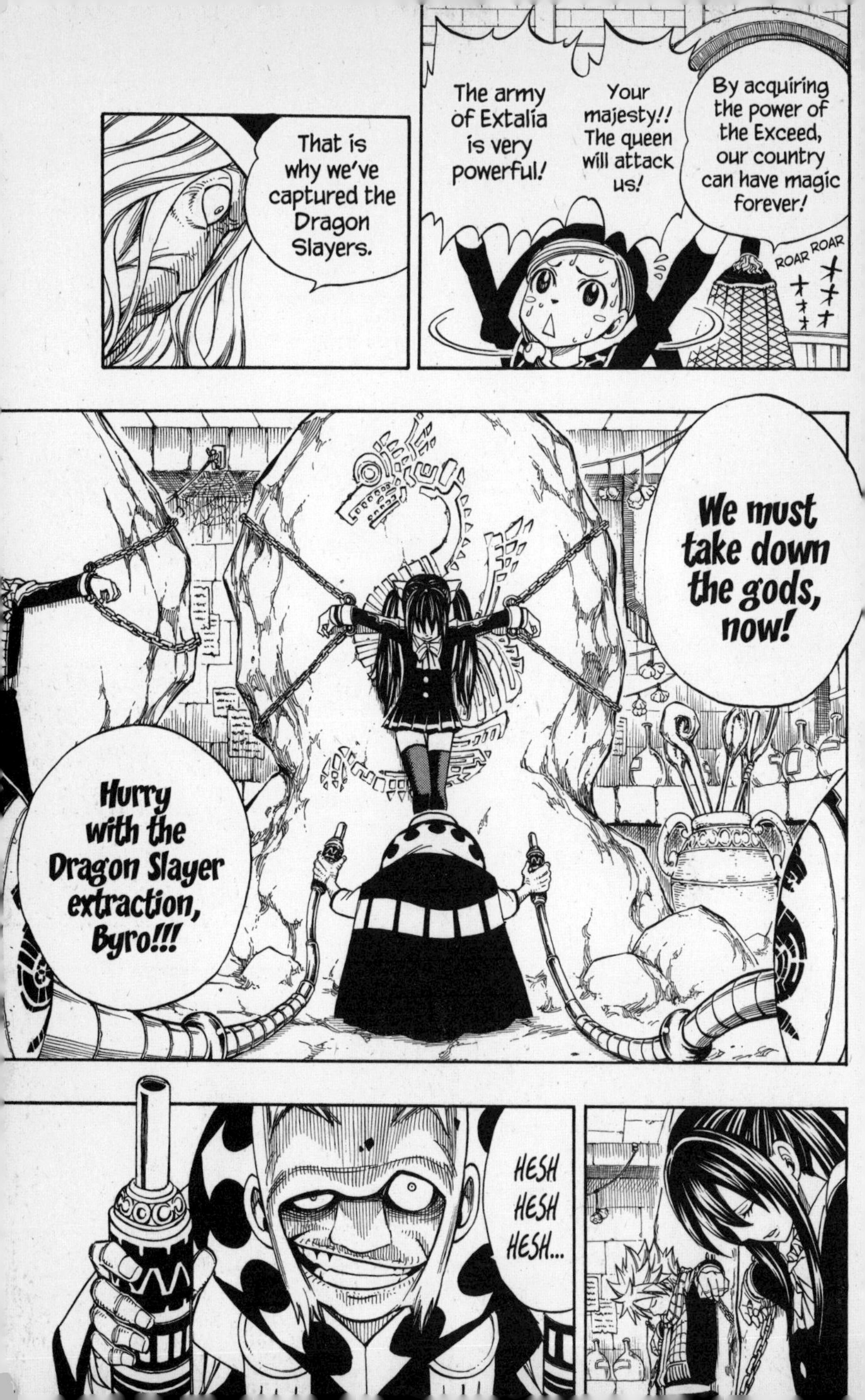
By acquiring the power of the Exceed, our country can have magic forever!
Your majesty!! The queen will attack us!
The army of Extalia is very powerful!
ROAR ROAR
That is why we've captured the Dragon Slayers.
We must take down the gods, now!
Hurry with the Dragon Slayer extraction, Byro!!!
HESH HESH HESH...

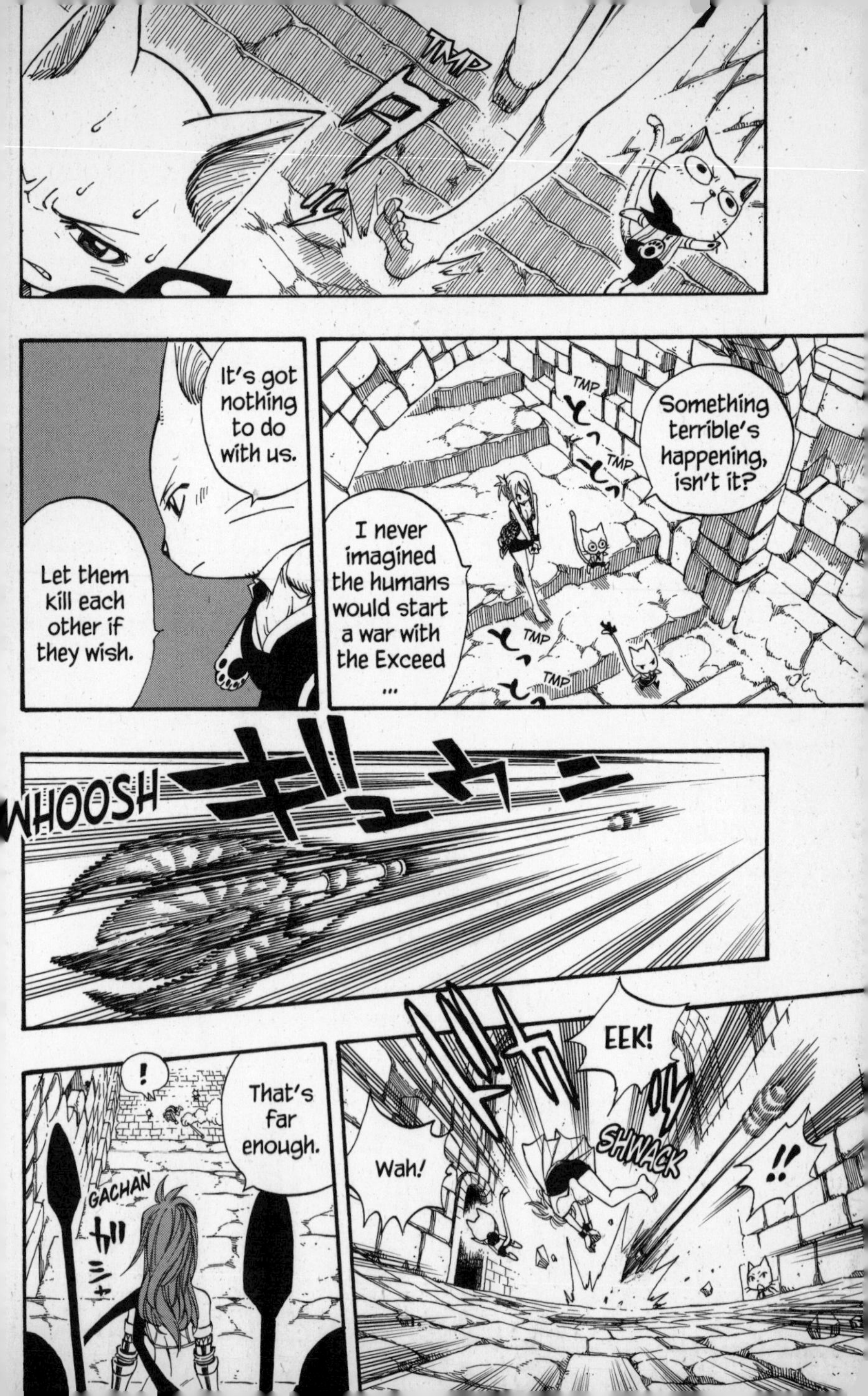
TMP
TMP
Something terrible's happening, isn't it?
TMP
I never imagined the humans would start a war with the Exceed ...
TMP
TMP
It's got nothing to do with us.
Let them kill each other if they wish.
WHOOSH
EEK!
SHWACK
!!
Wah!
!
That's far enough.
GACHAN

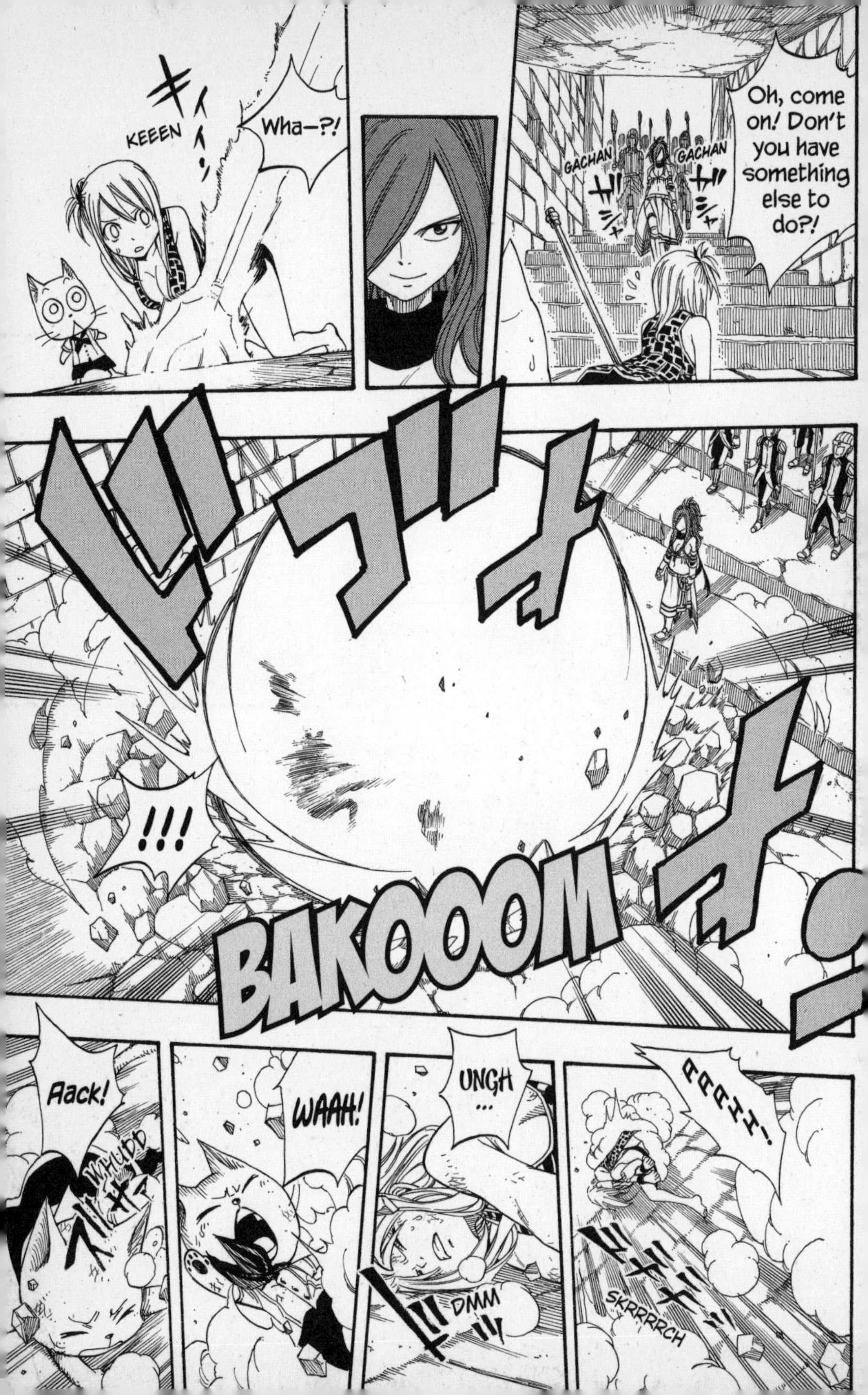
GACHAN
GACHAN
Oh, come on! Don't you have something else to do?!
Wha-?!
KEEEN
BAKOOOM
!!!
AAAHH!
SKRRRRCH
UNGH ...
DMM
WAAH!
Aack!
WHUDD

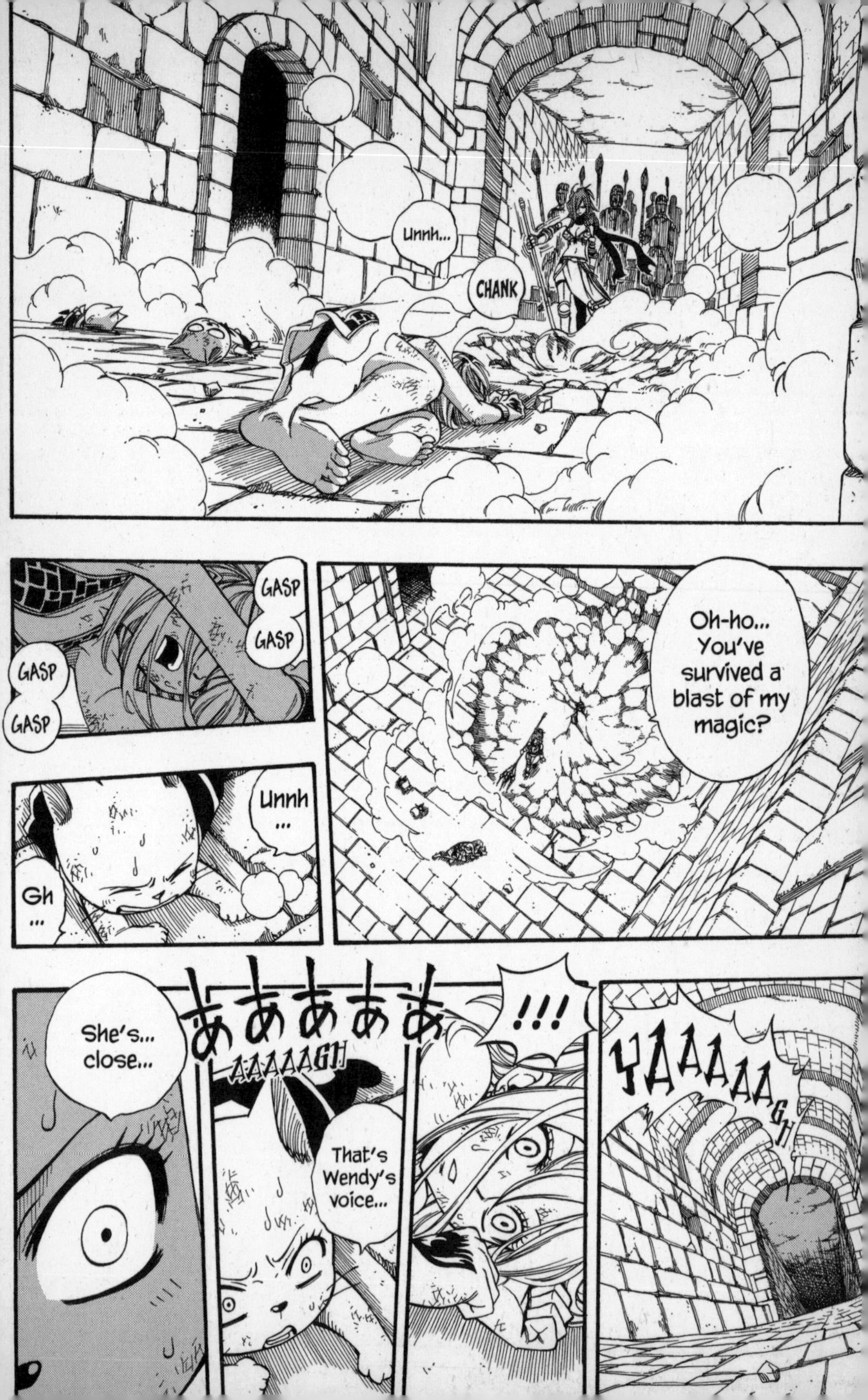

Unnh...
CHANK
Oh-ho... You've survived a blast of my magic?
GASP
GASP
GASP
GASP
Unnh...
Gh...
YAAAAAAGH
!!!
ああああああ
AAAAAAGH
That's Wendy's voice...
She's... close...

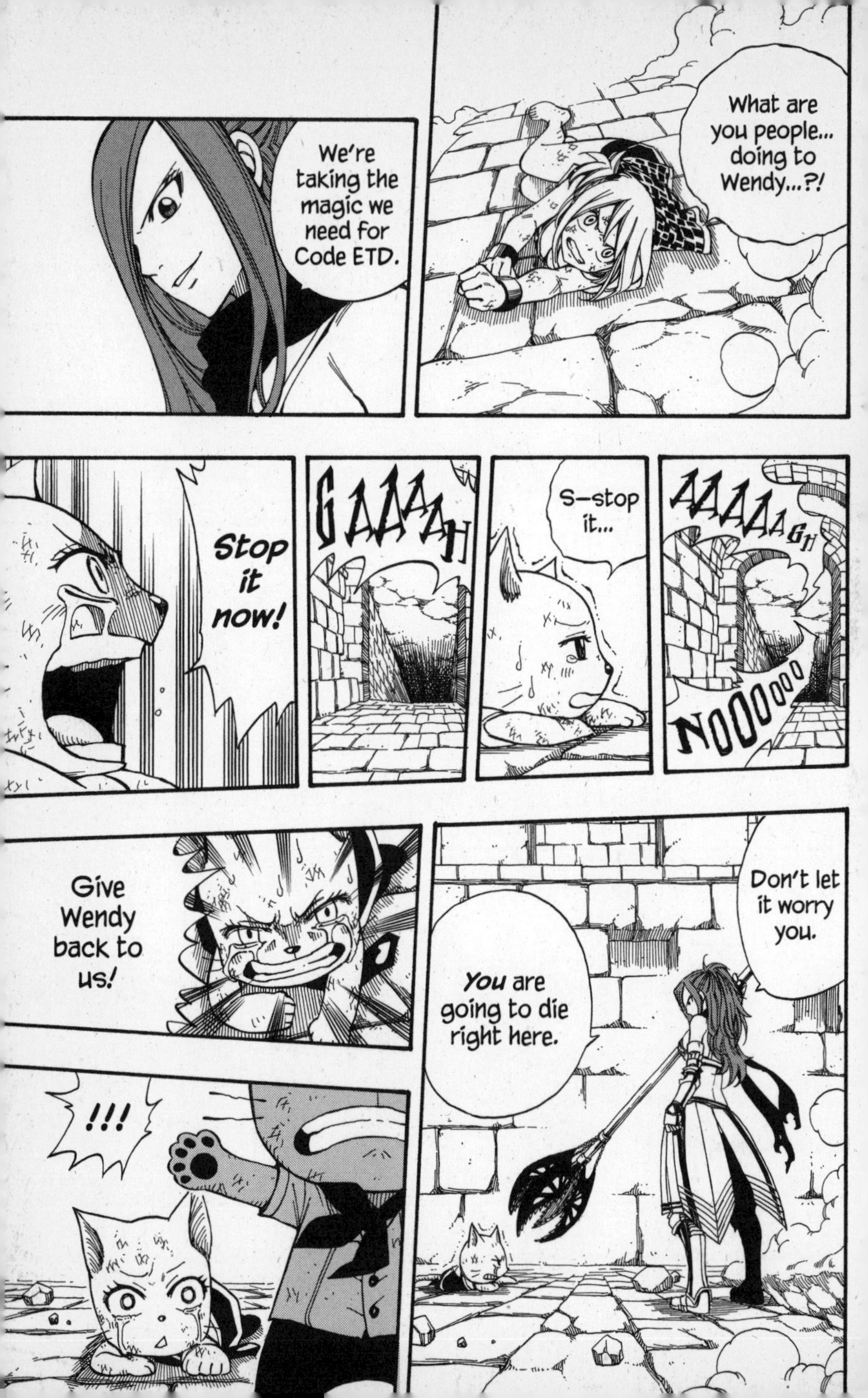
What are you people... doing to Wendy...?!
We're taking the magic we need for Code ETD.
AAAAAAGH
NOOOooo
S—stop it...
GAAAAAH
Stop it now!
Don't let it worry you.
You are going to die right here.
Give Wendy back to us!
!!!

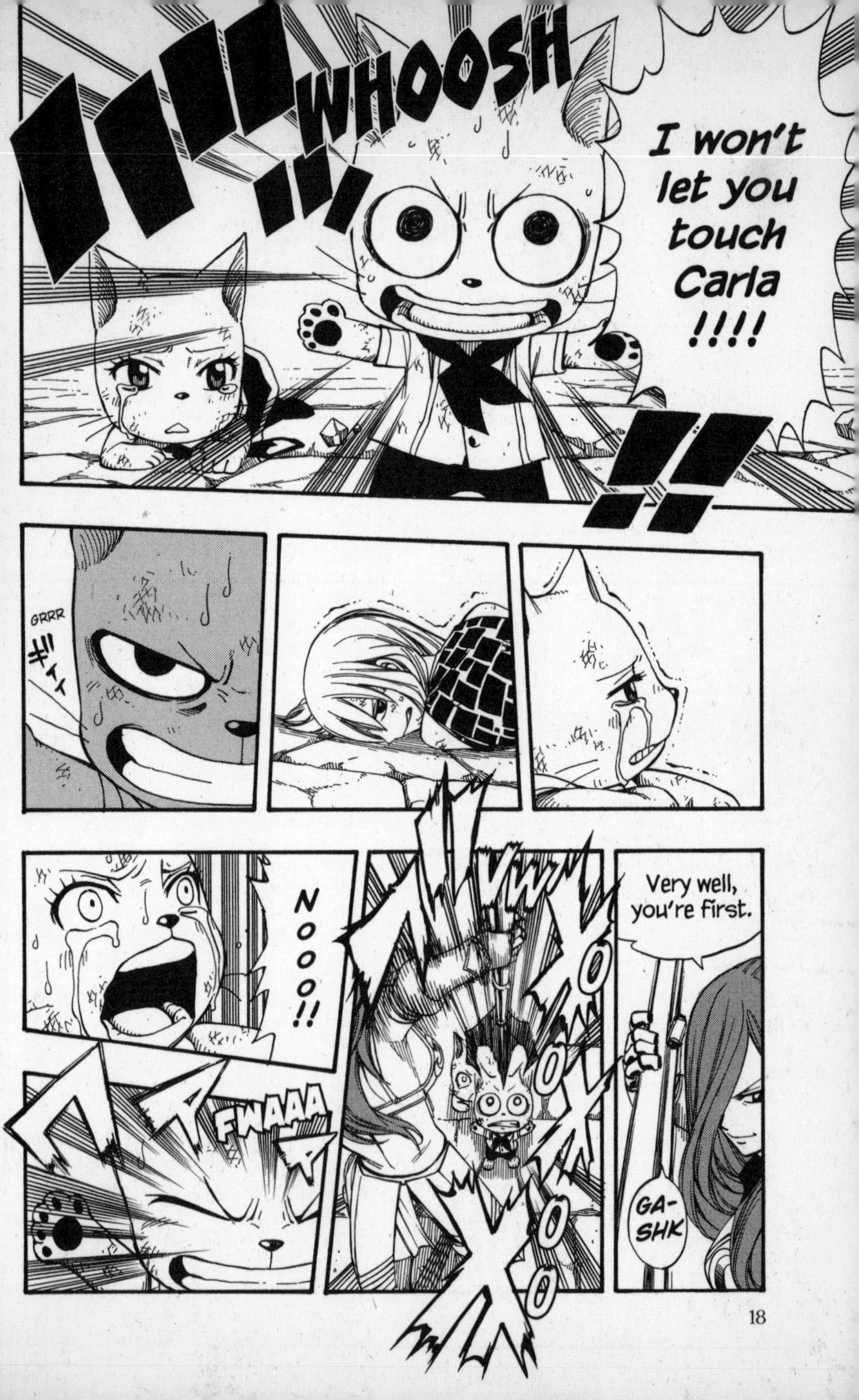

WHOOSH
I won't let you touch Carla !!!!
!!
GRRR
ギィィ
Very well, you're first.
GA-SHK
NOOOO!!
FWAAA

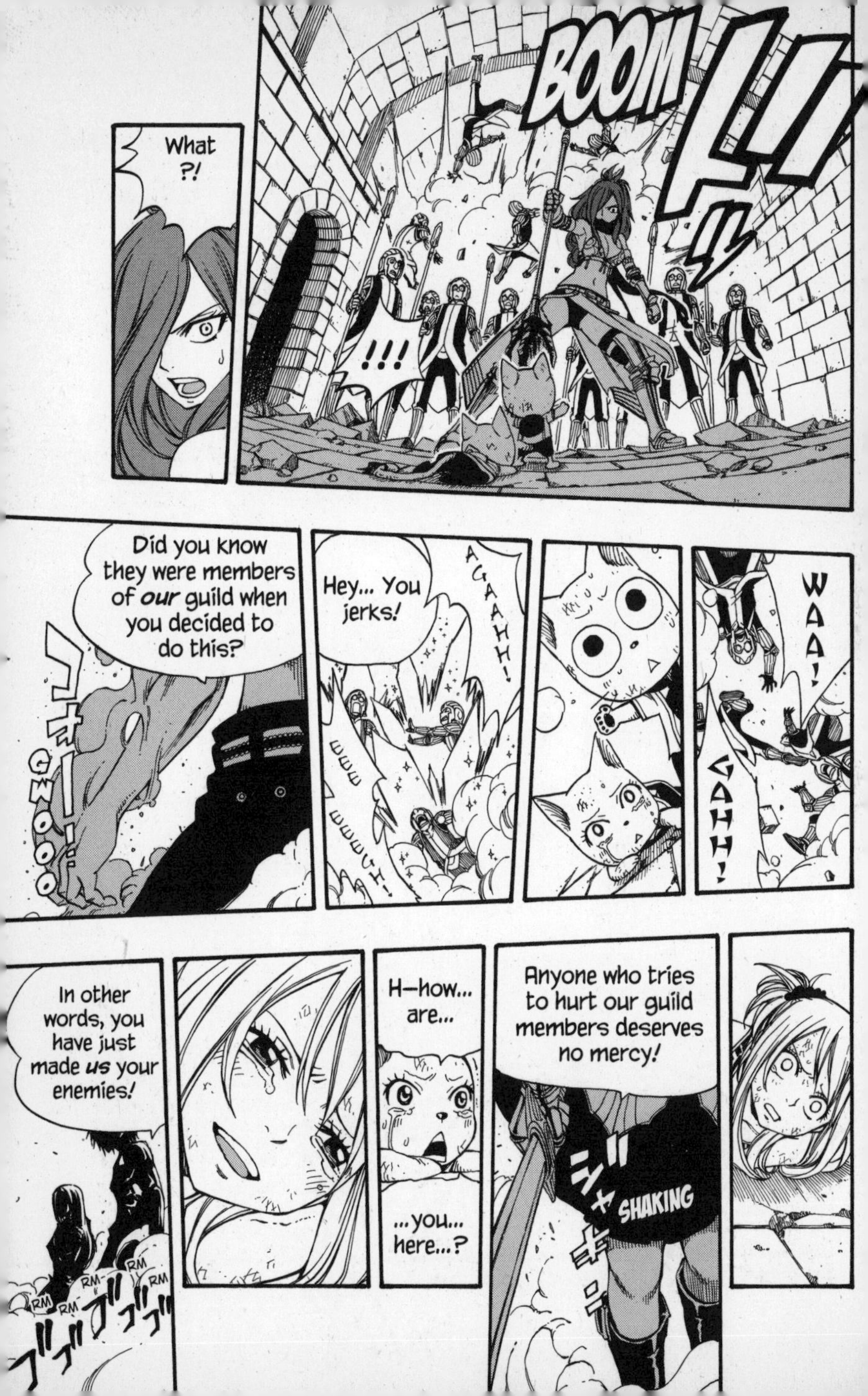
BOOM
What?!
!!!
WAA!
GAHH!
Hey... You jerks!
AGAAHH!
WWWWUGH!
Did you know they were members of *our* guild when you decided to do this?
GWOOOO
Anyone who tries to hurt our guild members deserves no mercy!
SHAKING
H—how... are...
...you... here...?
In other words, you have just made *us* your enemies!
RM RM RM RM RM

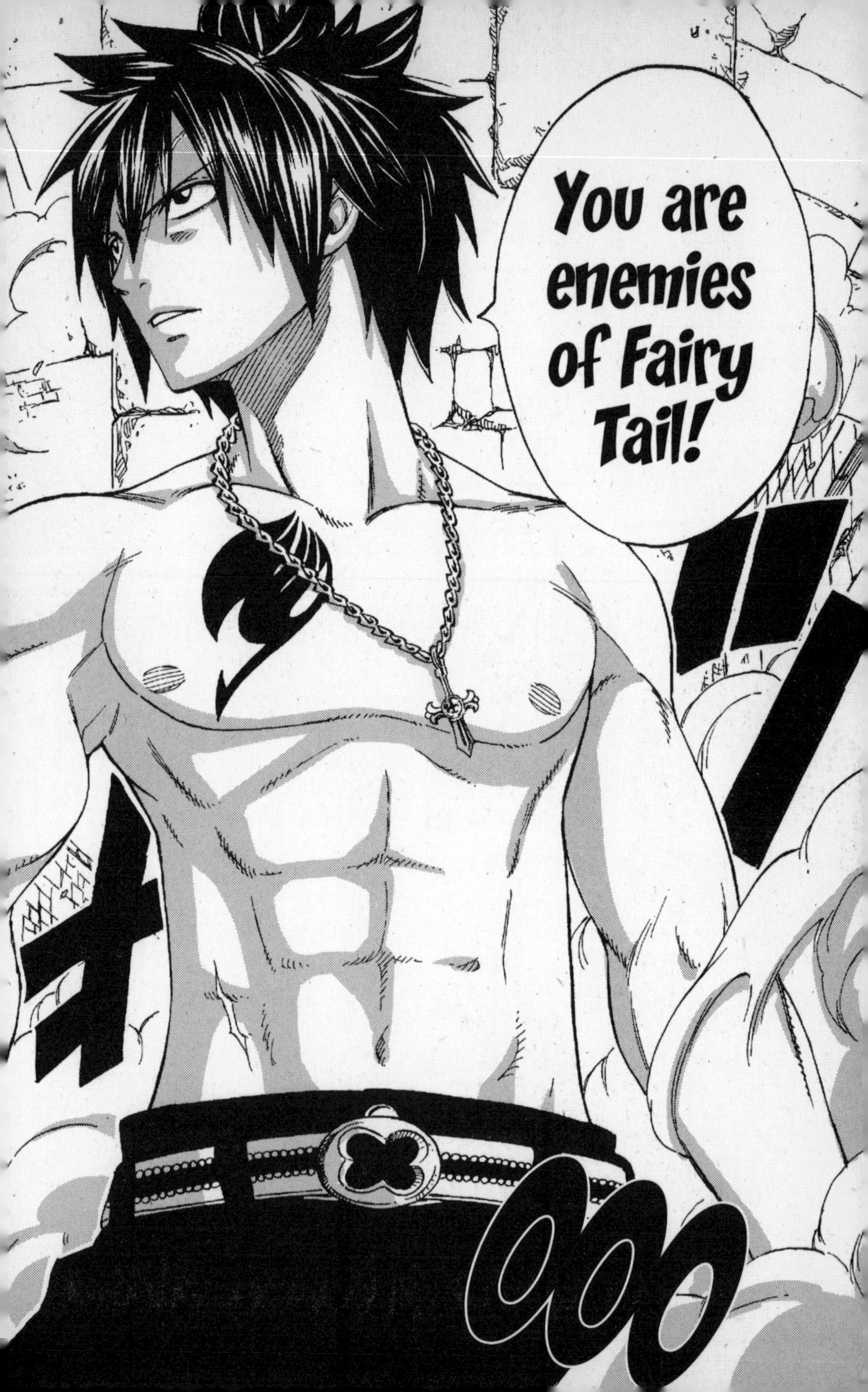
You are enemies of Fairy Tail!

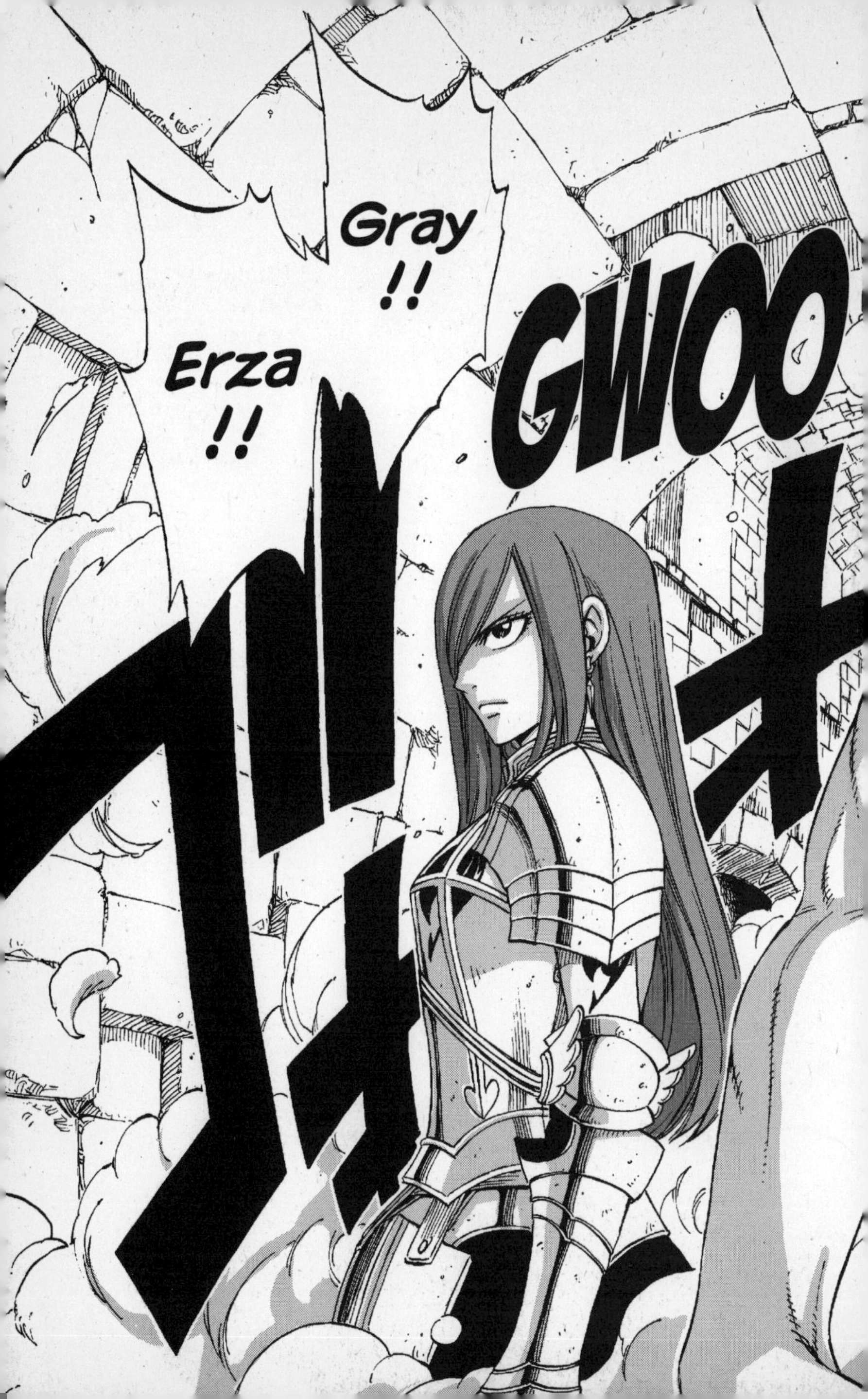
GWOO
Gray !!
Erza !!

FAIRY TAIL
フェアリーテイル

Chapter 180, Erza vs. Erza

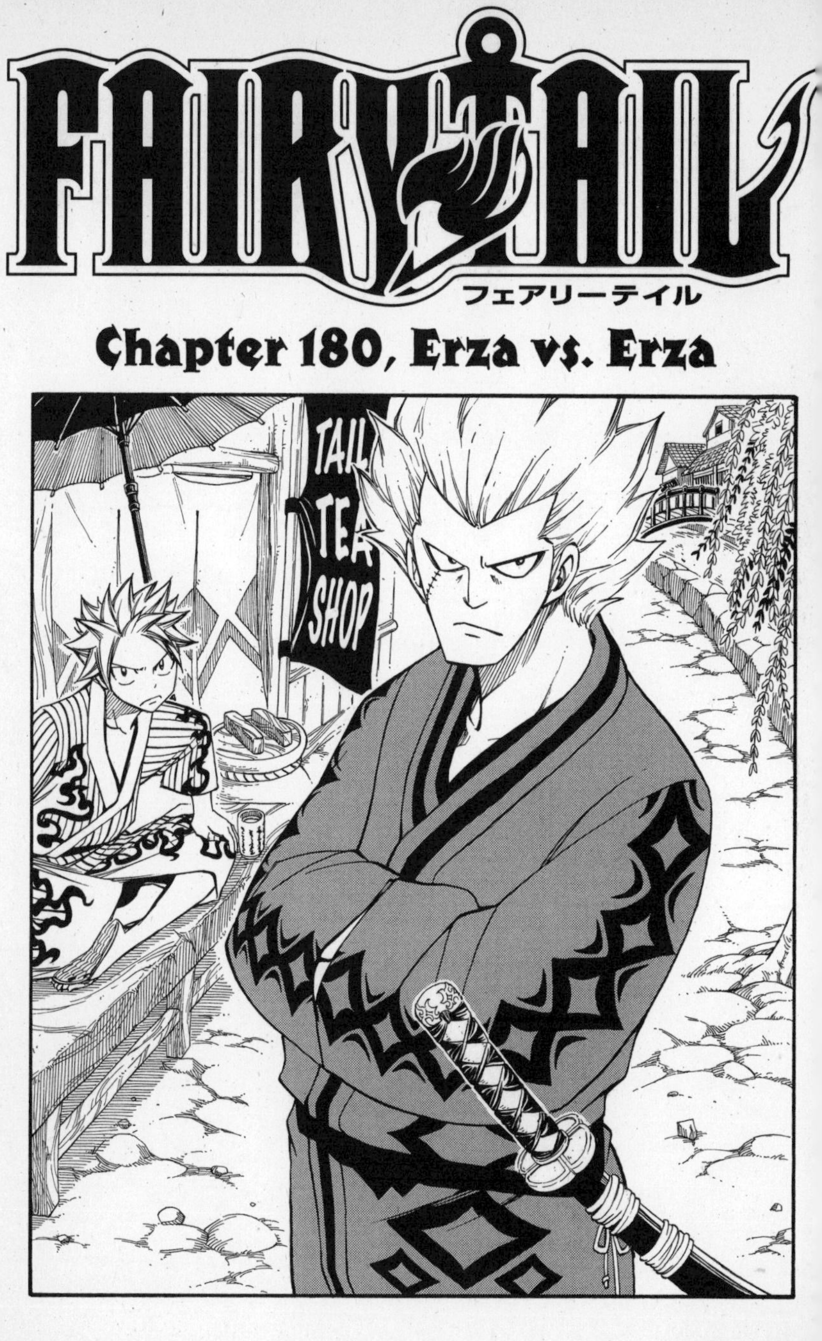
TAIL
TEA
SHOP

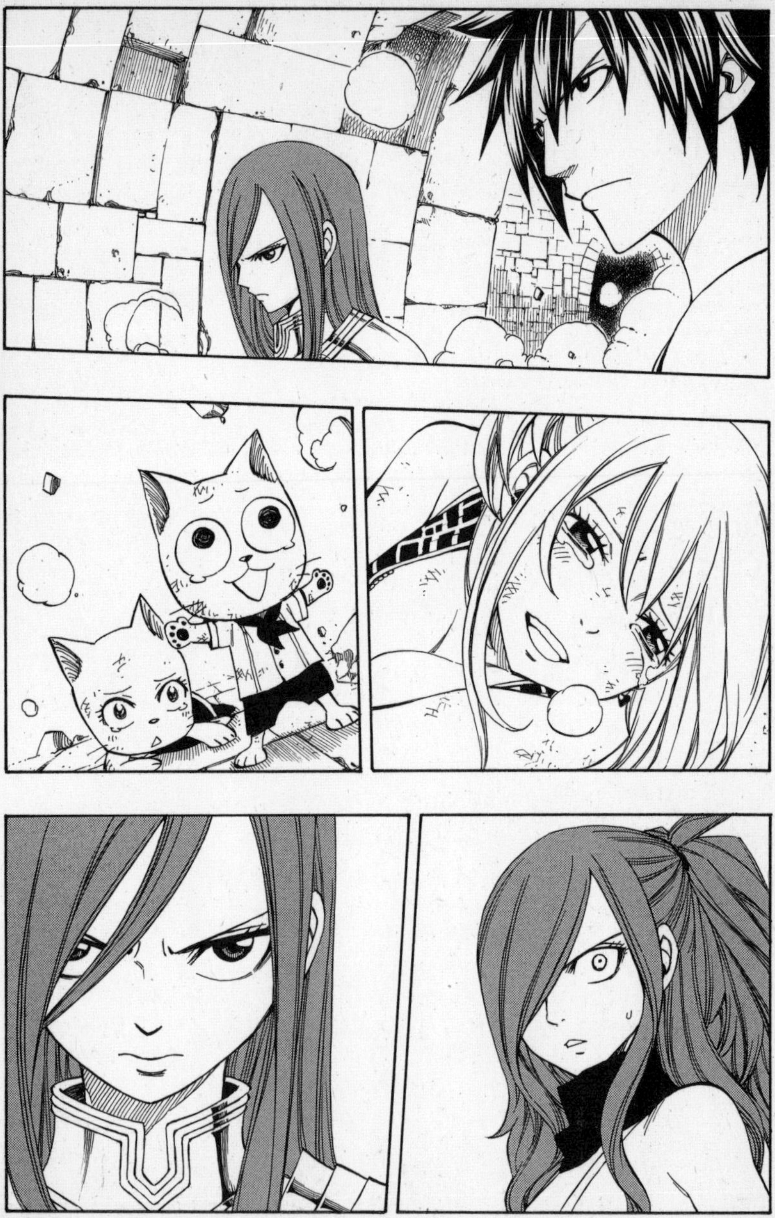

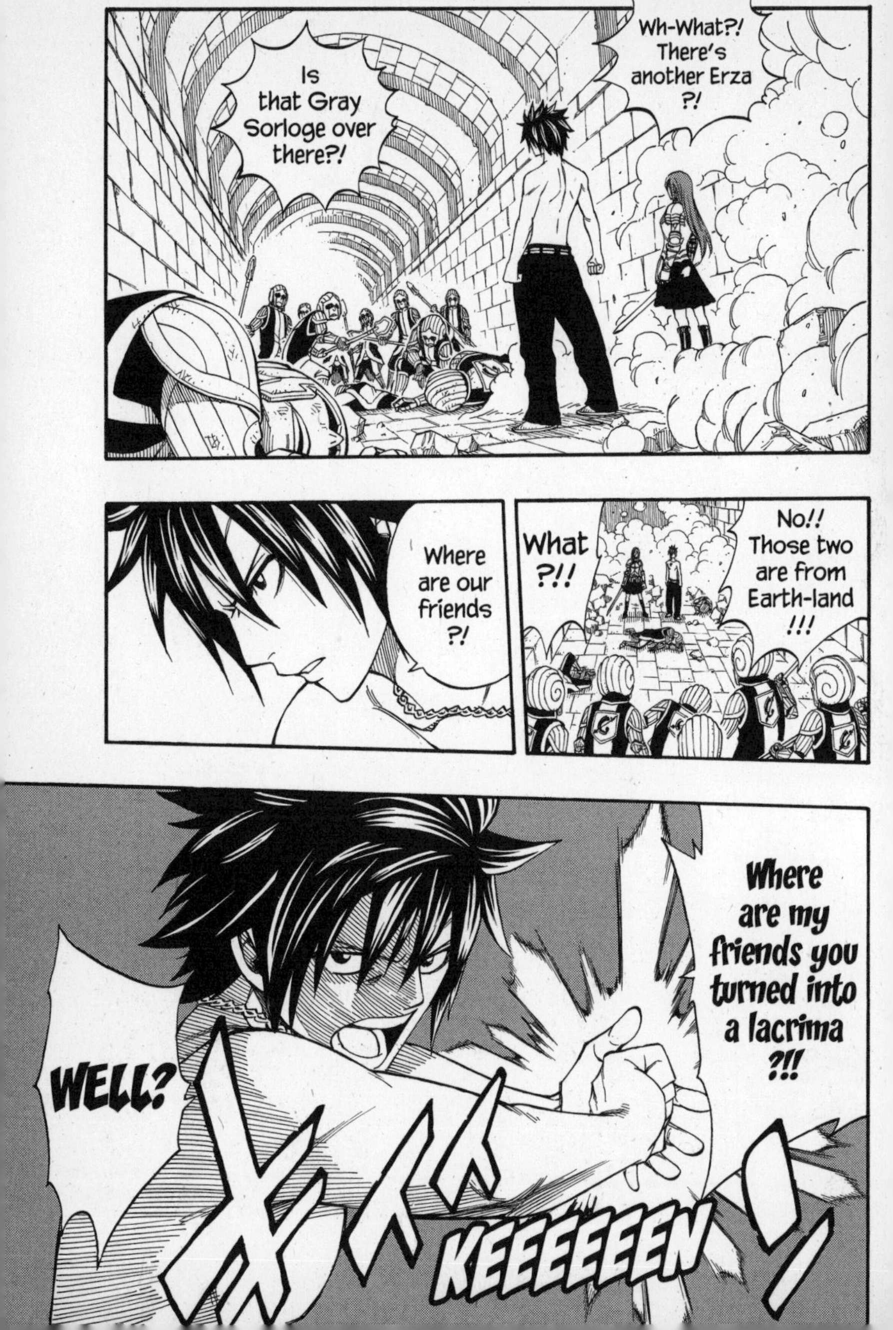
Wh-What?! There's another Erza ?!
Is that Gray Sorloge over there?!
No!! Those two are from Earth-land !!!
What ?!!
Where are our friends ?!
Where are my friends you turned into a lacrima ?!!
WELL?
KEEEEEEN

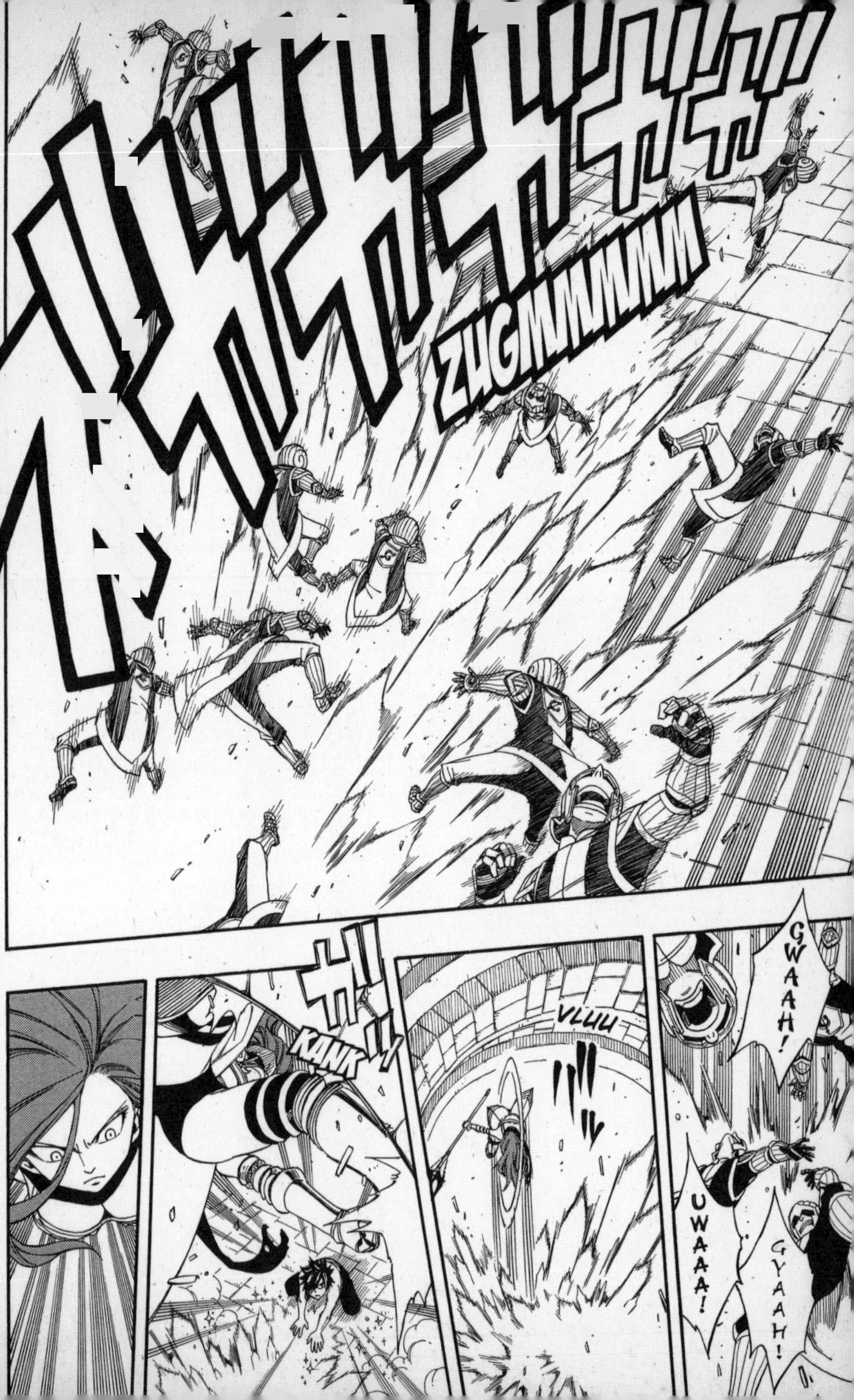
ZUGMMMMMM
GWAAH!
UWAAAA!
GYAAH!
VLUU
KANK

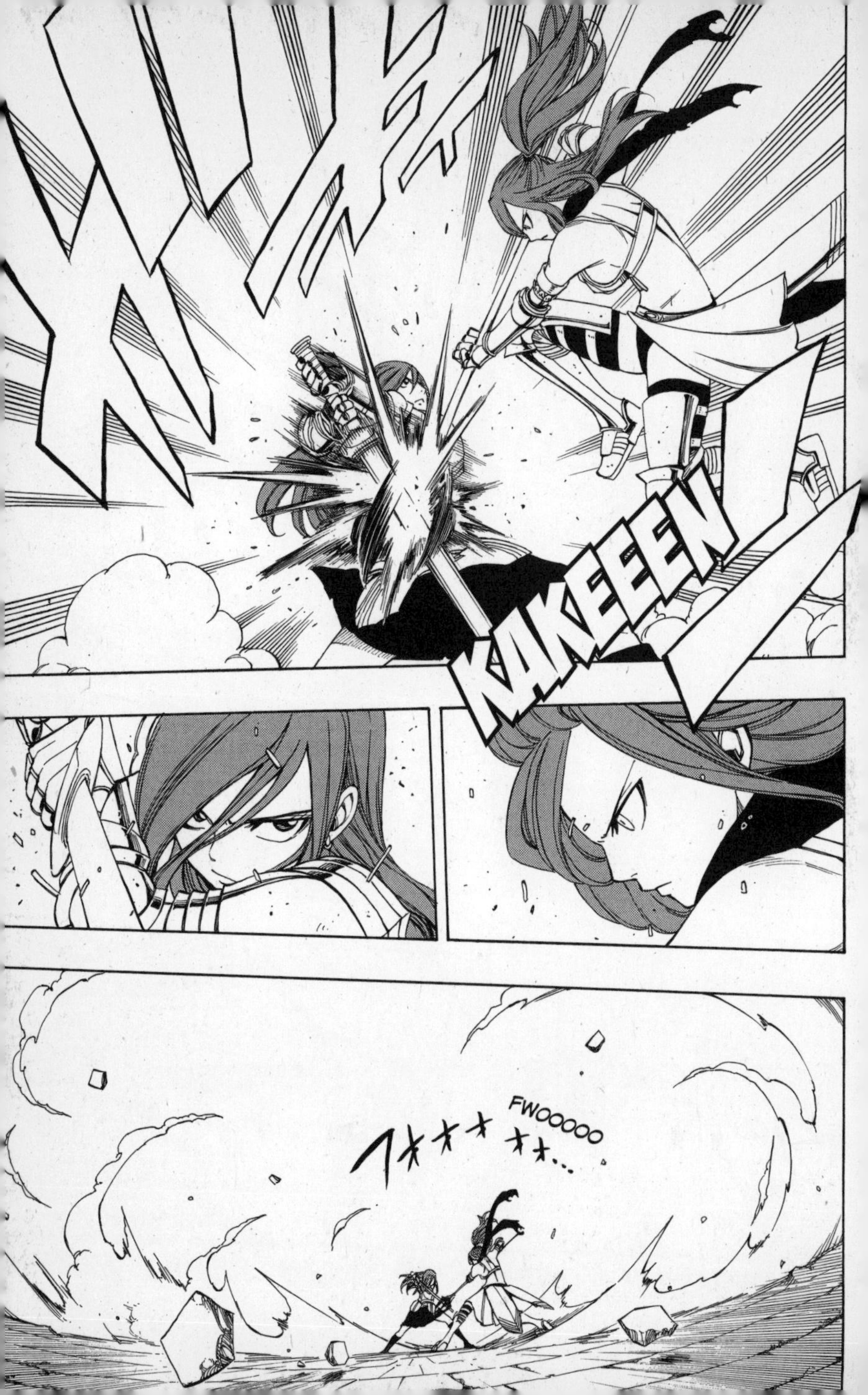
KAKEEEN
FWOOOOO

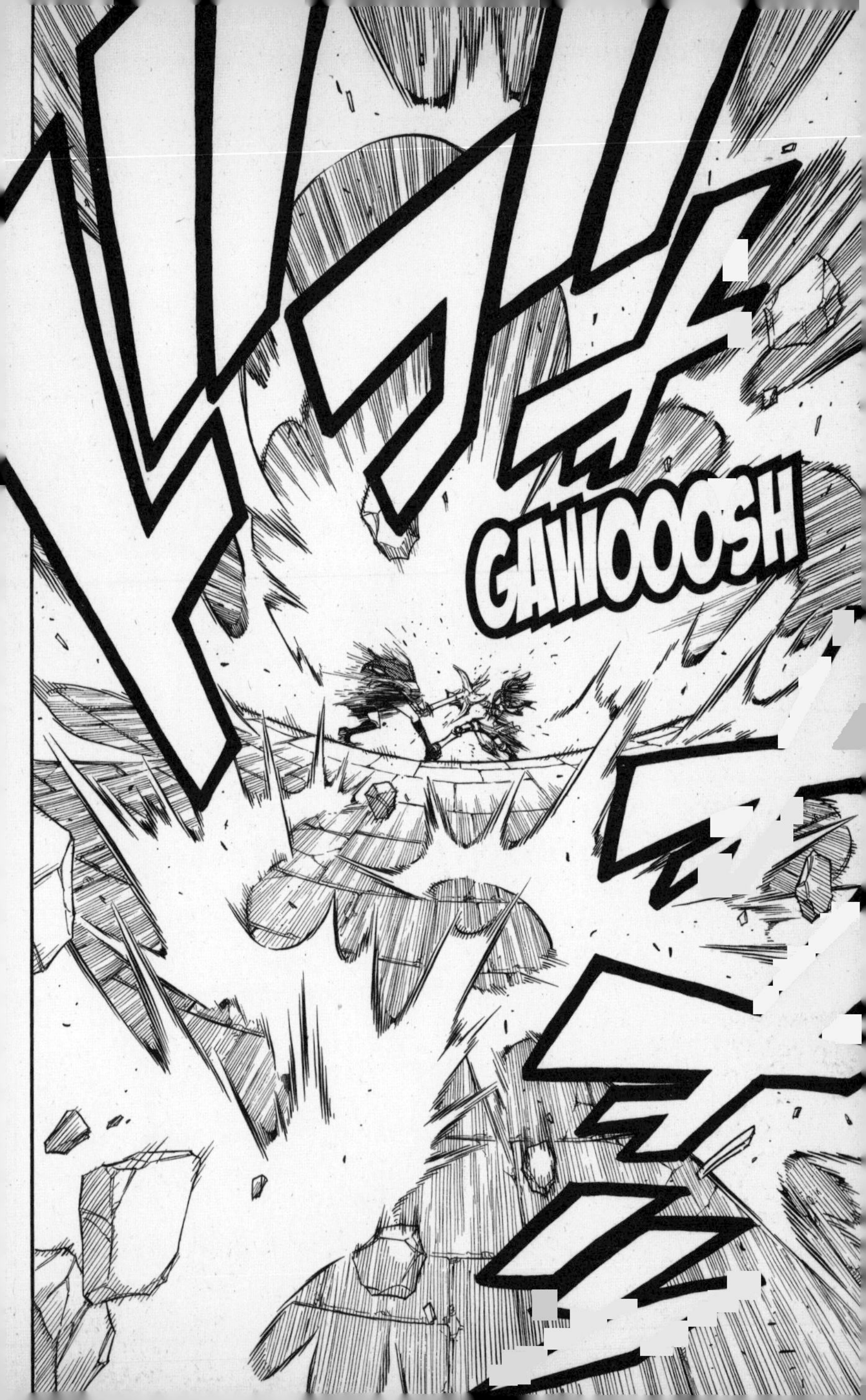
GAWOOOSH

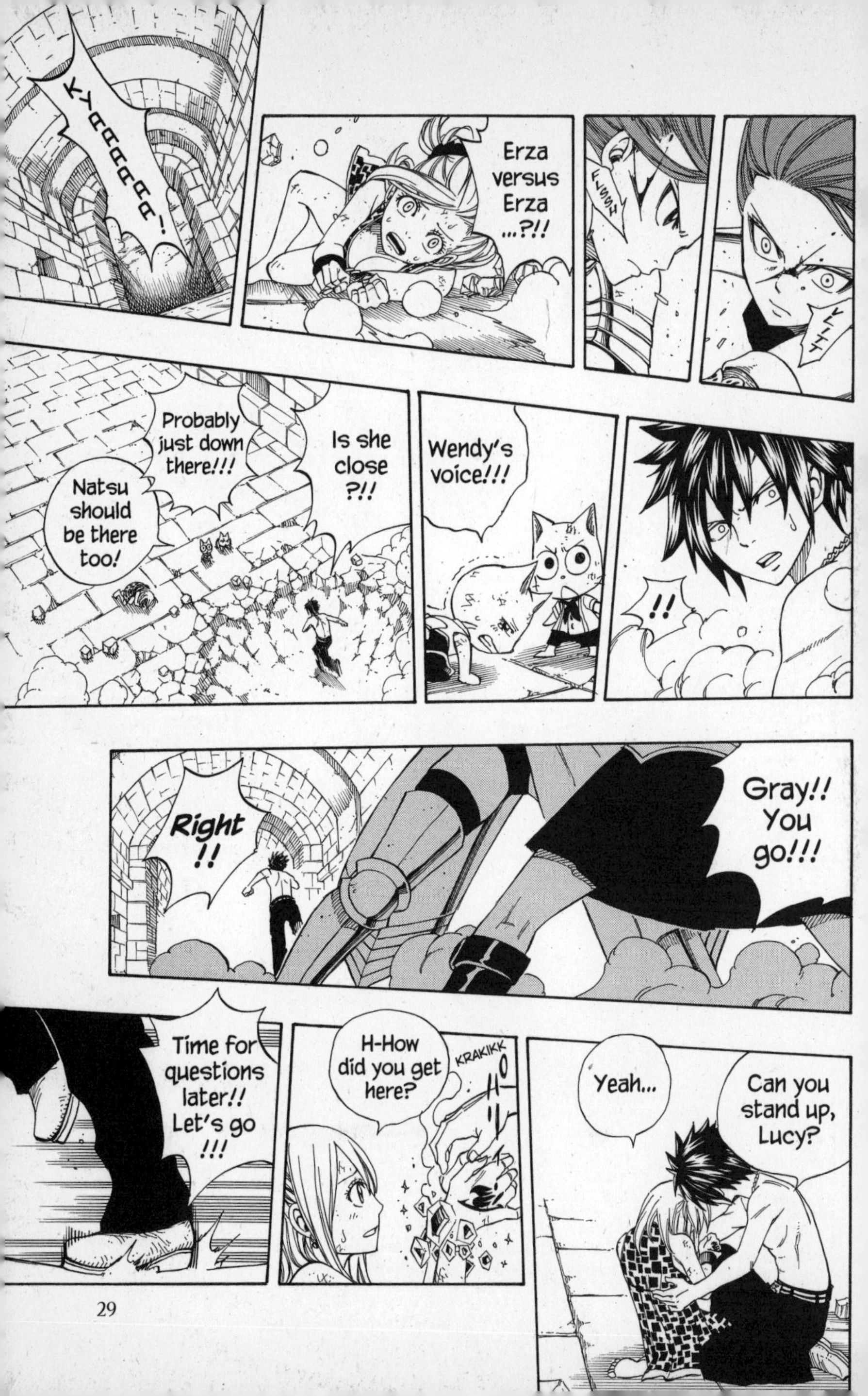
YLITT
FLISSH
Erza versus Erza ...?!!
KYAAAAAAAA!
!!
Wendy's voice!!!
Is she close ?!!
Probably just down there!!!
Natsu should be there too!
Gray!! You go!!!
Right !!
Can you stand up, Lucy?
Yeah...
H-How did you get here?
KRAKIKK
Time for questions later!! Let's go !!!

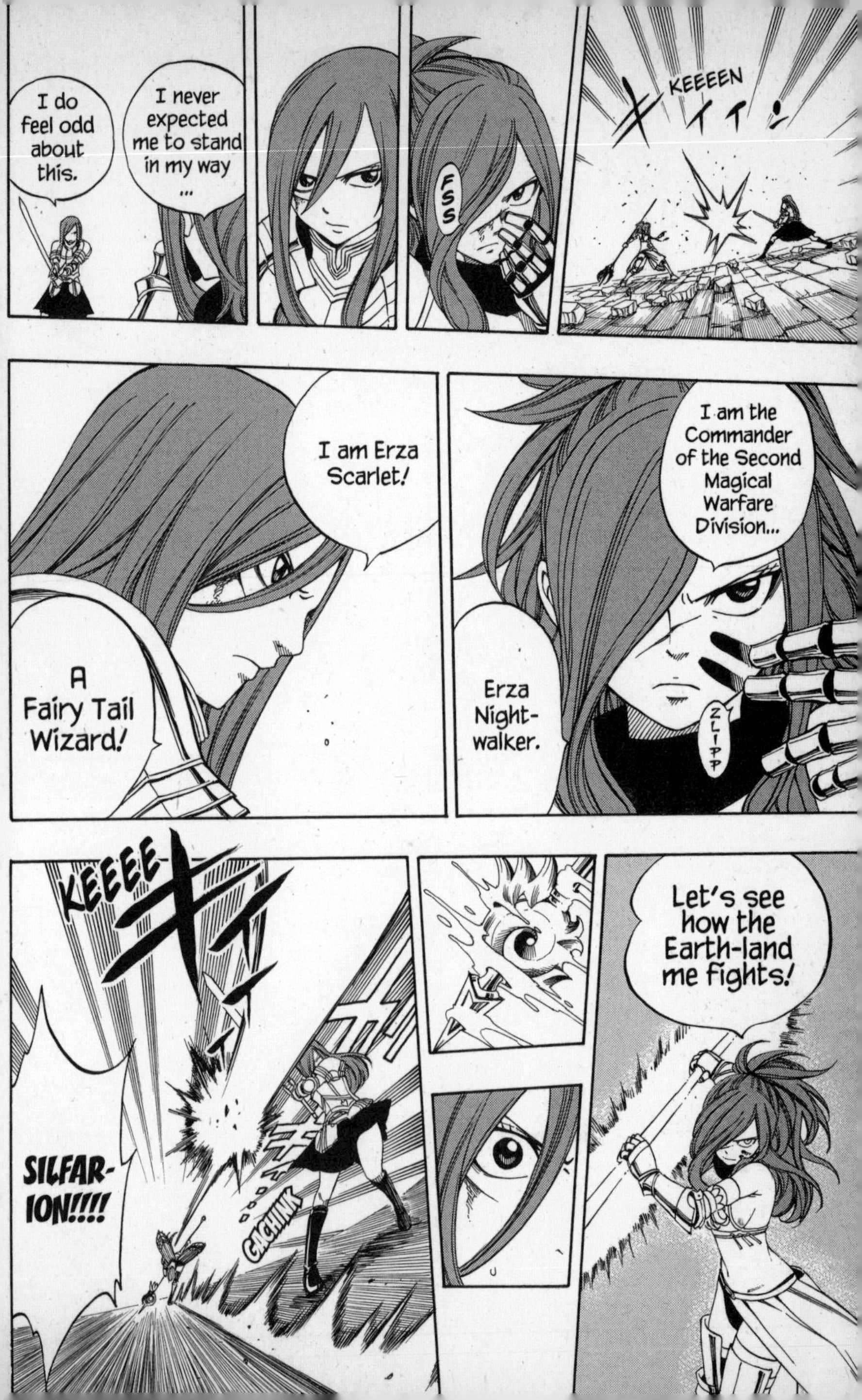
KEEEEN
FSS
I never expected me to stand in my way ...
I do feel odd about this.
I am the Commander of the Second Magical Warfare Division...
Erza Night-walker.
ZLIPP
I am Erza Scarlet!
A Fairy Tail Wizard!
Let's see how the Earth-land me fights!
KEEEEN
SILFAR-ION!!!!
CACHINK

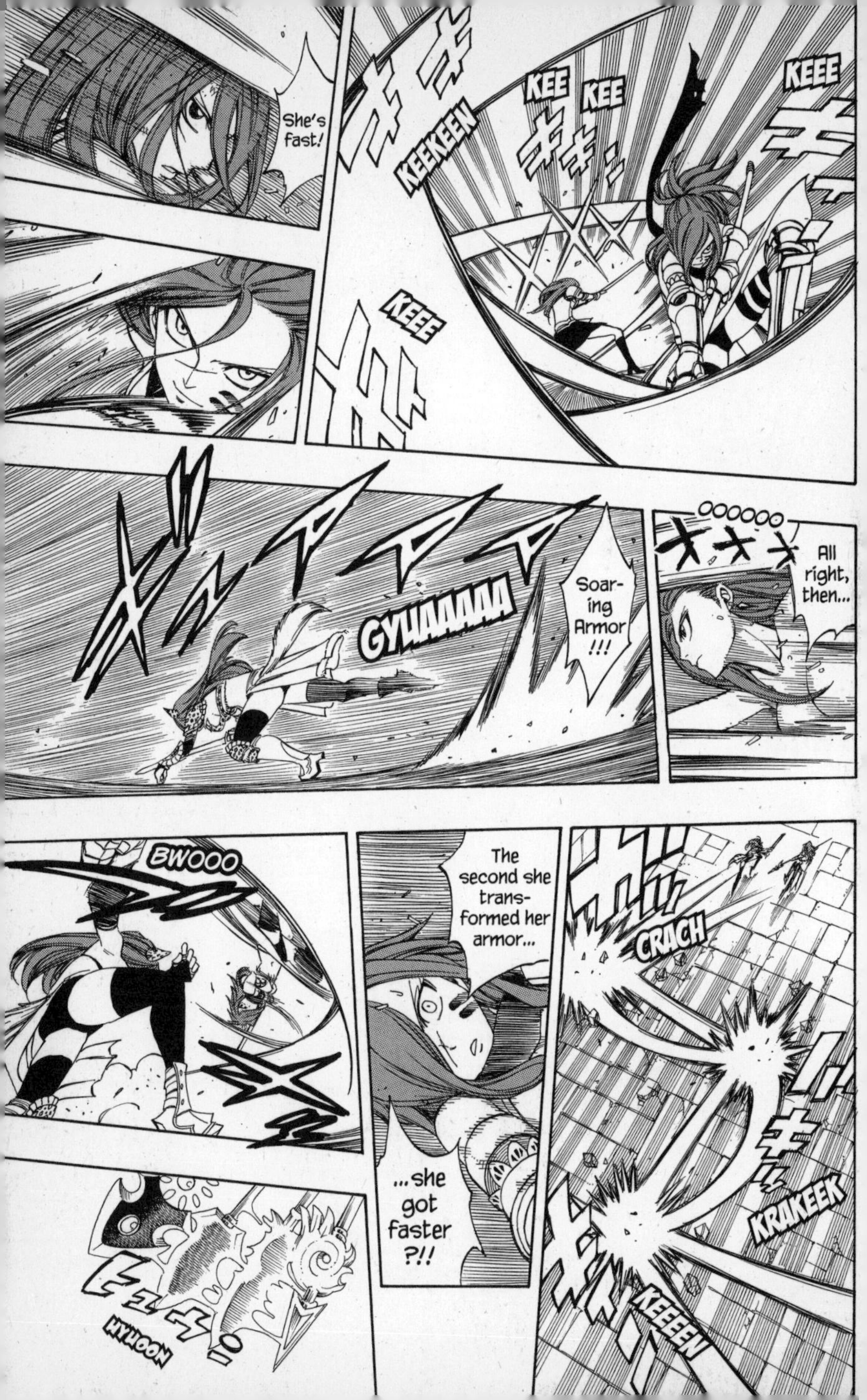
KEEE
KEE
KEE
KEEKEEN
KEEE
She's fast!
OOOOOO
All right, then...
Soar-ing Armor!!!
GYUAAAAA
KRAKEEK
CRACH
KEEEEN
The second she trans-formed her armor...
...she got faster?!!
BWOOO
HYUOON

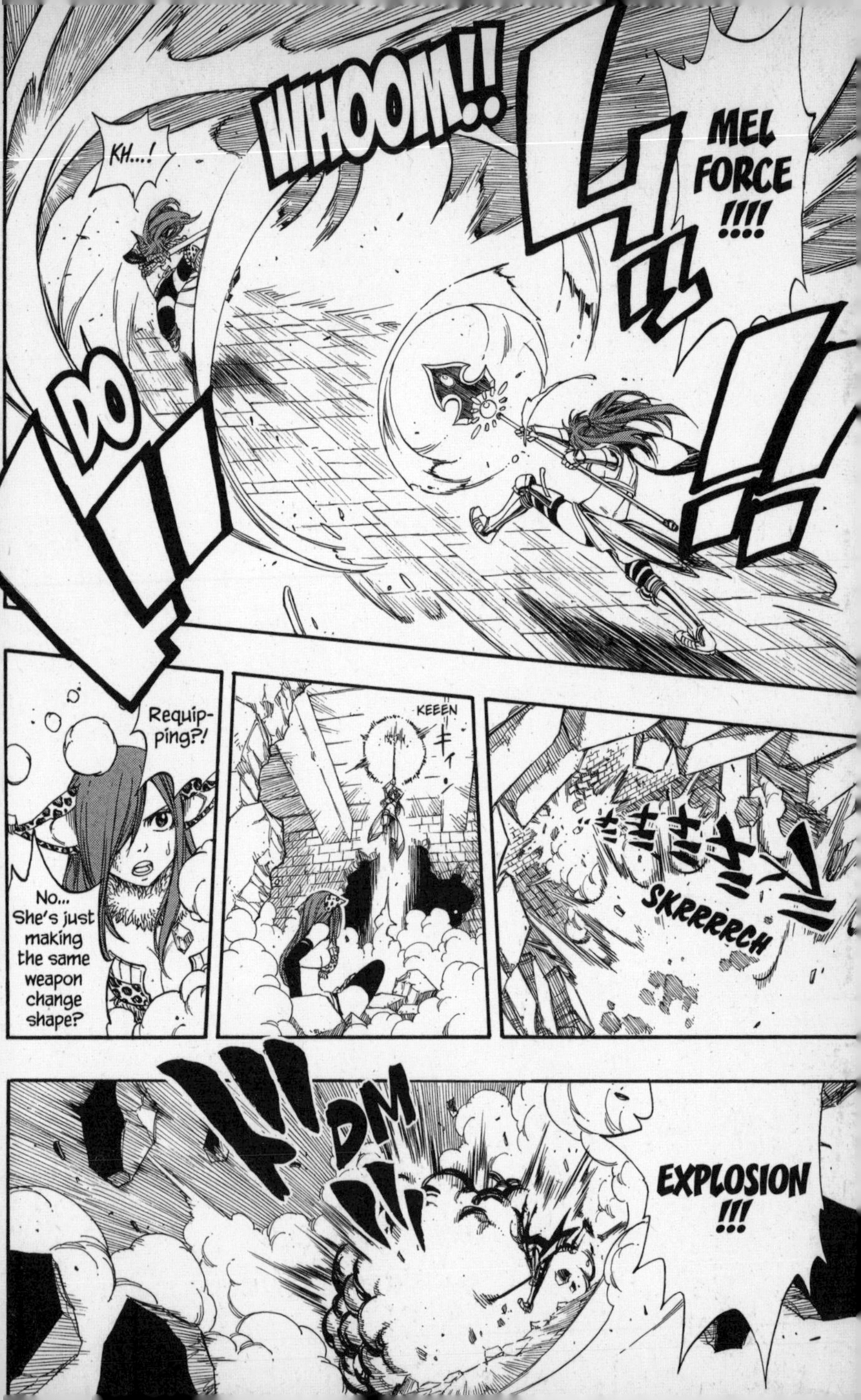
MEL FORCE !!!!
WHOOM!!
KH...!
DO
SKRRRRCH
KEEEN
Requip-ping?!
No... She's just making the same weapon change shape?
EXPLOSION !!!
DM

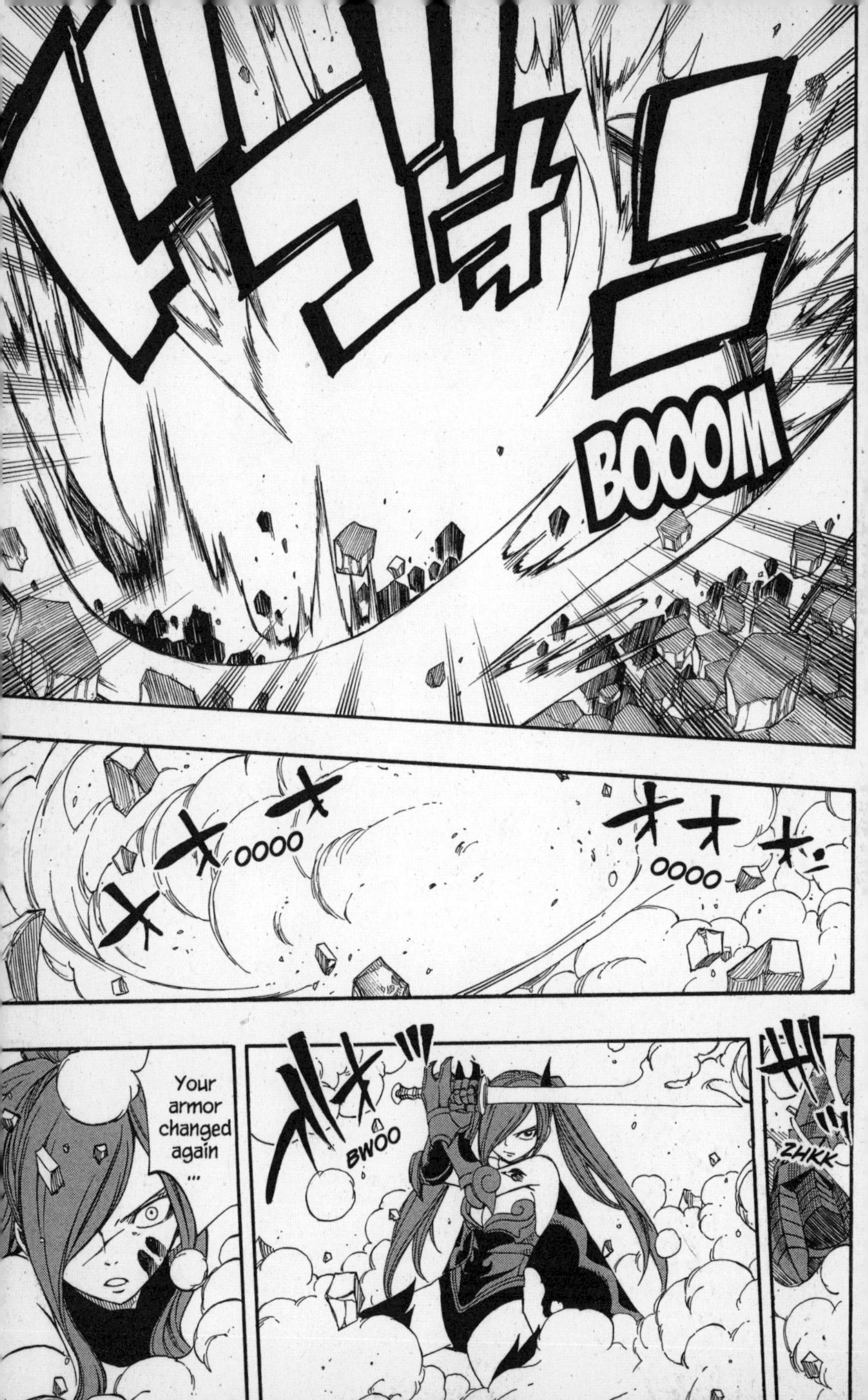
BOOOM
OOOO-
OOOO
ZHKK
BWOO
Your armor changed again ...

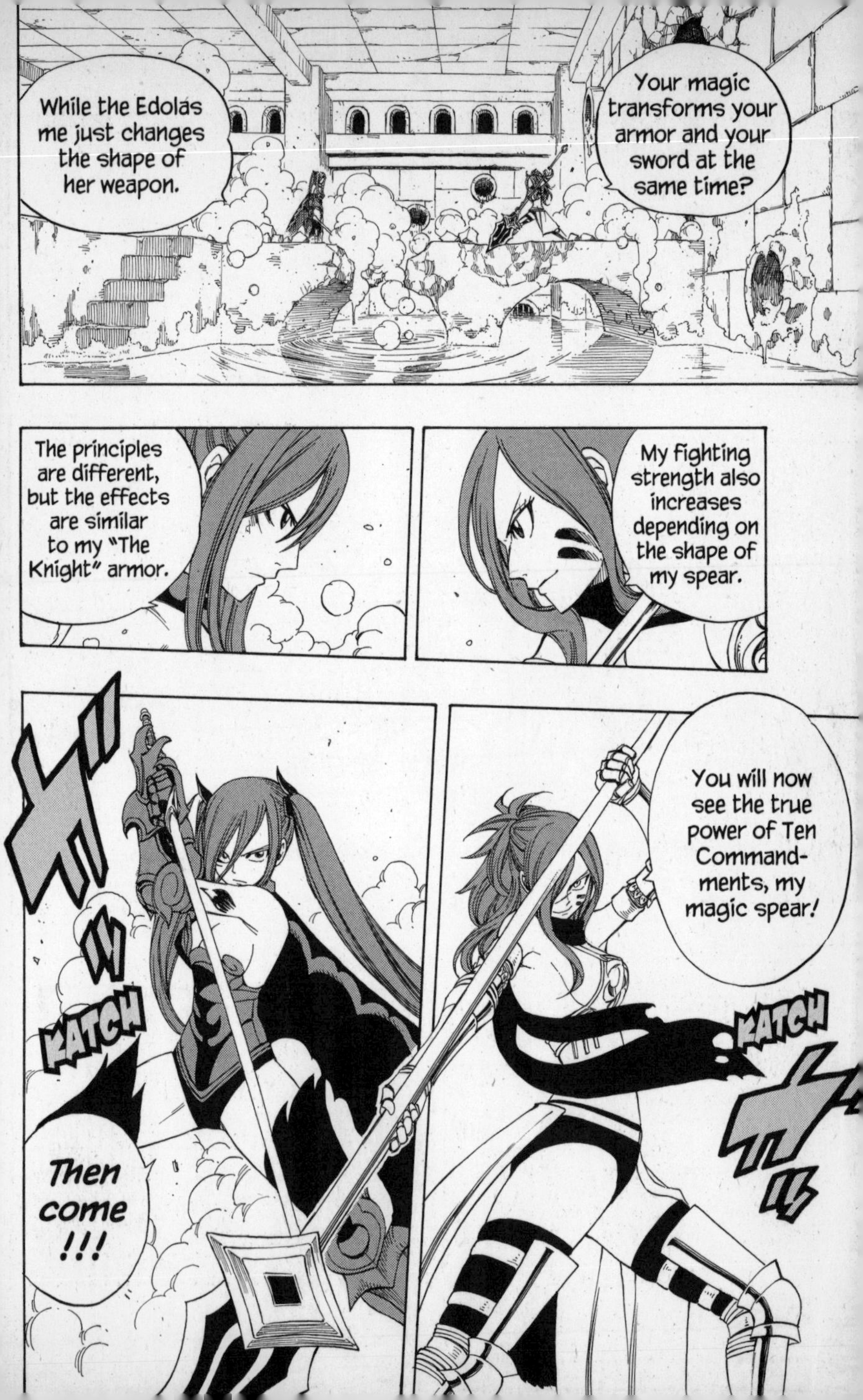
Your magic transforms your armor and your sword at the same time?
While the Edolas me just changes the shape of her weapon.
My fighting strength also increases depending on the shape of my spear.
The principles are different, but the effects are similar to my "The Knight" armor.
You will now see the true power of Ten Commandments, my magic spear!
KATCH
KATCH
Then come!!!

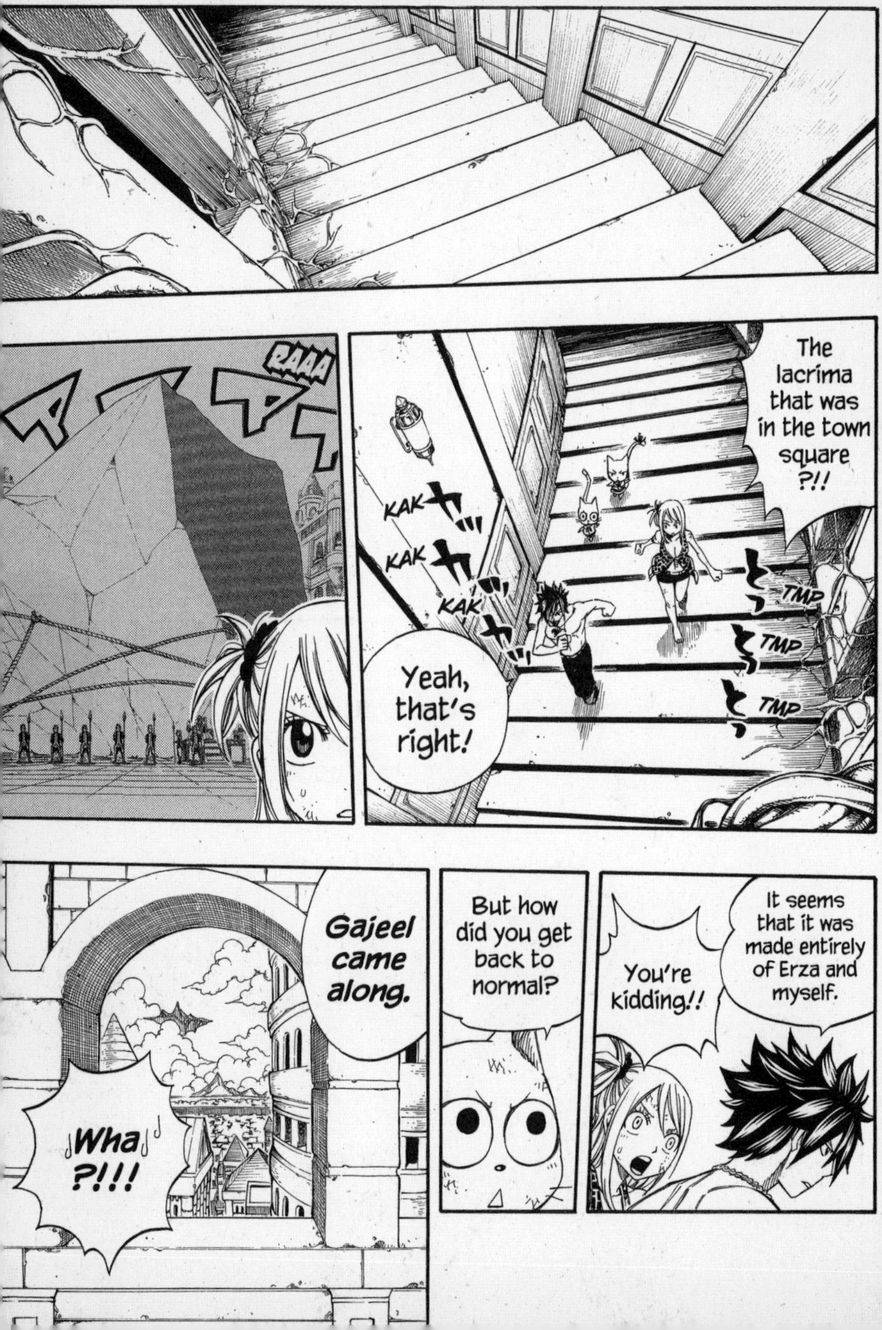
The lacrima that was in the town square?!!
TMP
TMP
TMP
KAK
KAK
KAK
Yeah, that's right!
RAAA
It seems that it was made entirely of Erza and myself.
You're kidding!!
But how did you get back to normal?
Gajeel came along.
Wha?!!!

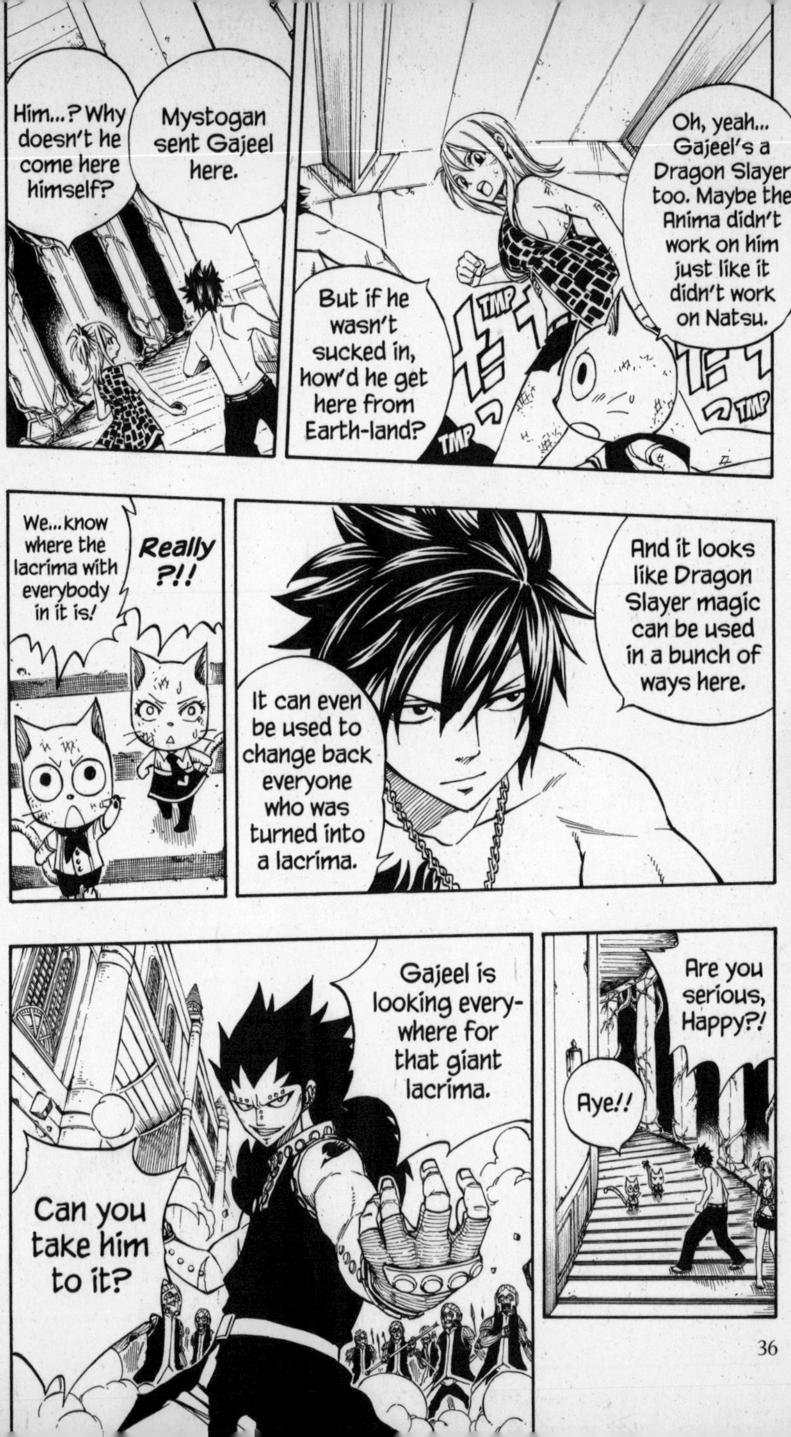
Oh, yeah... Gajeel's a Dragon Slayer too. Maybe the Anima didn't work on him just like it didn't work on Natsu.
TMP
TMP
TMP
But if he wasn't sucked in, how'd he get here from Earth-land?
Mystogan sent Gajeel here.
Him...? Why doesn't he come here himself?
And it looks like Dragon Slayer magic can be used in a bunch of ways here.
It can even be used to change back everyone who was turned into a lacrima.
Really?!!
We...know where the lacrima with everybody in it is!
Are you serious, Happy?!
Aye!!
Gajeel is looking every-where for that giant lacrima.
Can you take him to it?

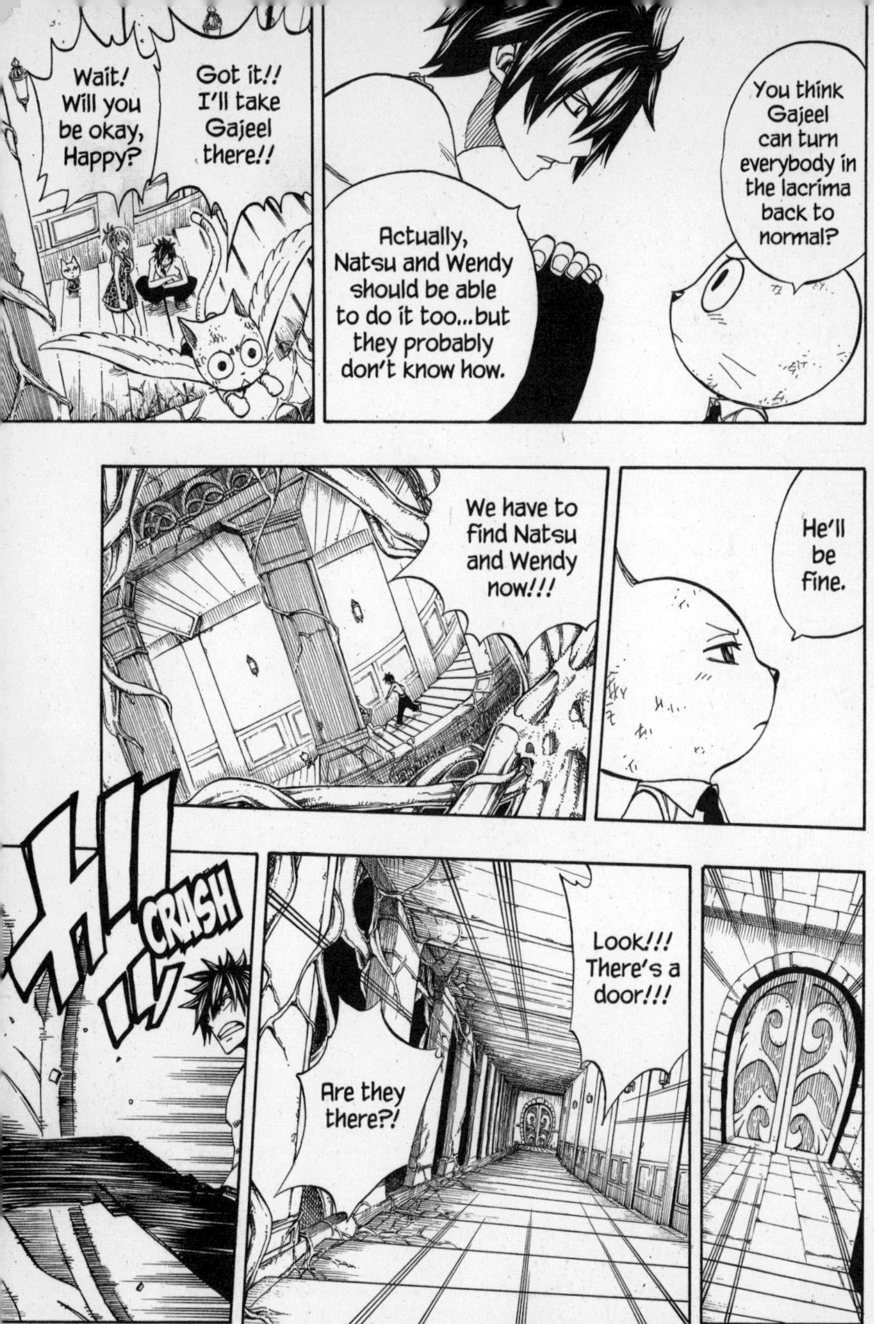

You think Gajeel can turn everybody in the lacrima back to normal?
Actually, Natsu and Wendy should be able to do it too...but they probably don't know how.
Got it!! I'll take Gajeel there!!
Wait! Will you be okay, Happy?
He'll be fine.
We have to find Natsu and Wendy now!!!
Look!!! There's a door!!!
Are they there?!
CRASH

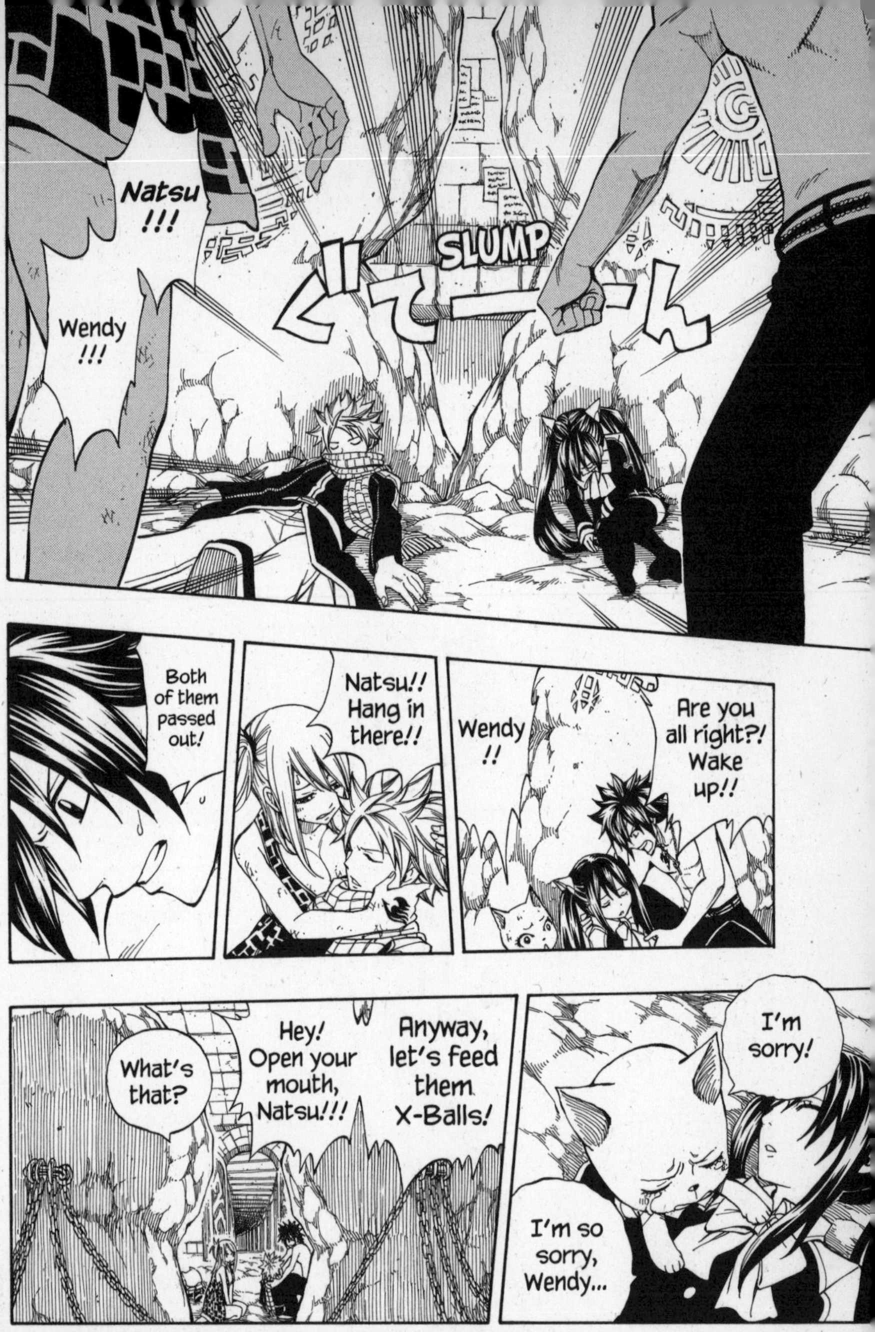
SLUMP
Natsu!!!
Wendy!!!
Are you all right?! Wake up!!
Wendy!!
Natsu!! Hang in there!!
Both of them passed out!
I'm sorry!
I'm so sorry, Wendy...
Anyway, let's feed them X-Balls!
Hey! Open your mouth, Natsu!!!
What's that?

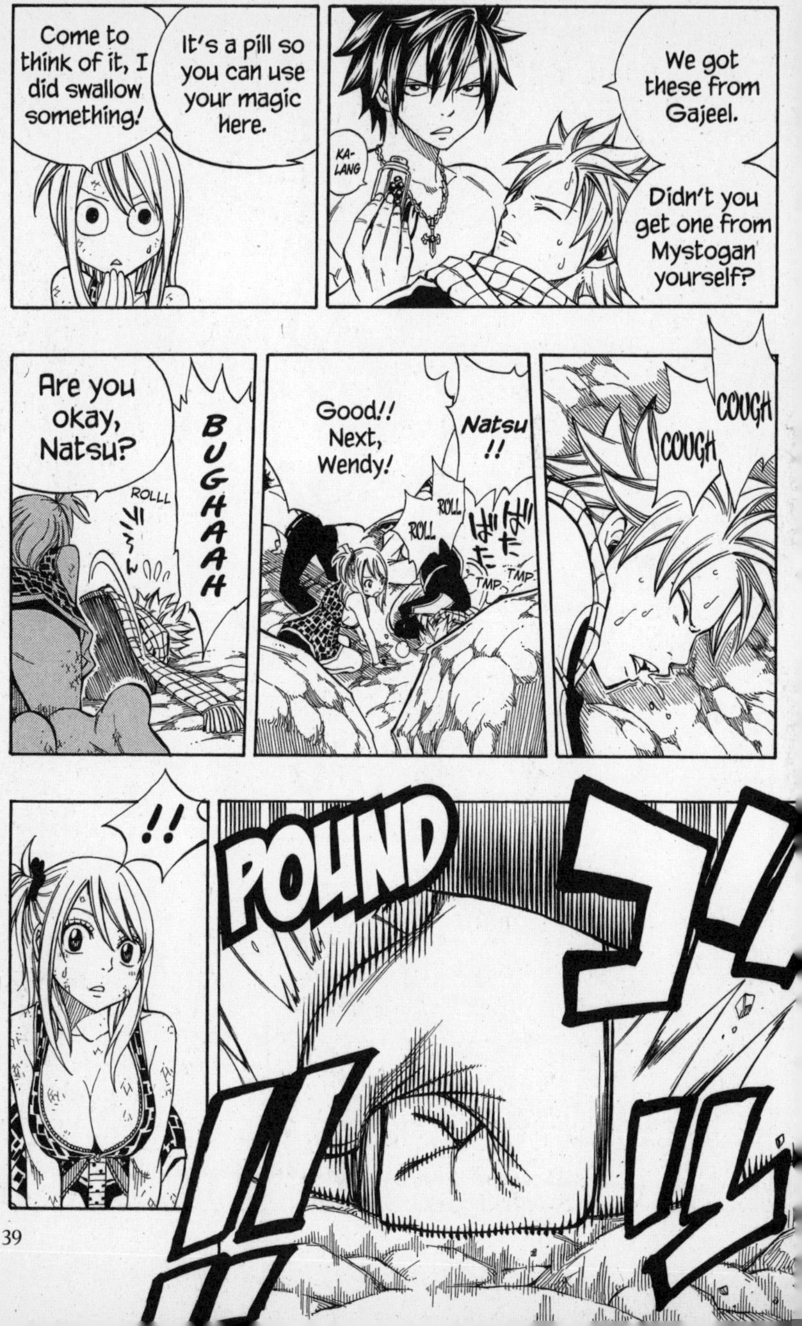
We got these from Gajeel.
KA-LANG
Didn't you get one from Mystogan yourself?
It's a pill so you can use your magic here.
Come to think of it, I did swallow something!
COUGH
COUGH
Natsu!!
Good!! Next, Wendy!
ROLL
ROLL
ばたばた
TMP
TMP
BUGHAAAH
Are you okay, Natsu?
ROLLL
POUND
!!

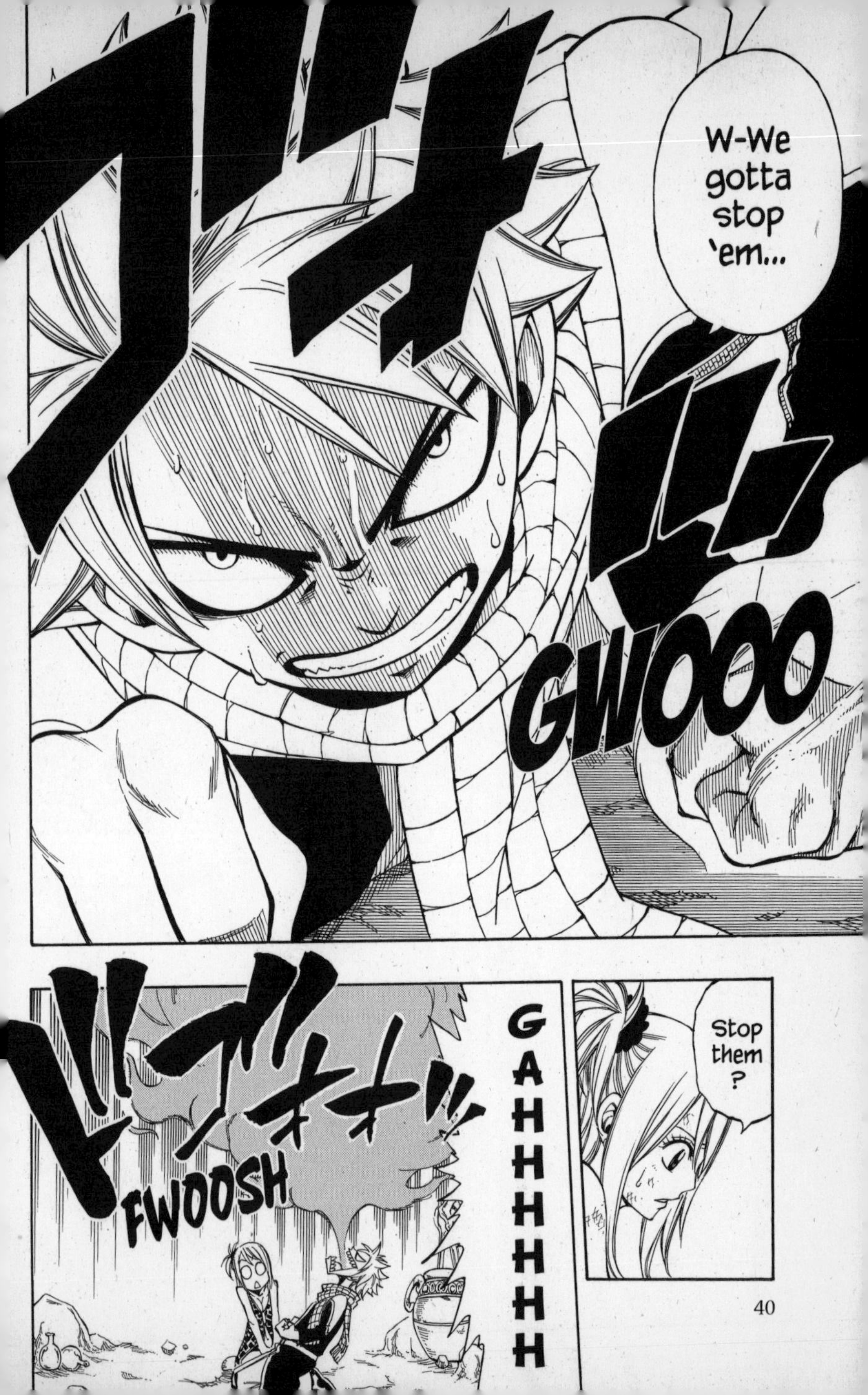
W-We gotta stop 'em...
GWOOO
Stop them?
FWOOSH
GAHHHHHHHH

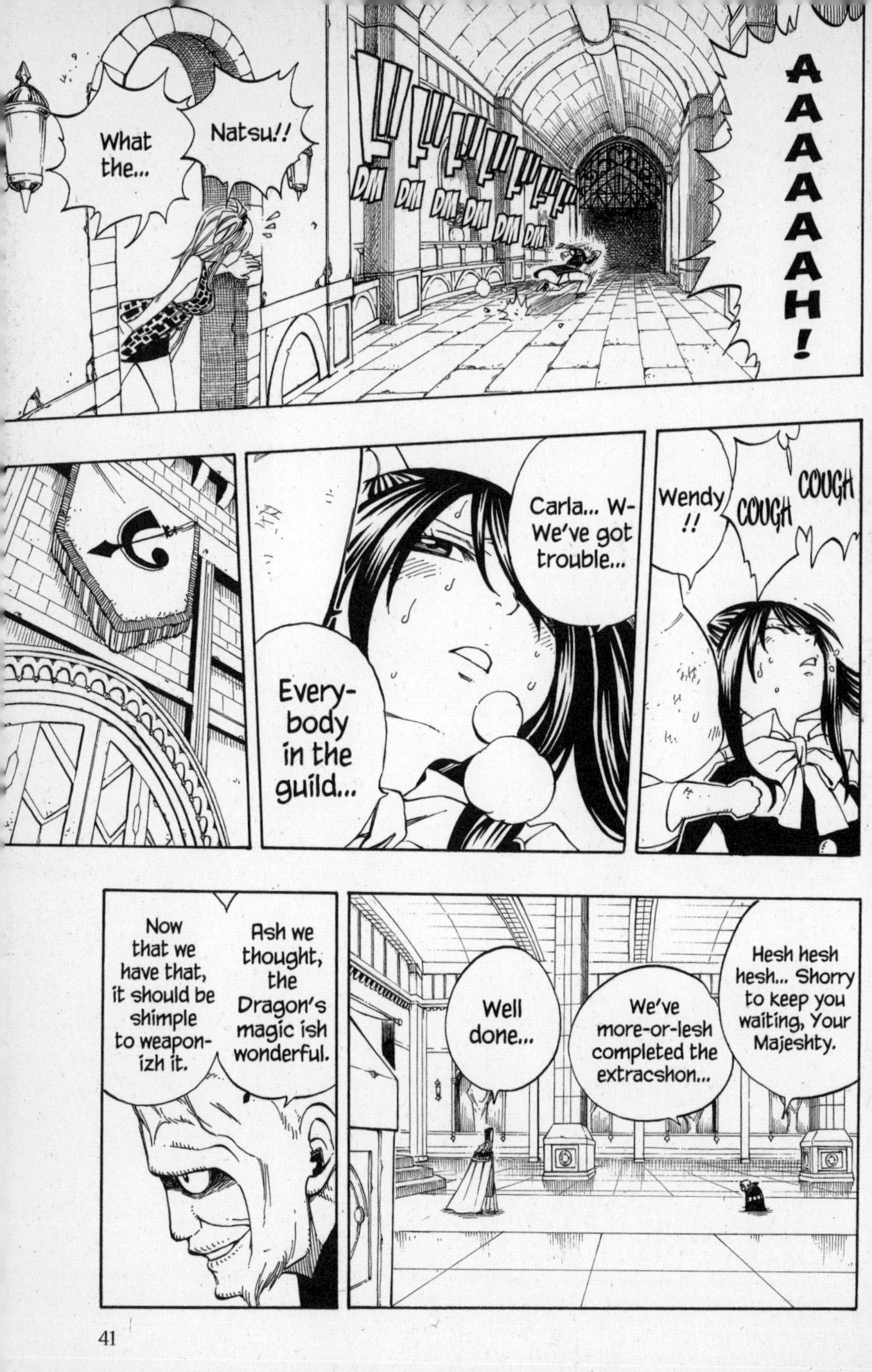
AAAAAAH!
Natsu!!
What the...
DM DM DM DM DM DM
COUGH
COUGH
Wendy !!
Carla... W- We've got trouble...
Every-body in the guild...
Hesh hesh... Shorry to keep you waiting, Your Majeshty.
We've more-or-lesh completed the extracshon...
Well done...
Ash we thought, the Dragon's magic ish wonderful.
Now that we have that, it should be shimple to weapon-izh it.

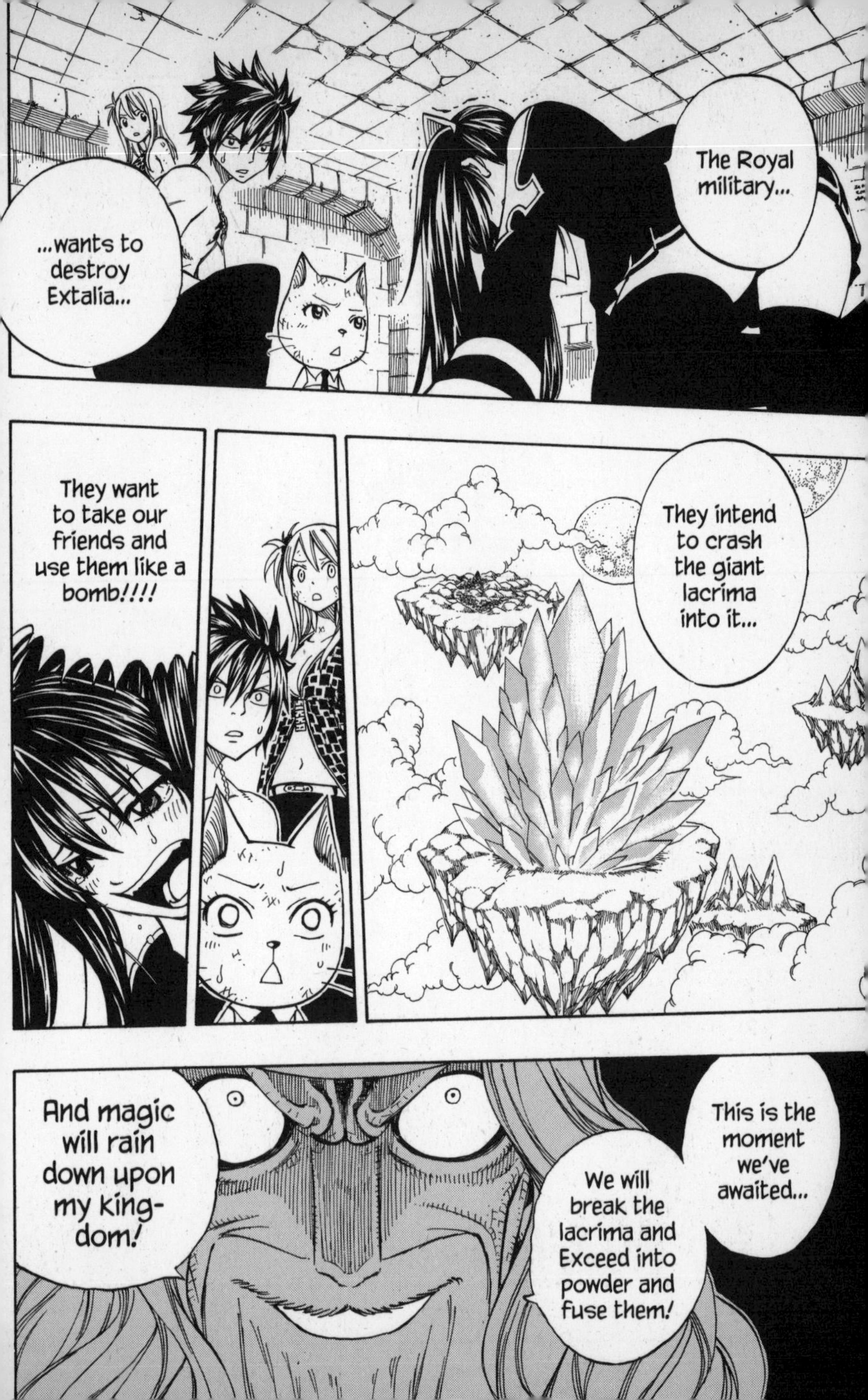
The Royal military...
...wants to destroy Extalia...
They intend to crash the giant lacrima into it...
They want to take our friends and use them like a bomb!!!!
This is the moment we've awaited...
We will break the lacrima and Exceed into powder and fuse them!
And magic will rain down upon my king-dom!

FAIRY TAIL
フェアリーテイル

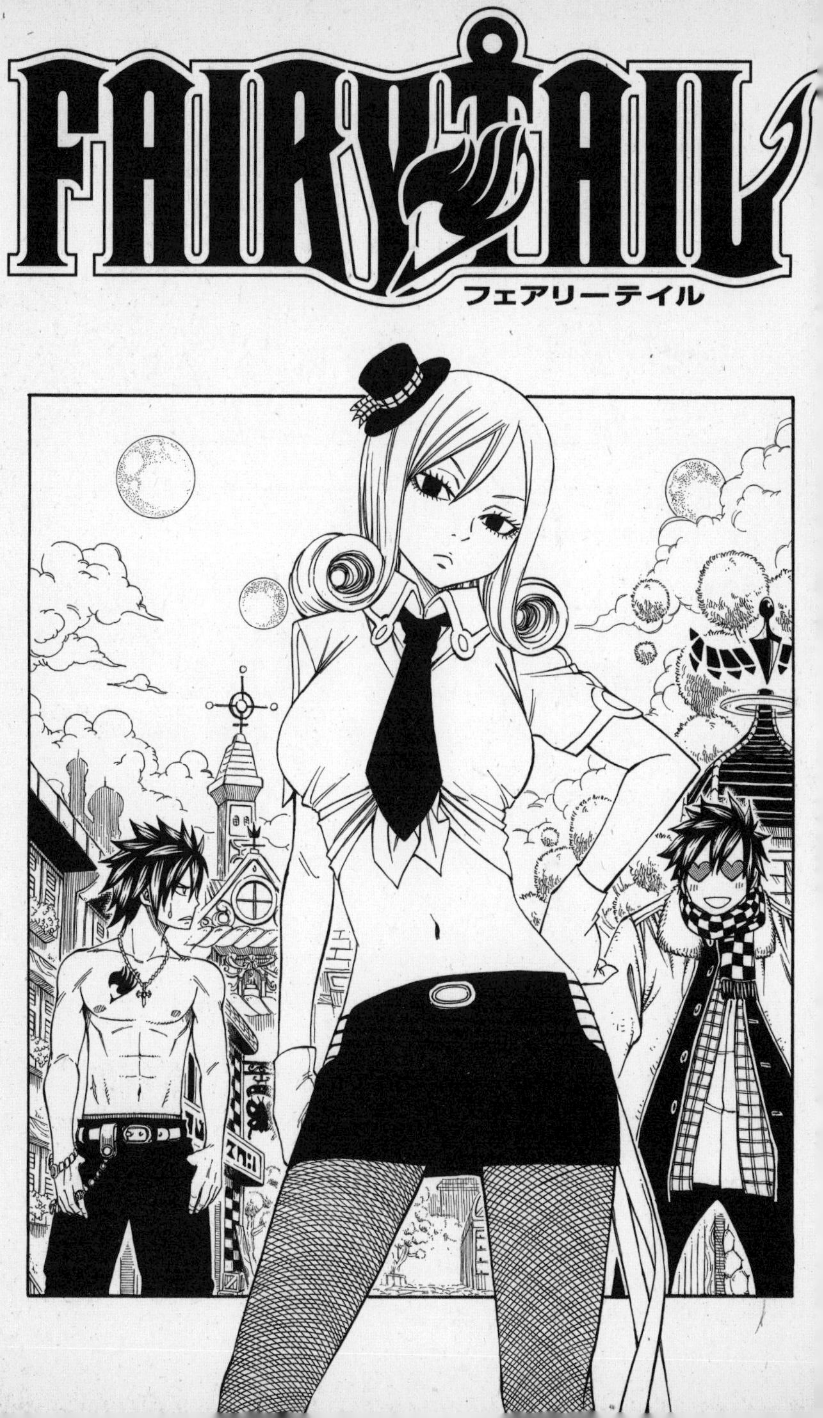

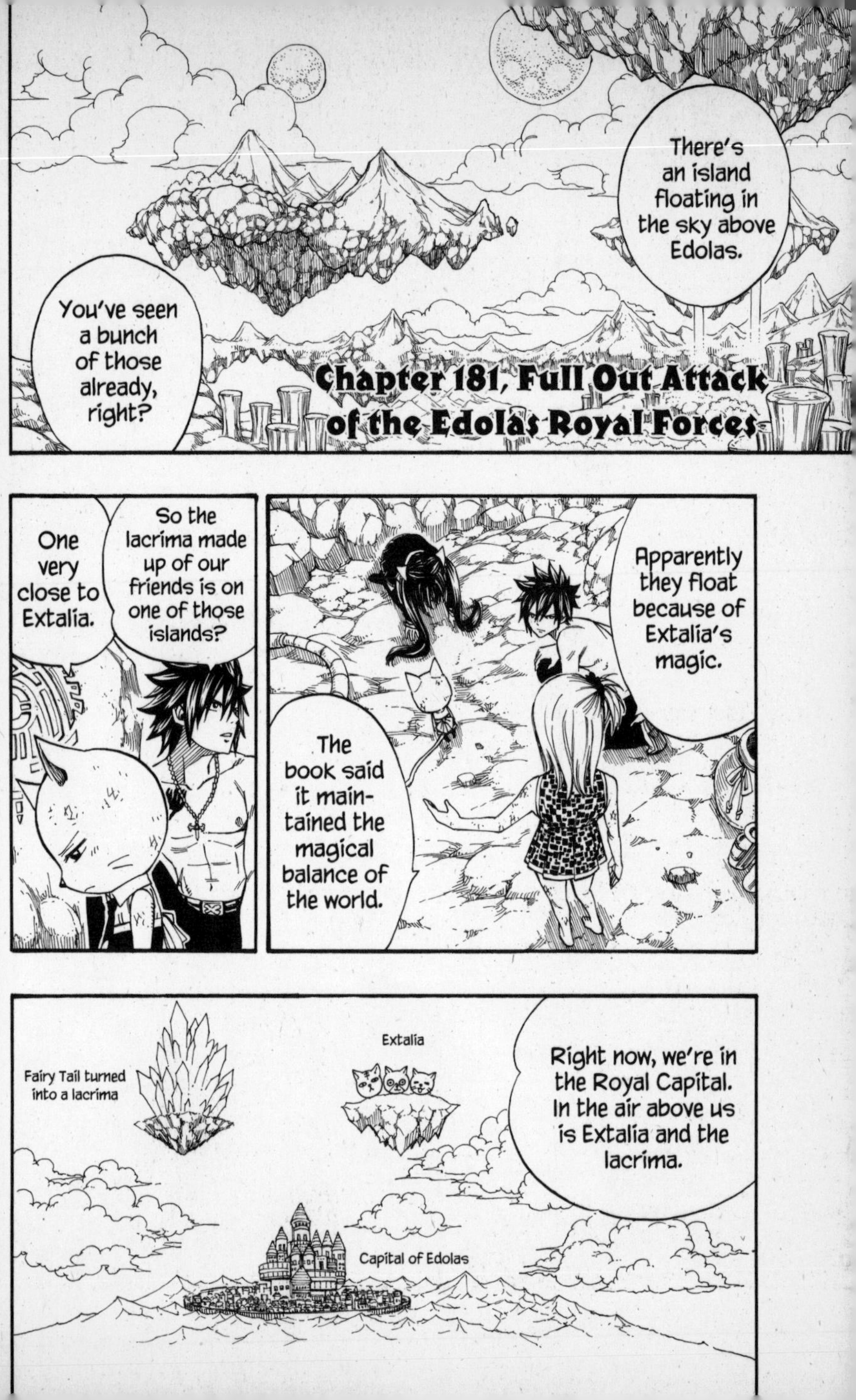
There's an island floating in the sky above Edolas.
You've seen a bunch of those already, right?
Chapter 181, Full Out Attack of the Edolas Royal Forces
Apparently they float because of Extalia's magic.
The book said it maintained the magical balance of the world.
So the lacrima made up of our friends is on one of those islands?
One very close to Extalia.
Right now, we're in the Royal Capital. In the air above us is Extalia and the lacrima.
Extalia
Fairy Tail turned into a lacrima
Capital of Edolas

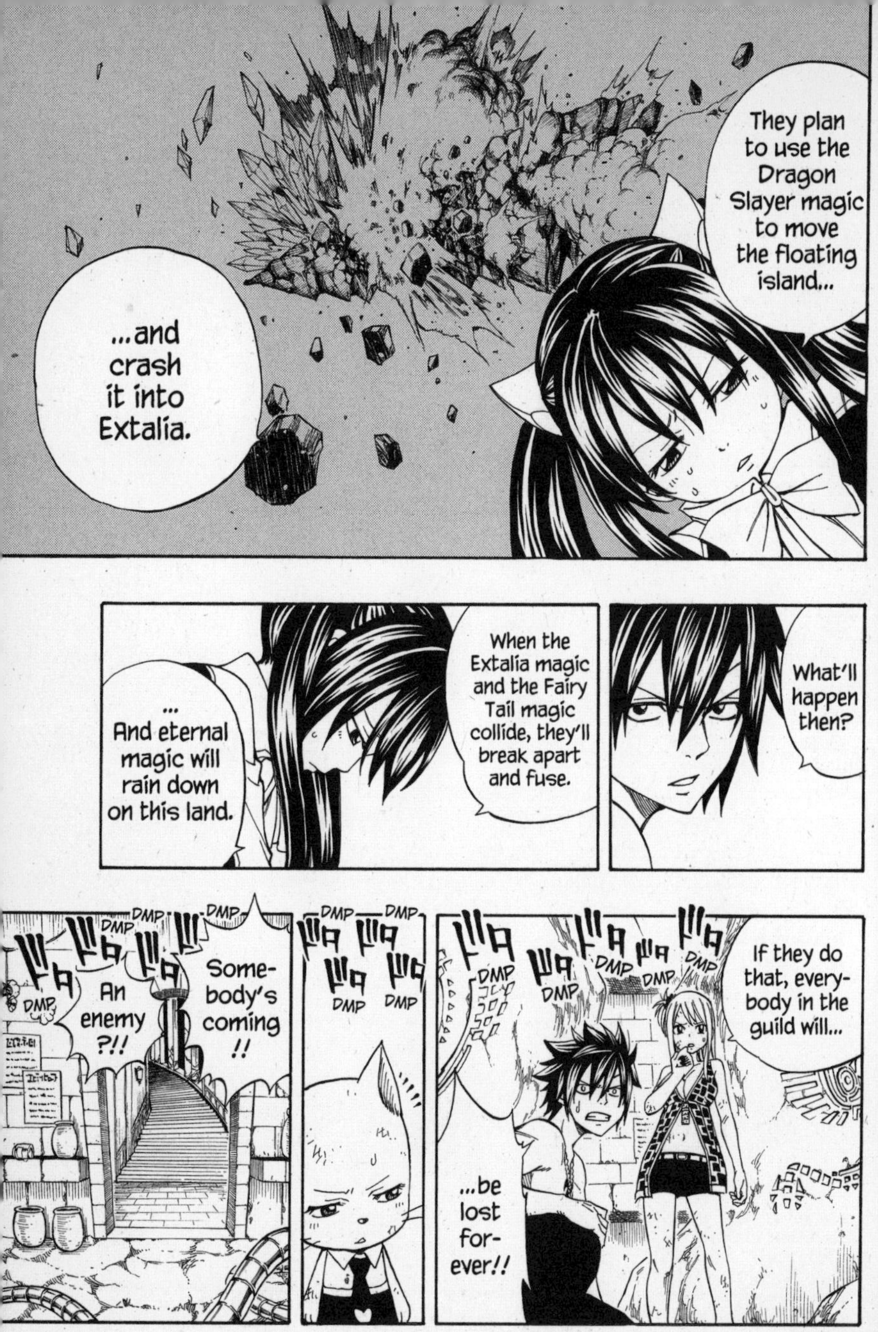
They plan to use the Dragon Slayer magic to move the floating island...
...and crash it into Extalia.
What'll happen then?
When the Extalia magic and the Fairy Tail magic collide, they'll break apart and fuse.
... And eternal magic will rain down on this land.
If they do that, everybody in the guild will...
...be lost forever!!
DMP DMP DMP DMP DMP DMP
DMP DMP DMP DMP
Somebody's coming!!
An enemy?!!
DMP DMP DMP DMP

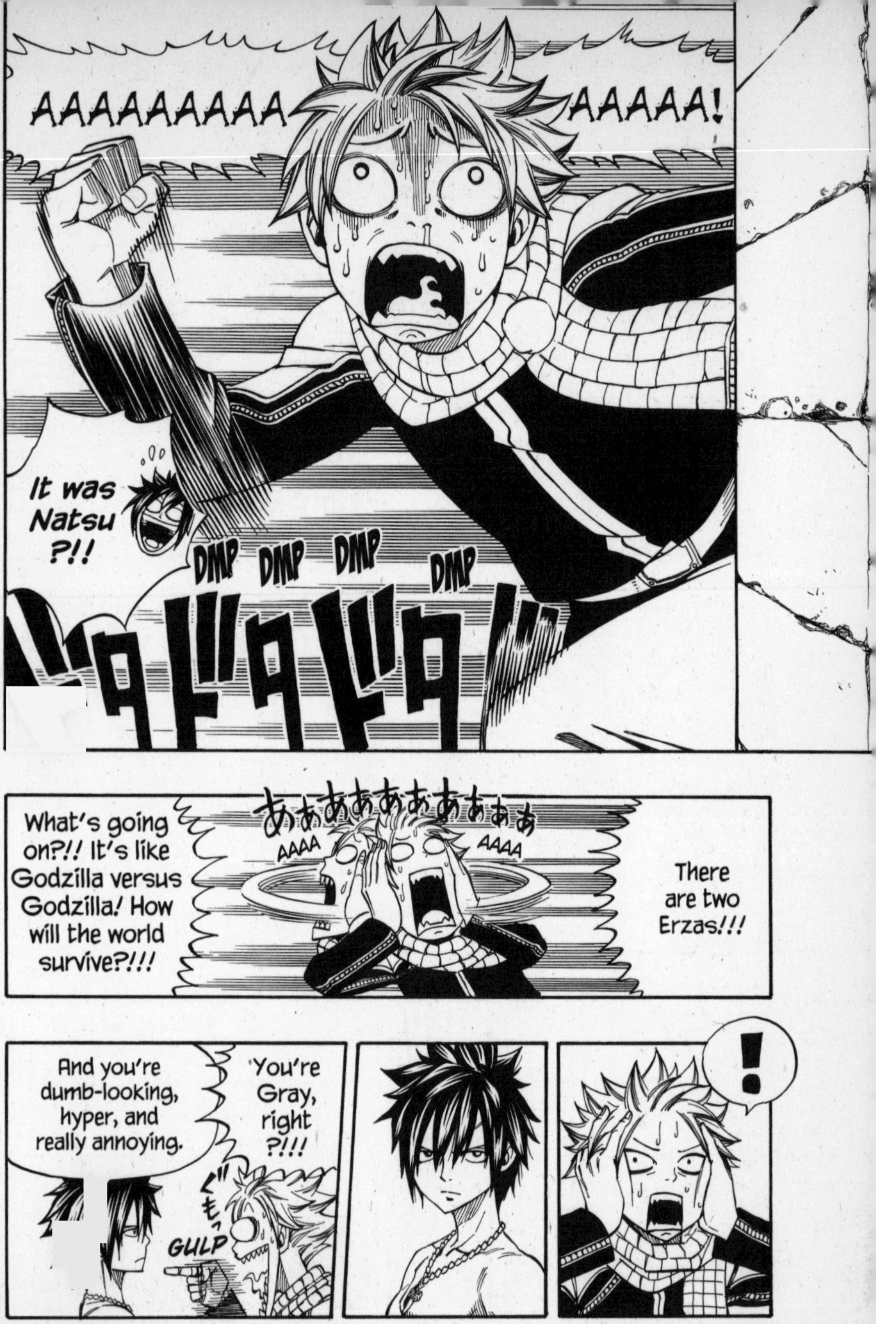
AAAAAAAAA
AAAAA!
It was Natsu?!!
DMP DMP DMP DMP
あぁぁぁぁぁぁぁぁぁ
AAAA
AAAA
There are two Erzas!!!
What's going on?!! It's like Godzilla versus Godzilla! How will the world survive?!!!
!
You're Gray, right?!!!
And you're dumb-looking, hyper, and really annoying.
ぐもっ
GULP

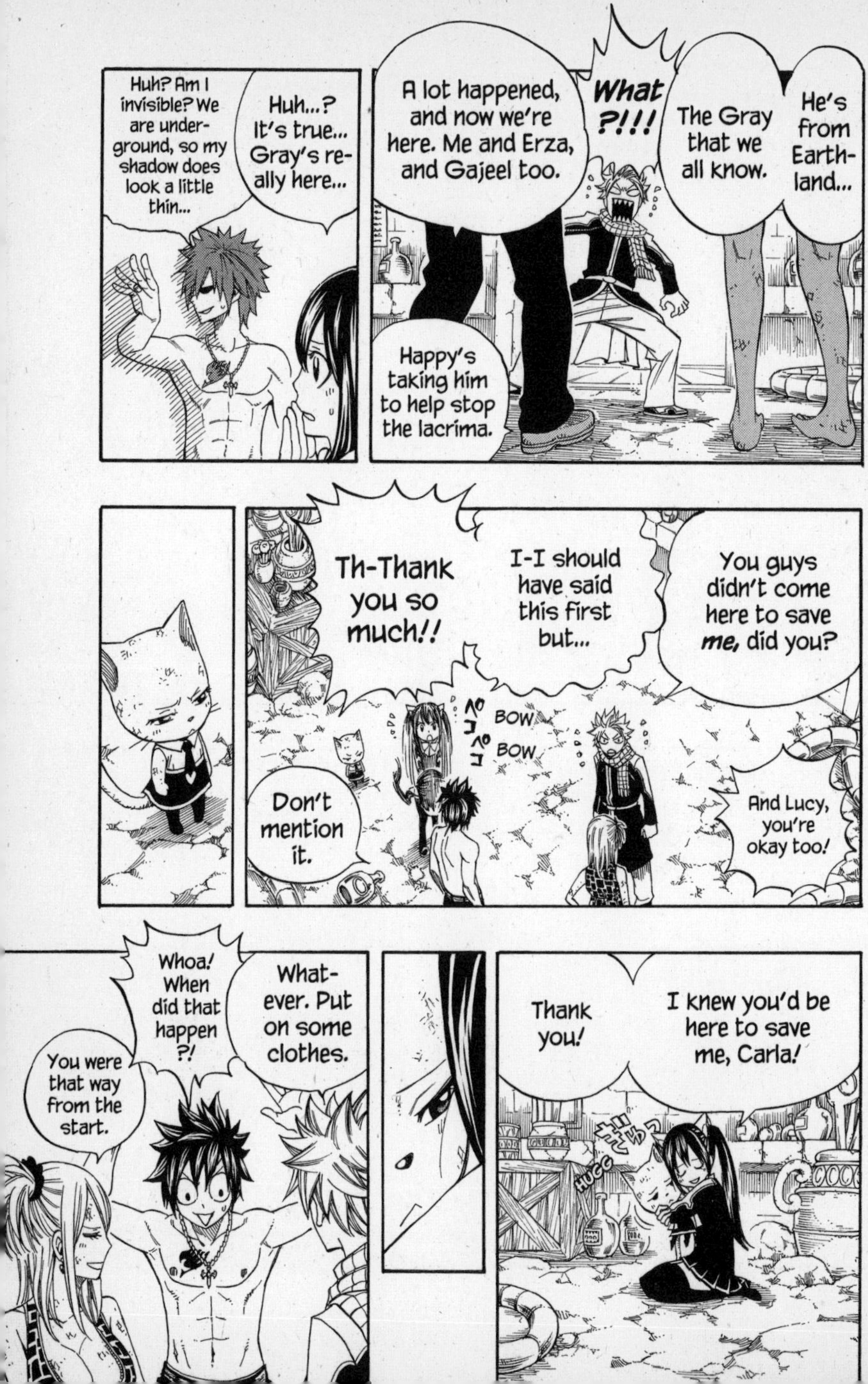
He's from Earth-land...
The Gray that we all know.
What?!!!
A lot happened, and now we're here. Me and Erza, and Gajeel too.
Happy's taking him to help stop the lacrima.
Huh...? It's true... Gray's re-ally here...
Huh? Am I invisible? We are under-ground, so my shadow does look a little thin...
You guys didn't come here to save *me*, did you?
I-I should have said this first but...
Th-Thank you so much!!
BOW BOW
And Lucy, you're okay too!
Don't mention it.
I knew you'd be here to save me, Carla!
Thank you!
HUGG
What-ever. Put on some clothes.
Whoa! When did that happen?!
You were that way from the start.

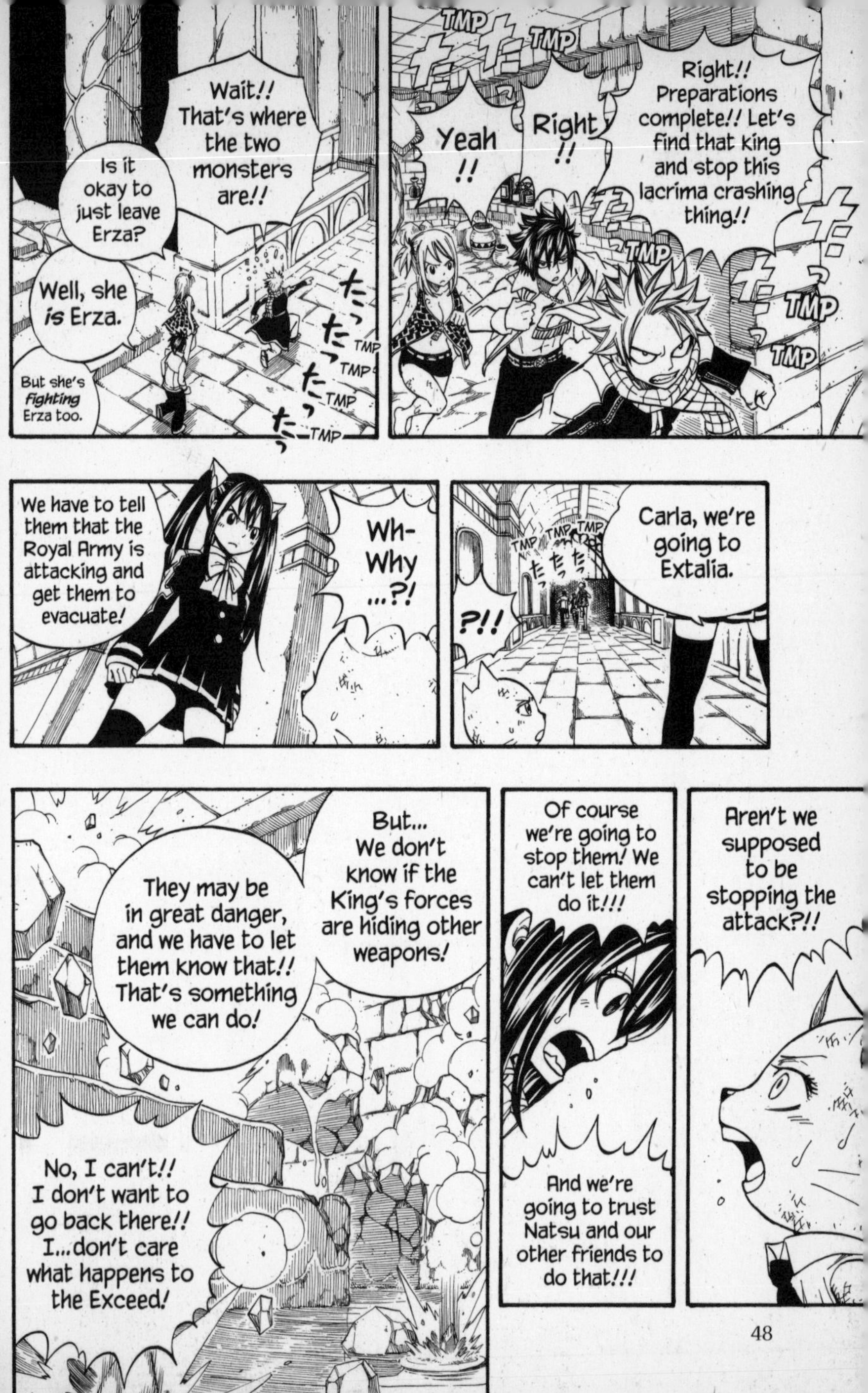

TMP TMP
Right!! Preparations complete!! Let's find that king and stop this lacrima crashing thing!!
Right !!
Yeah !!
TMP
TMP
TMP
Wait!! That's where the two monsters are!!
Is it okay to just leave Erza?
Well, she *is* Erza.
But she's *fighting* Erza too.
TMP
TMP
TMP
TMP
Carla, we're going to Extalia.
TMP TMP TMP
?!!
Wh- Why ...?!
We have to tell them that the Royal Army is attacking and get them to evacuate!
Aren't we supposed to be stopping the attack?!!
Of course we're going to stop them! We can't let them do it!!!
And we're going to trust Natsu and our other friends to do that!!!
But... We don't know if the King's forces are hiding other weapons!
They may be in great danger, and we have to let them know that!! That's something we can do!
No, I can't!! I don't want to go back there!! I...don't care what happens to the Exceed!

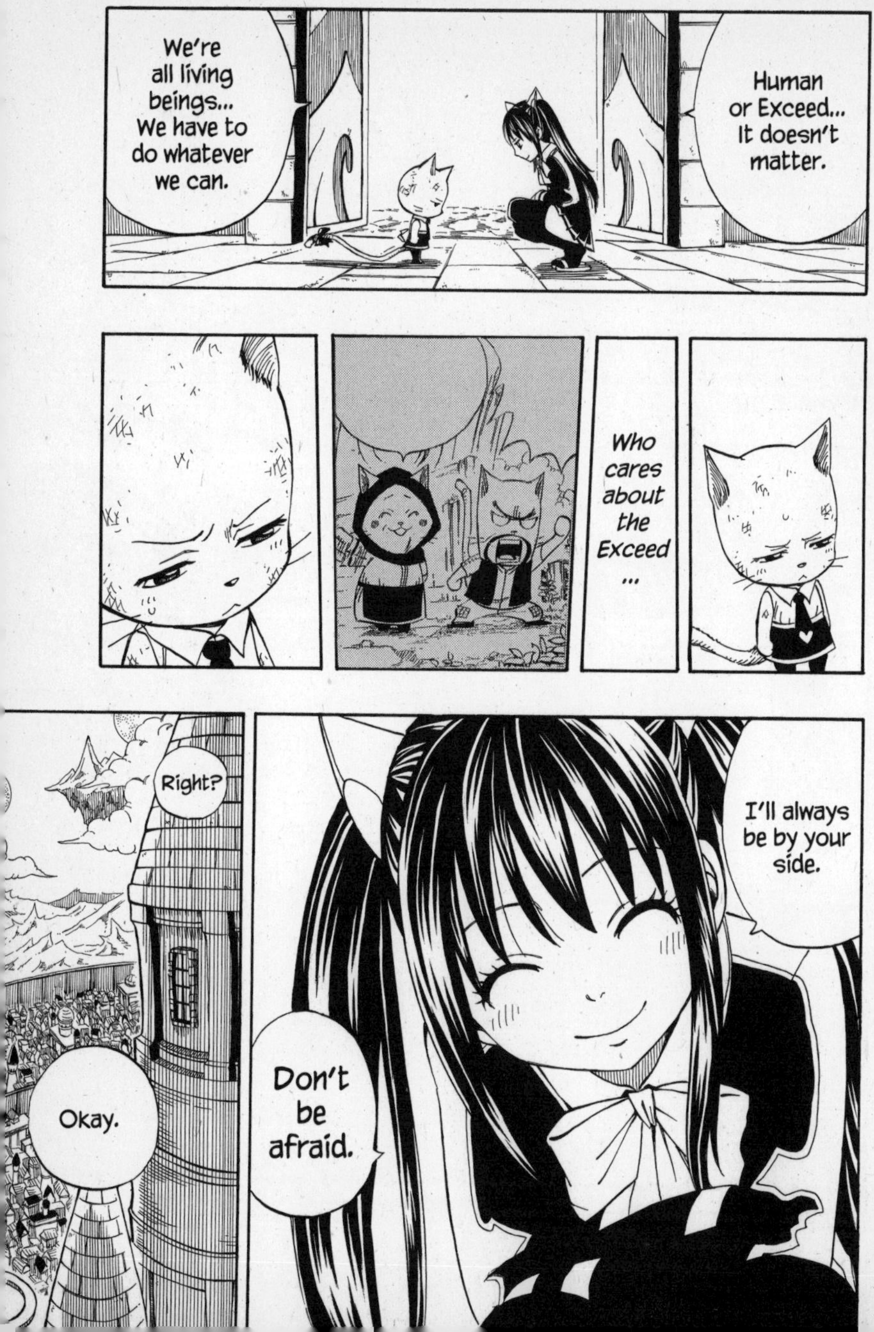
Human or Exceed... It doesn't matter.
We're all living beings... We have to do whatever we can.
Who cares about the Exceed ...
I'll always be by your side.
Don't be afraid.
Right?
Okay.

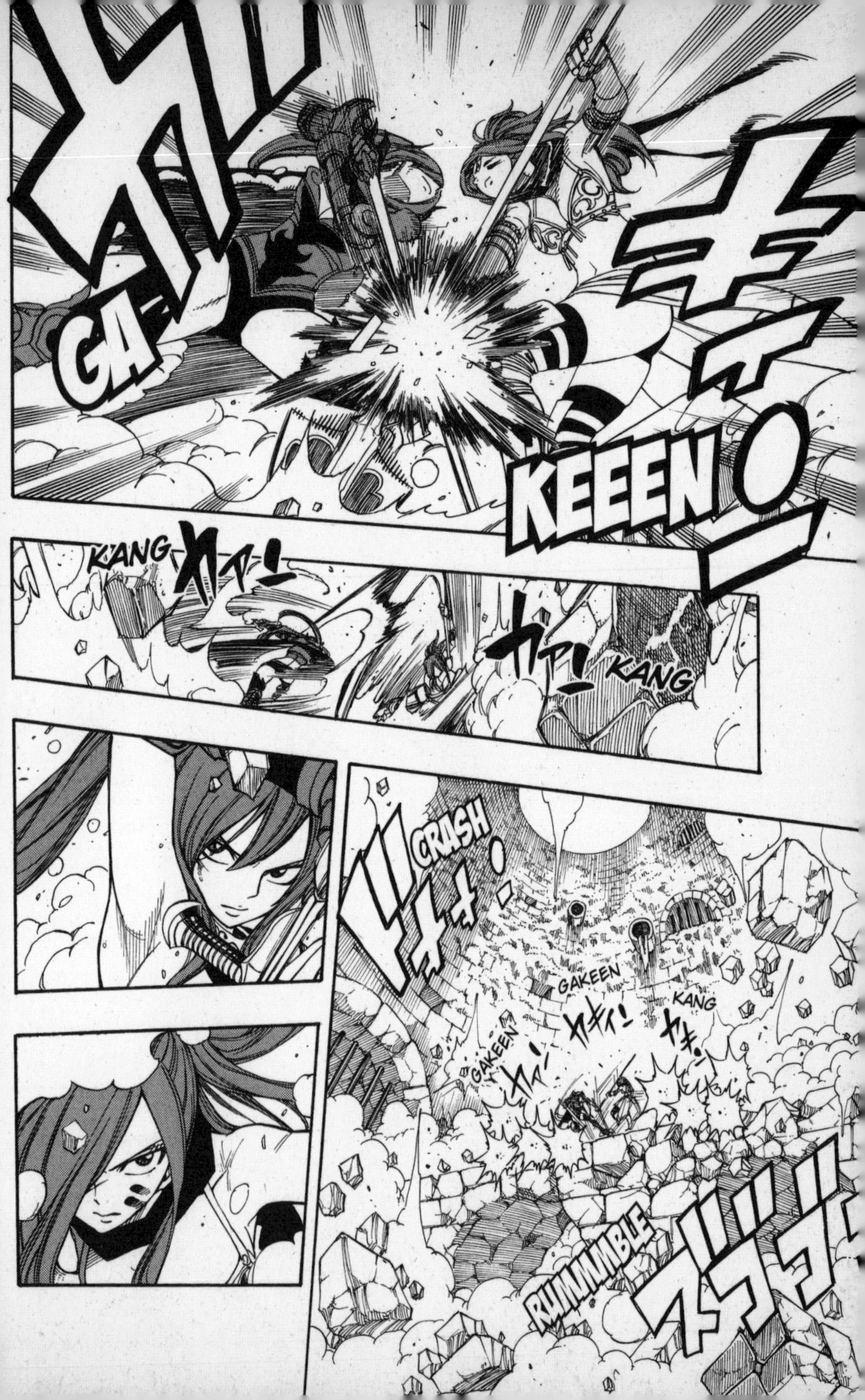

GA
KEEEN
KANG
KANG
CRASH
KANG
GAKEEN
GAKEEN
RUMMMBLE

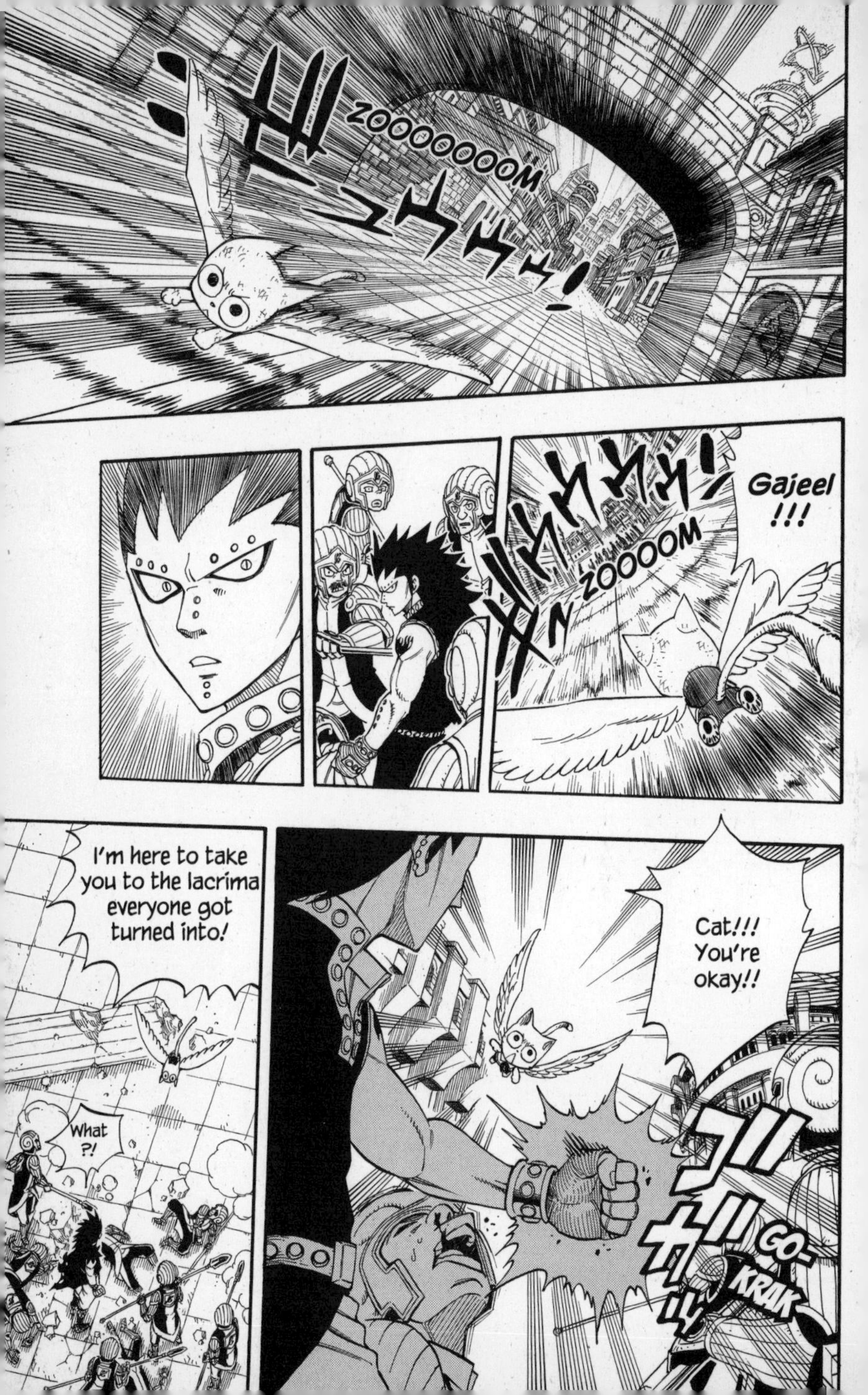

ZOOOOOOOOM
Gajeel !!!
ZOOOOM
Cat!!! You're okay!!
GO-KRAK
I'm here to take you to the lacrima everyone got turned into!
What ?!

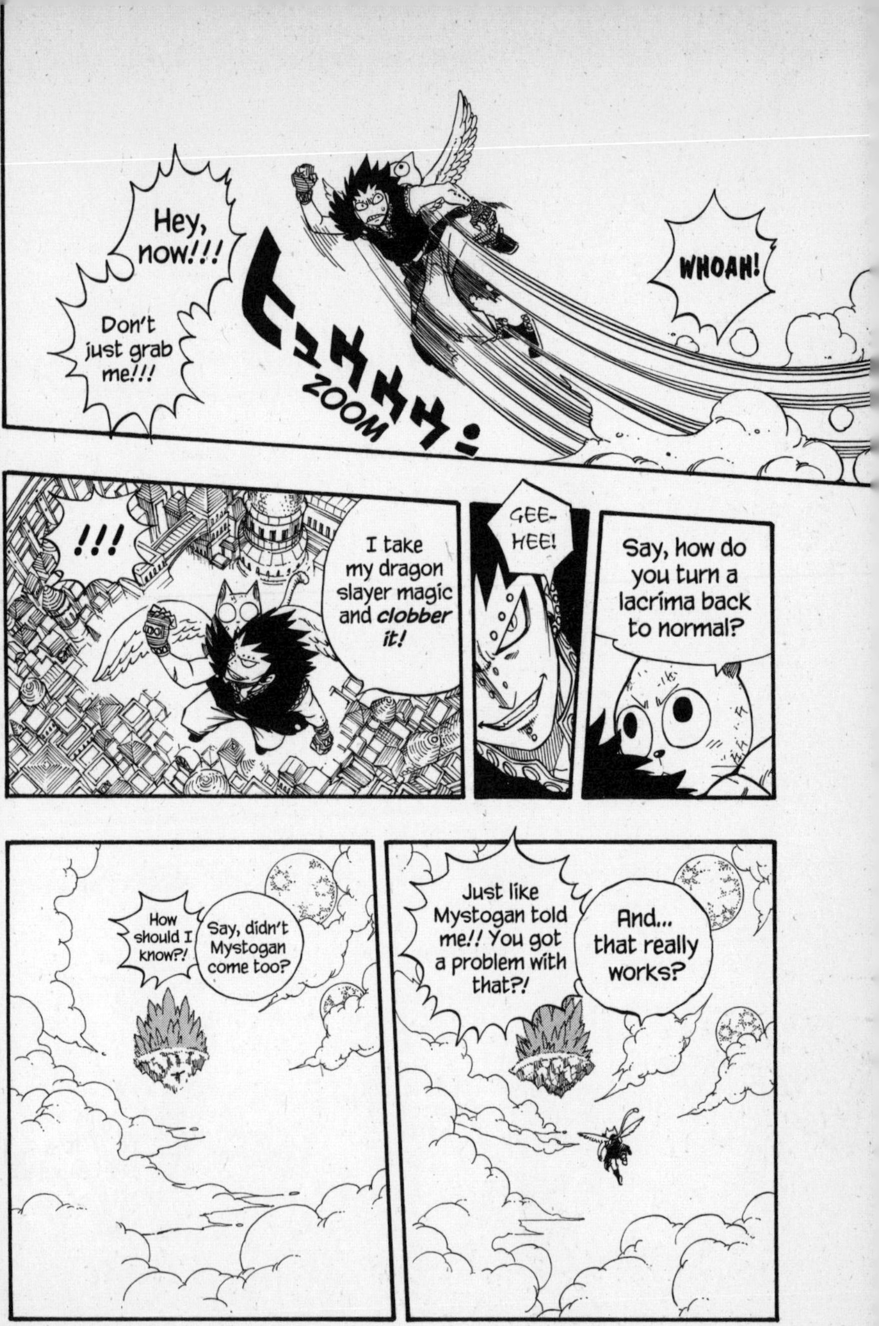
WHOAH!
ZOOM
Hey, now!!!
Don't just grab me!!!
Say, how do you turn a lacrima back to normal?
GEE-HEE!
I take my dragon slayer magic and *clobber it!*
!!!
And... that really works?
Just like Mystogan told me!! You got a problem with that?!
Say, didn't Mystogan come too?
How should I know?!

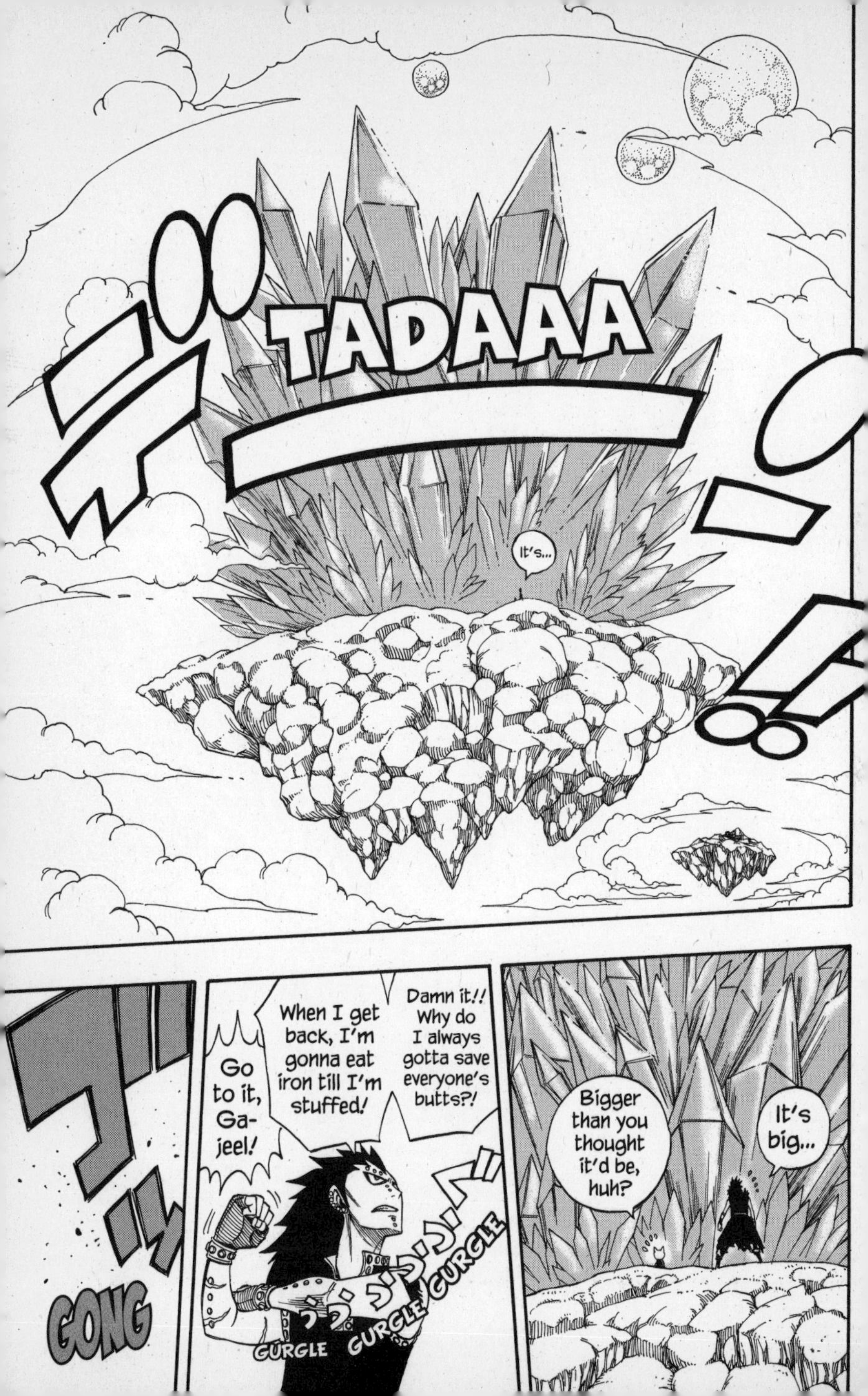
TADAAA
It's...
It's big...
Bigger than you thought it'd be, huh?
Damn it!! Why do I always gotta save everyone's butts?!
When I get back, I'm gonna eat iron till I'm stuffed!
Go to it, Ga-jeel!
GURGLE
GURGLE
GURGLE
GONG

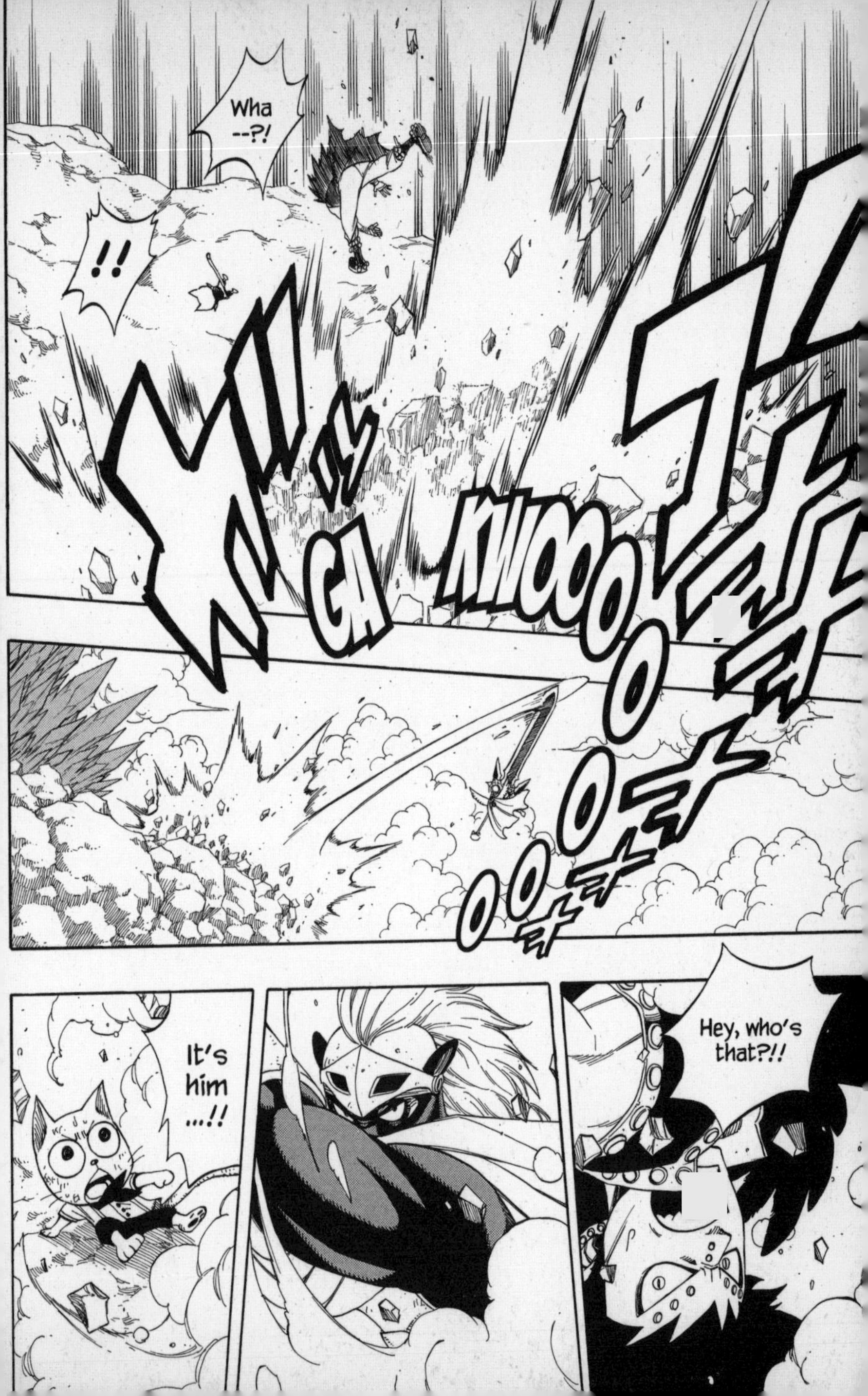
Wha --?!
!!
GA
KWOOOO
Hey, who's that?!!
It's him ...!!

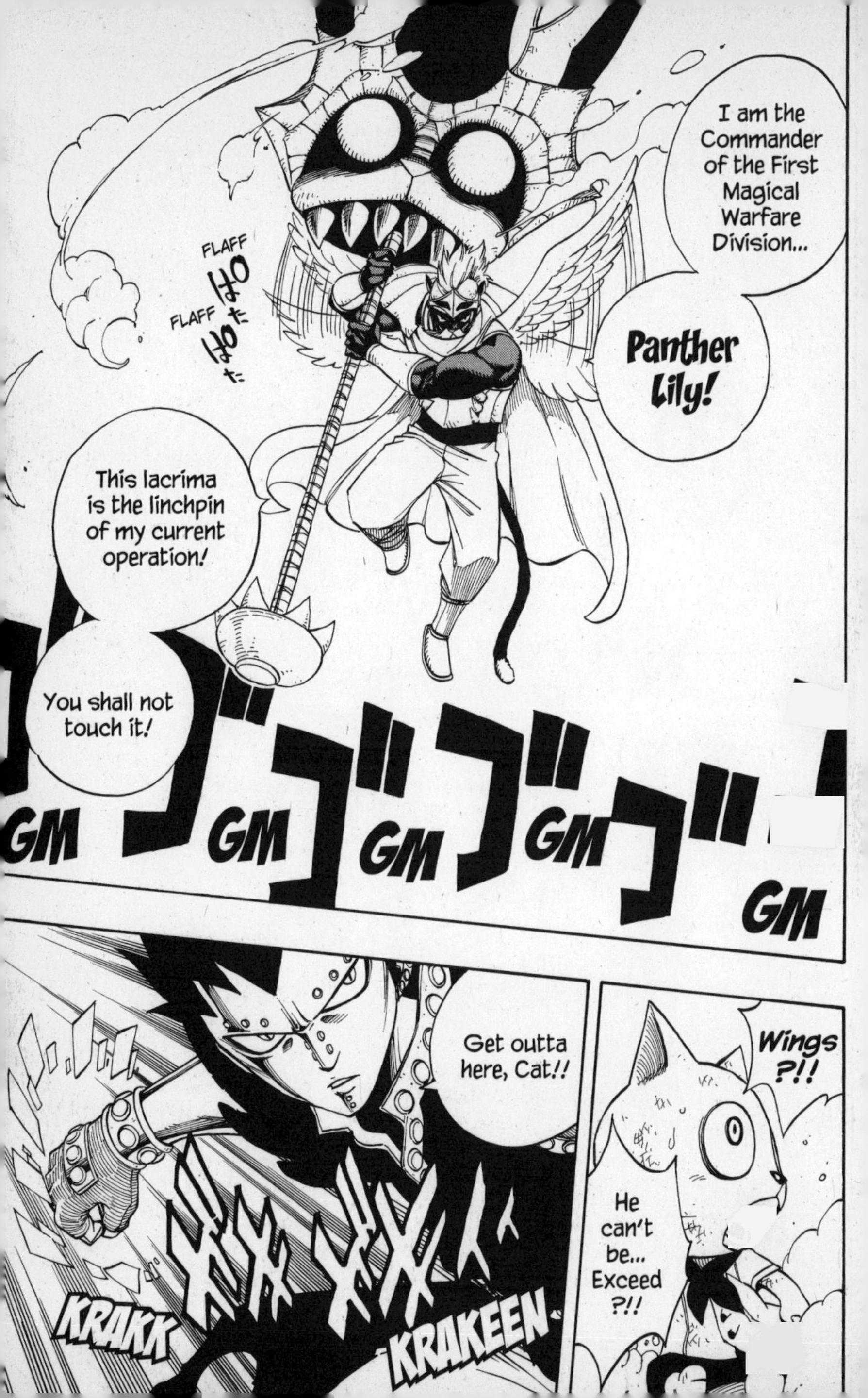
I am the Commander of the First Magical Warfare Division...
Panther Lily!
FLAFF
FLAFF
This lacrima is the linchpin of my current operation!
You shall not touch it!
GM GM GM GM GM
Wings?!!
He can't be... Exceed?!!
Get outta here, Cat!!
KRAKEEN
KRAKK

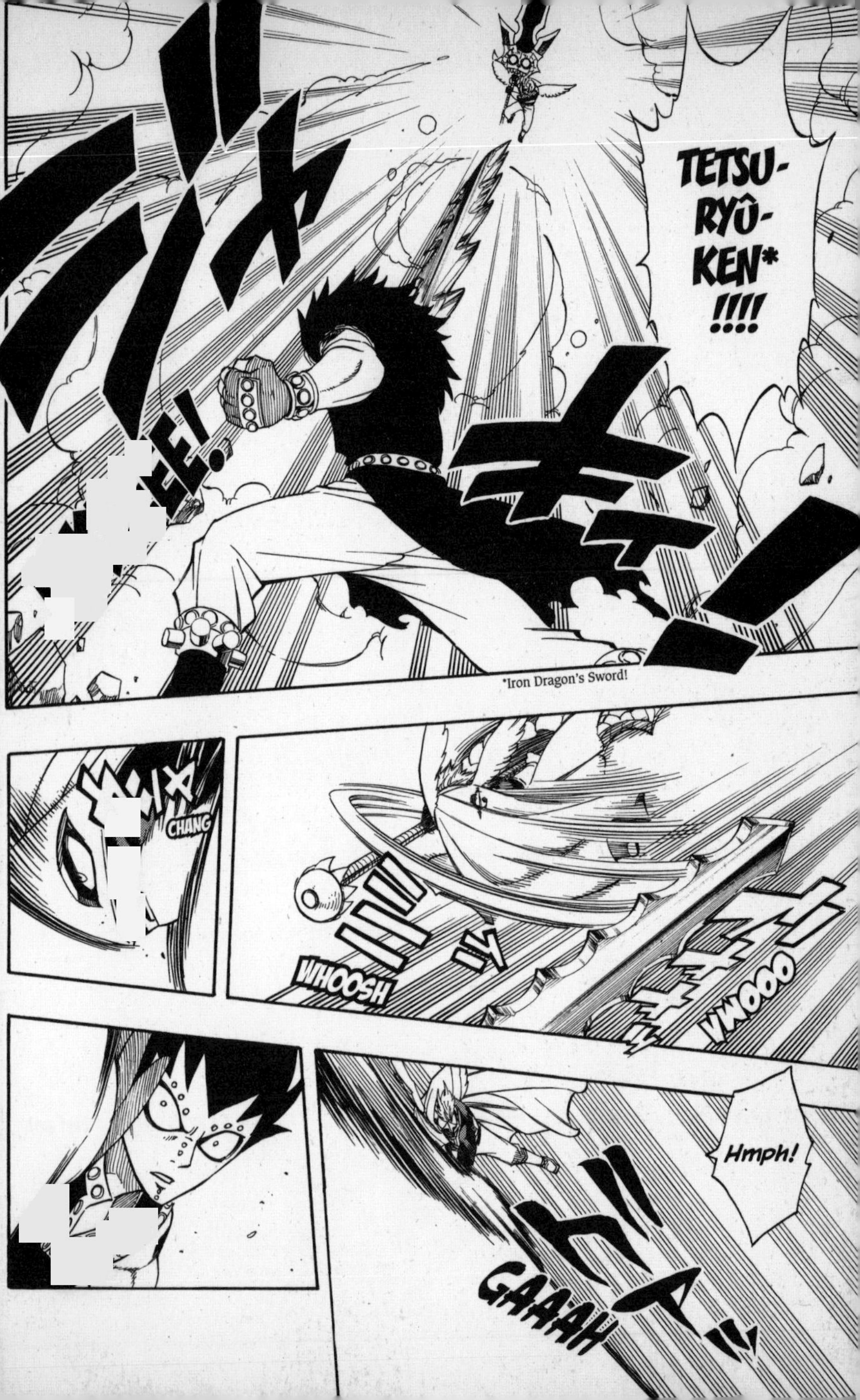
TETSU-RYÛ-KEN*!!!!
*Iron Dragon's Sword!
VWOOO
WHOOSH
CHANG
Hmph!
GAAAH

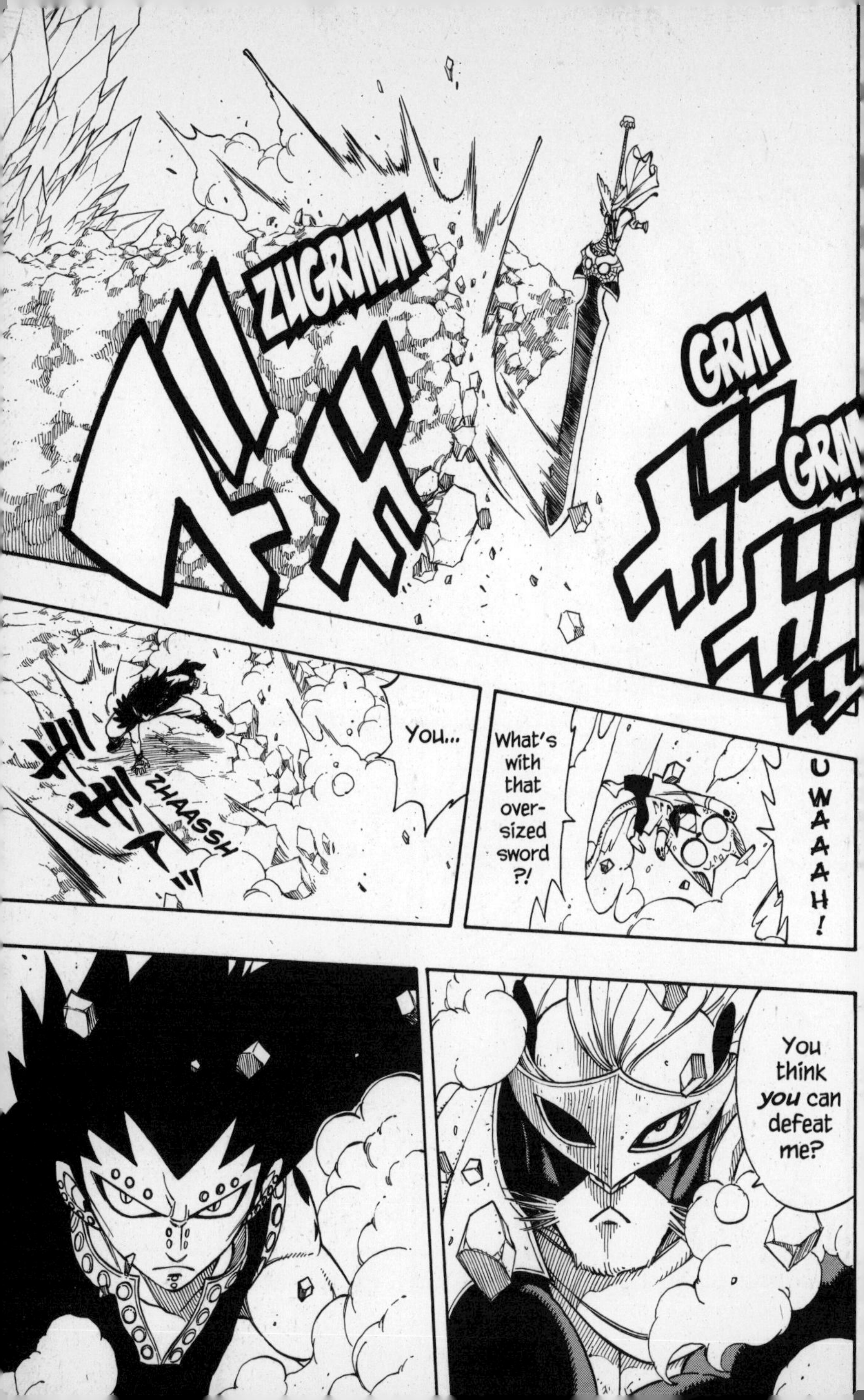
GRM
GRM
ZUGRMMM
UWAAAAH!
What's with that over-sized sword?!
You...
ZHAASSH
You think *you* can defeat me?

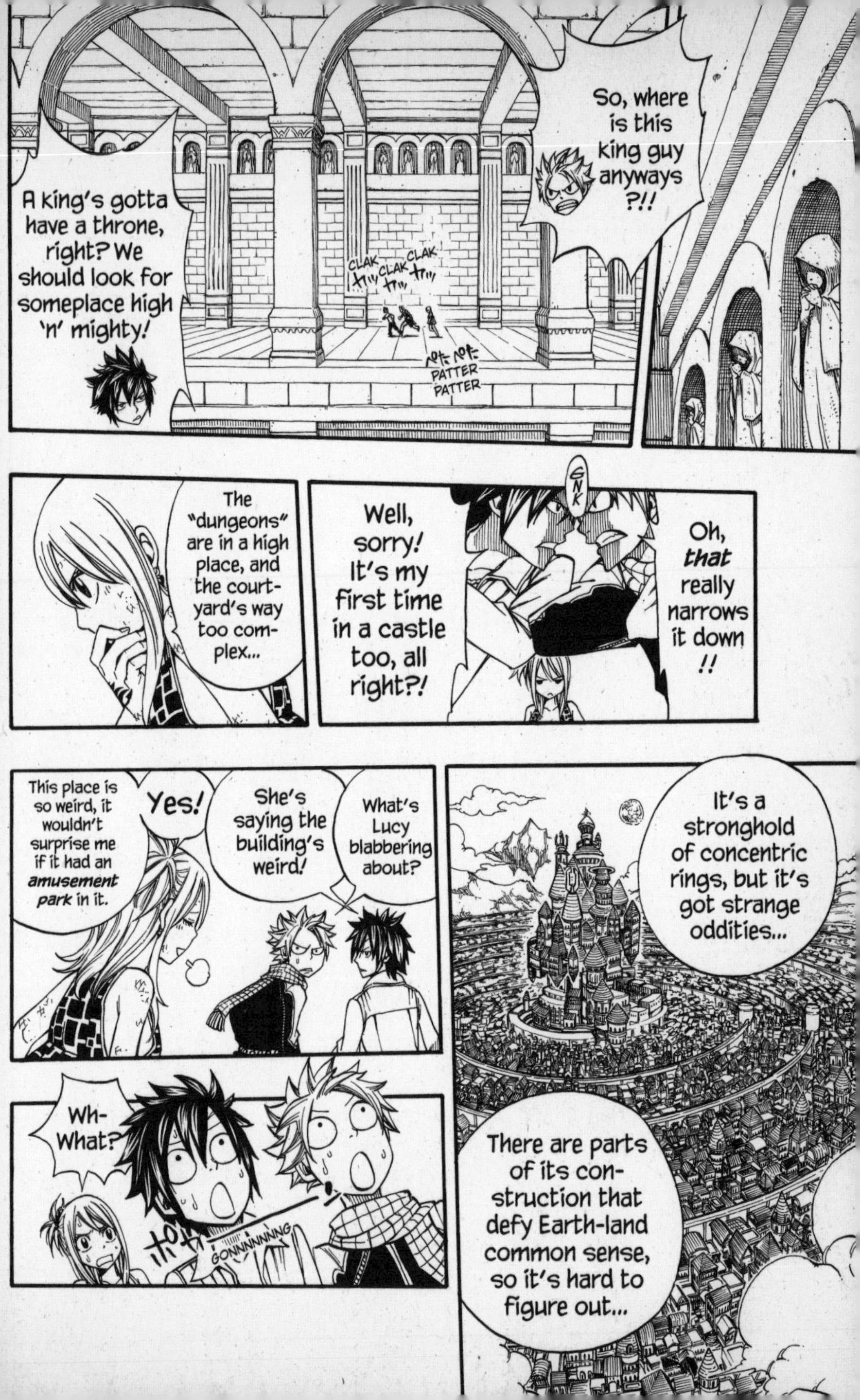
So, where is this king guy anyways ?!!
A king's gotta have a throne, right? We should look for someplace high 'n' mighty!
CLAK CLAK CLAK
PATTER PATTER
Oh, *that* really narrows it down !!
GNK
Well, sorry! It's my first time in a castle too, all right?!
The "dungeons" are in a high place, and the court-yard's way too com-plex...
It's a stronghold of concentric rings, but it's got strange oddities...
There are parts of its con-struction that defy Earth-land common sense, so it's hard to figure out...
What's Lucy blabbering about?
She's saying the building's weird!
Yes!
This place is so weird, it wouldn't surprise me if it had an ***amusement park*** in it.
Wh- What?
GONNNNNNNG

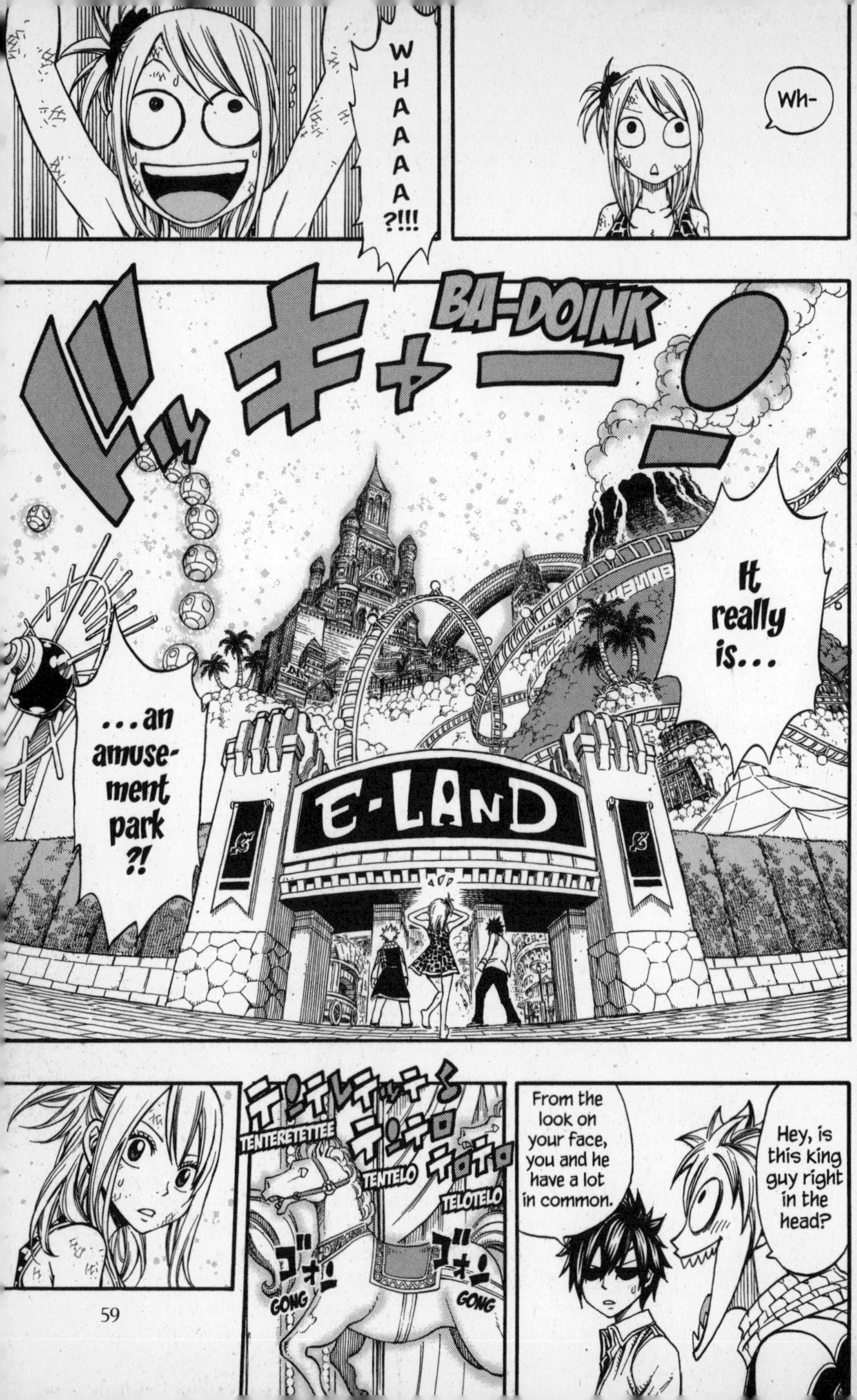
Wh-
WHAAAAA?!!!
BA-DOINK
It really is...
...an amusement park?!
Hey, is this king guy right in the head?
From the look on your face, you and he have a lot in common.
TENTERETETTEE
TENTELO
TELOTELO
GONG
GONG

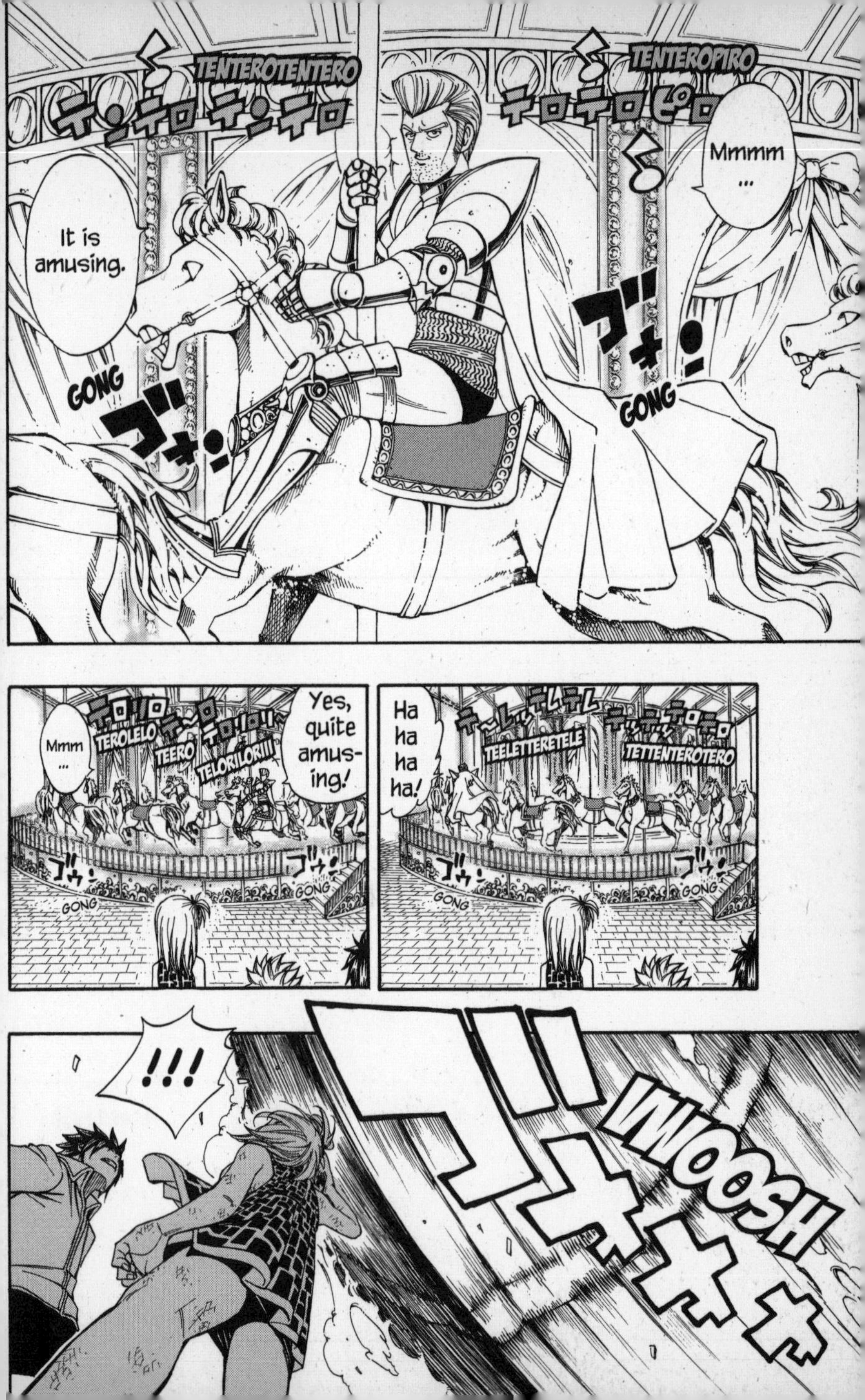
TENTEROPIRO
Mmmm ...
TENTEROTENTERO
It is amusing.
GONG
GONG
TETTENTEROTERO
TEELETTERETELE
Ha ha ha ha!
GONG
GONG
Yes, quite amusing!
TELORILORI
TEERO
TEROLELO
Mmm ...
GONG
GONG
WHOOSH
!!!

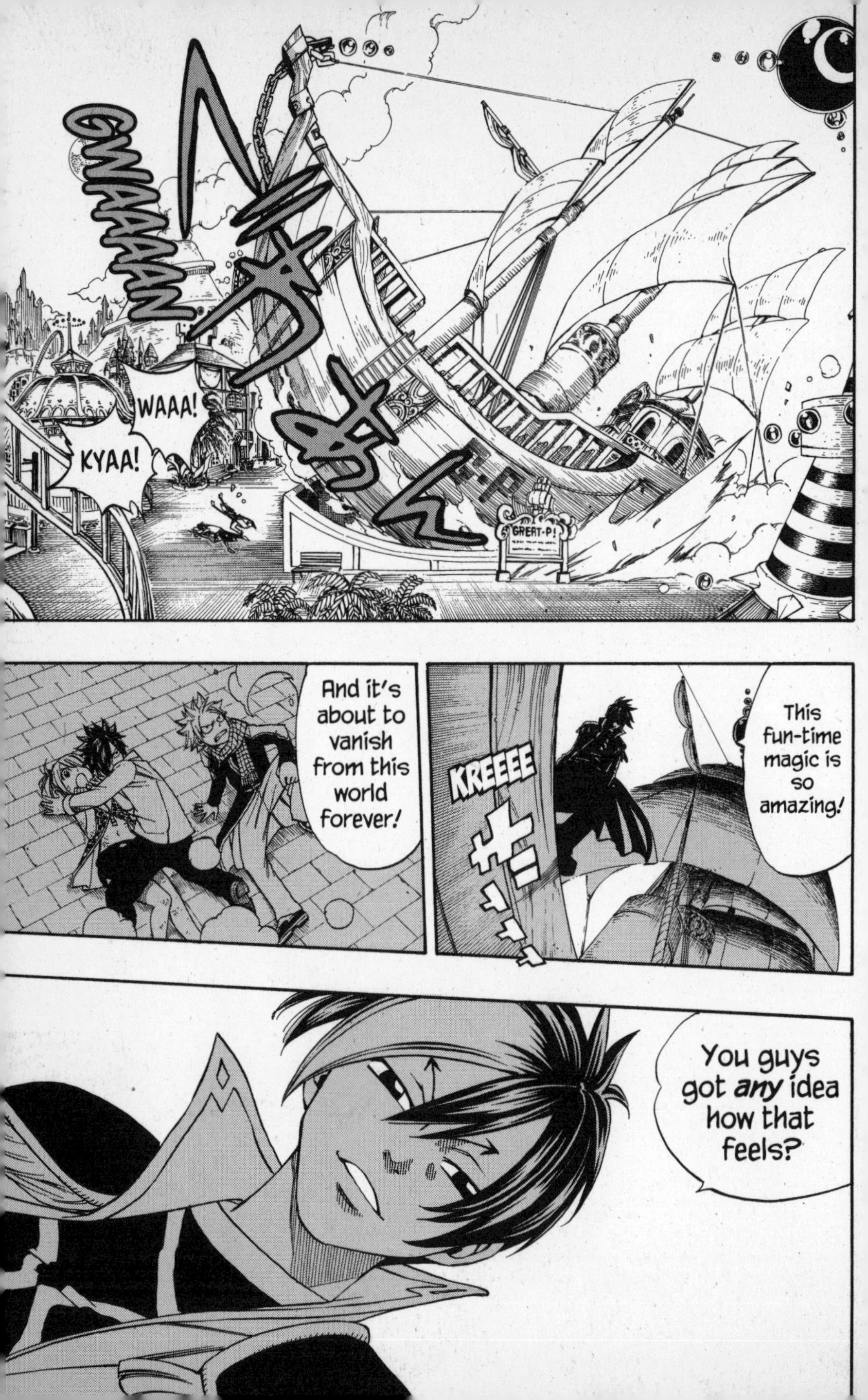
GWAAAAN
WAAA!
KYAA!
GREAT-P!
KREEEE
This fun-time magic is so amazing!
And it's about to vanish from this world forever!
You guys got *any* idea how that feels?

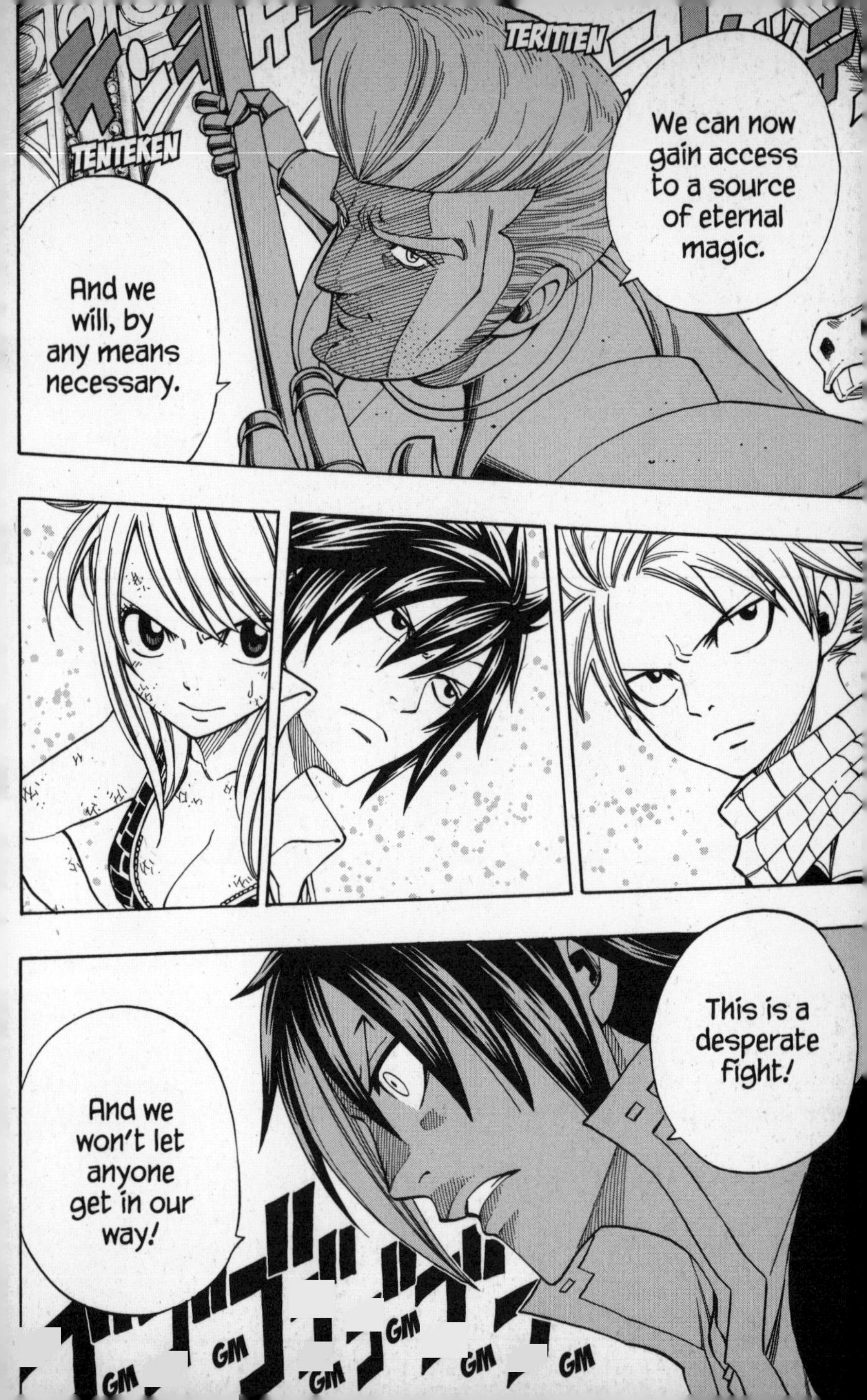
TERITTEN
We can now gain access to a source of eternal magic.
TENTEKEN
And we will, by any means necessary.
This is a desperate fight!
And we won't let anyone get in our way!
GM GM GM GM GM GM

FAIRYTAIL

フェアリーテイル

Chapter 182,
It's People's Lives, Right?!!!

HiRO · MaSHiMa

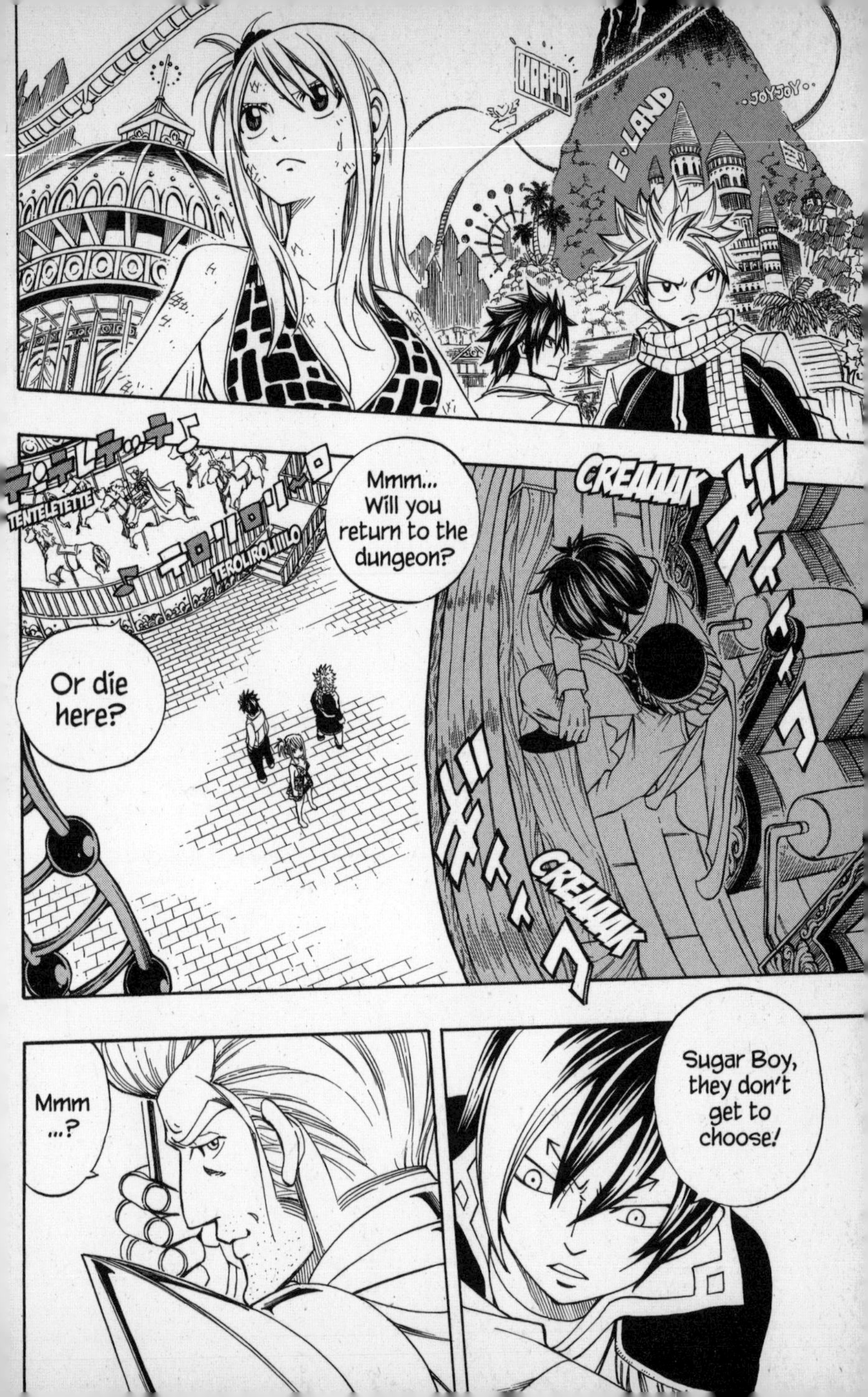
HAPPY
JOYJOY
E·LAND
CREAAAK
CREAAAK
Mmm... Will you return to the dungeon?
TENTELETETTE
TEROLIROLIIILO
Or die here?
Sugar Boy, they don't get to choose!
Mmm ...?

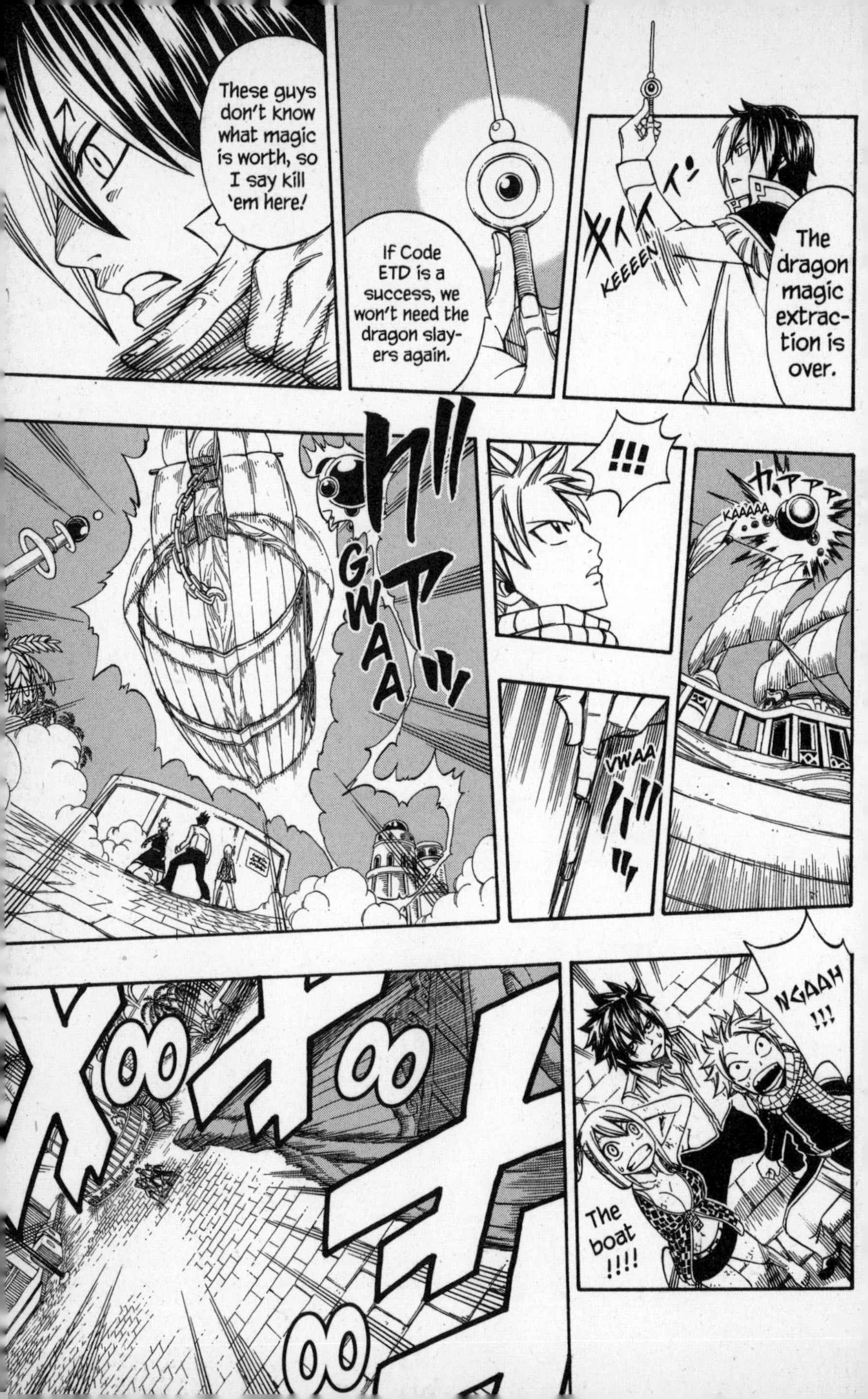

The dragon magic extraction is over.
KEEEEN
If Code ETD is a success, we won't need the dragon slayers again.
These guys don't know what magic is worth, so I say kill 'em here!
KAAAAA
!!!
VWAA
GWAAA
NGAAH !!!
The boat !!!!

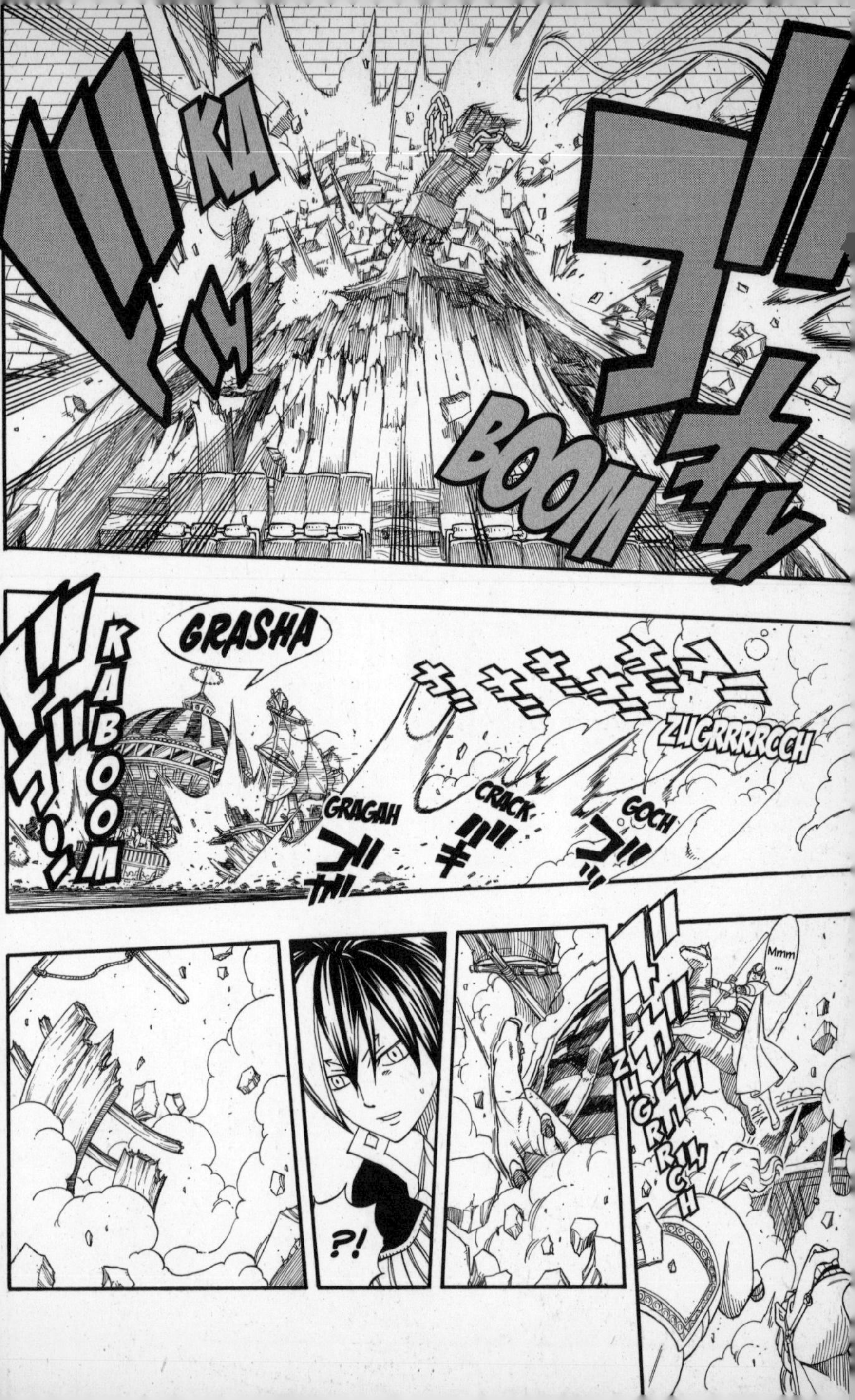
BOOM
KA
ZUGRRRRCCH
GOCH
CRACK
GRAGAH
GRASHA
KABOOM
Mmm...
ZUGRRCH
?!

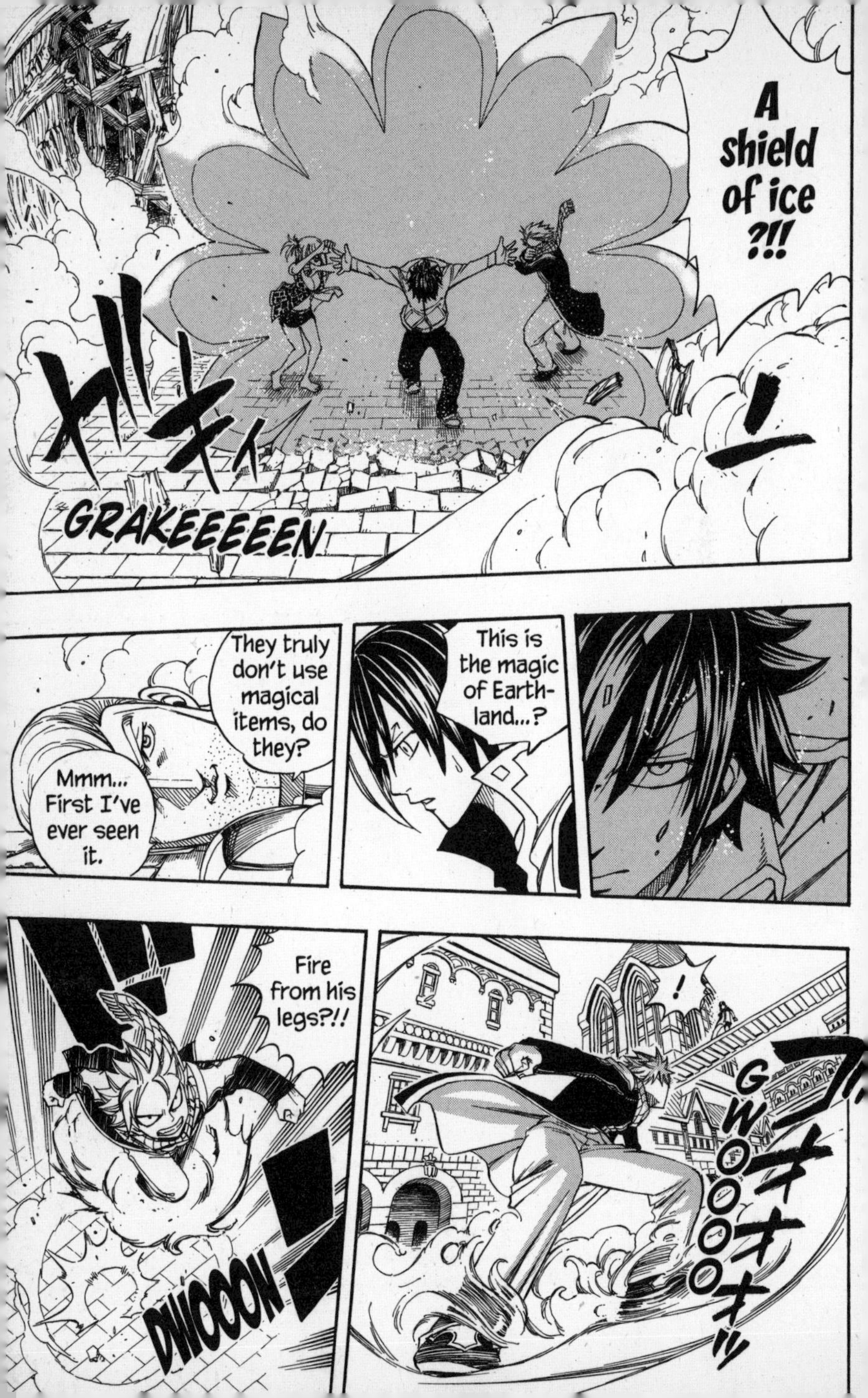
A shield of ice ?!!
GRAKEEEEEEN
This is the magic of Earth-land...?
They truly don't use magical items, do they?
Mmm... First I've ever seen it.
!
GWOOOOO
Fire from his legs?!!
DWOOON

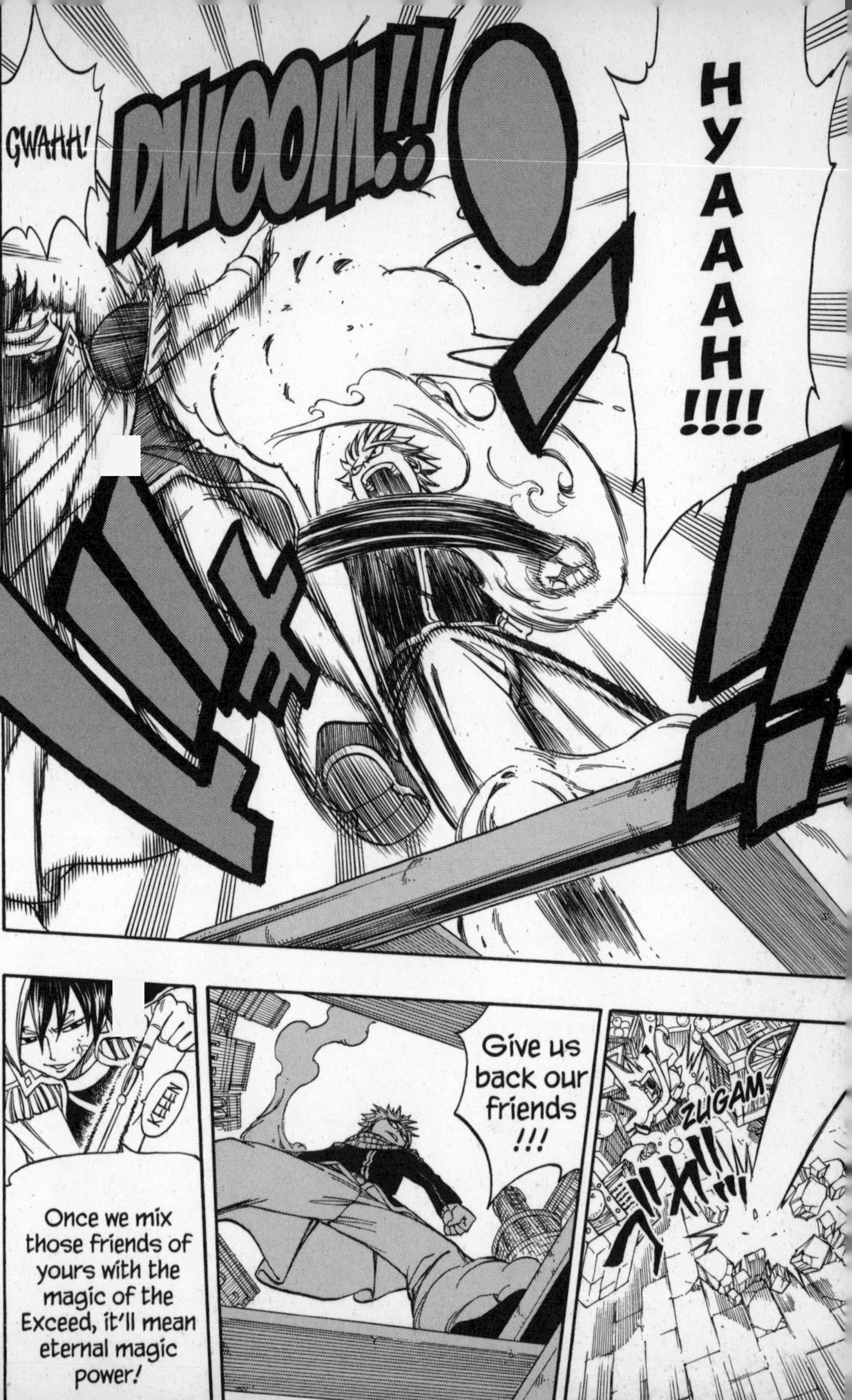
HYAAAH!!!!
DWOOM!!
GWAHH!
ZUGAM
Give us back our friends!!!
KEEEN
Once we mix those friends of yours with the magic of the Exceed, it'll mean eternal magic power!

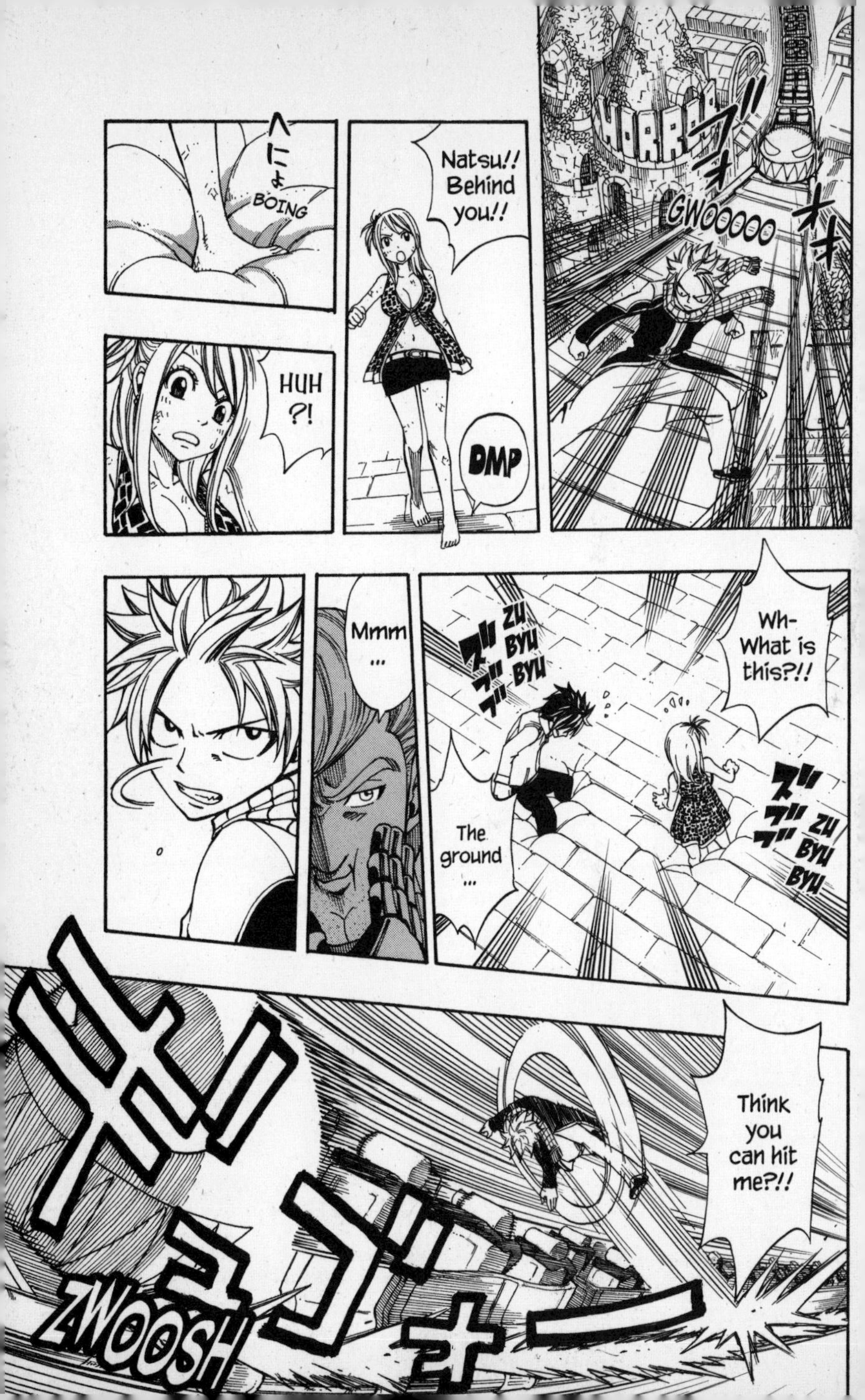

GWOOOOO
Natsu!! Behind you!!
DMP
へにょ
BOING
HUH ?!
Wh- What is this?!!
ZU BYU BYU
The ground ...
ZU BYU BYU
Mmm ...
Think you can hit me?!!
ZWOOSH

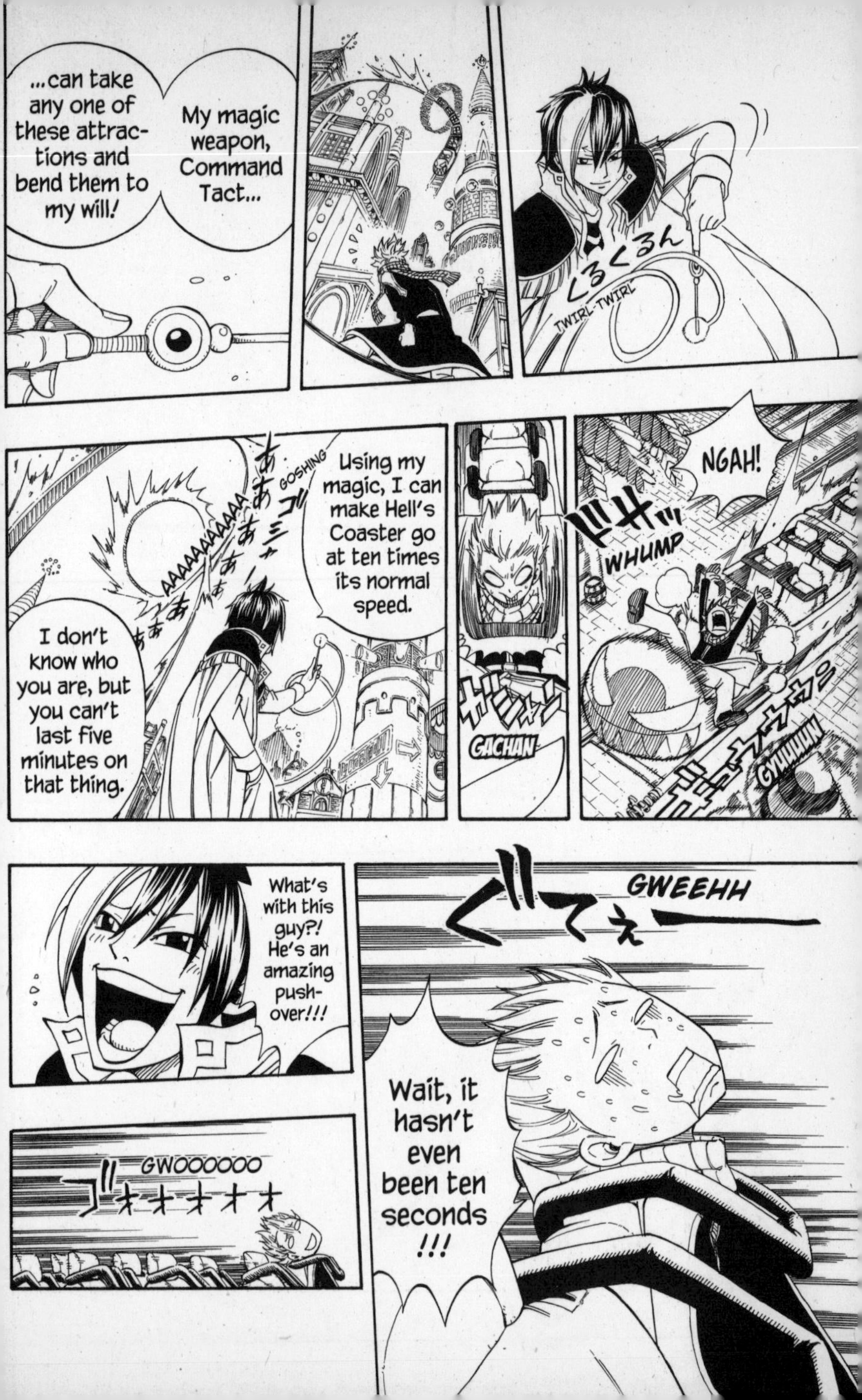
くるくるん
TWIRL-TWIRL
My magic weapon, Command Tact...
...can take any one of these attractions and bend them to my will!
NGAH!
ドサッ
WHUMP
ギュウウン
GYUUUN
ガシャン
GACHAN
Using my magic, I can make Hell's Coaster go at ten times its normal speed.
GOSHING
I don't know who you are, but you can't last five minutes on that thing.
ぐえー
GWEEHH
Wait, it hasn't even been ten seconds!!!
What's with this guy?! He's an amazing push-over!!!
ゴオオオオオ
GWOOOOOO

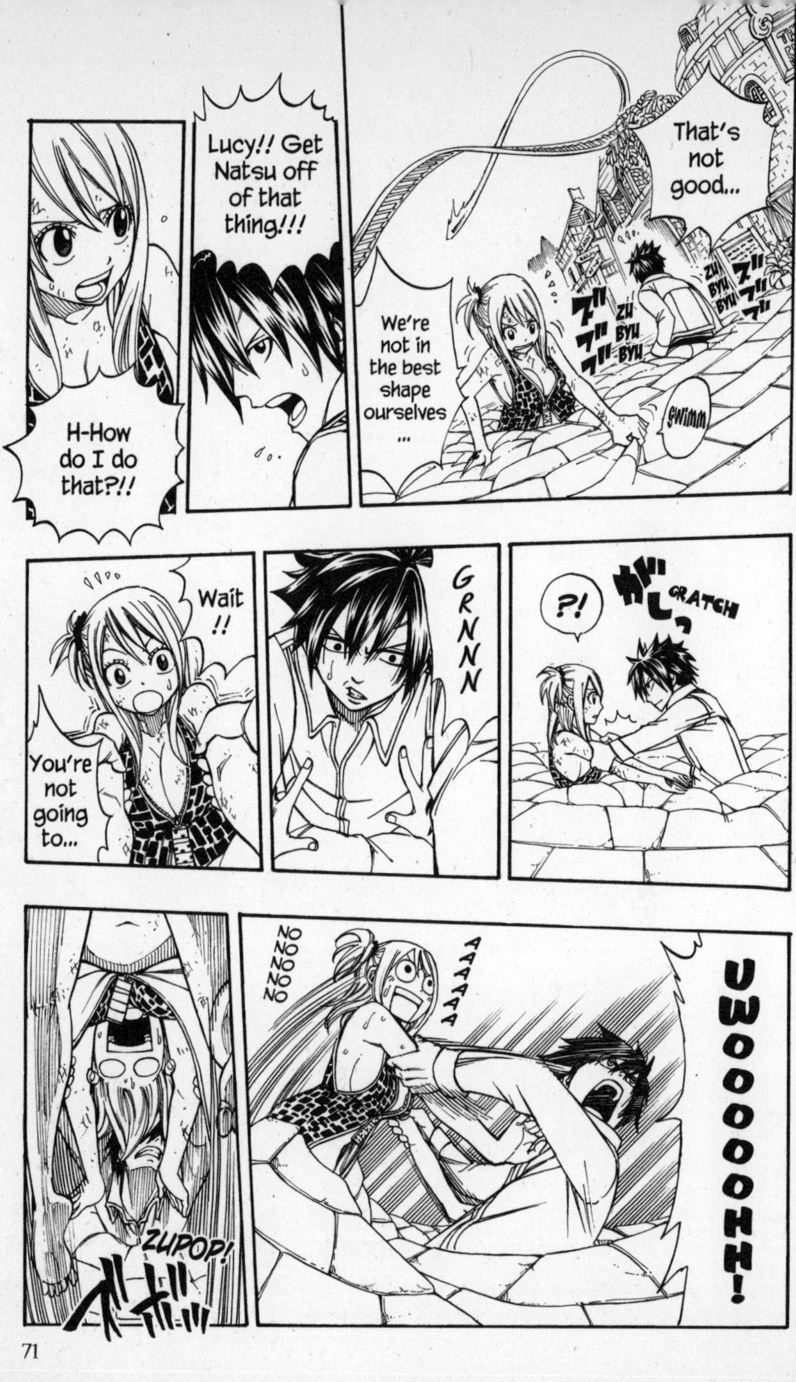

That's not good...
We're not in the best shape ourselves ...
ZU BYU ZU BYU
ZU BYU-BYU
SWIMM
Lucy!! Get Natsu off of that thing!!!
H-How do I do that?!!
?!
GRATCH
GRNNN
Wait!!
You're not going to...
UWOOOOOOOH!
AAAAAA
NO NO NO NO NO
ZUPOP!

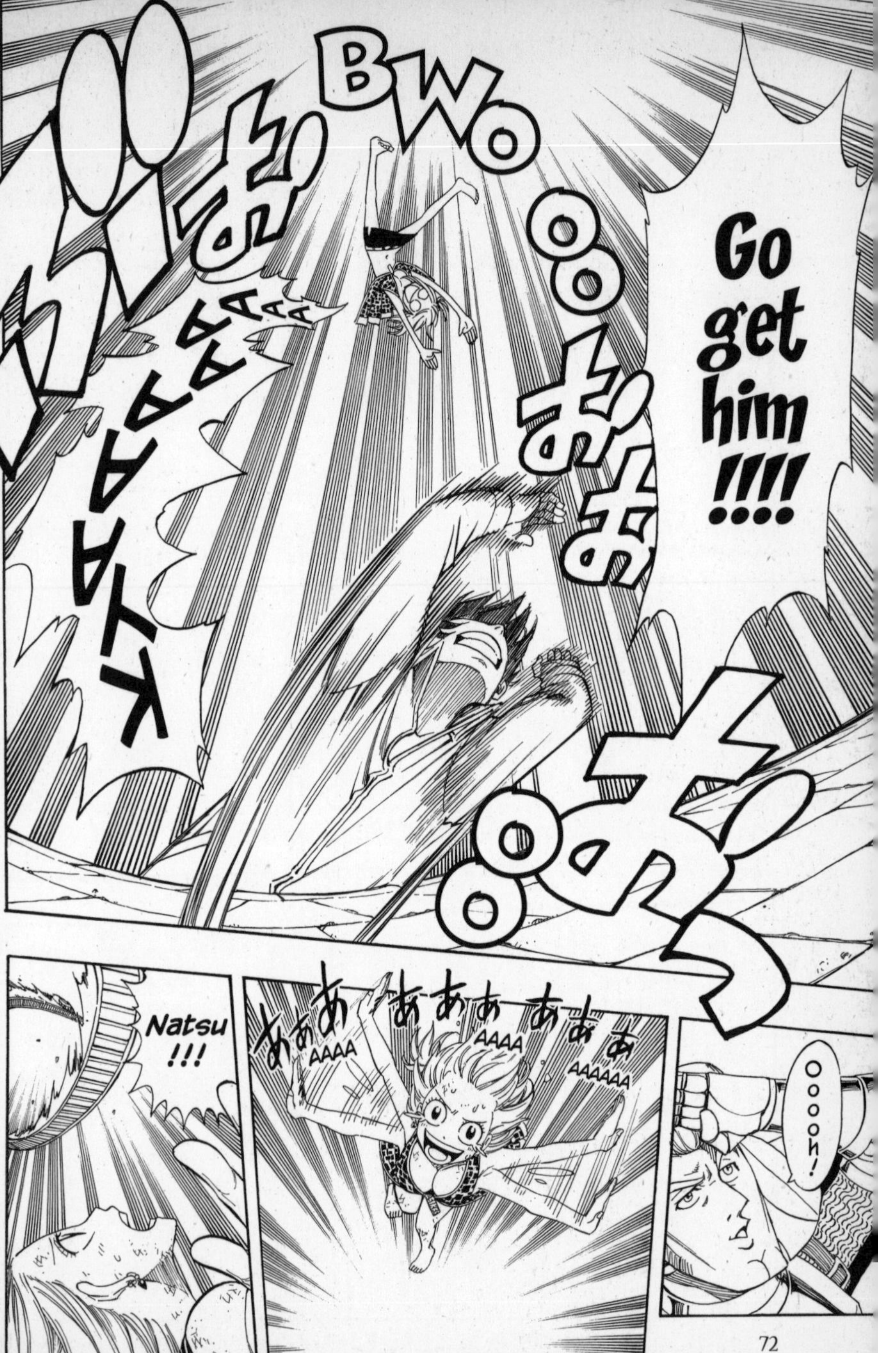
Go get him!!!!
BWOOO
Ooooh!
AAAA
AAAA
AAAAAA
Natsu!!!

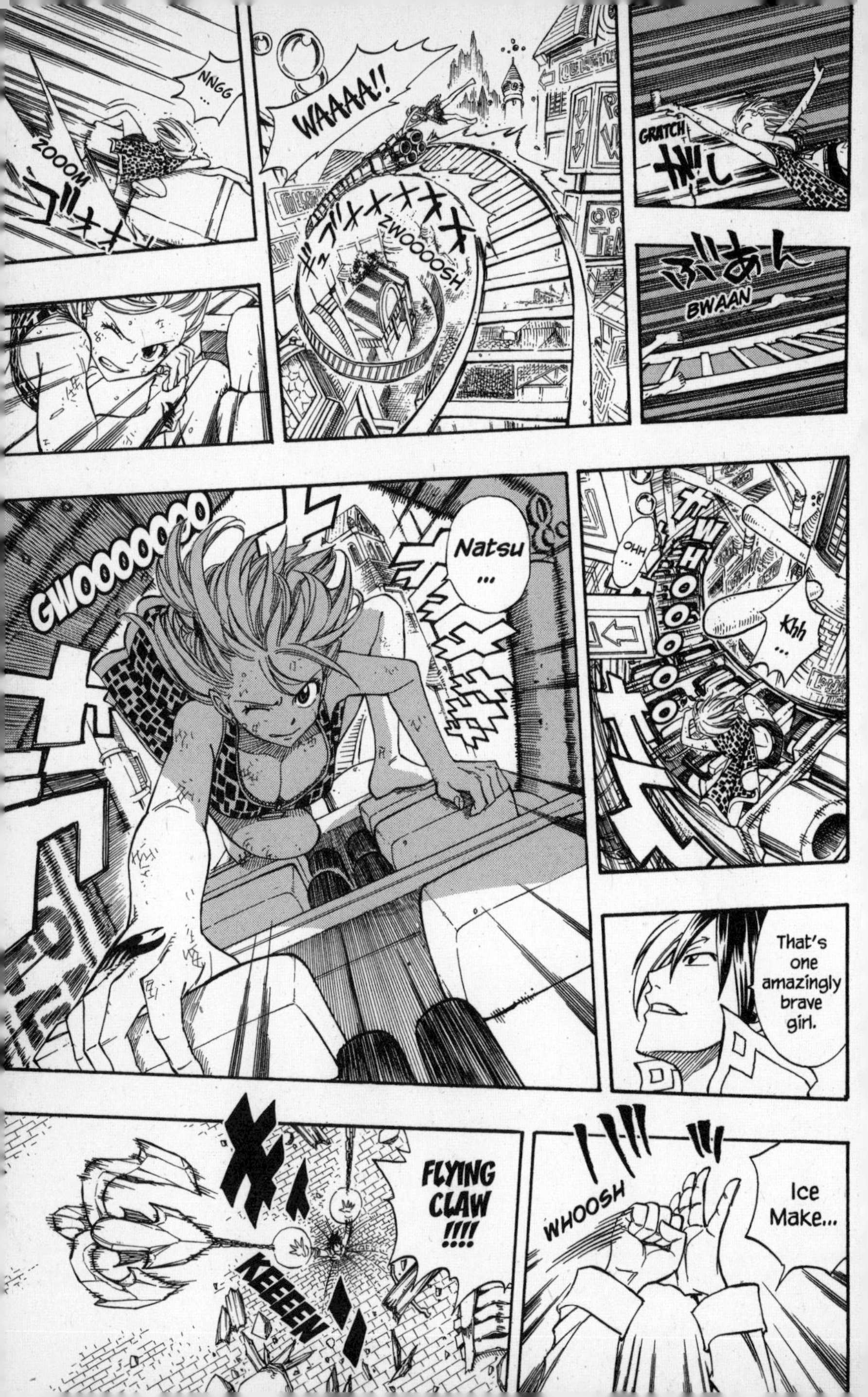

GRATCH
BWAAN
WAAAA!!
ZWOOOOOSH
NNGG...
ZOOOM
OHH...
WHOOOOOOO
Khh...
That's one amazingly brave girl.
Natsu...
GWOOOOOOO
Ice Make...
WHOOSH
FLYING CLAW!!!!
KEEEEN

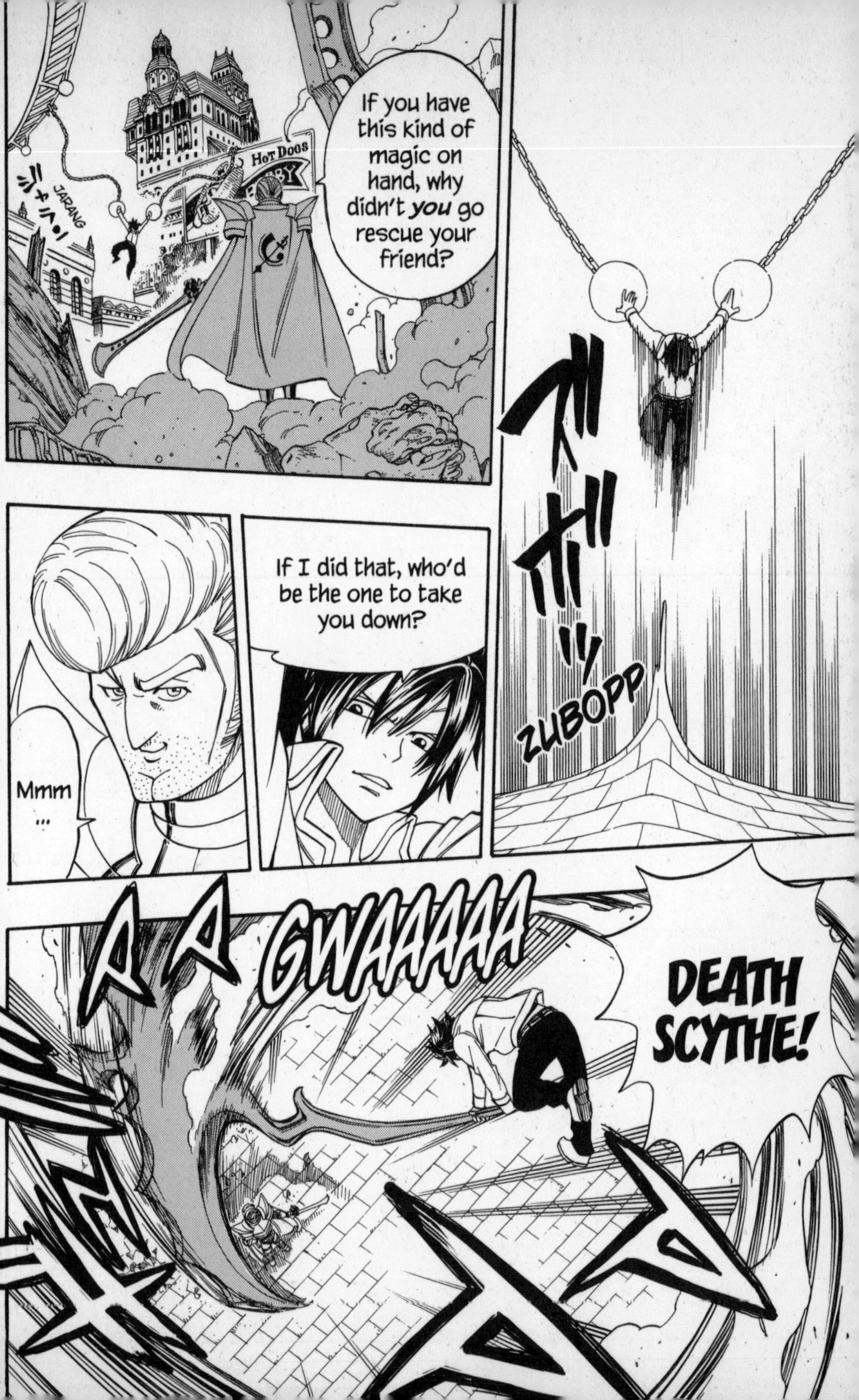
ZUBOPP
If you have this kind of magic on hand, why didn't *you* go rescue your friend?
HOT DOGS
JARANG
If I did that, who'd be the one to take you down?
Mmm ...
DEATH SCYTHE!
GWAAAAAA

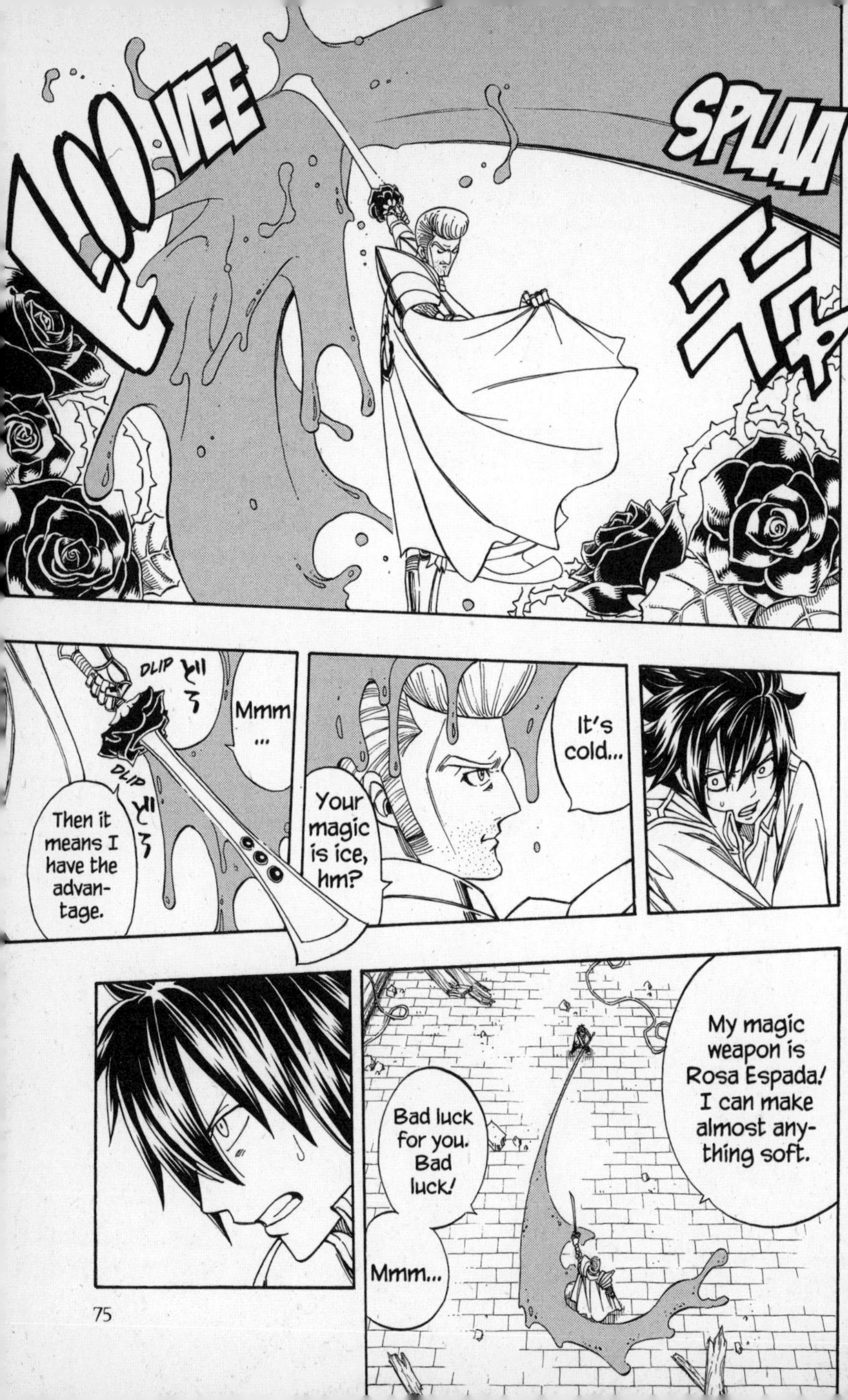
SPLAAA
ZOOOVEE
It's cold...
Your magic is ice, hm?
DLIP
Mmm...
DLIP
Then it means I have the advantage.
My magic weapon is Rosa Espada! I can make almost anything soft.
Bad luck for you. Bad luck!
Mmm...

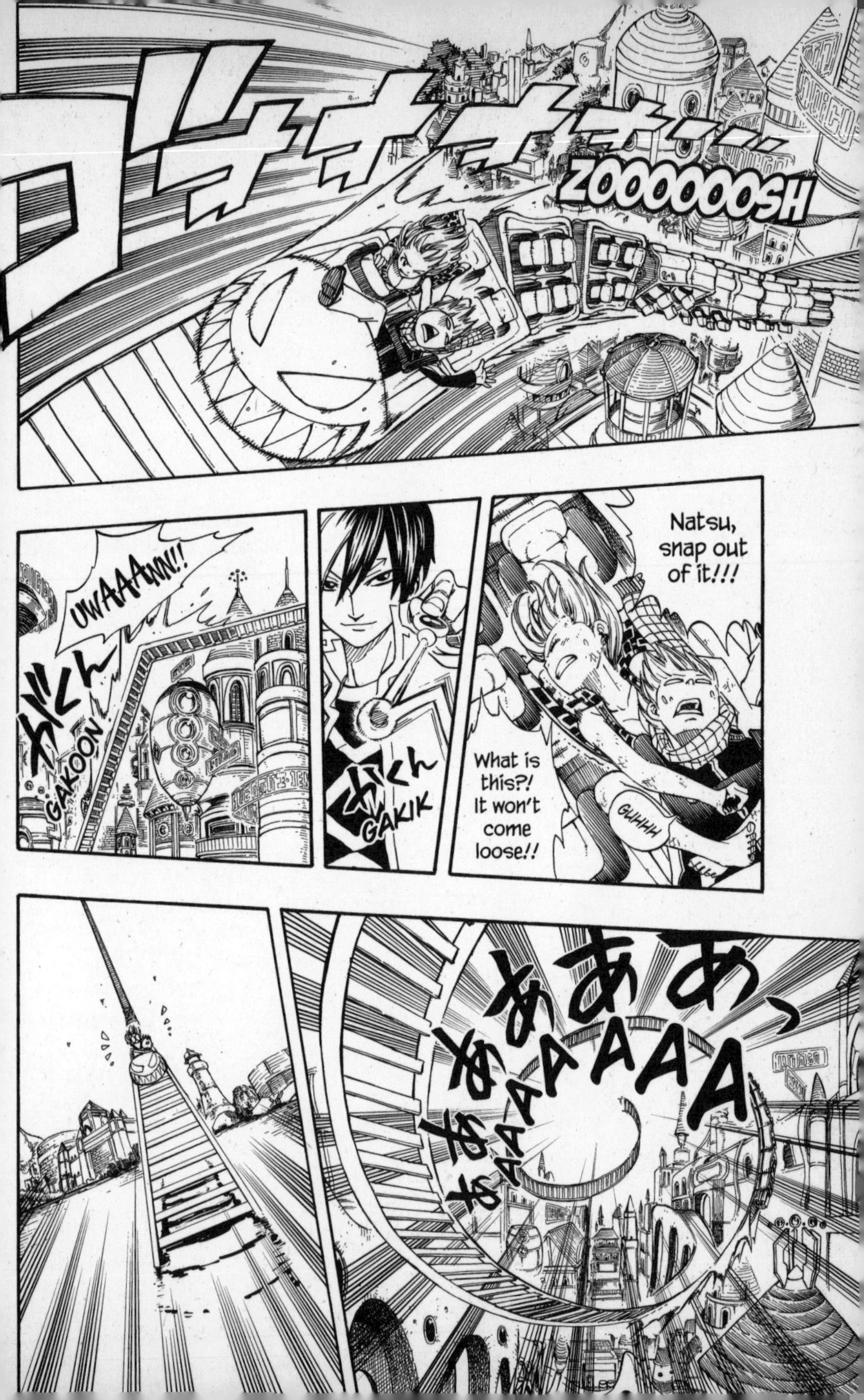

ゴォオオオ…
ZOOOOOOOSH
Natsu, snap out of it!!!
What is this?! It won't come loose!!
GUHHH
ガキッ
GAKIK
UWAAANN!!
ガコン
GAKOON
あああ、
AAAAA
ああああ
AAAA

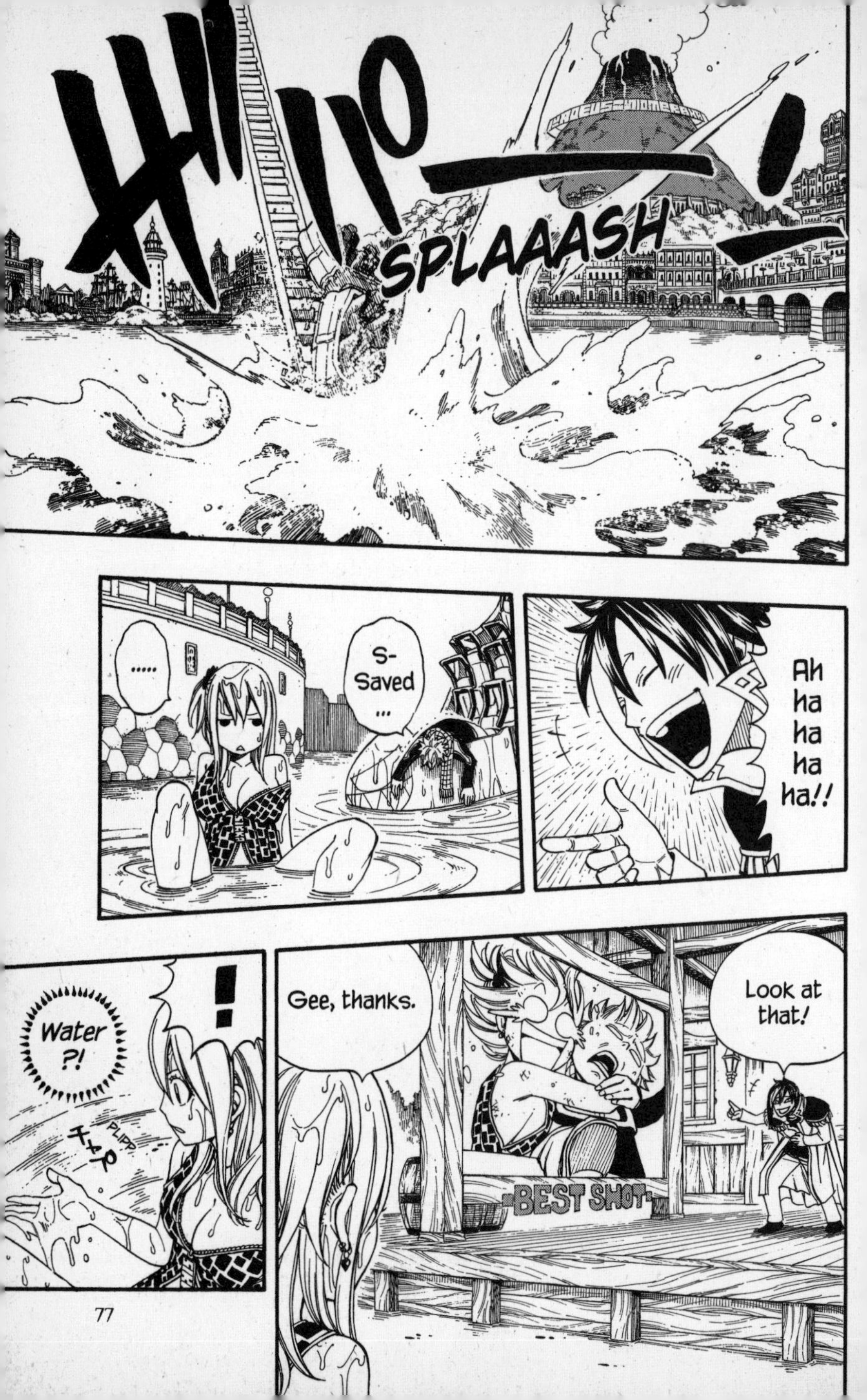
SPLAAASH
Ah ha ha ha ha!!
S- Saved ...
.....
Look at that!
BEST SHOT
Gee, thanks.
!
Water ?!
PLIPP

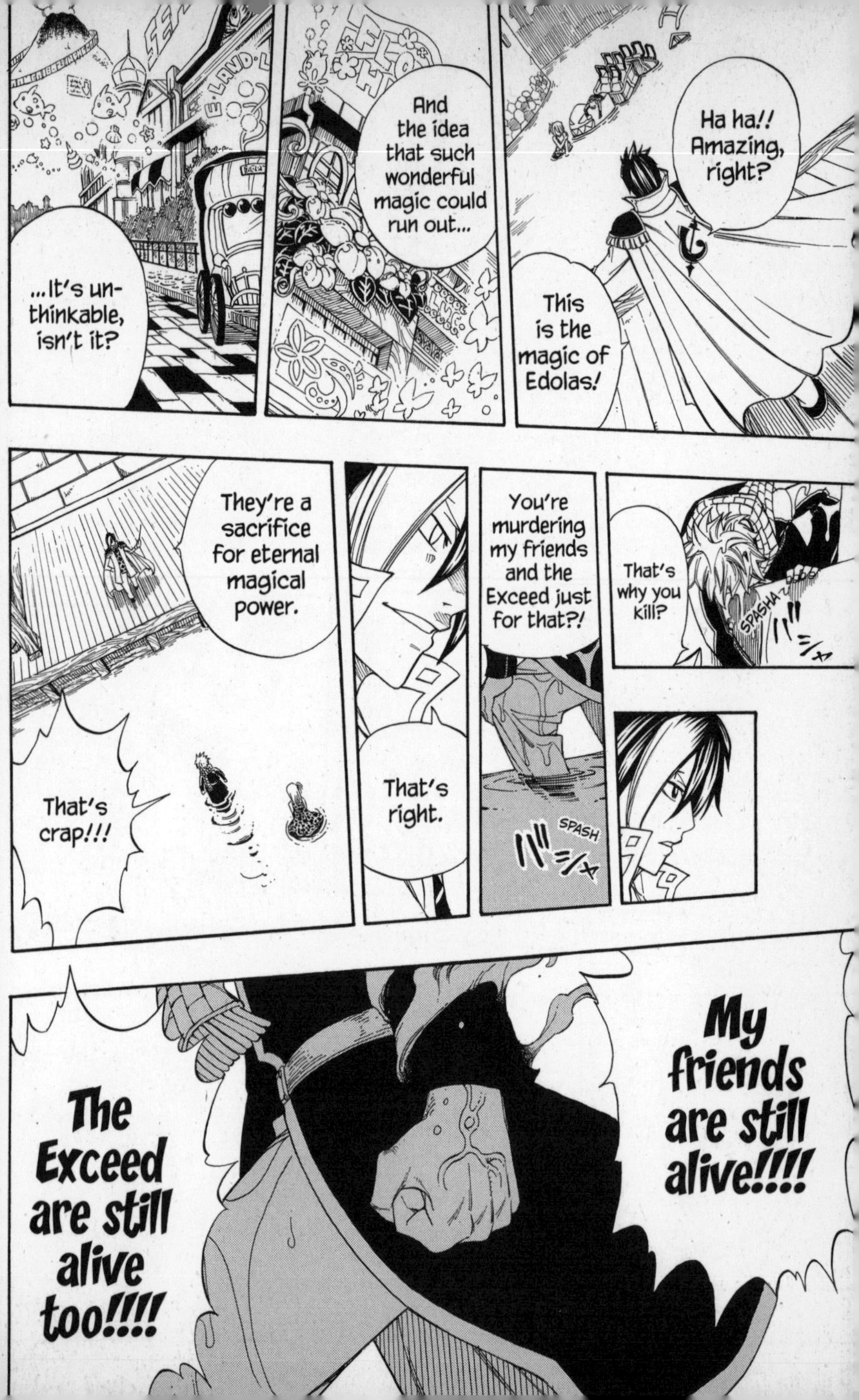
Ha ha!! Amazing, right?
This is the magic of Edolas!
And the idea that such wonderful magic could run out...
...It's unthinkable, isn't it?
That's why you kill?
SPASHA
You're murdering my friends and the Exceed just for that?!
SPASH
That's right.
They're a sacrifice for eternal magical power.
That's crap!!!
My friends are still alive!!!!
The Exceed are still alive too!!!!

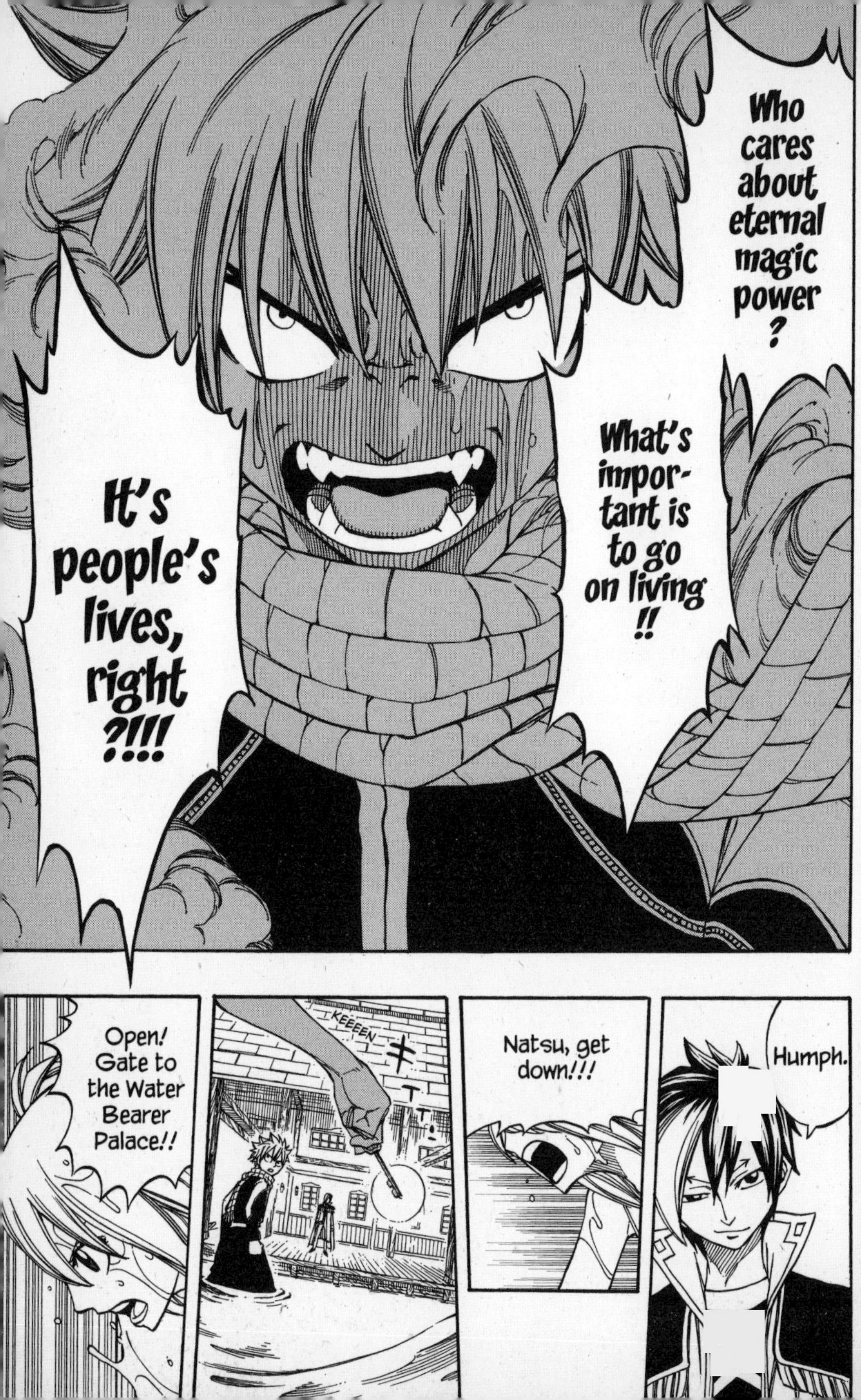
Who cares about eternal magic power?
What's important is to go on living!!
It's people's lives, right?!!!
Humph.
Natsu, get down!!!
KEEEEN
Open! Gate to the Water Bearer Palace!!

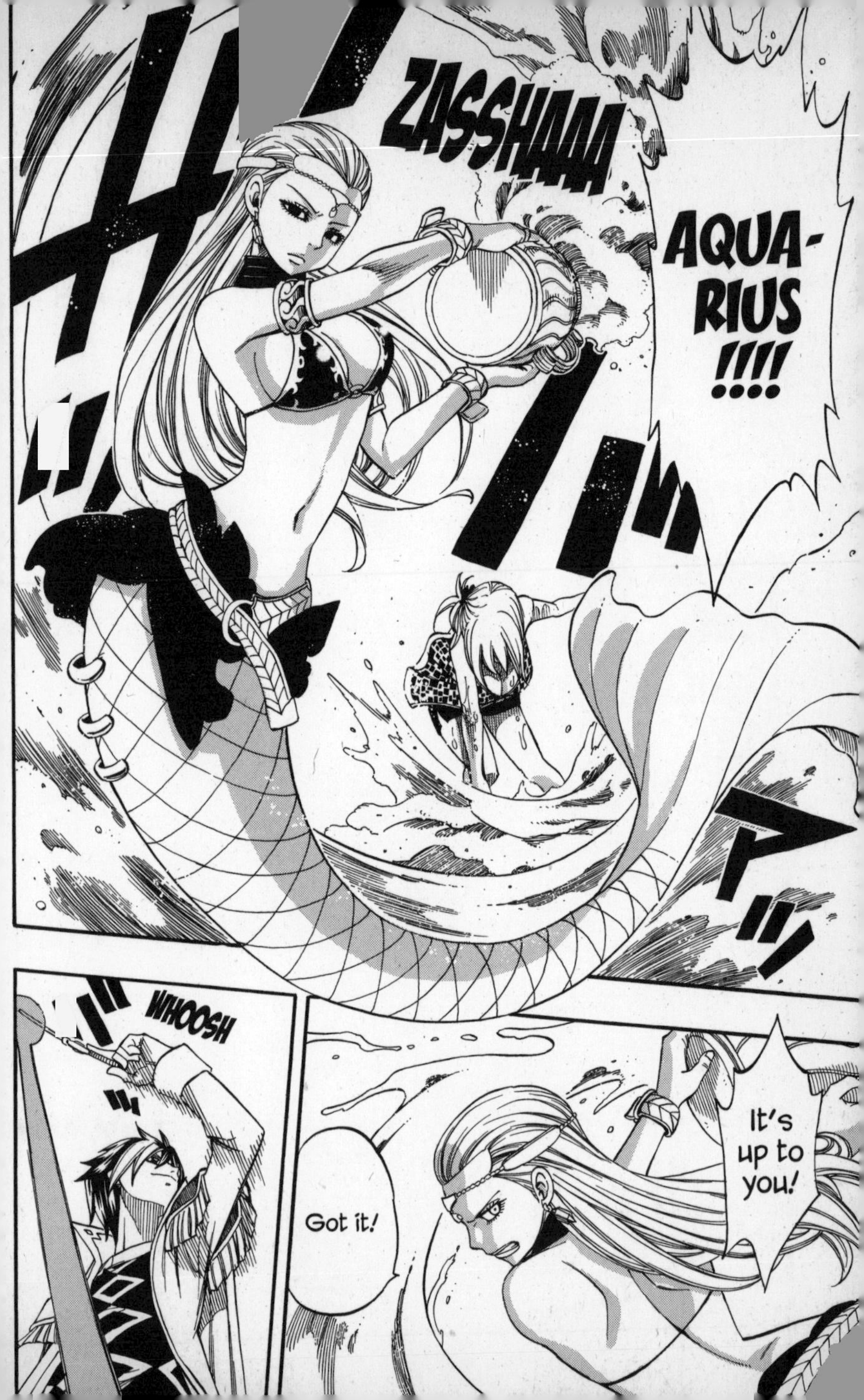
ZASSHAAA
AQUA-RIUS!!!!
It's up to you!
Got it!
WHOOSH

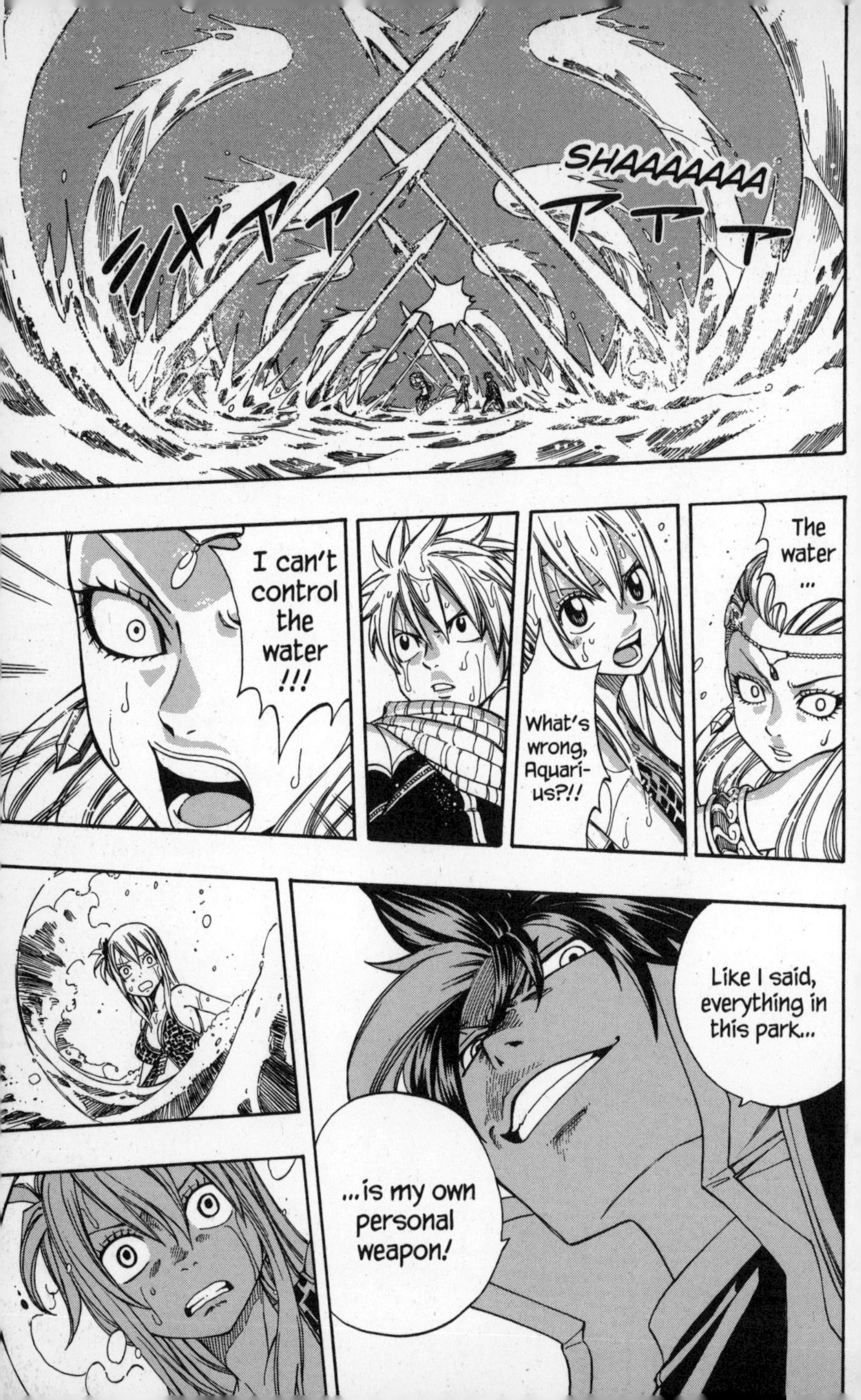
SHAAAAAAA
The water ...
What's wrong, Aquari-us?!!
I can't control the water!!!
Like I said, everything in this park...
...is my own personal weapon!

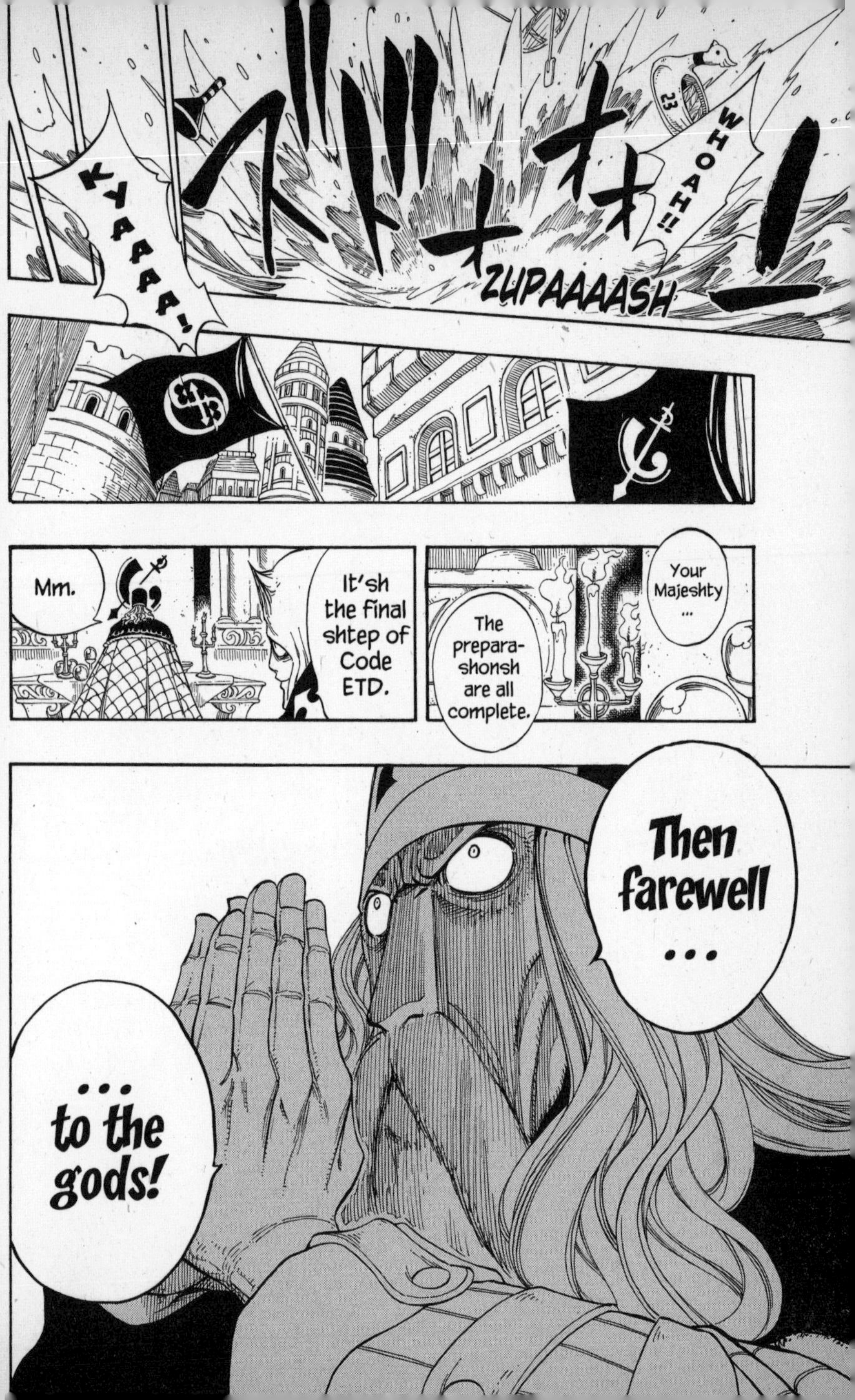
WHOAH!!
ZUPAAAASH
KYAAAA!
Your Majeshty ...
The prepara-shonsh are all complete.
It'sh the final shtep of Code ETD.
Mm.
Then farewell ...
... to the gods!

FAIRY TAIL
フェアリーテイル

Chapter 183, Monster Academy

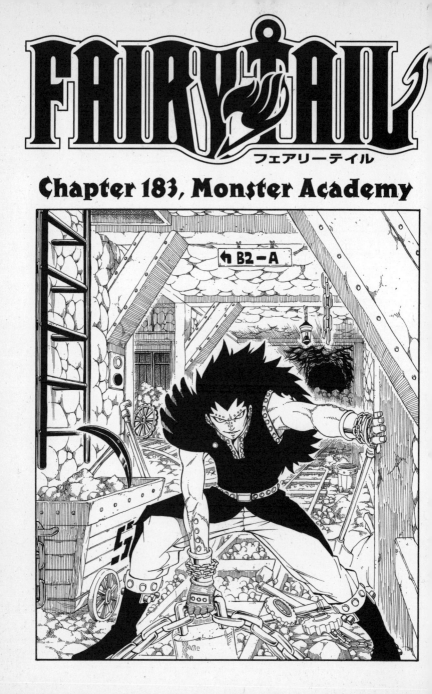

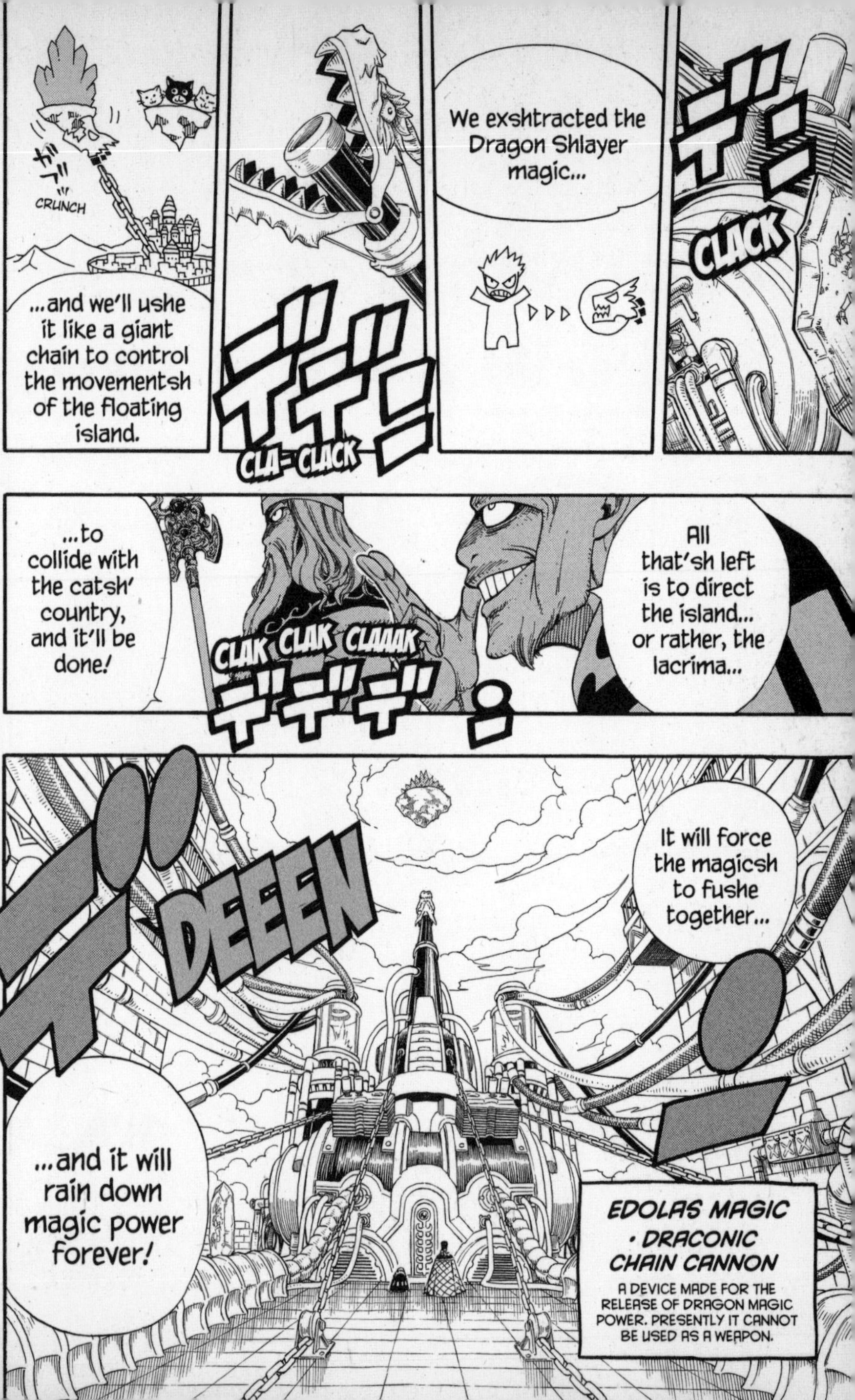
CLACK
We exshtracted the Dragon Shlayer magic...
CLA-CLACK
...and we'll ushe it like a giant chain to control the movementsh of the floating island.
ガブ
CRUNCH
All that'sh left is to direct the island... or rather, the lacrima...
...to collide with the catsh' country, and it'll be done!
CLAK CLAK CLAAAK
It will force the magicsh to fushe together...
DEEEN
EDOLAS MAGIC
• DRACONIC CHAIN CANNON
A DEVICE MADE FOR THE RELEASE OF DRAGON MAGIC POWER. PRESENTLY IT CANNOT BE USED AS A WEAPON.
...and it will rain down magic power forever!

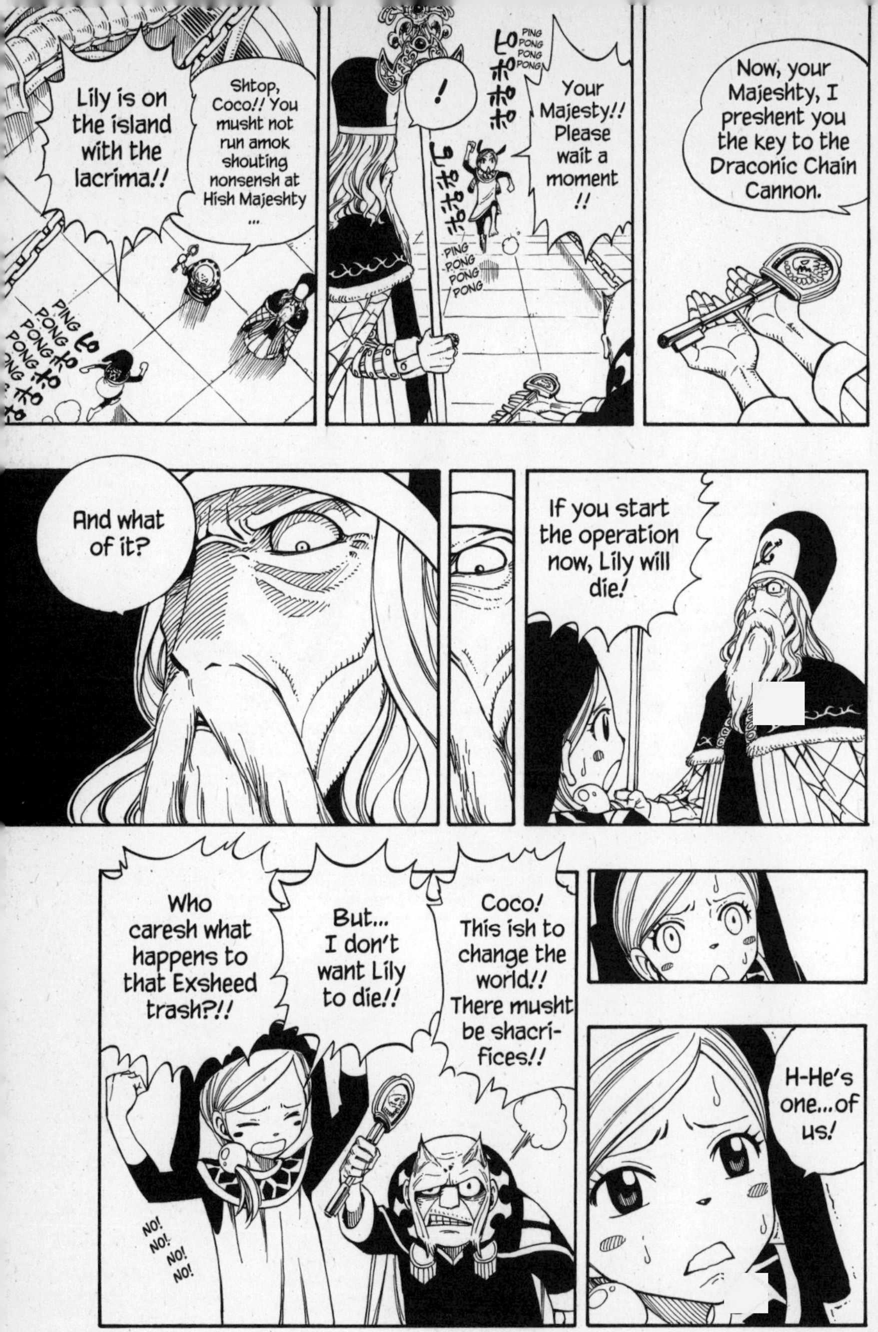
Now, your Majeshty, I preshent you the key to the Draconic Chain Cannon.
!
PING PONG PONG PONG
Your Majesty!! Please wait a moment!!
PING PONG PONG PONG
Shtop, Coco!! You musht not run amok shouting nonsensh at Hish Majeshty ...
Lily is on the island with the lacrima!!
PING PONG PONG PONG
If you start the operation now, Lily will die!
And what of it?
H-He's one...of us!
Coco! This ish to change the world!! There musht be shacrifices!!
But... I don't want Lily to die!!
Who caresh what happens to that Exsheed trash?!!
NO! NO! NO! NO!

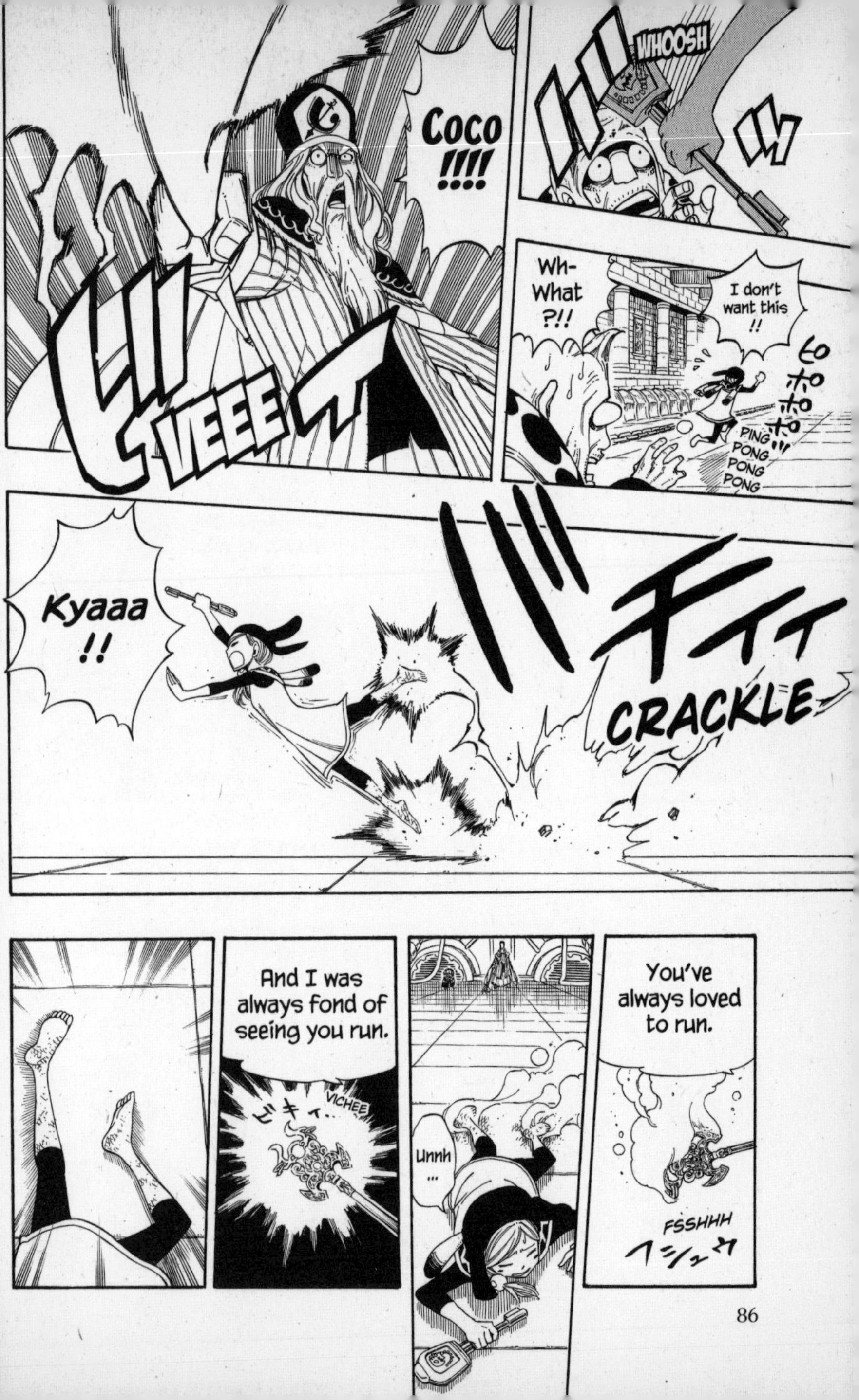

WHOOSH
I don't want this !!
Wh-What ?!!
PING PONG PONG PONG
Coco !!!!
VEEE
CRACKLE
Kyaaa !!
You've always loved to run.
FSSHHH
Unnh ...
And I was always fond of seeing you run.
VICHEE

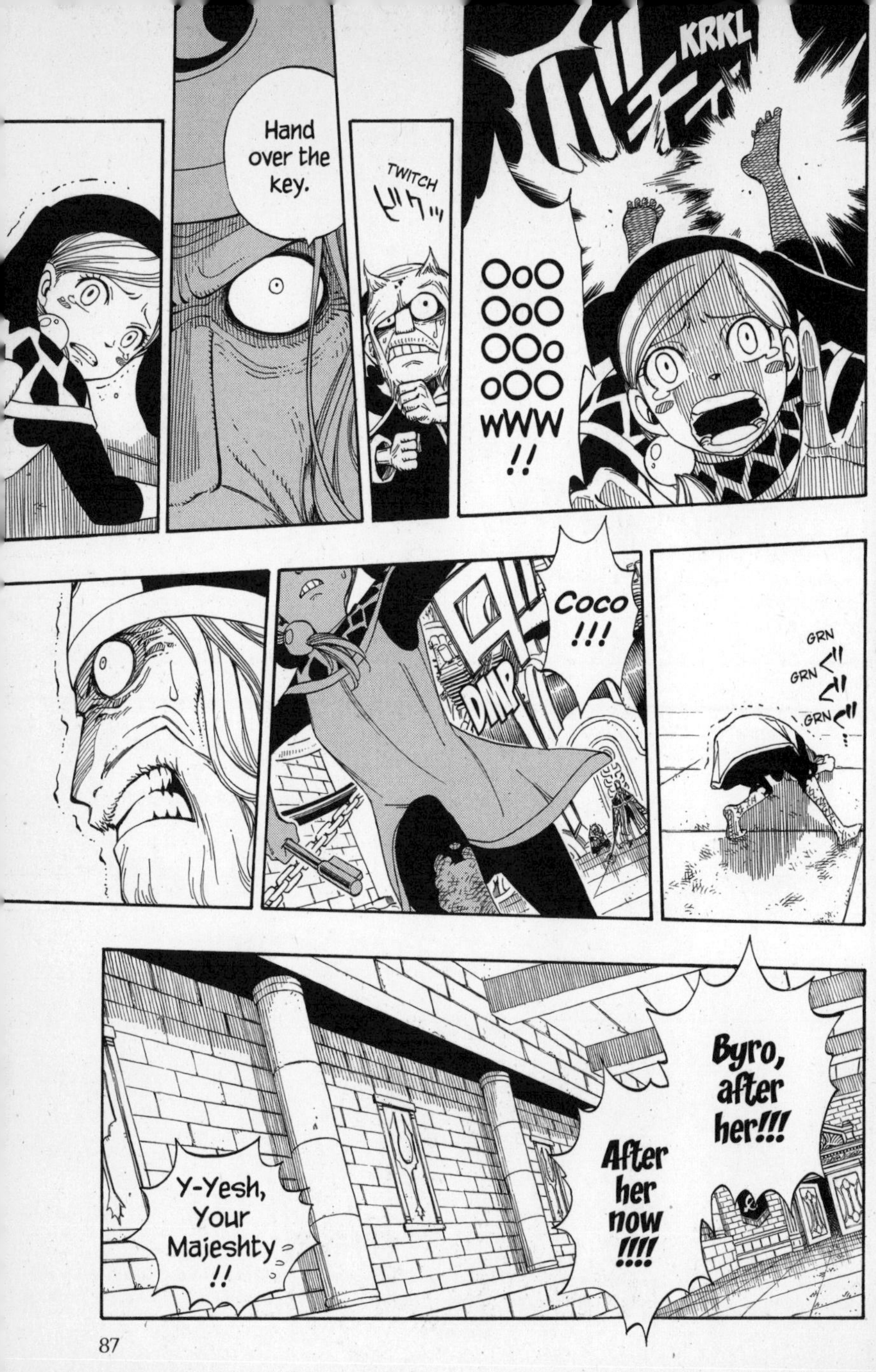
KRKL
OoO OoO OOo oOO www!!
TWITCH
Hand over the key.
GRN GRN GRN
Coco!!!
DMP
Byro, after her!!!
After her now!!!!
Y-Yesh, Your Majeshty!!

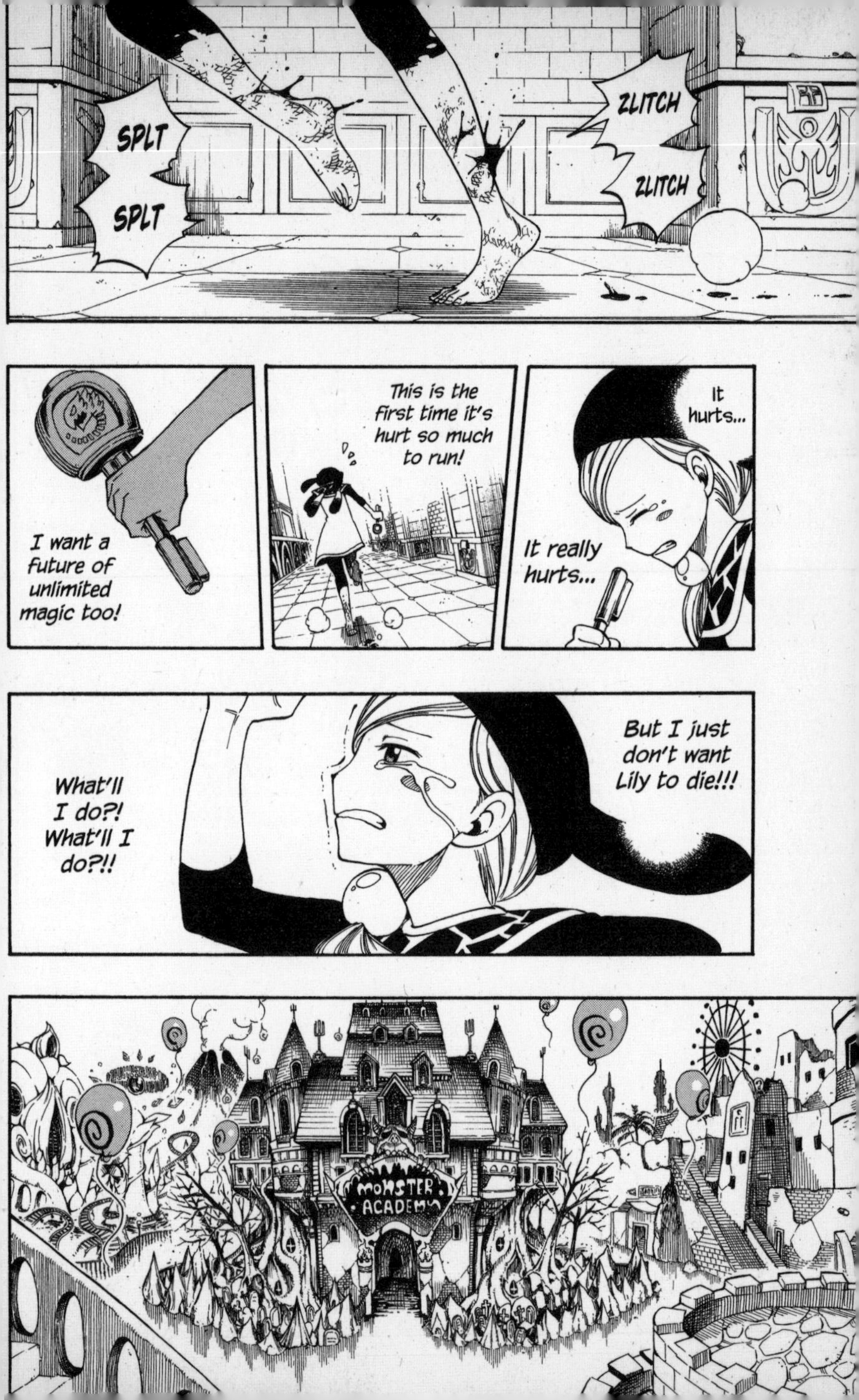
ZLITCH
ZLITCH
SPLT
SPLT
It hurts...
It really hurts...
This is the first time it's hurt so much to run!
I want a future of unlimited magic too!
But I just don't want Lily to die!!!
What'll I do?! What'll I do?!!
MONSTER ACADEMY

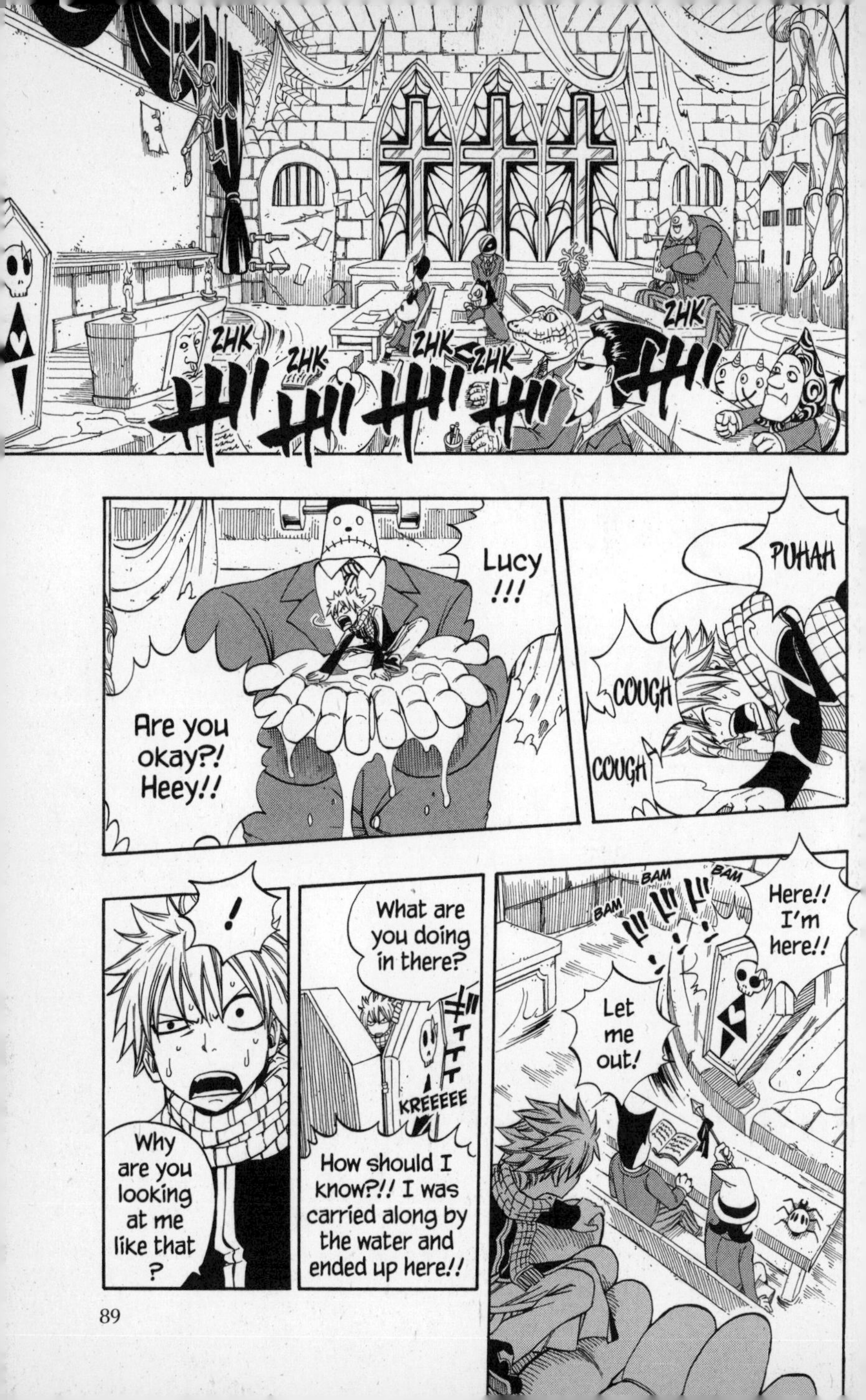
ZHK
ZHK
ZHK
ZHK
ZHK
PUHAH
COUGH
COUGH
Lucy!!!
Are you okay?! Heey!!
BAM
BAM
BAM
Here!! I'm here!!
Let me out!
What are you doing in there?
KREEEEE
How should I know?!! I was carried along by the water and ended up here!!
!
Why are you looking at me like that?

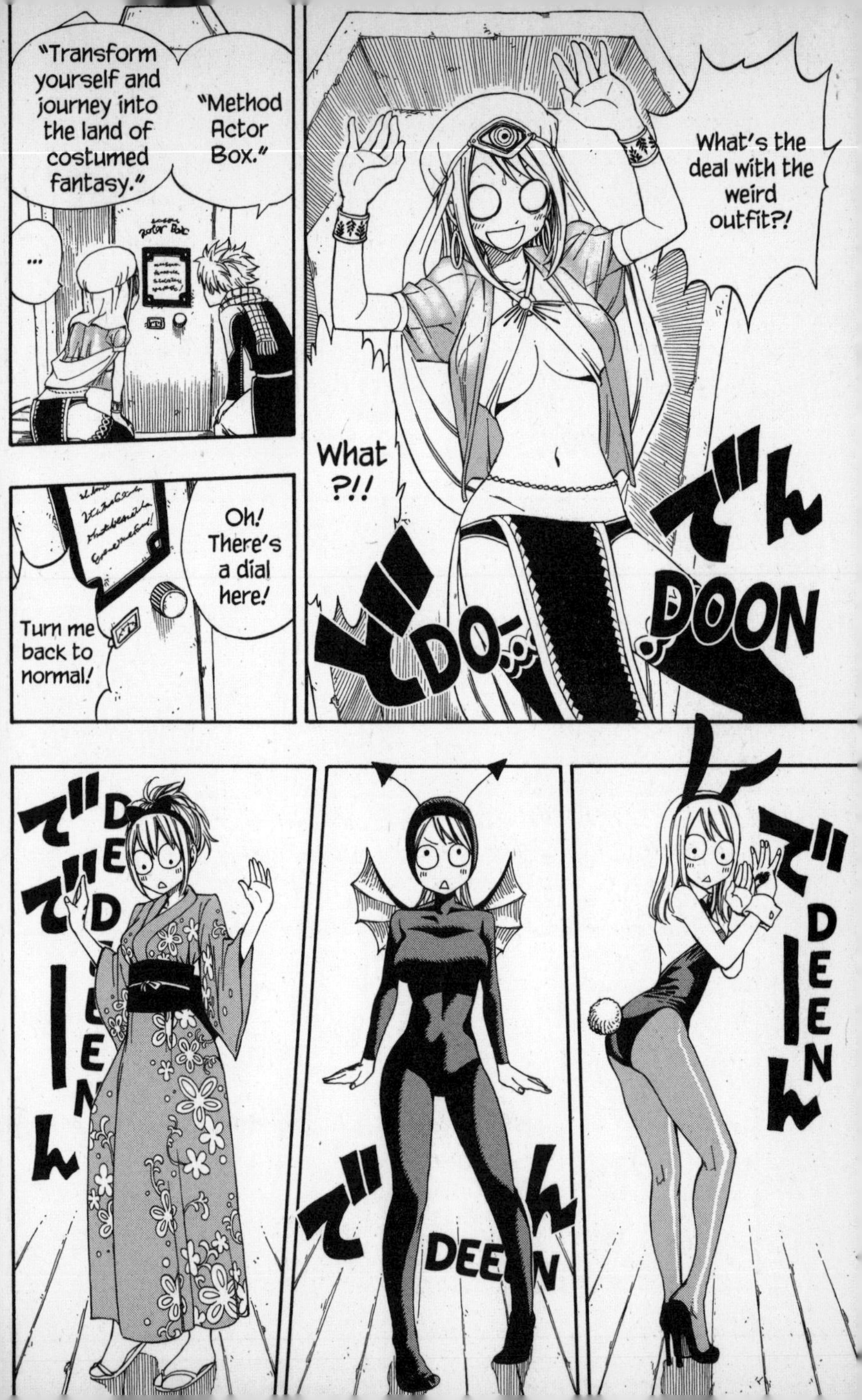

What's the deal with the weird outfit?!
What ?!!
DO-
DOON
"Method Actor Box."
"Transform yourself and journey into the land of costumed fantasy."
...
Oh! There's a dial here!
Turn me back to normal!
DEEN
DEEN

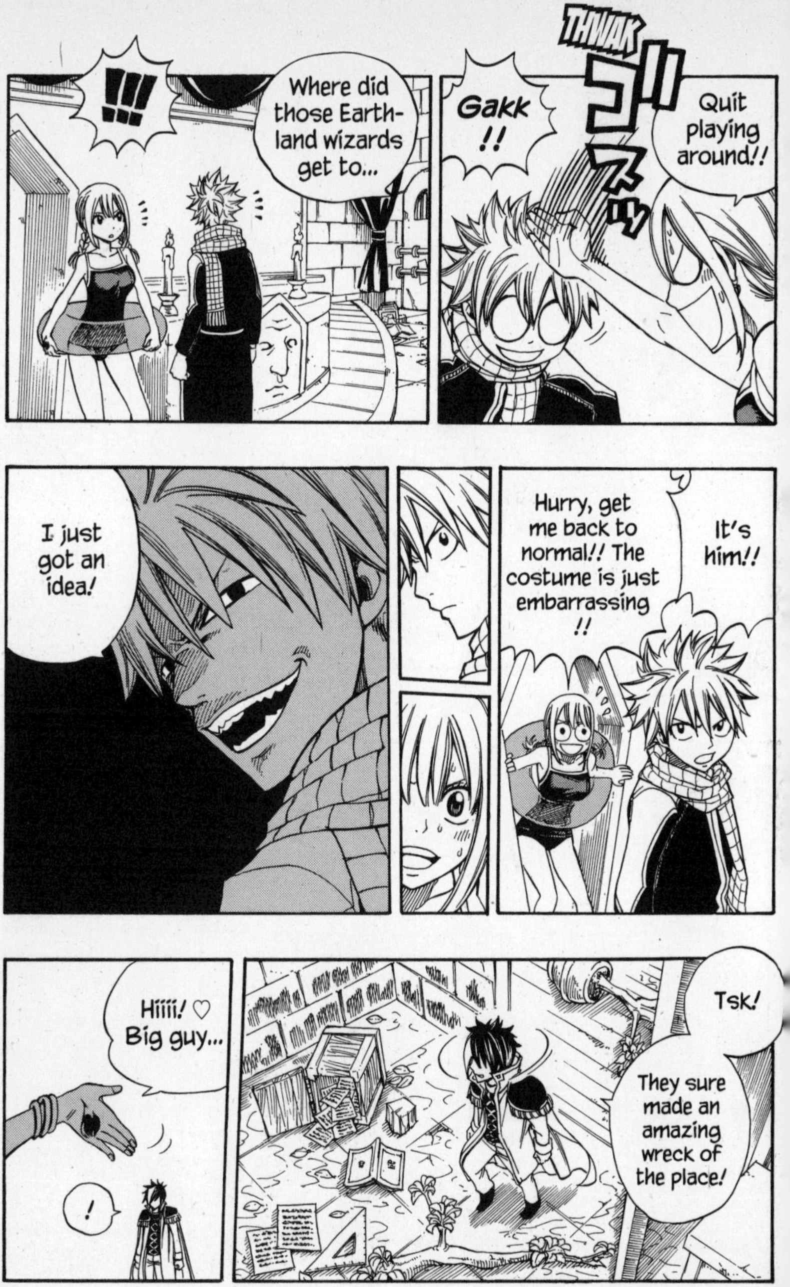
Quit playing around!!
THWAK
Gakk!!
Where did those Earth-land wizards get to...
!!!
It's him!!
Hurry, get me back to normal!! The costume is just embarrassing!!
I just got an idea!
Tsk!
They sure made an amazing wreck of the place!
Hiiii! ♡ Big guy...
!

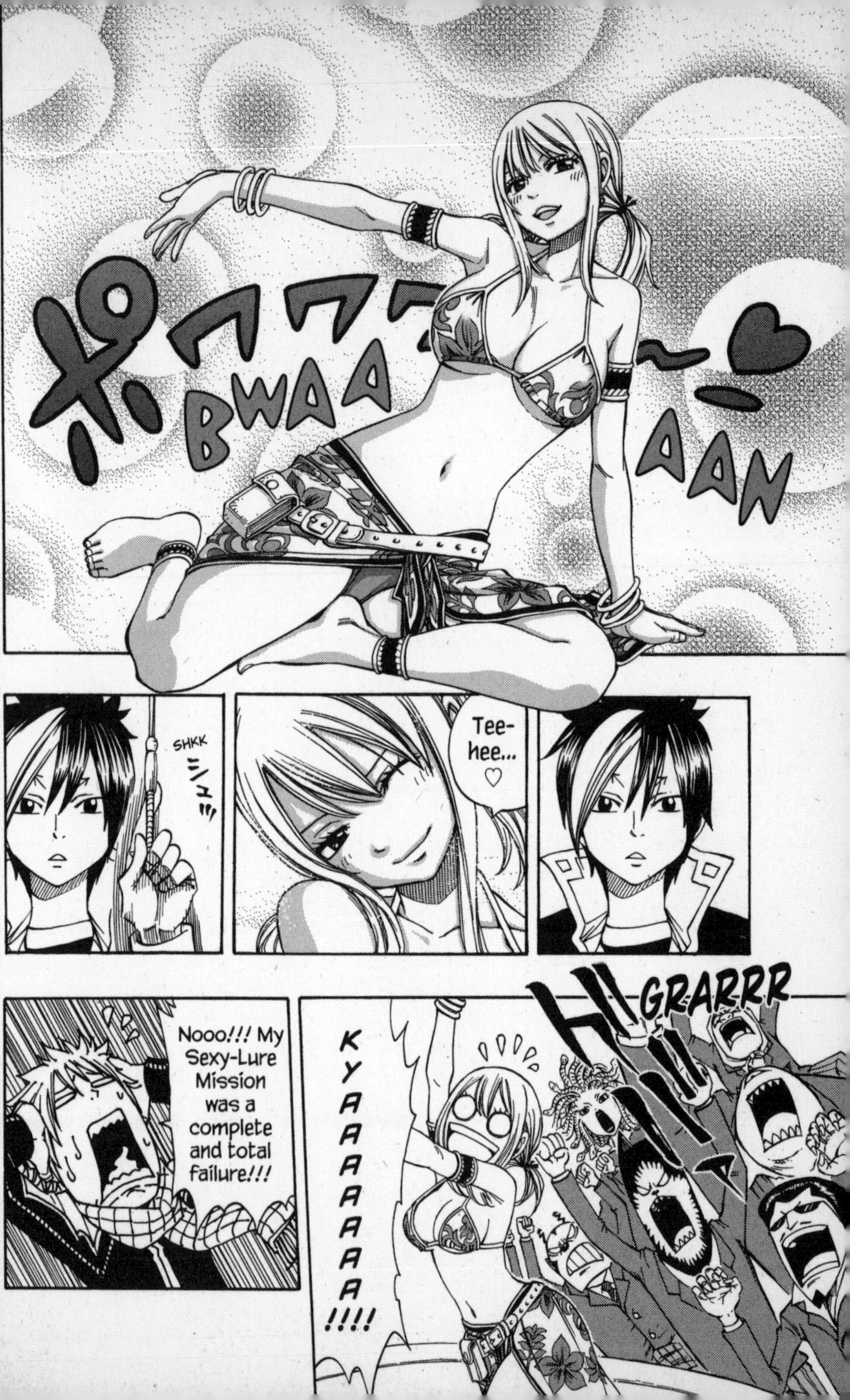
BWAA~AAN
Tee-hee... ♡
SHKK
GRARRR
KYAAAAAAAAA!!!!
Nooo!!! My Sexy-Lure Mission was a complete and total failure!!!

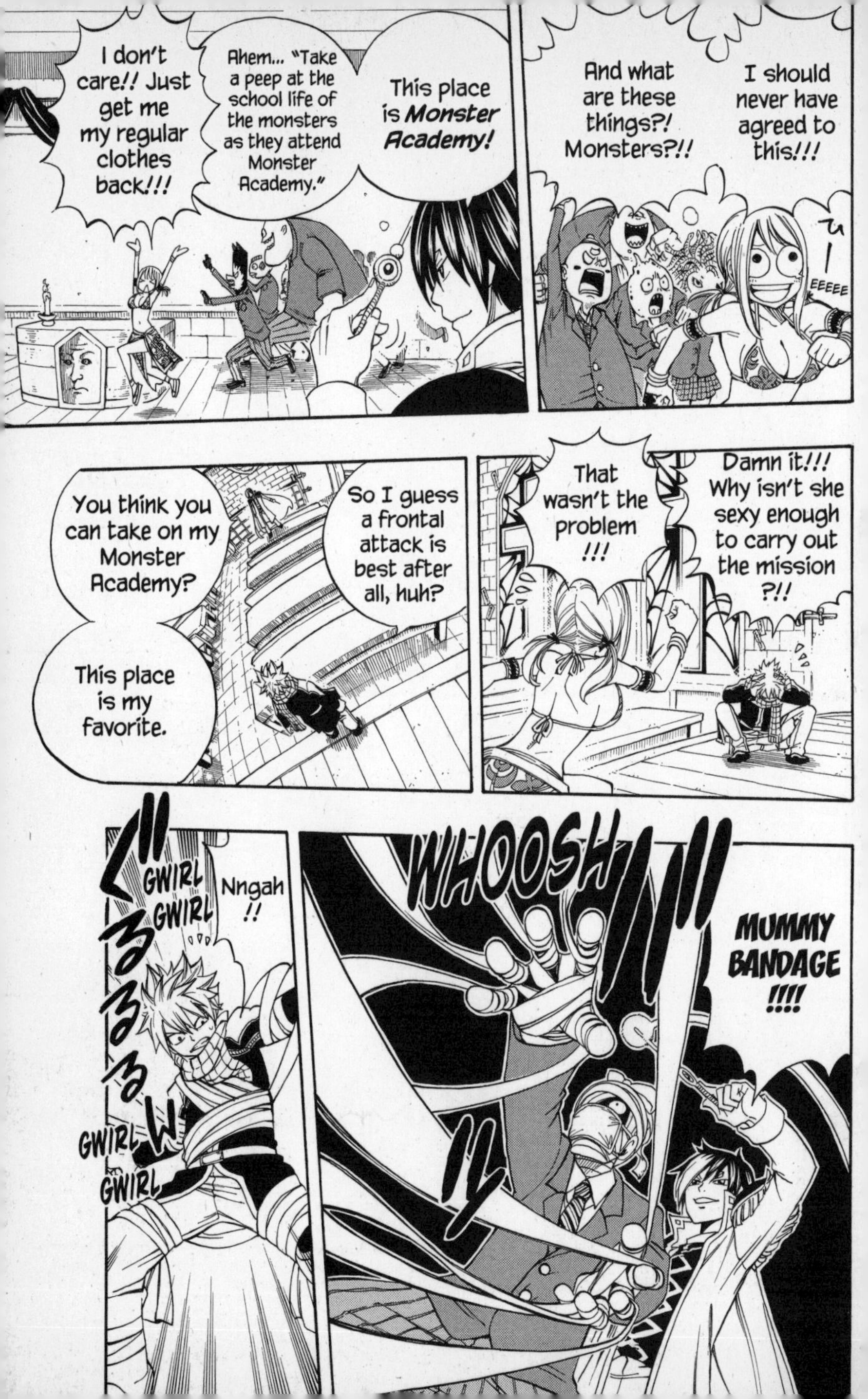
I should never have agreed to this!!!
And what are these things?! Monsters?!!
EEEEE
This place is ***Monster Academy!***
Ahem... "Take a peep at the school life of the monsters as they attend Monster Academy."
I don't care!! Just get me my regular clothes back!!!
Damn it!!! Why isn't she sexy enough to carry out the mission?!!
That wasn't the problem!!!
So I guess a frontal attack is best after all, huh?
You think you can take on my Monster Academy?
This place is my favorite.
WHOOSH
MUMMY BANDAGE!!!!
Nngah!!
GWIRL GWIRL
GWIRL GWIRL

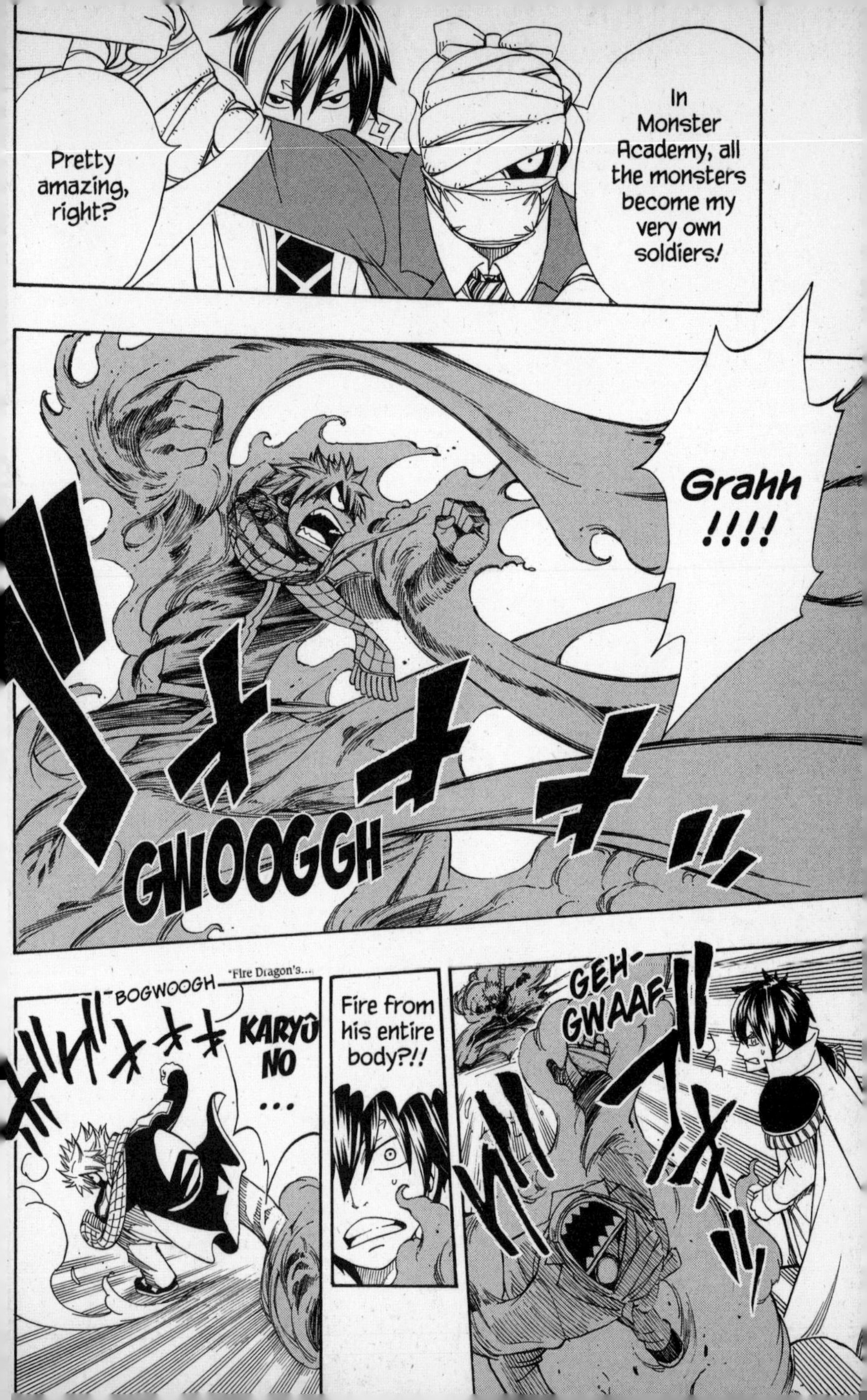
In Monster Academy, all the monsters become my very own soldiers!
Pretty amazing, right?
Grahh !!!!
GWOOGGH
GEH-GWAAF
Fire from his entire body?!!
BOGWOOGH
KARYÛ NO ...
*Fire Dragon's...

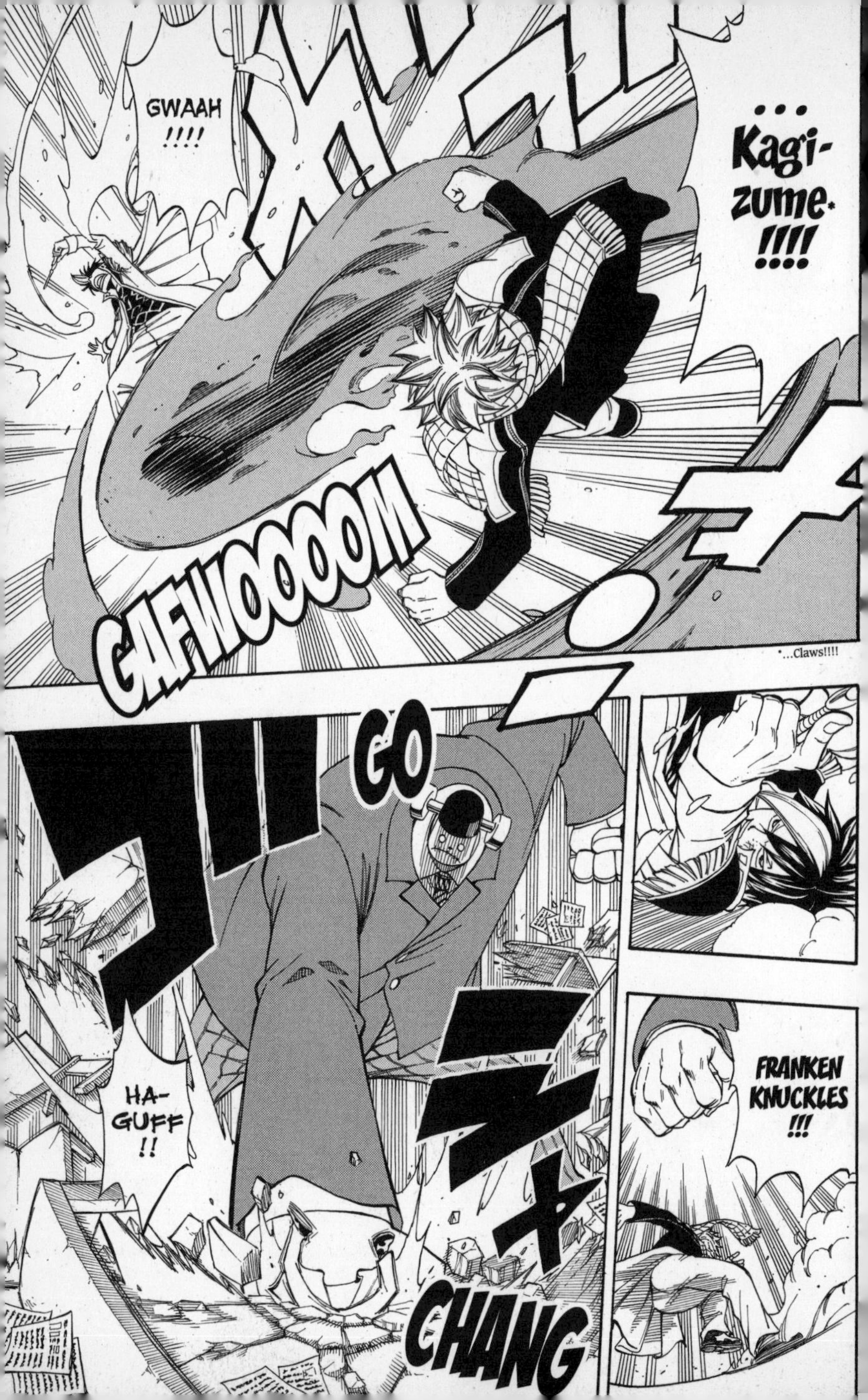
...Kagi-zume*!!!!
GWAAH!!!!
GAFWOOOOM
*...Claws!!!!
FRANKEN KNUCKLES!!!
GO
HA-GUFF!!
CHANG

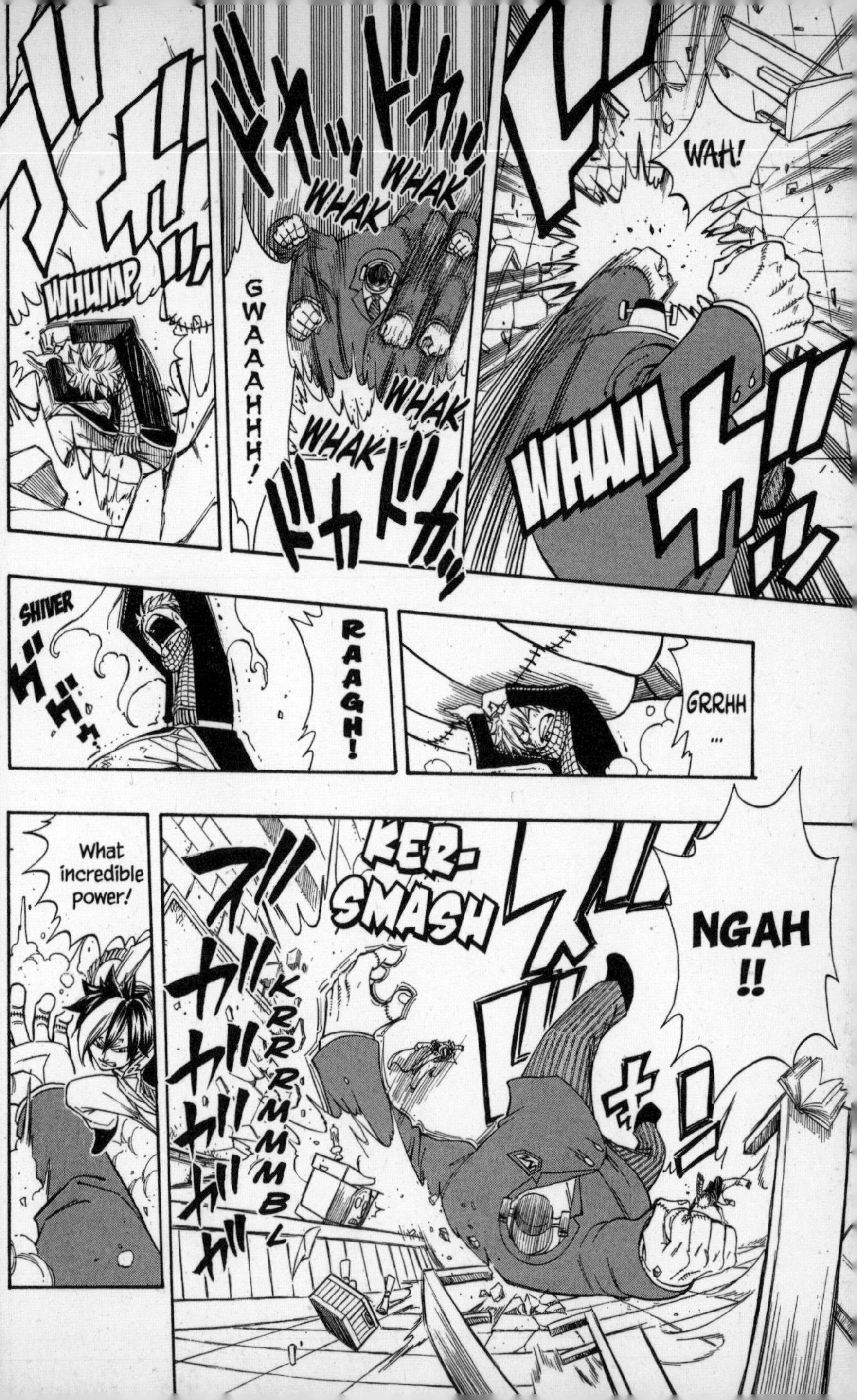
WAH!
WHAM
WHAK
WHAK
GWAAAAHHH!
WHAK
WHAK
WHUMP
GRRHH
...
RAAGH!
SHIVER
NGAH!!
KER-SMASH
KRRRRMMMBL
What incredible power!

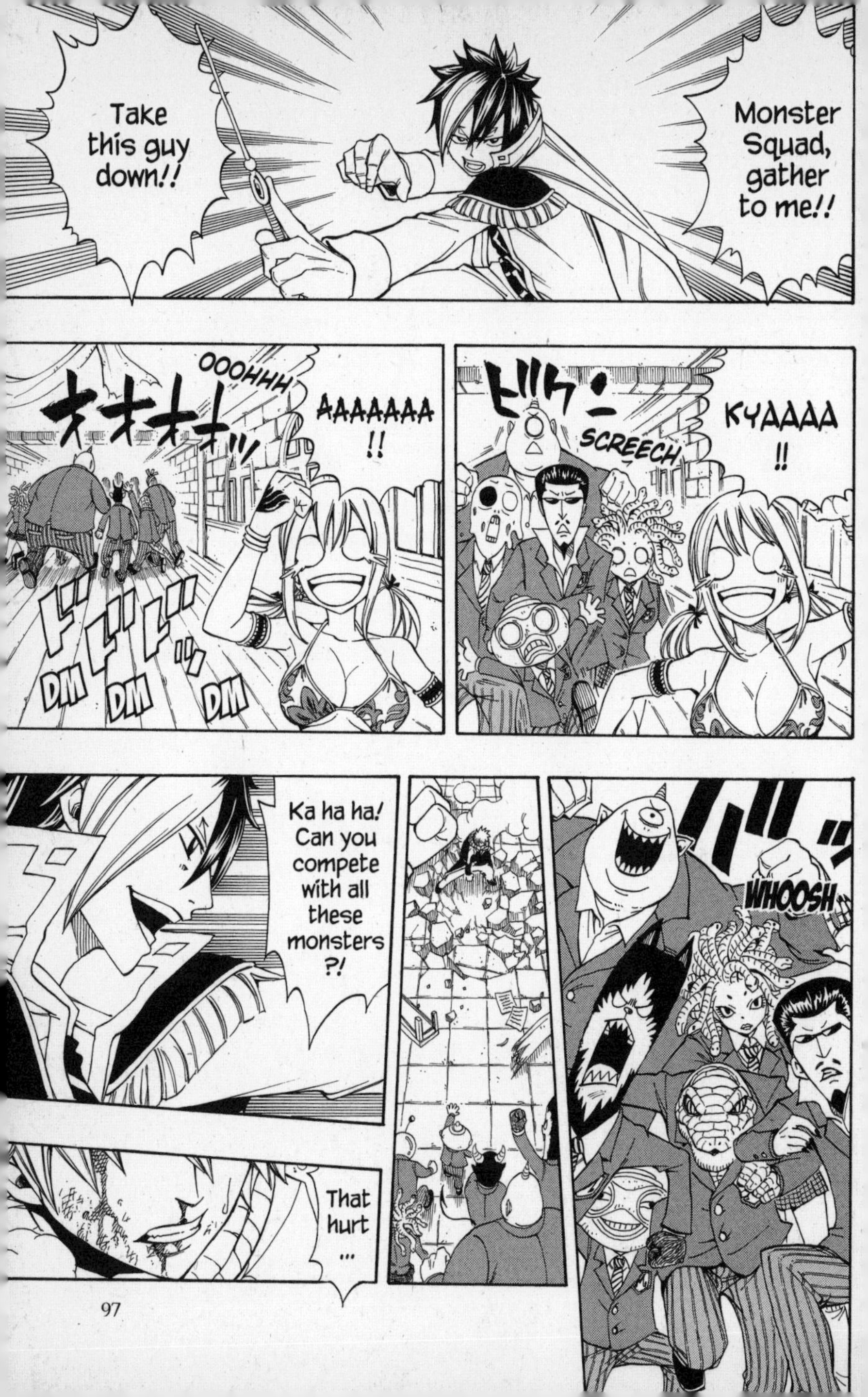
Monster Squad, gather to me!!
Take this guy down!!
SCREECH
KYAAAA!!
OOOHHH
AAAAAAA!!
DM DM DM
WHOOSH
Ka ha ha! Can you compete with all these monsters?!
That hurt...

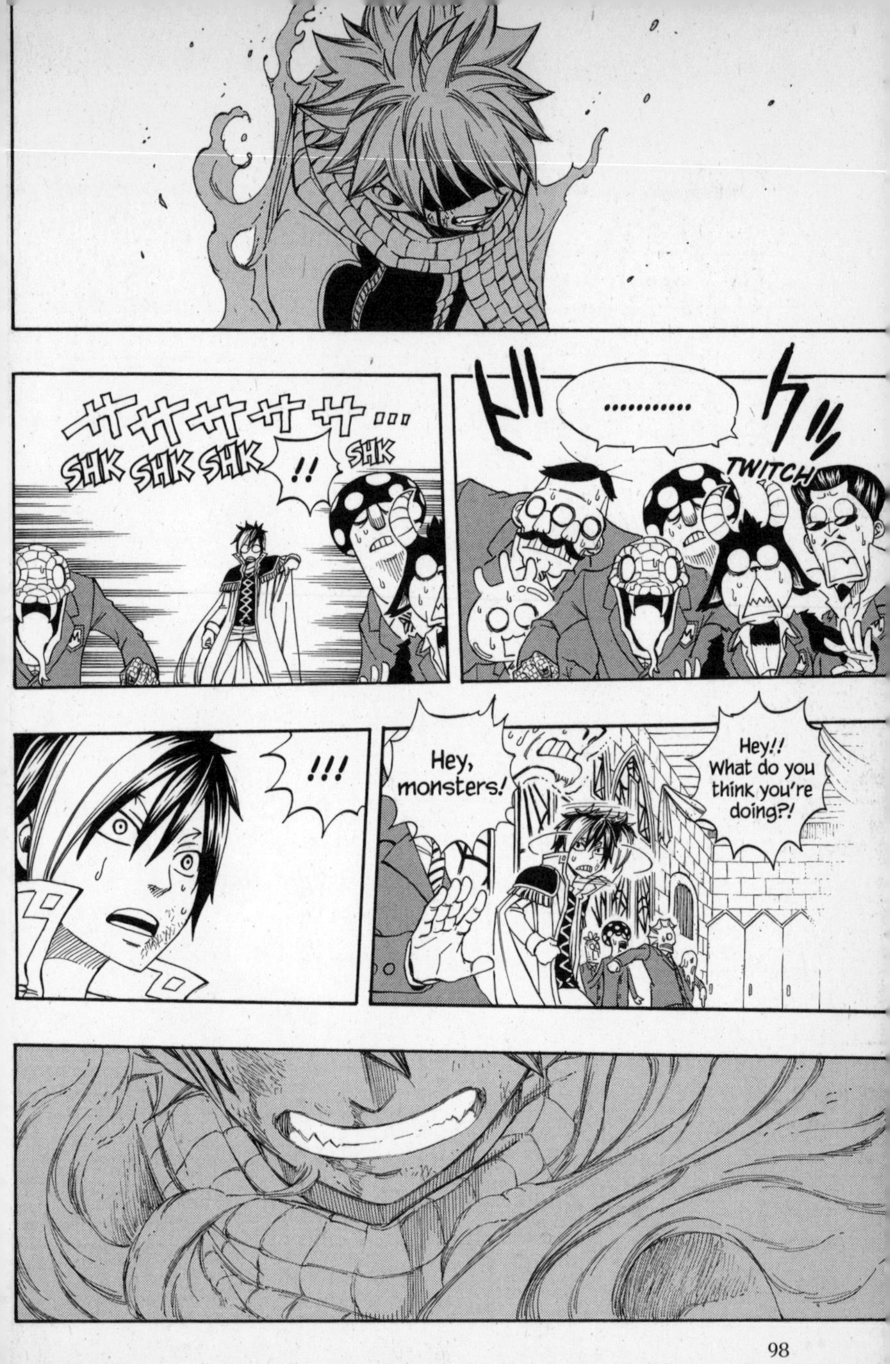
…………
TWITCH
SHK SHK SHK
!!
SHK
Hey!! What do you think you're doing?!
Hey, monsters!
!!!

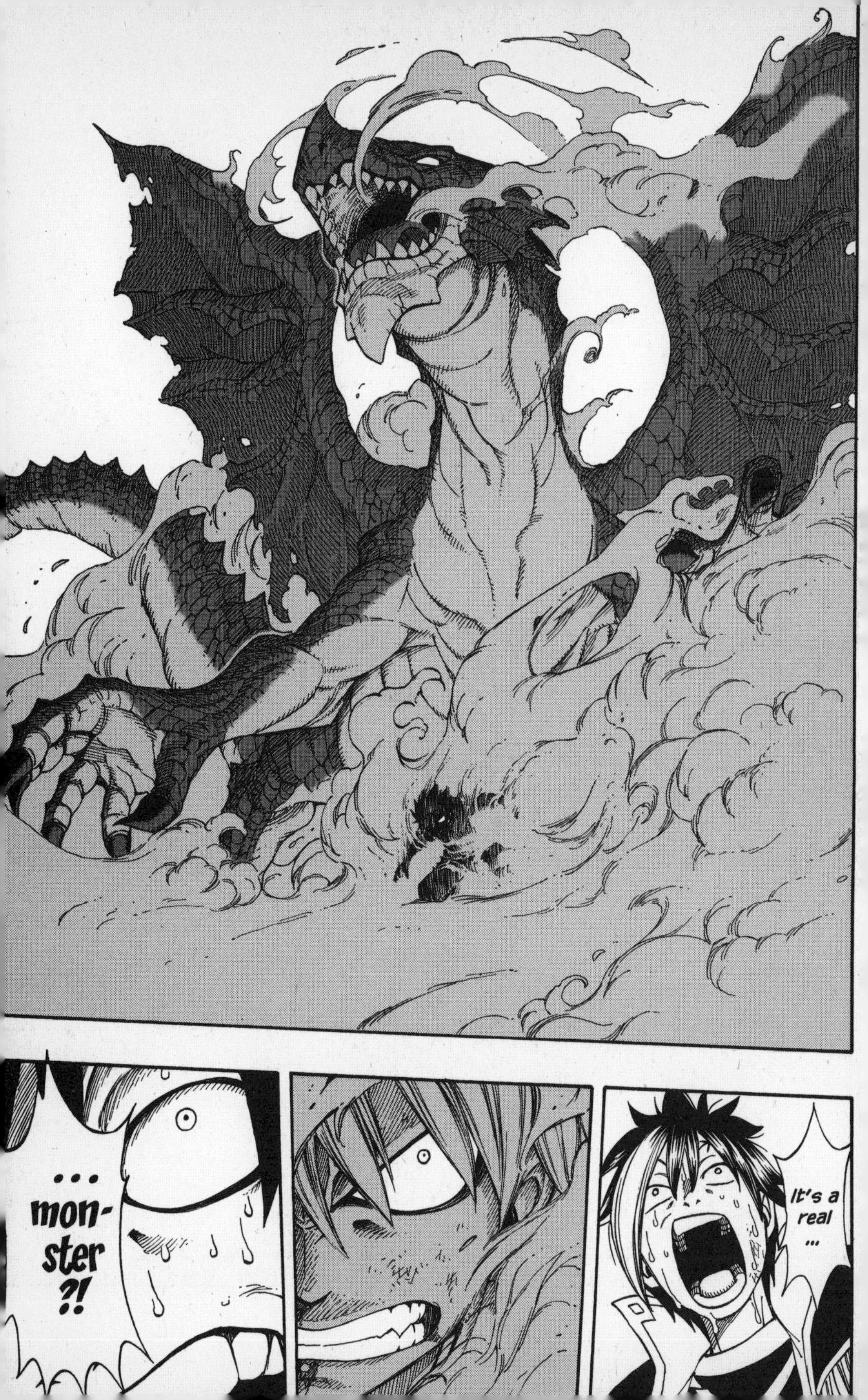
It's a real ...
... monster ?!

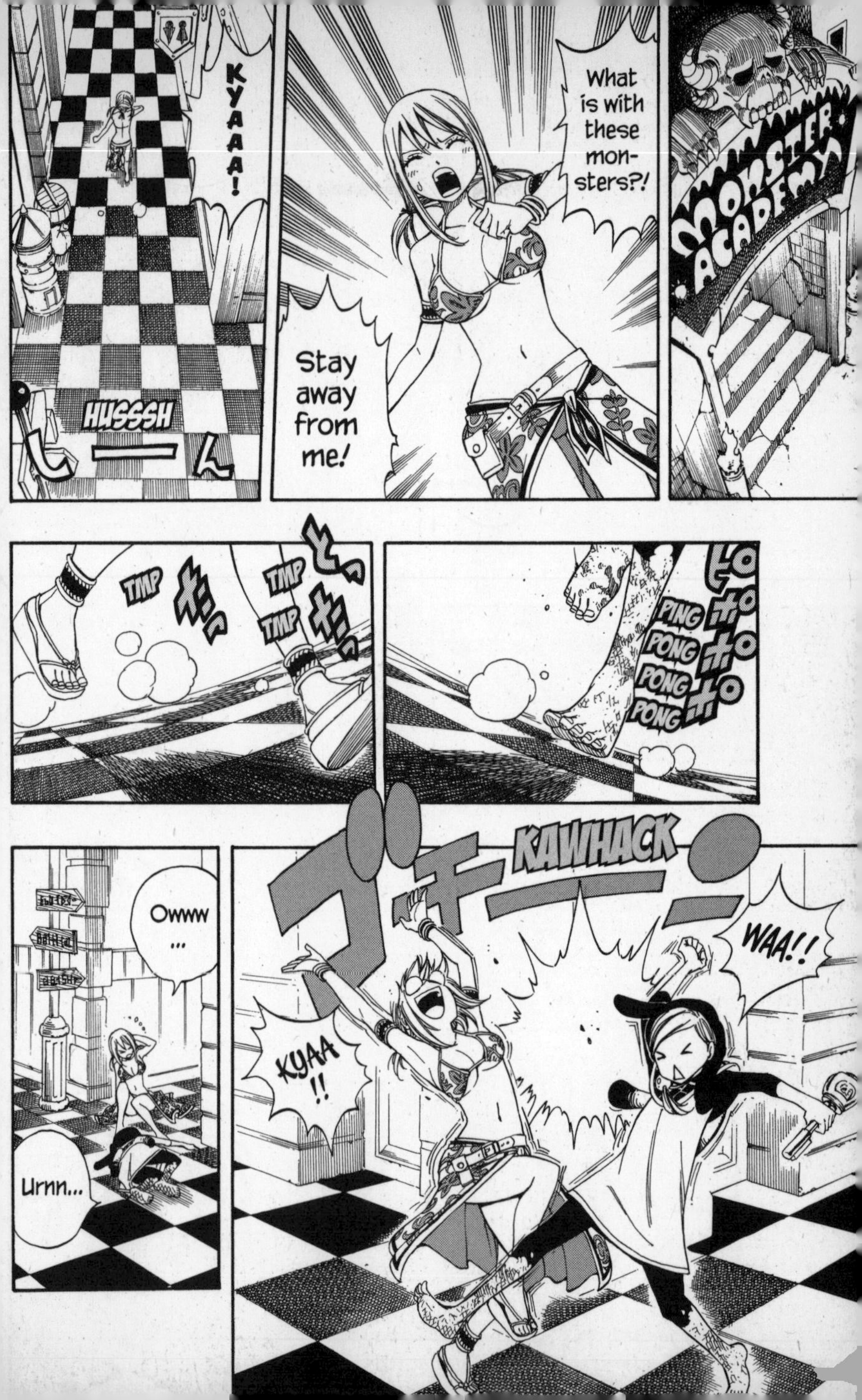

MONSTER ACADEM
What is with these mon-sters?!
Stay away from me!
KYAAAA!
HUSSSH
しーーん
ピポポポ
PING PONG PONG PONG
とっ
TMP TMP
たっ
TMP
たっ
ゴチーン
KAWHACK
WAA!!
KYAA!!
Owww ...
Urnn...

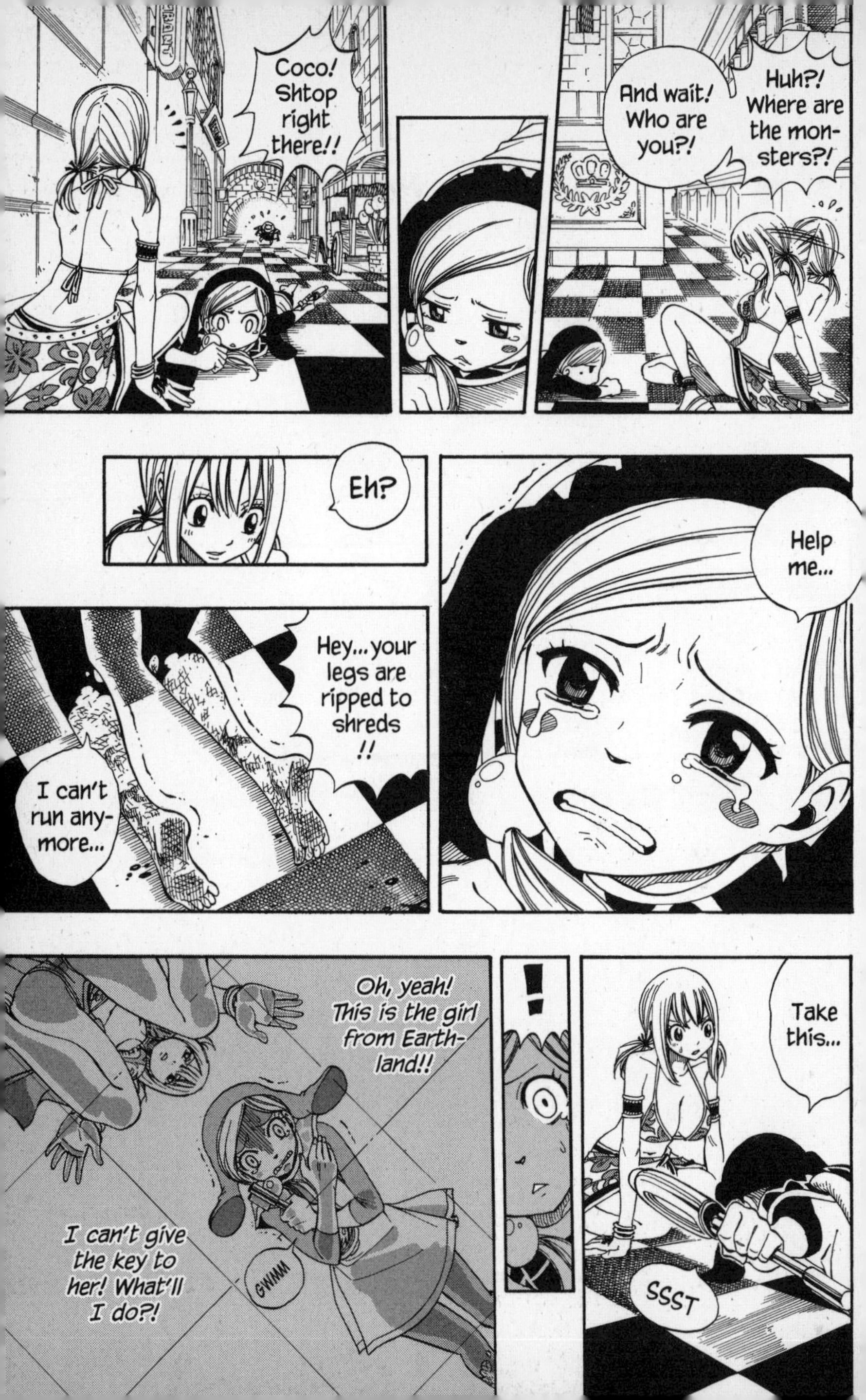
Huh?! Where are the monsters?!
And wait! Who are you?!
Coco! Shtop right there!!
Help me...
Eh?
Hey...your legs are ripped to shreds!!
I can't run anymore...
Take this...
SSST
!
Oh, yeah! This is the girl from Earthland!!
I can't give the key to her! What'll I do?!
GWMM

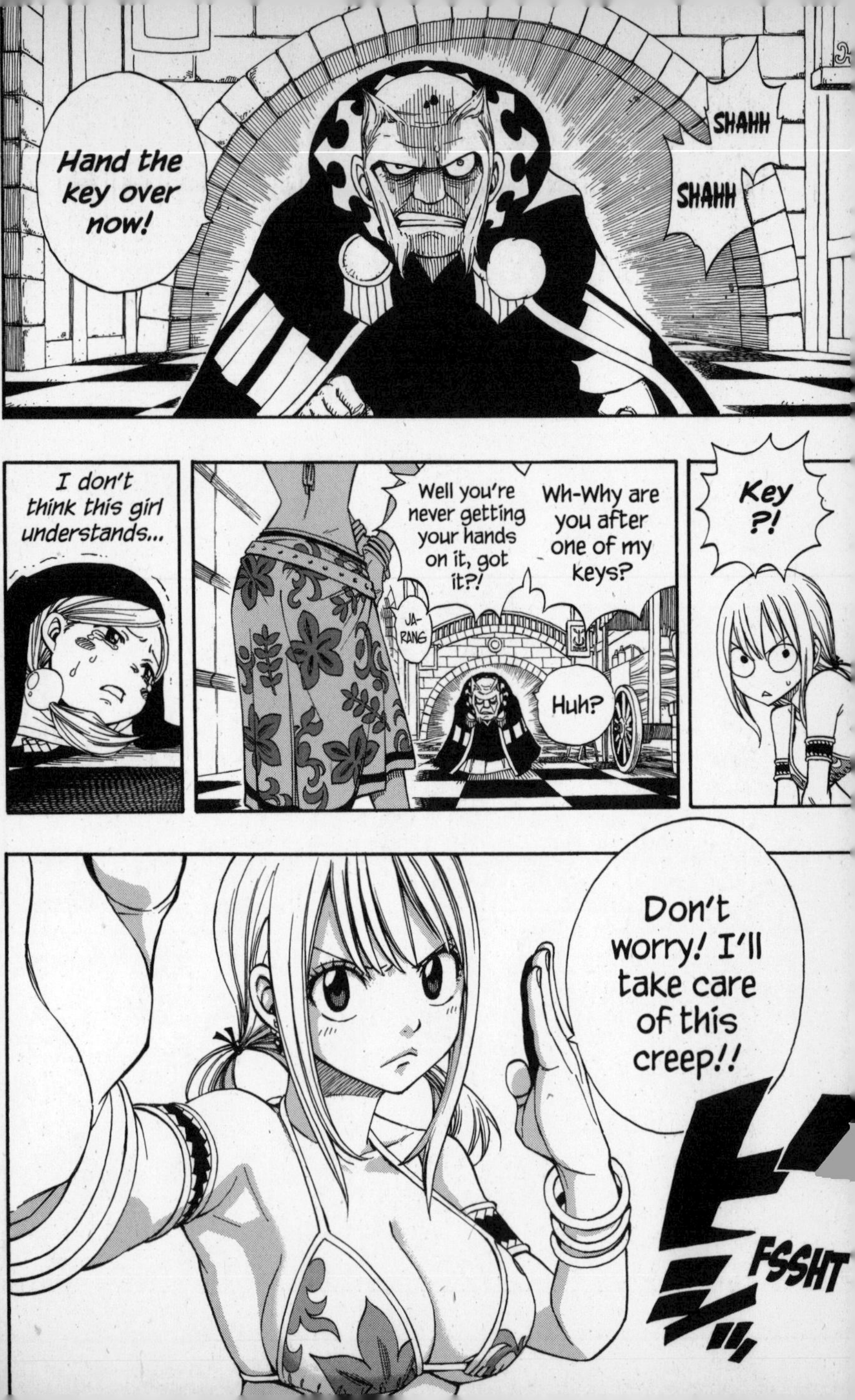
SHAHH
SHAHH
Hand the key over now!
Key?!
Wh-Why are you after one of my keys?
Well you're never getting your hands on it, got it?!
JA-RANG
Huh?
I don't think this girl understands...
Don't worry! I'll take care of this creep!!
FSSHT

FAIRY TAIL

フェアリーテイル

Chapter 184, For the Pride of the Great Celestial River

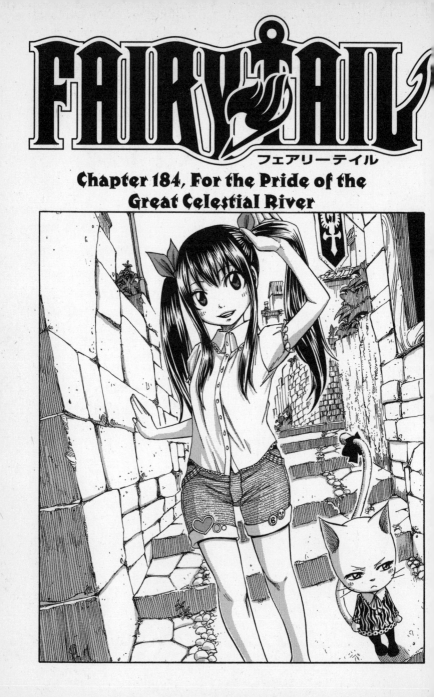

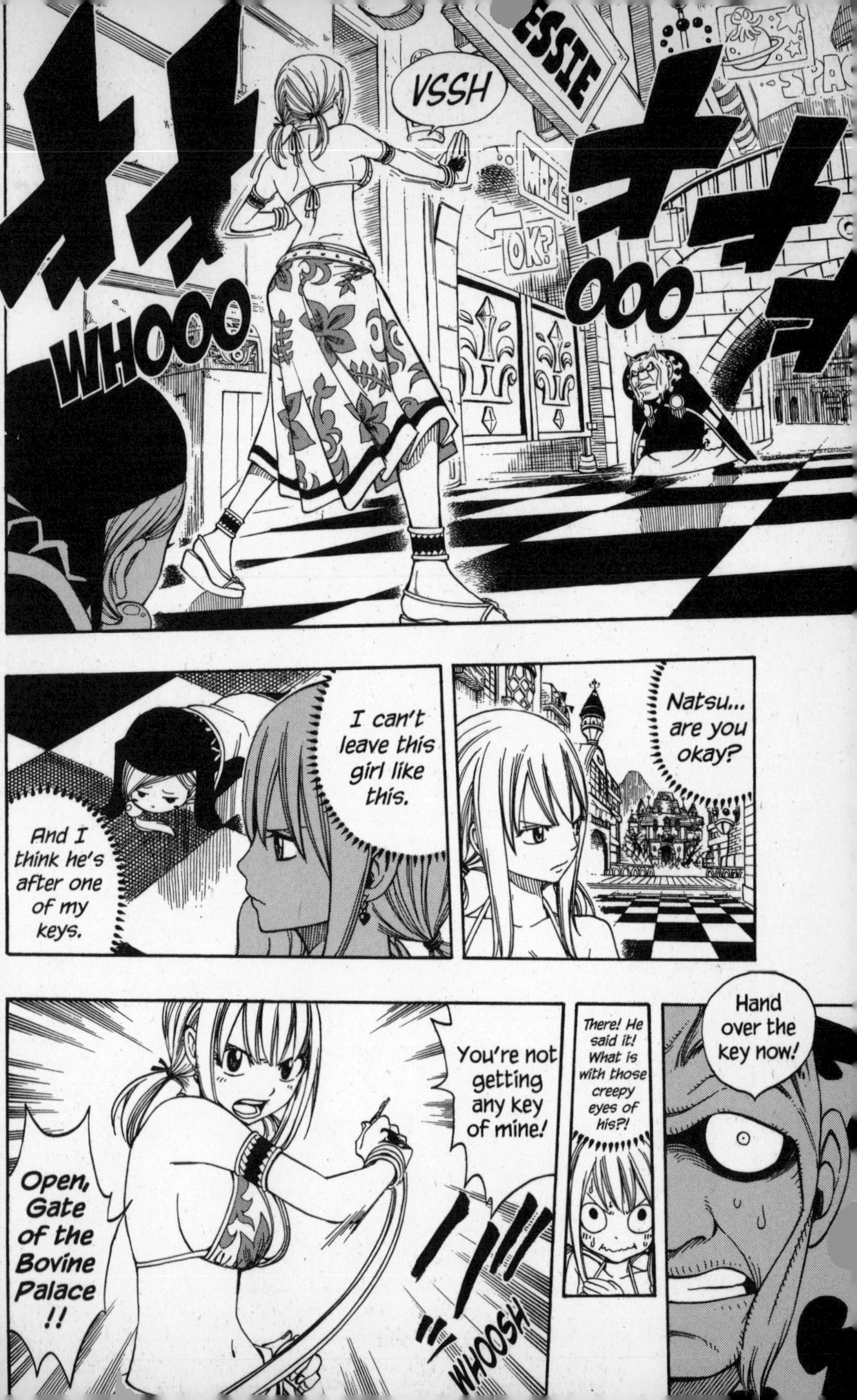
VSSH
WHOOO
OOO
Natsu... are you okay?
I can't leave this girl like this.
And I think he's after one of my keys.
Hand over the key now!
There! He said it! What is with those creepy eyes of his?!
You're not getting any key of mine!
Open, Gate of the Bovine Palace!!
WHOOSH

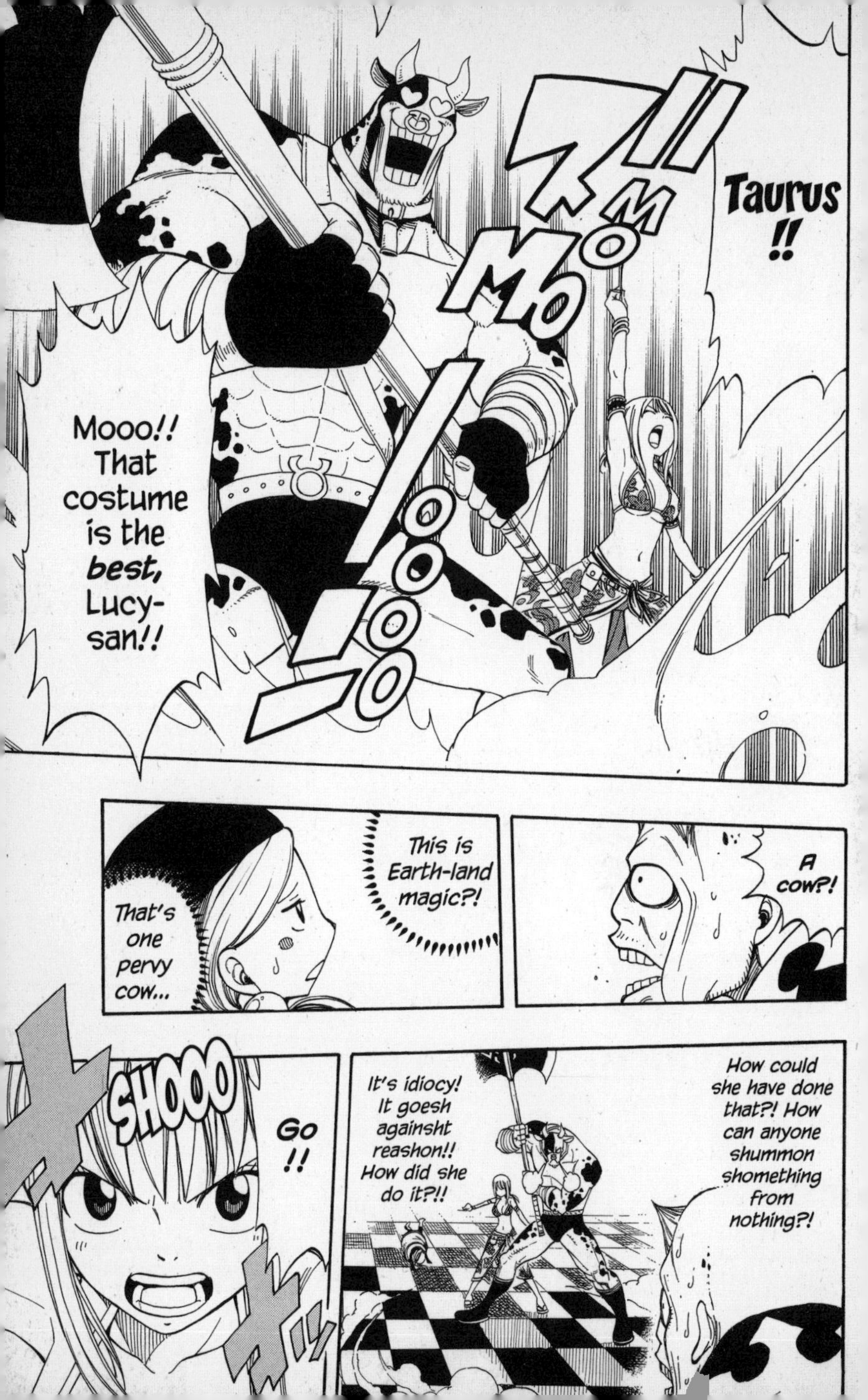
Taurus!!
Mooo!! That costume is the *best,* Lucy-san!!
A cow?!
This is Earth-land magic?!
That's one pervy cow...
How could she have done that?! How can anyone shummon shomething from nothing?!
It's idiocy! It goesh againsht reashon!! How did she do it?!!
SHOOO
Go!!

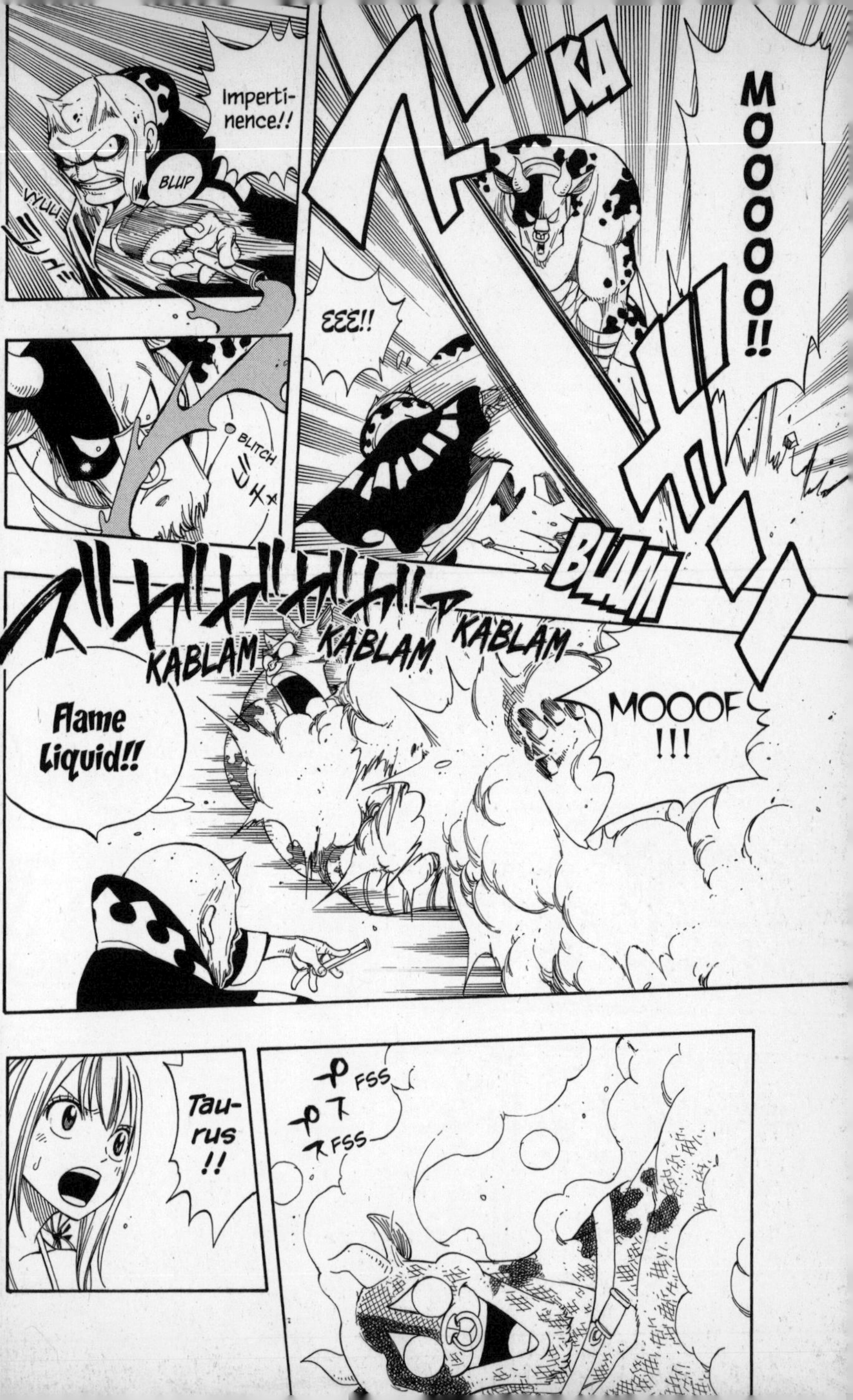
KA
MOOOOOO!!
EEE!!
BLAM
Imperti-nence!!
BLUP
VYUU
BLITCH
MOOOF!!!
KABLAM
KABLAM
KABLAM
Flame Liquid!!
FSS
FSS
Tau-rus!!

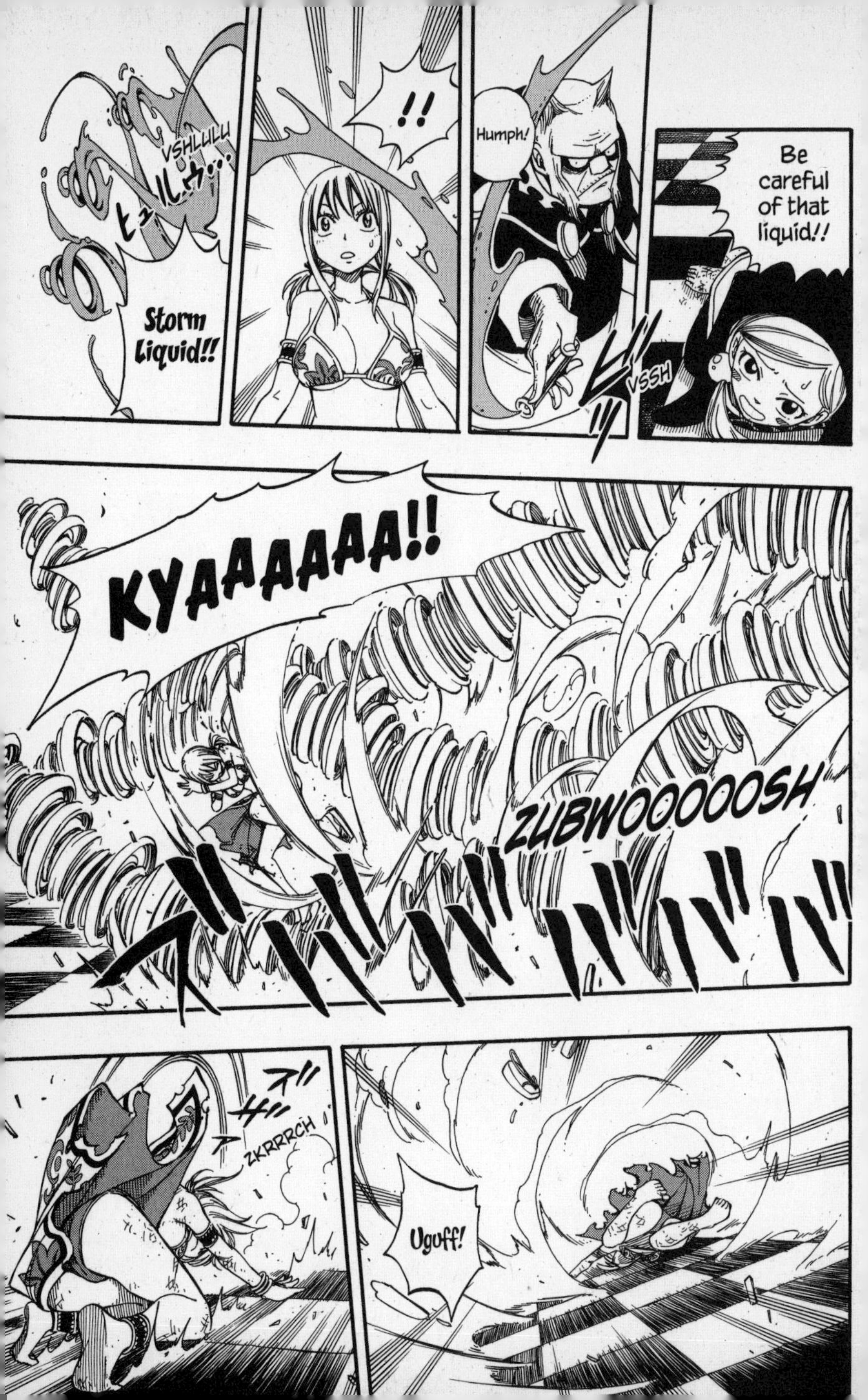
Be careful of that liquid!!
Humph!
VSSH
!!
VSHLULU
Storm Liquid!!
KYAAAAAA!!
ZUBWOOOOOSH
Uguff!
ZKRRRCH

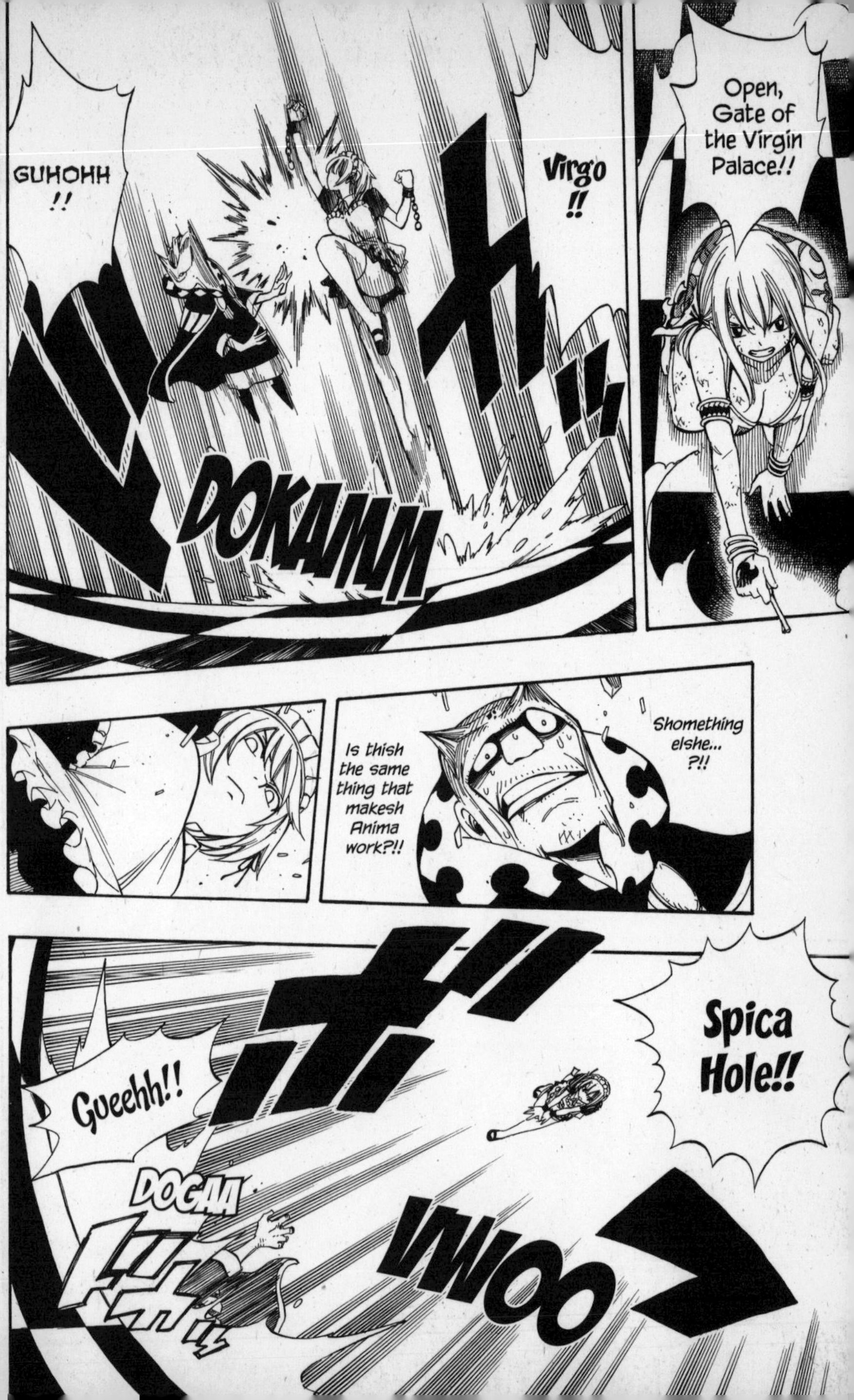
Open, Gate of the Virgin Palace!!
Virgo!!
GUHOHH!!
DOKAMM
Shomething elshe...?!!
Is thish the same thing that makesh Anima work?!!
Spica Hole!!
VWOO
Gueehh!!
DOGAA

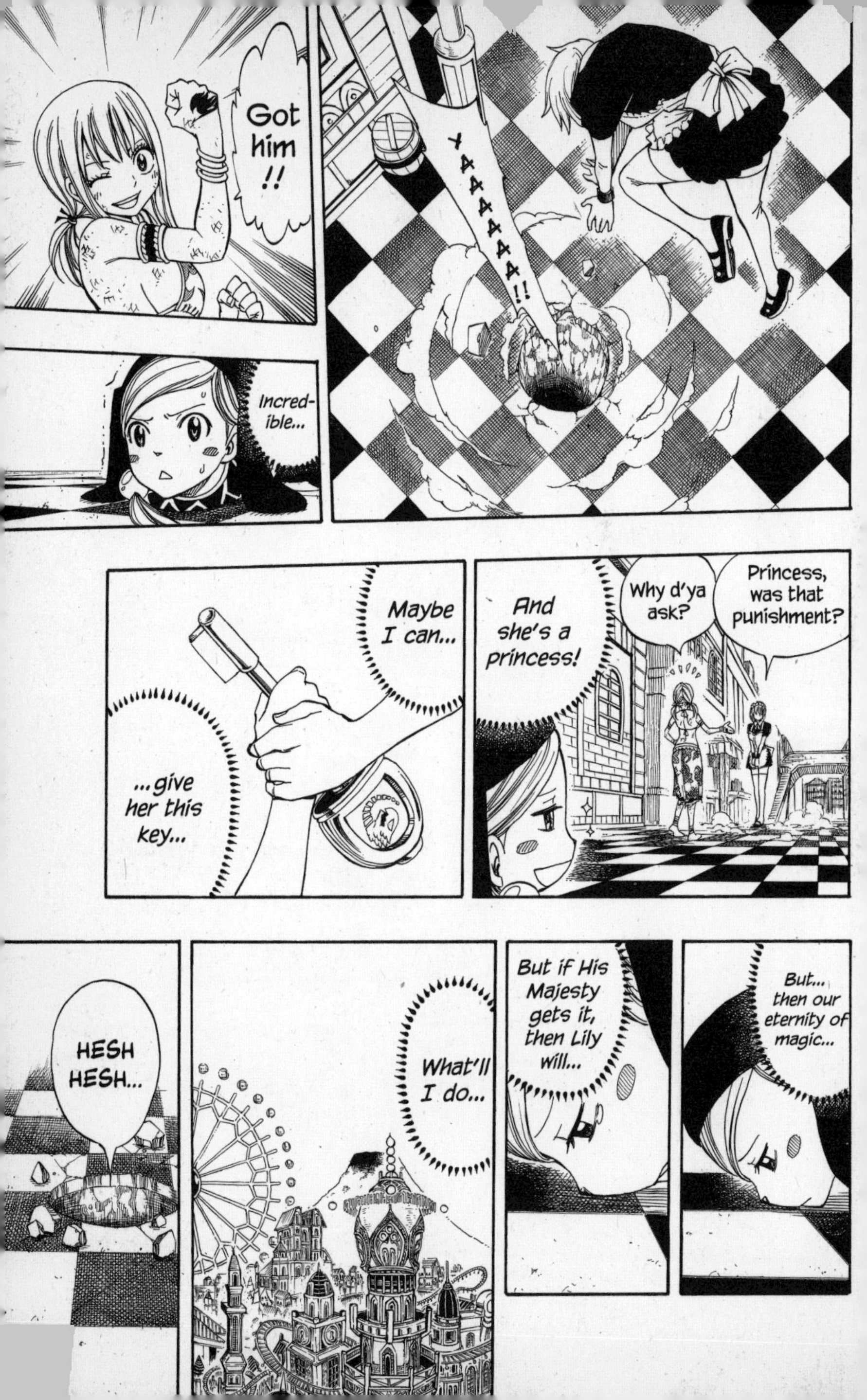
YAAAAAA!!
Got him!!
Incred-ible...
Princess, was that punishment?
Why d'ya ask?
And she's a princess!
Maybe I can...
...give her this key...
But... then our eternity of magic...
But if His Majesty gets it, then Lily will...
What'll I do...
HESH HESH...

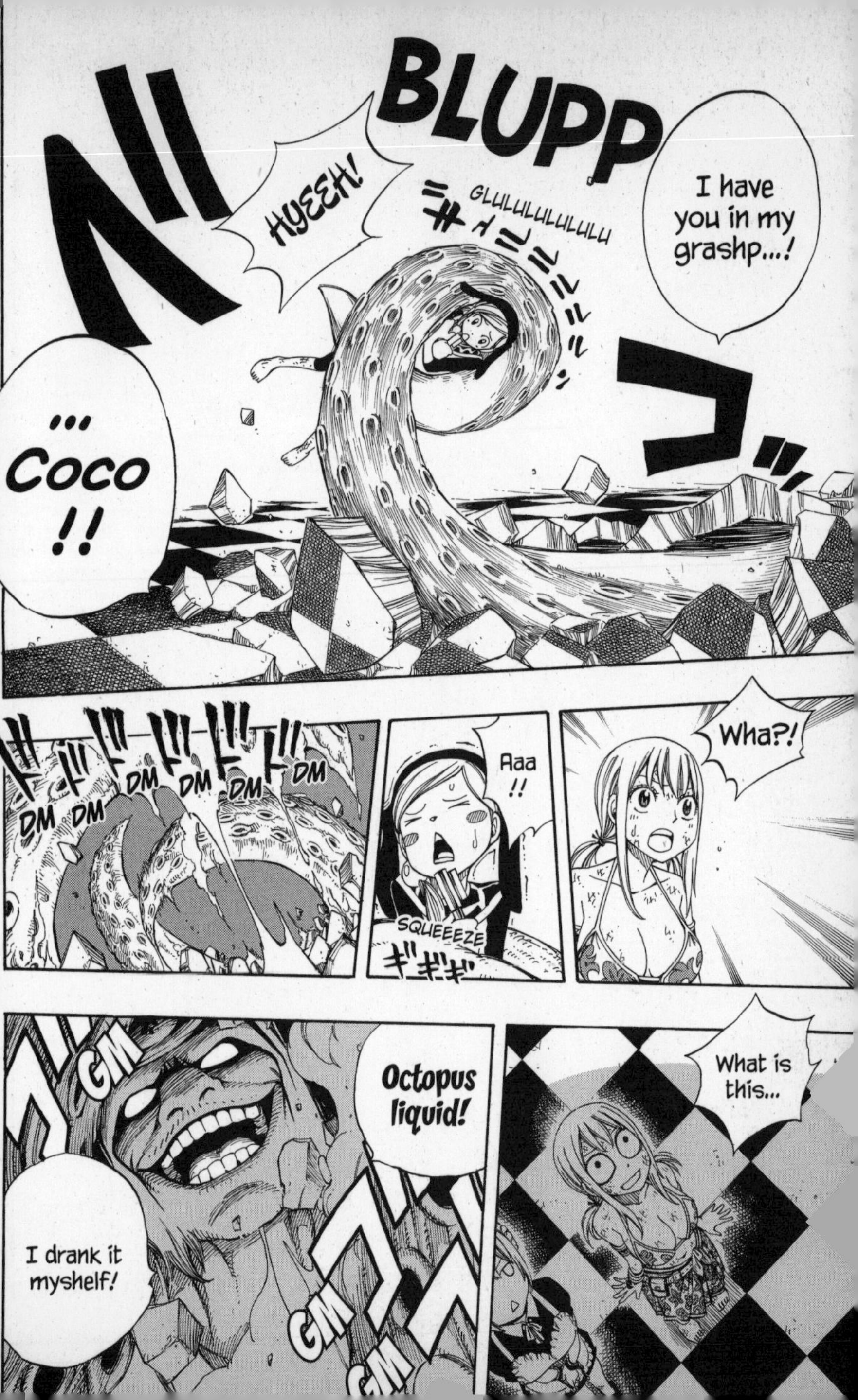
BLUPP
I have you in my grashp...!
HYEEH!
GLULULULULULU
...Coco!!
Wha?!
Aaa!!
SQUEEEZE
ギギギ
DM DM DM DM DM DM
What is this...
Octopus liquid!
I drank it myshelf!
GM GM GM

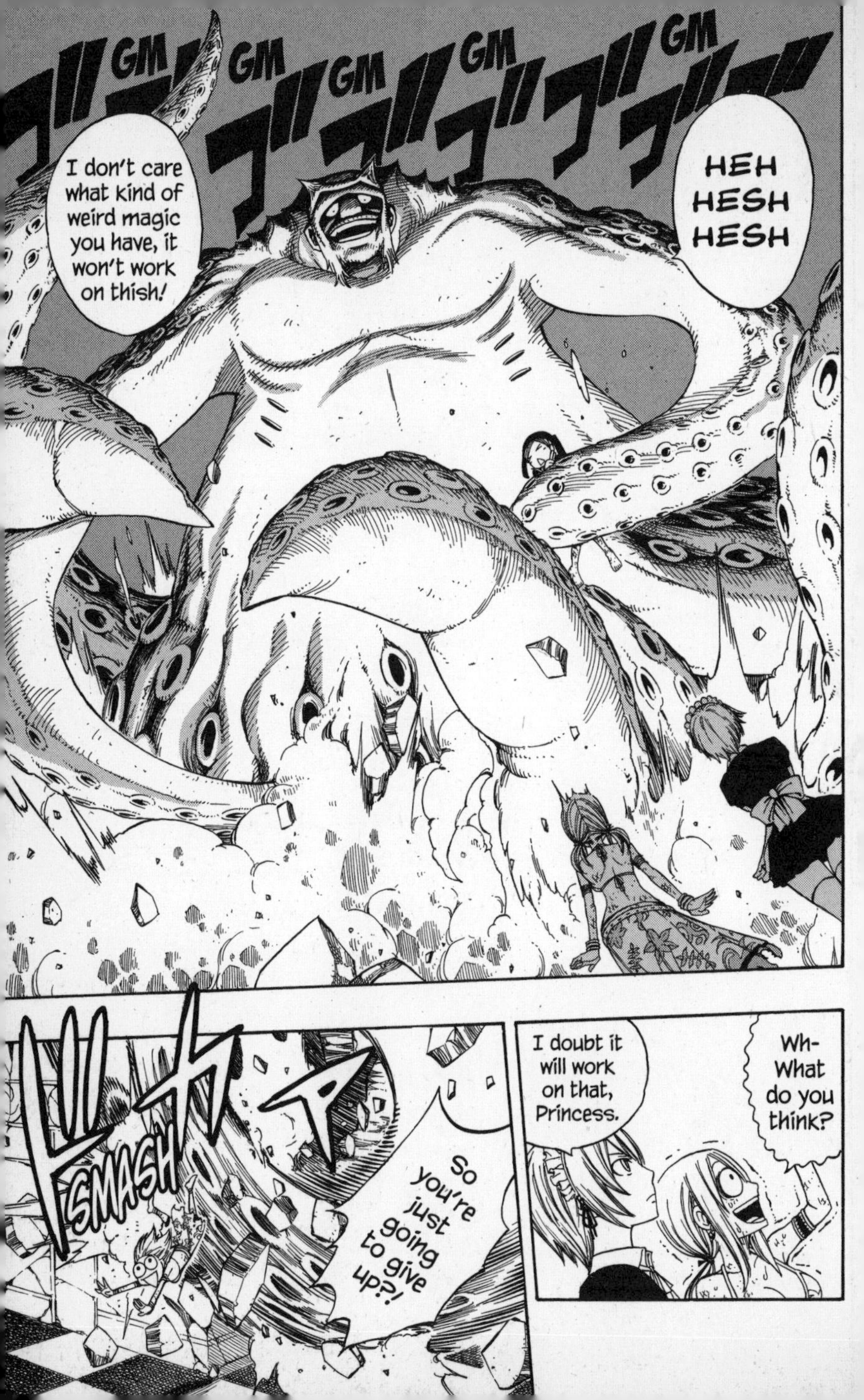
GM GM GM GM GM
HEH HESH HESH
I don't care what kind of weird magic you have, it won't work on thish!
Wh- What do you think?
I doubt it will work on that, Princess.
So you're just going to give up?!
SMASH

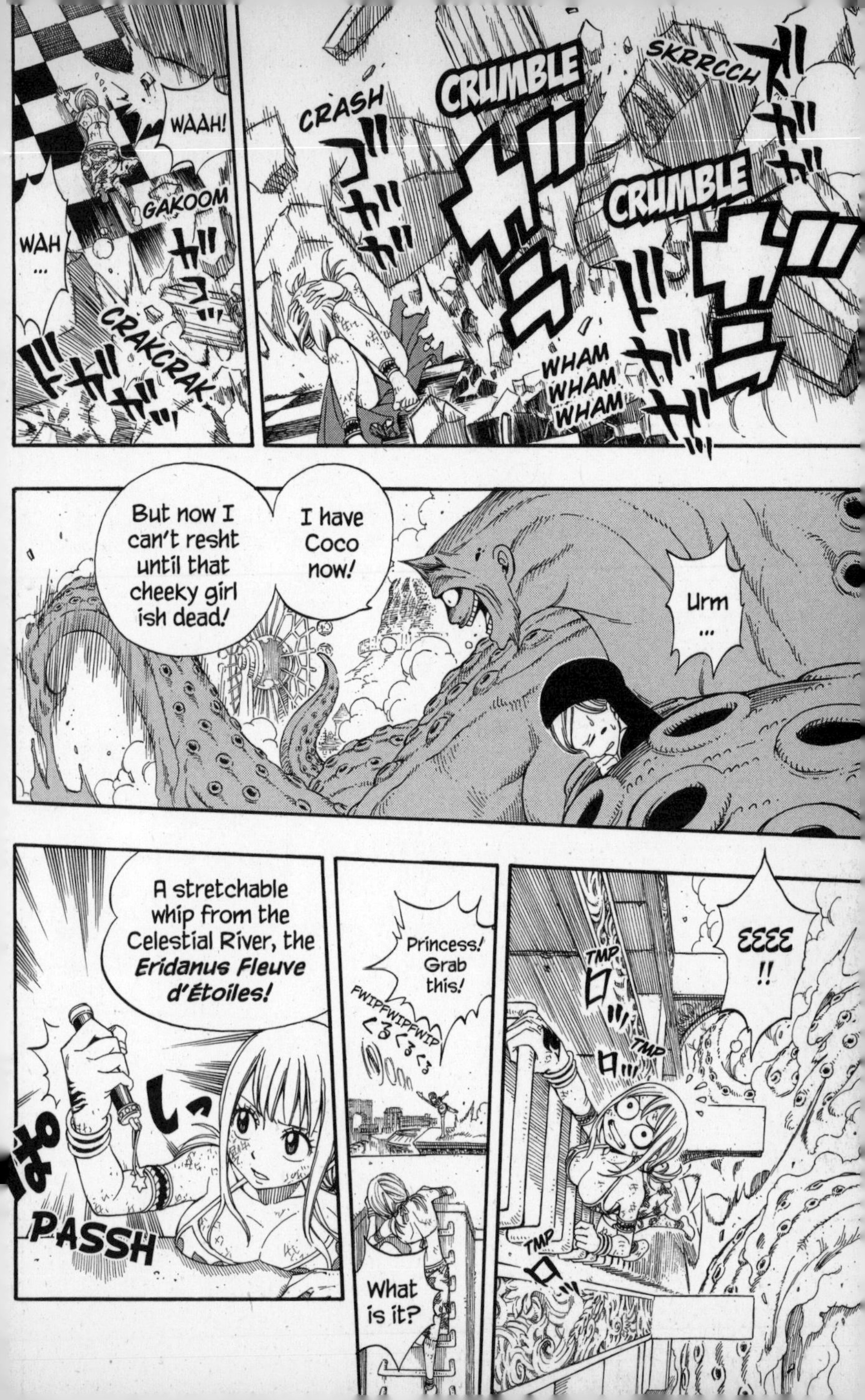
SKRRCCH
CRUMBLE
CRUMBLE
CRASH
WHAM
WHAM
WHAM
WAAH!
GAKOOM
WAH ...
CRAKCRAK
I have Coco now!
But now I can't resht until that cheeky girl ish dead!
Urm ...
ƐƐƐƐ!!
TMP
TMP
TMP
Princess! Grab this!
FWIPFWIPFWIP
What is it?
A stretchable whip from the Celestial River, the *Eridanus Fleuve d'Étoiles!*
PASSH

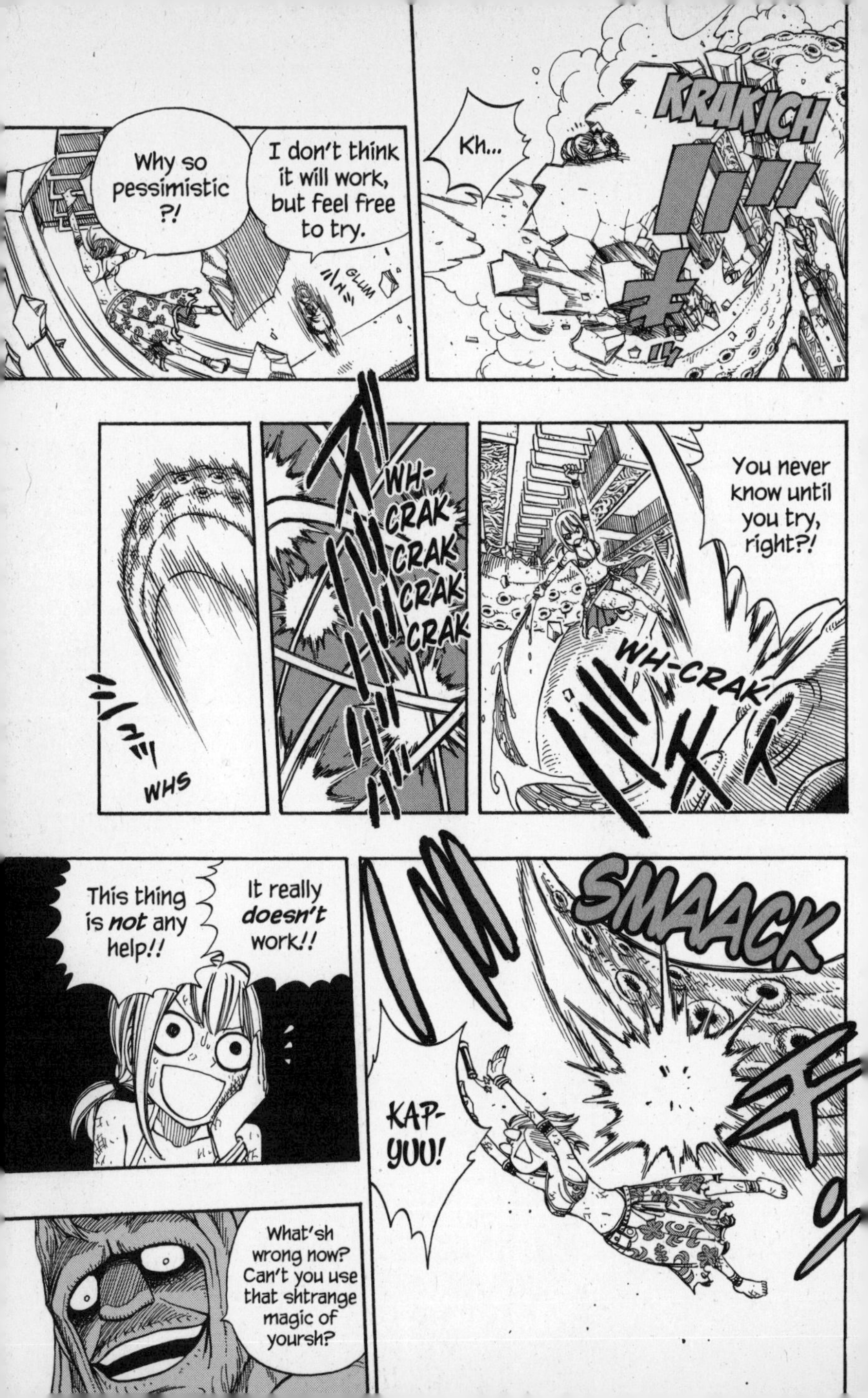
KRAKICH
Kh...
I don't think it will work, but feel free to try.
Why so pessimistic?!
GLUM
You never know until you try, right?!
WH-CRAK
WH-CRAK CRAK CRAK CRAK
WHS
SMAACK
KAP-YUU!
It really *doesn't* work!!
This thing is *not* any help!!
What'sh wrong now? Can't you use that shtrange magic of yoursh?

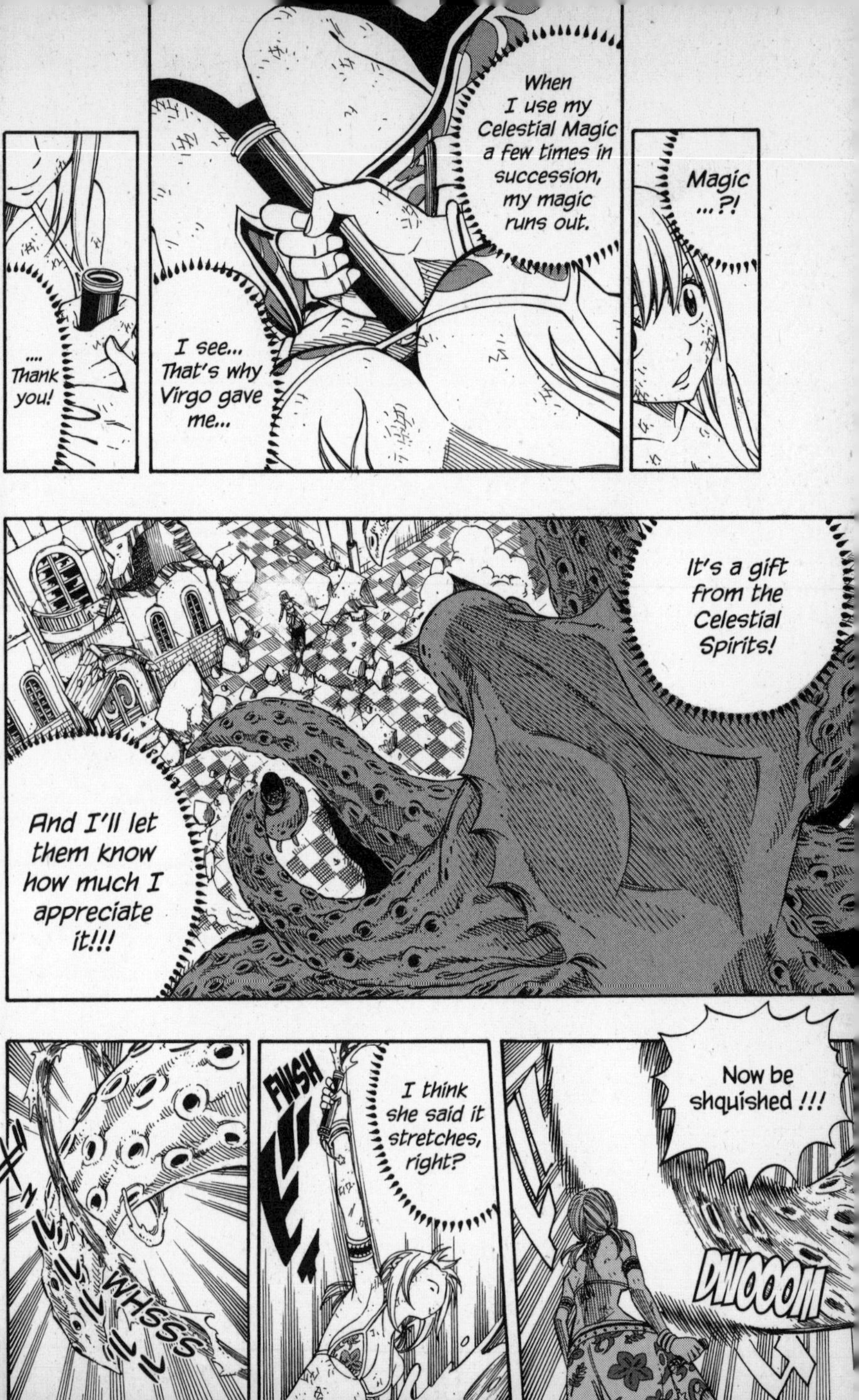
Magic ...?!
When I use my Celestial Magic a few times in succession, my magic runs out.
I see... That's why Virgo gave me...
.... Thank you!
It's a gift from the Celestial Spirits!
And I'll let them know how much I appreciate it!!!
Now be shquished !!!
DWOOOM
I think she said it stretches, right?
FWSH
WHSSS

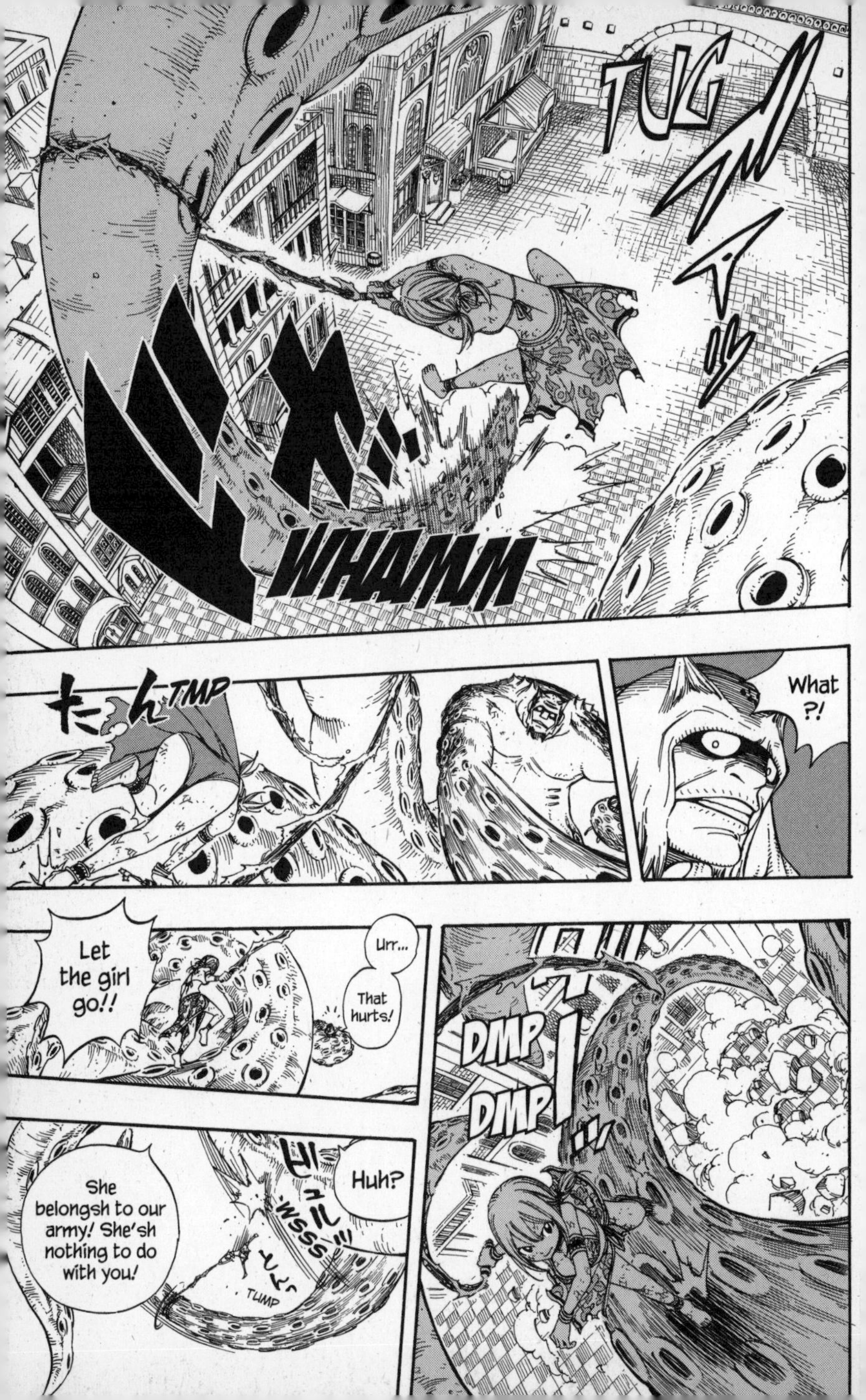
TUG
WHAMM
What?!
TMP
DMP
DMP
Urr...
That hurts!
Let the girl go!!
Huh?
WSSS
She belongsh to our army! She'sh nothing to do with you!
TUMP

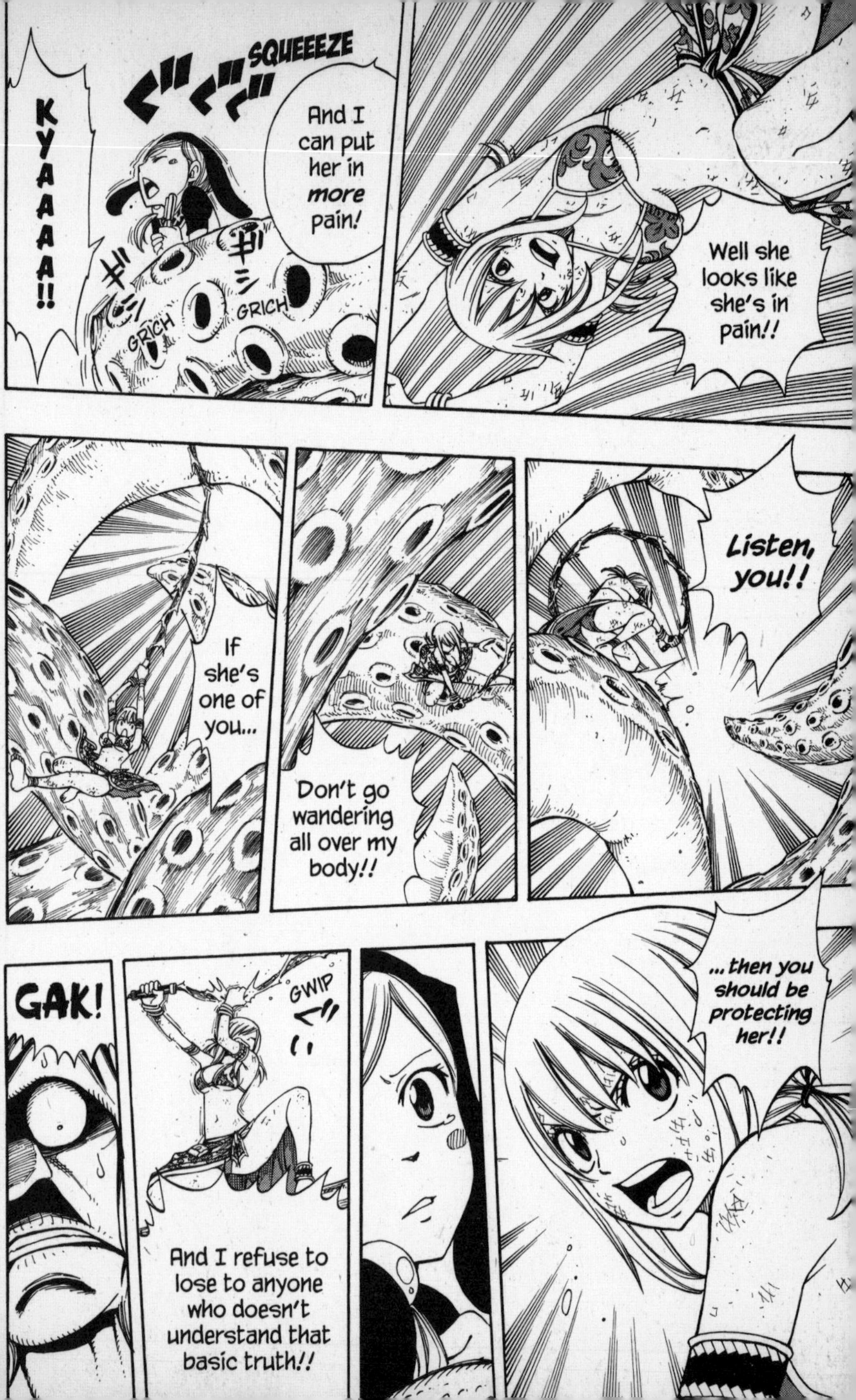
Well she looks like she's in pain!!
SQUEEEZE
And I can put her in *more* pain!
KYAAAAA!!
GRICH
GRICH
Listen, you!!
Don't go wandering all over my body!!
If she's one of you...
...then you should be protecting her!!
GWIP
And I refuse to lose to anyone who doesn't understand that basic truth!!
GAK!

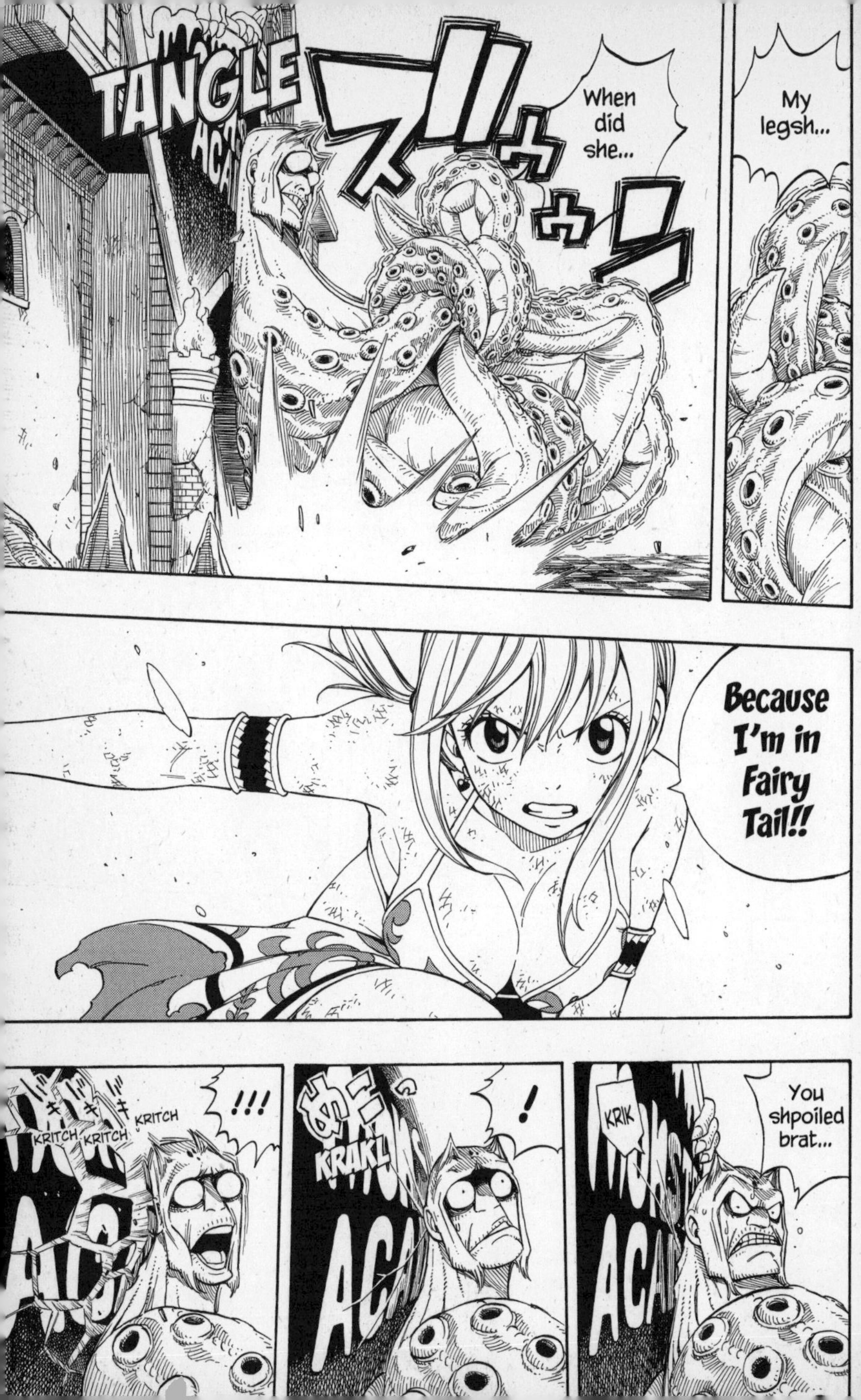
My legsh...
TANGLE
When did she...
Because I'm in Fairy Tail!!
KRIK
You shpoiled brat...
KRAKL
!
KRITCH KRITCH KRITCH
!!!

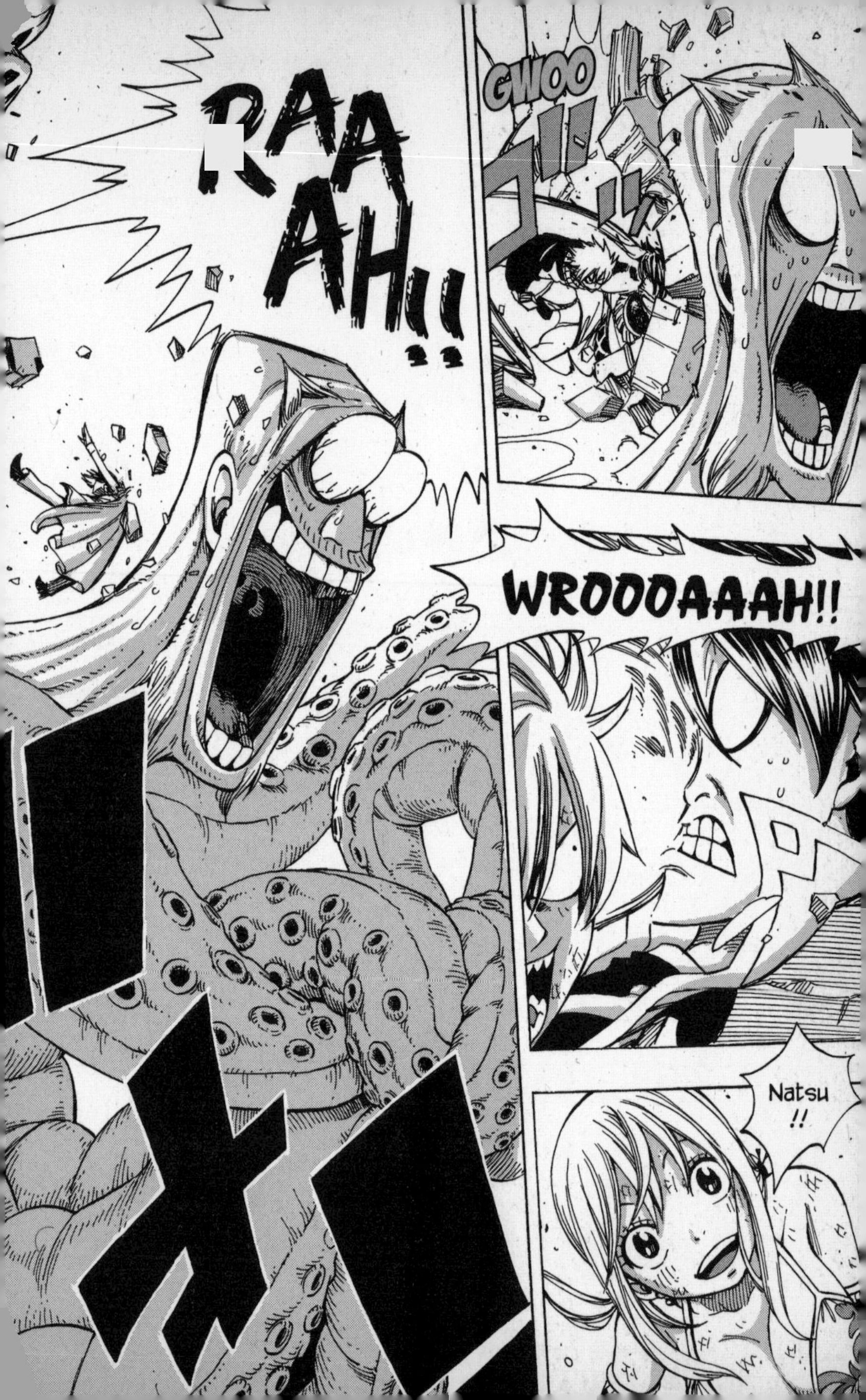
GWOO
WROOOOAAAH!!
Natsu !!
RAAAH!!

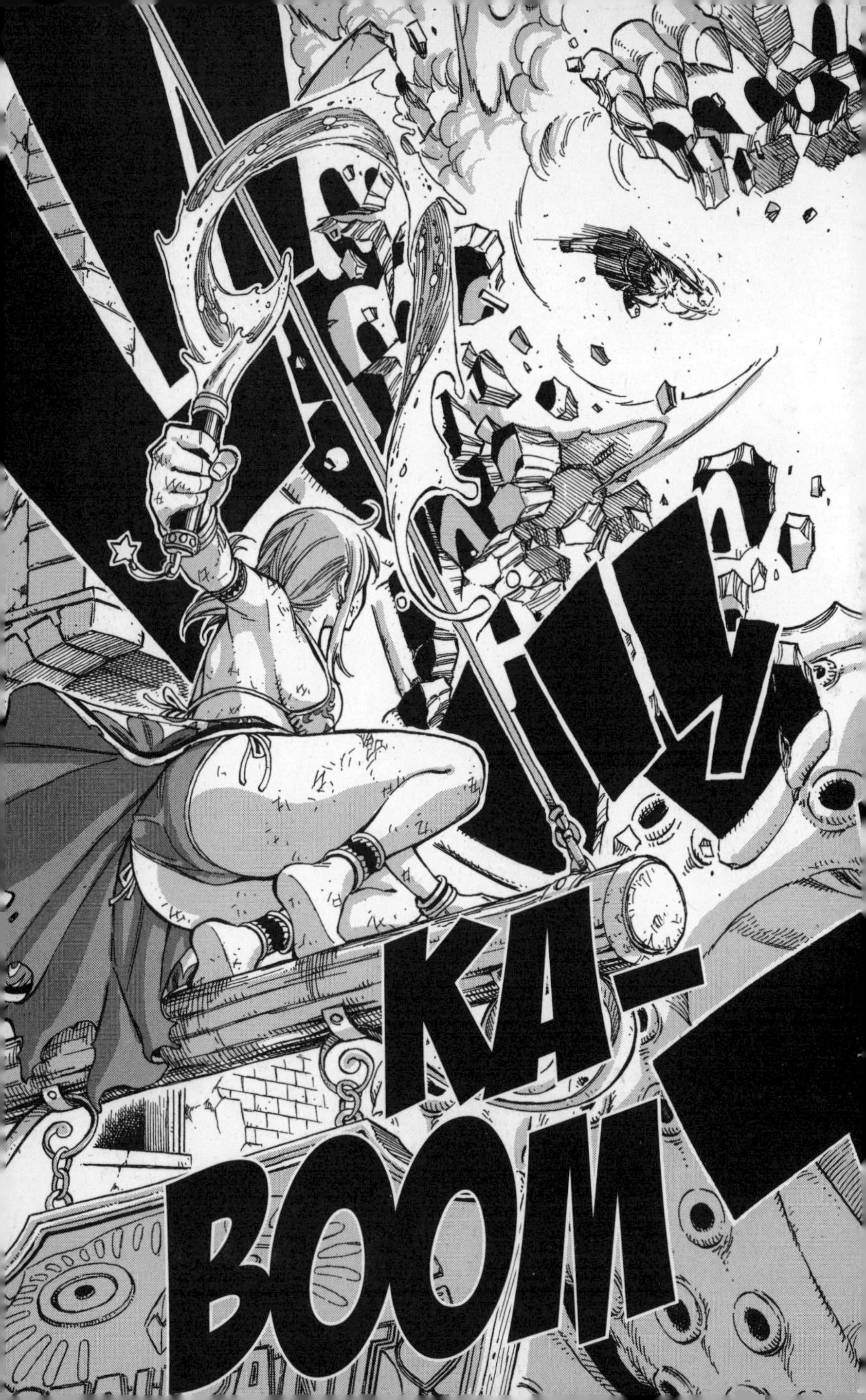
KA-BOOM

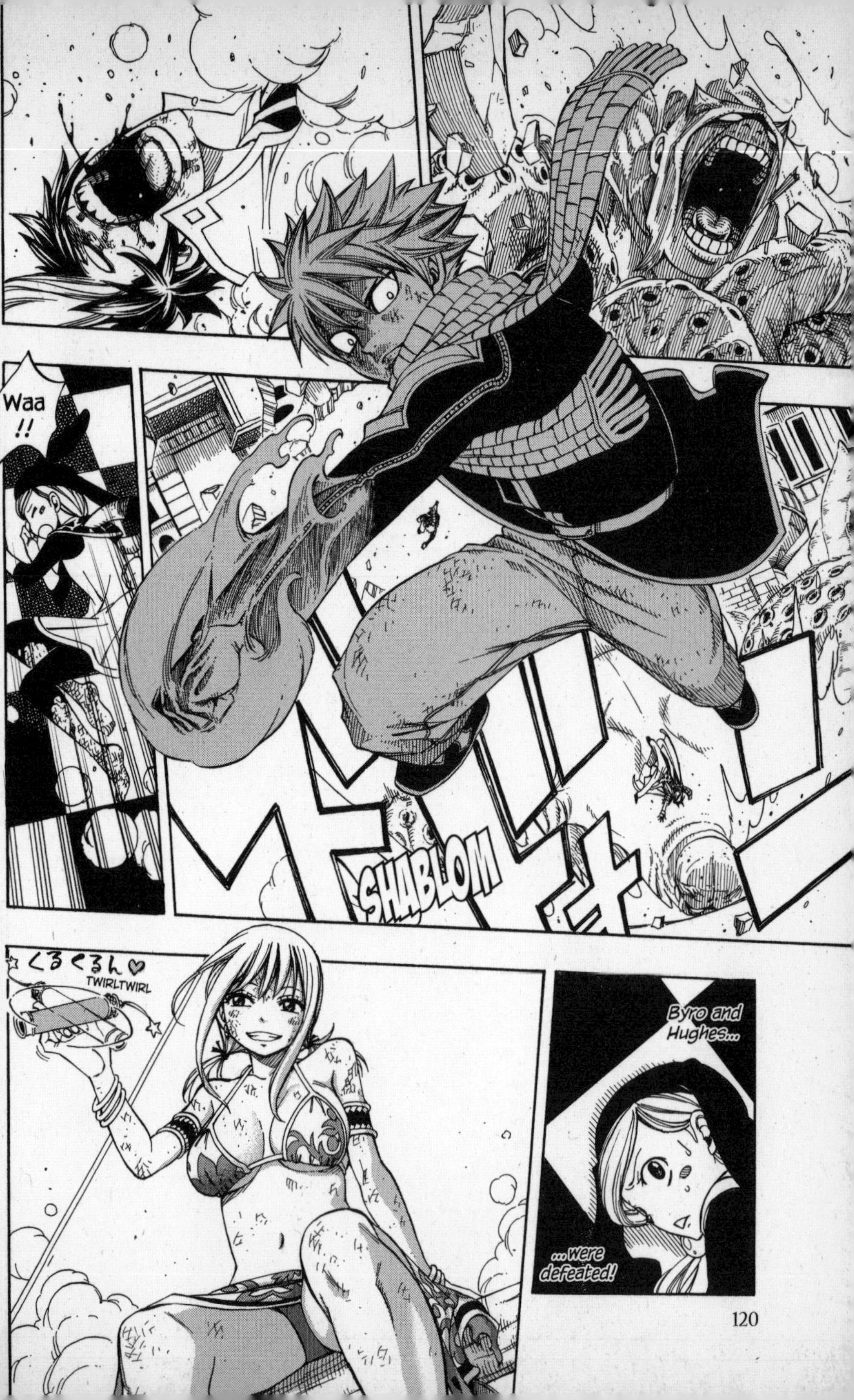
SHABLOM
Waa !!
Byro and Hughes...
...were defeated!
くるくるん
TWIRLTWIRL

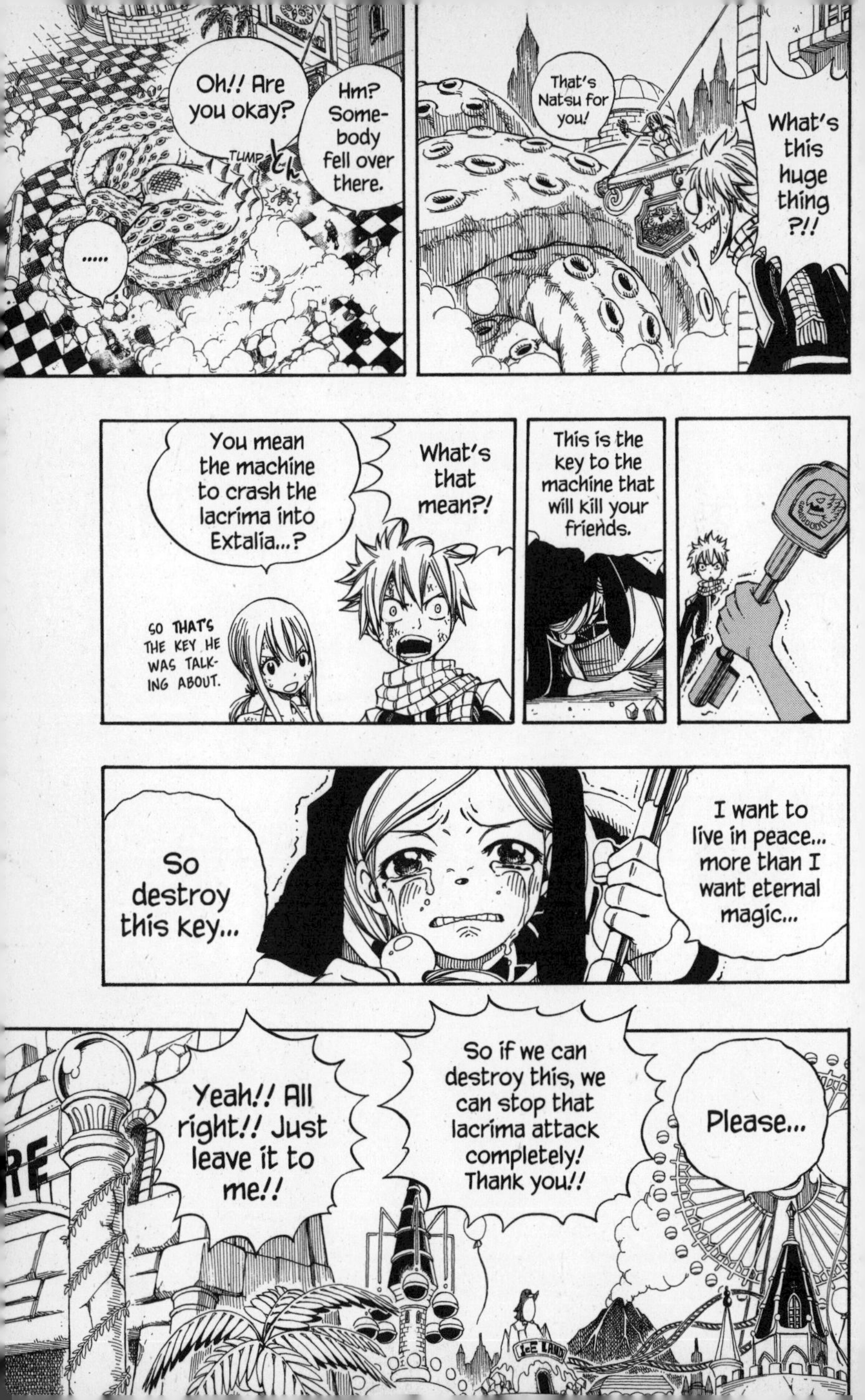
What's this huge thing?!!
That's Natsu for you!
Hm? Somebody fell over there.
Oh!! Are you okay?
TUMP
.....
This is the key to the machine that will kill your friends.
What's that mean?!
You mean the machine to crash the lacrima into Extalia...?
SO THAT'S THE KEY HE WAS TALKING ABOUT.
I want to live in peace... more than I want eternal magic...
So destroy this key...
Please...
So if we can destroy this, we can stop that lacrima attack completely! Thank you!!
Yeah!! All right!! Just leave it to me!!

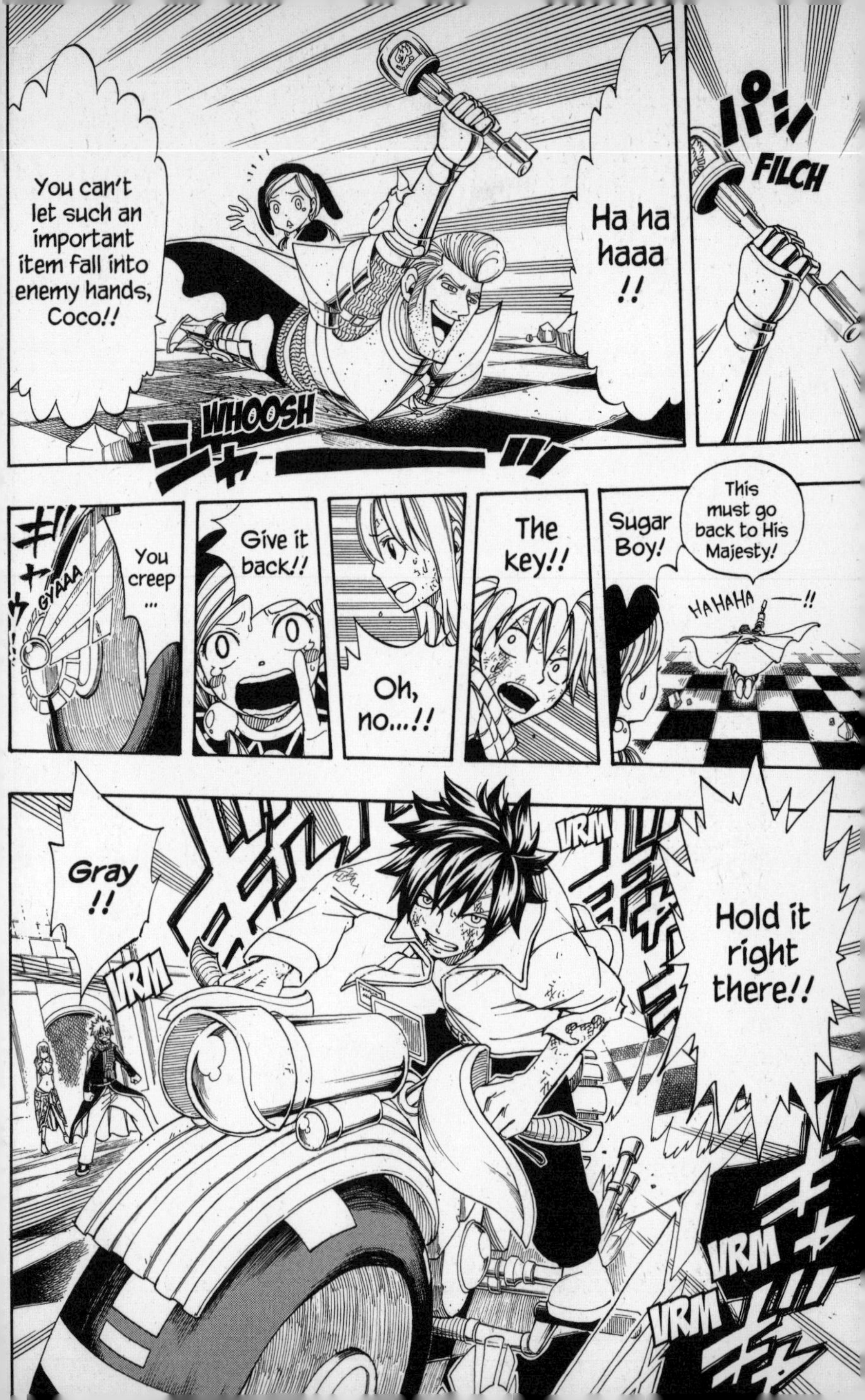
パッ
FILCH
Ha ha haaa!!
You can't let such an important item fall into enemy hands, Coco!!
WHOOSH
This must go back to His Majesty!
Sugar Boy!
HAHAHA—!!
The key!!
Oh, no...!!
Give it back!!
You creep...
GYAAA
Hold it right there!!
VRM
VRM
VRM
VRM
Gray!!

FAIRY TAIL
フェアリーテイル

Chapter 185, Ice Boy

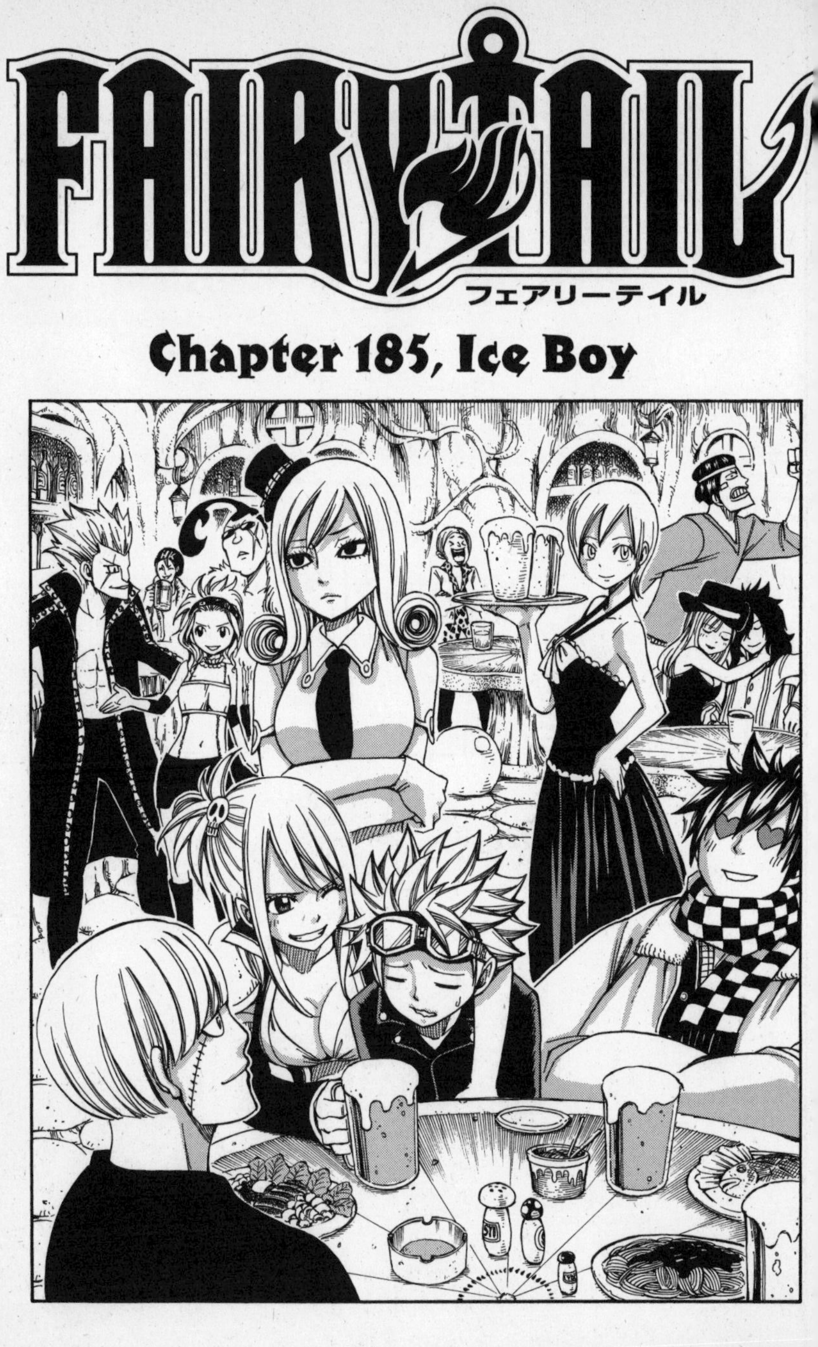

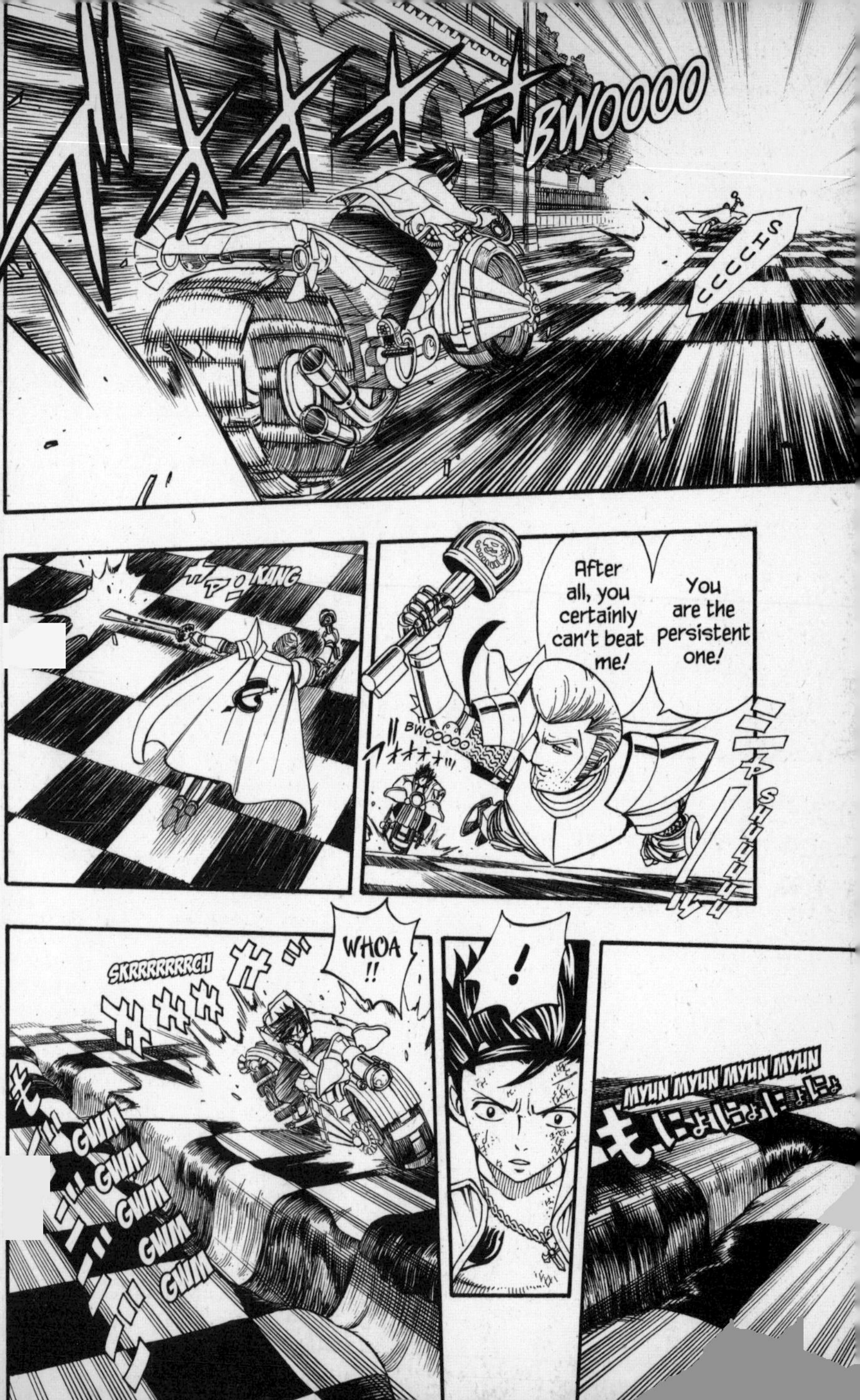
BWOOOO
SHUUUU
After all, you certainly can't beat me!
You are the persistent one!
BWOOOOO
SHUUUUUU
KANG
MYUN MYUN MYUN MYUN
!
WHOA !!
SKRRRRRRRCH
GWM
GWM
GWM
GWM
GWM

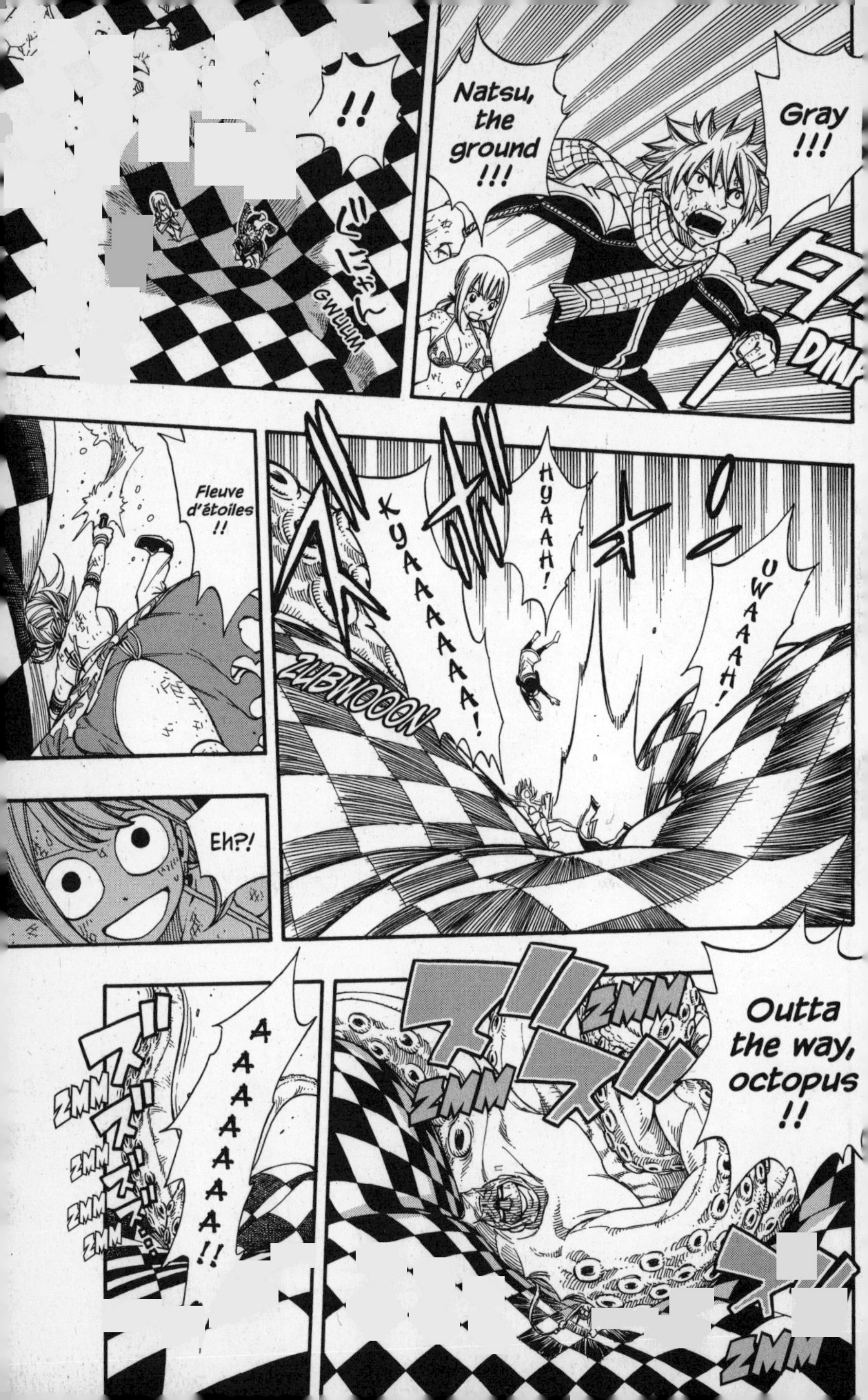
Gray!!!
DMP
Natsu, the ground!!!
!!
GWUUUM
UWAAAAH!
HYAAAH!
KYAAAAAAAA!
ZUBWOOON
Fleuve d'étoiles!!
Eh?!
Outta the way, octopus!!
ZMM
ZMM
ZMM
AAAAAAAA!!
ZMM
ZMM
ZMM
ZMM

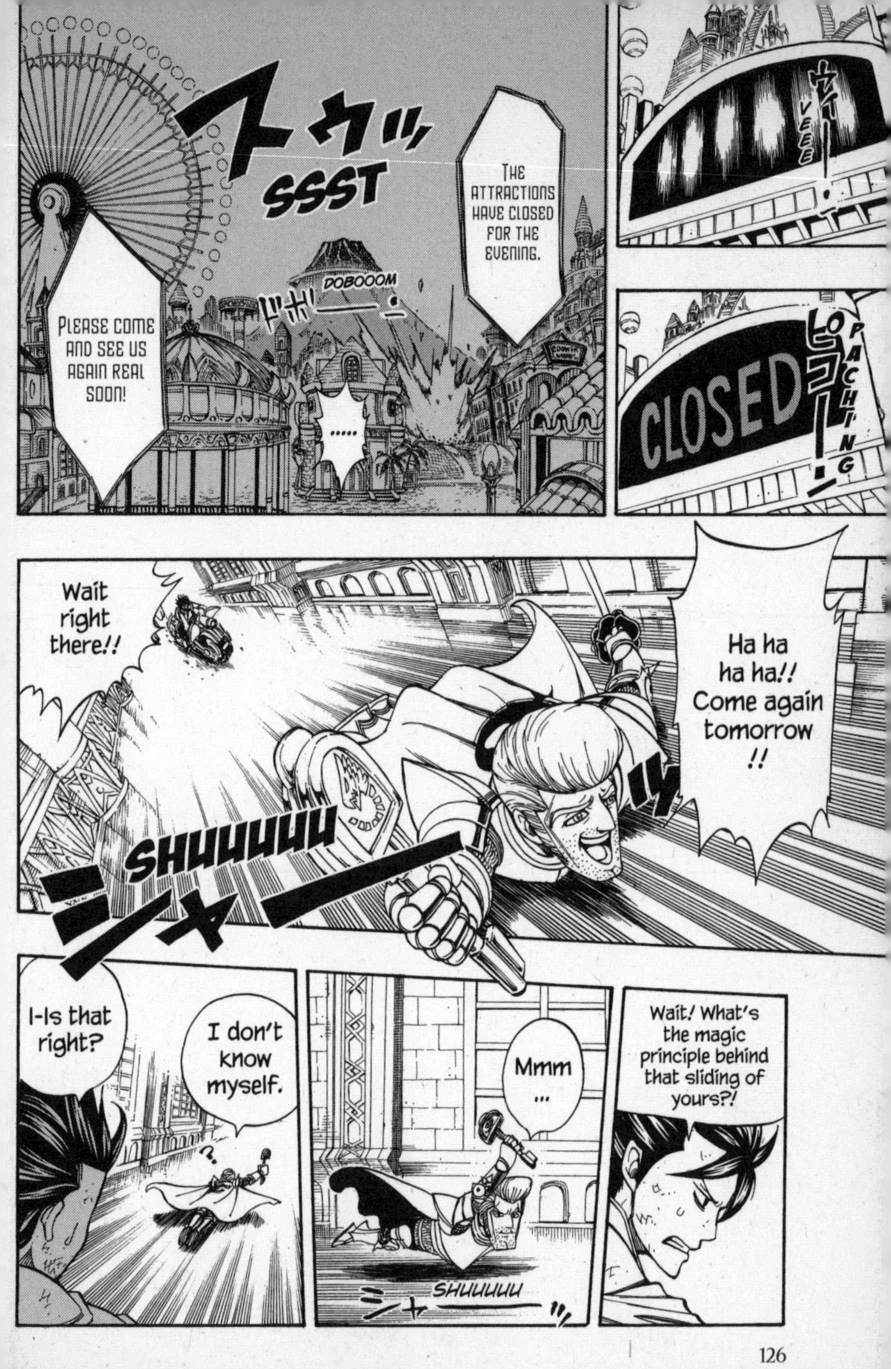
VEEE
CLOSED
PACHING
THE ATTRACTIONS HAVE CLOSED FOR THE EVENING.
SSST
DOBOOOM
.....
PLEASE COME AND SEE US AGAIN REAL SOON!
Ha ha ha ha!! Come again tomorrow !!
SHUUUUU
Wait right there!!
Wait! What's the magic principle behind that sliding of yours?!
Mmm ...
SHUUUUU
I don't know myself.
I-Is that right?

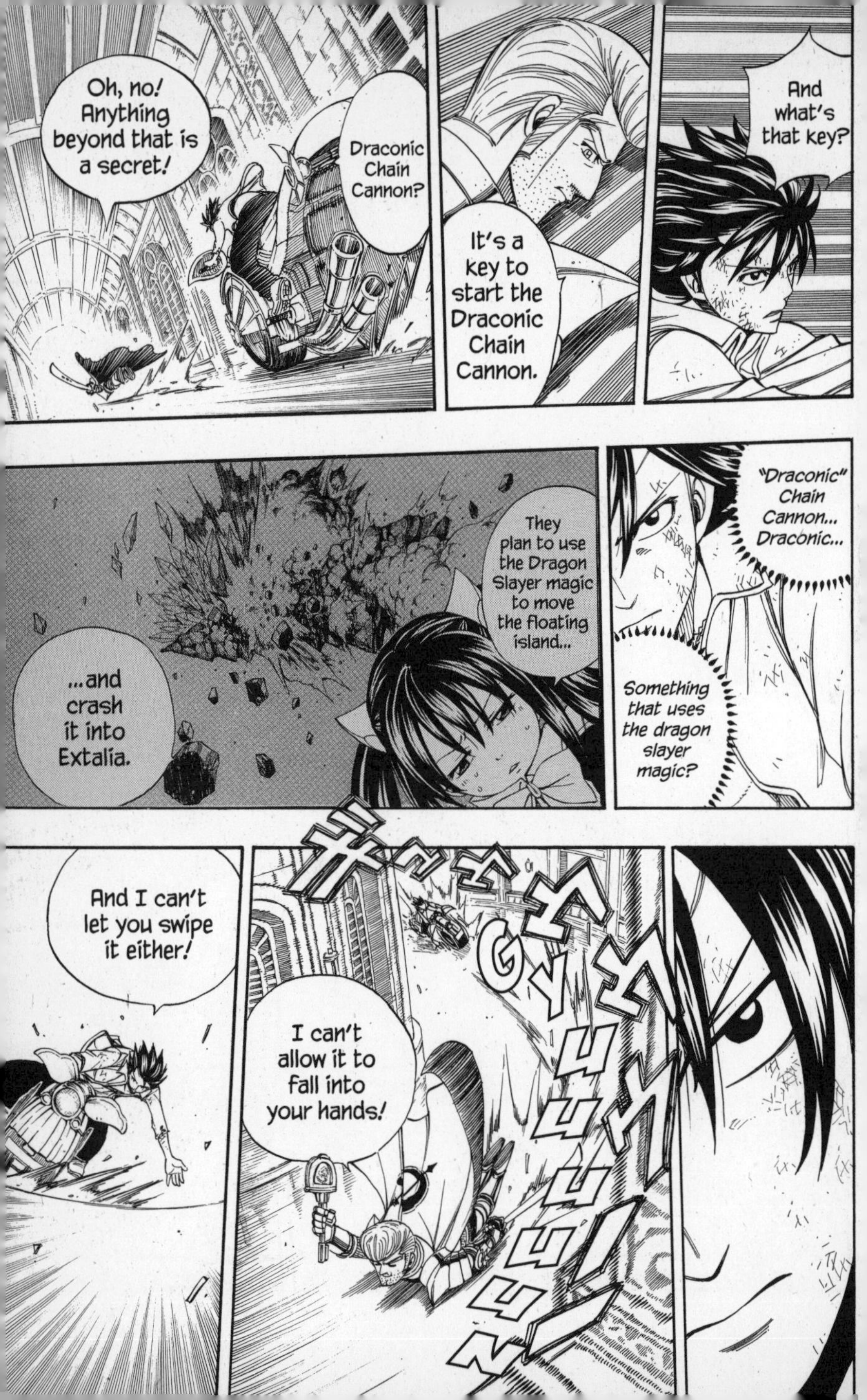
And what's that key?
It's a key to start the Draconic Chain Cannon.
Draconic Chain Cannon?
Oh, no! Anything beyond that is a secret!
"Draconic" Chain Cannon... Draconic...
Something that uses the dragon slayer magic?
They plan to use the Dragon Slayer magic to move the floating island...
...and crash it into Extalia.
I can't allow it to fall into your hands!
And I can't let you swipe it either!

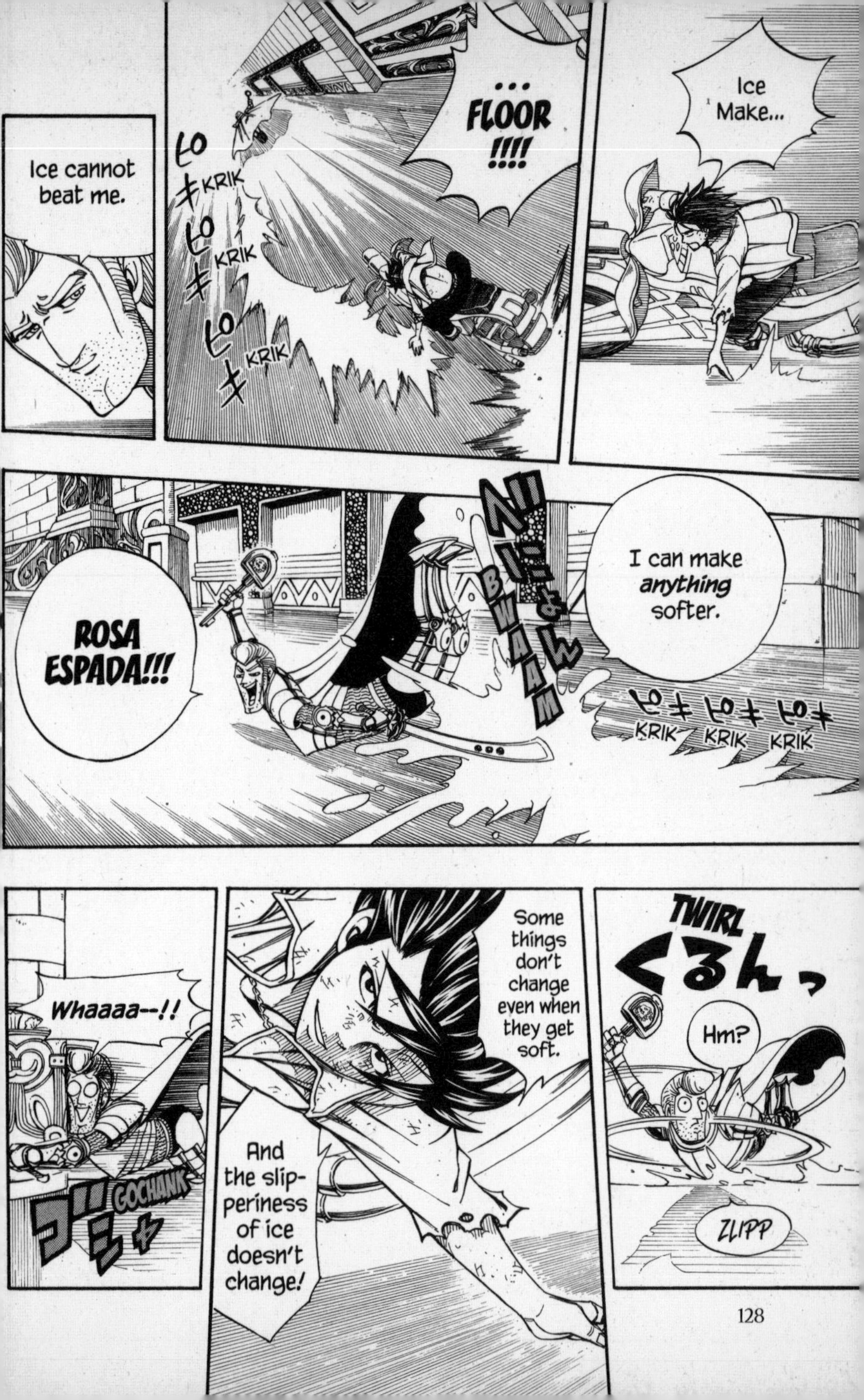

Ice Make...
...FLOOR!!!!
ピキ KRIK
ピキ KRIK
ピキ KRIK
Ice cannot beat me.
I can make *anything* softer.
ピキ KRIK ピキ KRIK ピキ KRIK
ぐにょん BWAAAM
ROSA ESPADA!!!
くるんっ TWIRL
Hm?
ZLIPP
Some things don't change even when they get soft.
And the slip-periness of ice doesn't change!
Whaaaa--!!
ゴシャ GOCHANK

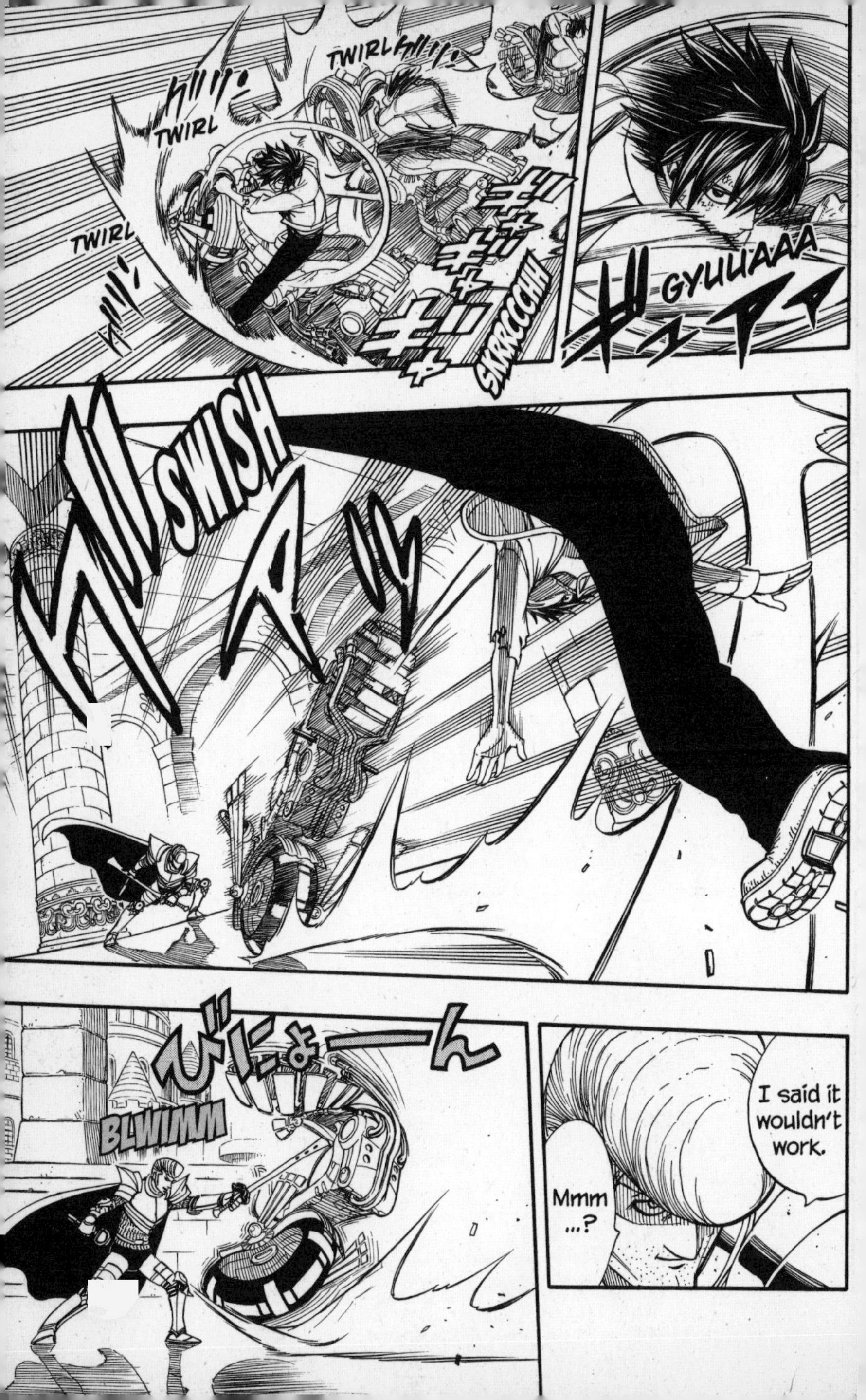

GYULIAAA
TWIRL
TWIRL
TWIRL
SKRRCCCHH
SWISH
I said it wouldn't work.
Mmm ...?
びにょーん
BLWIMM

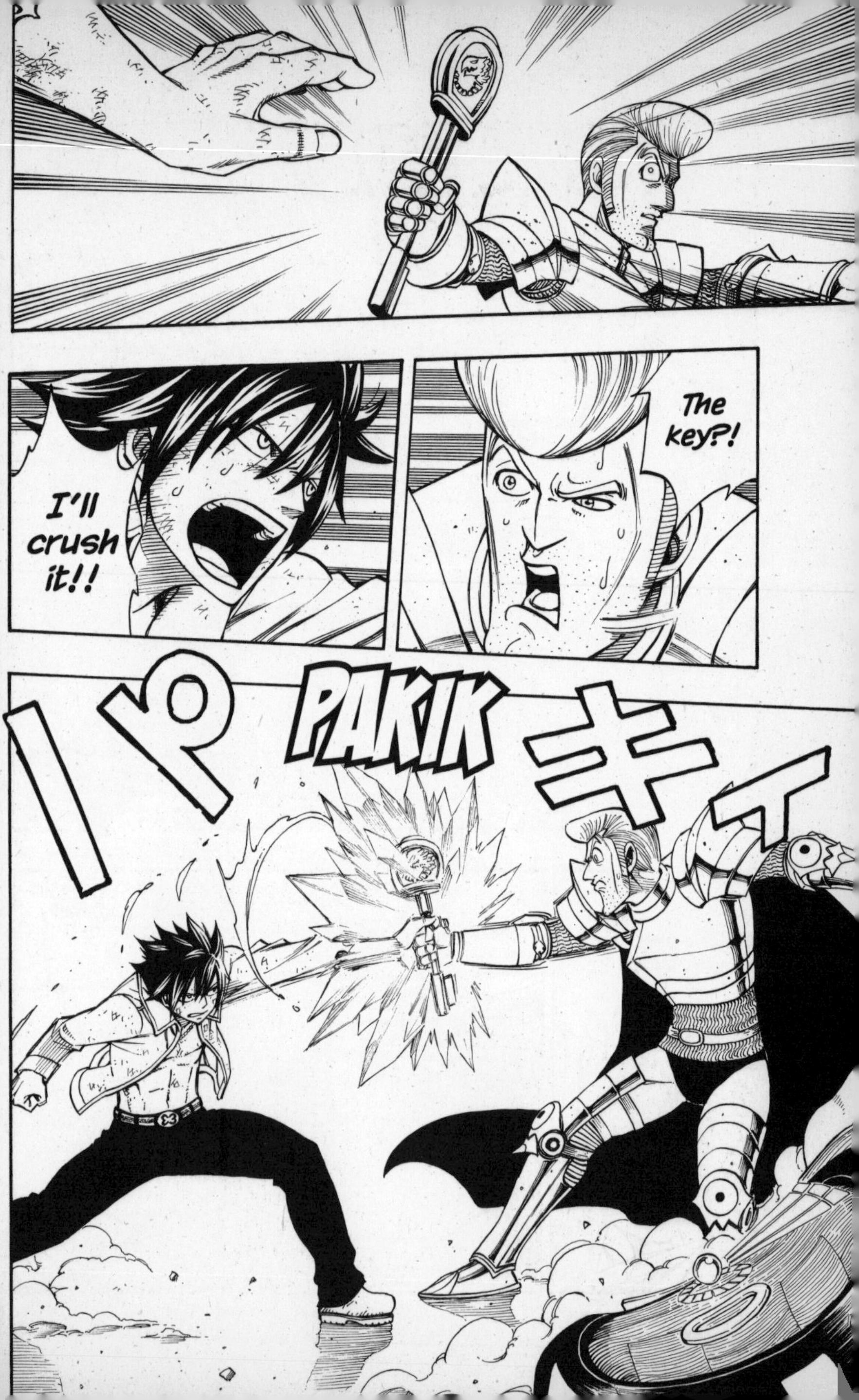
The key?!
I'll crush it!!
パキィ
PAKIK

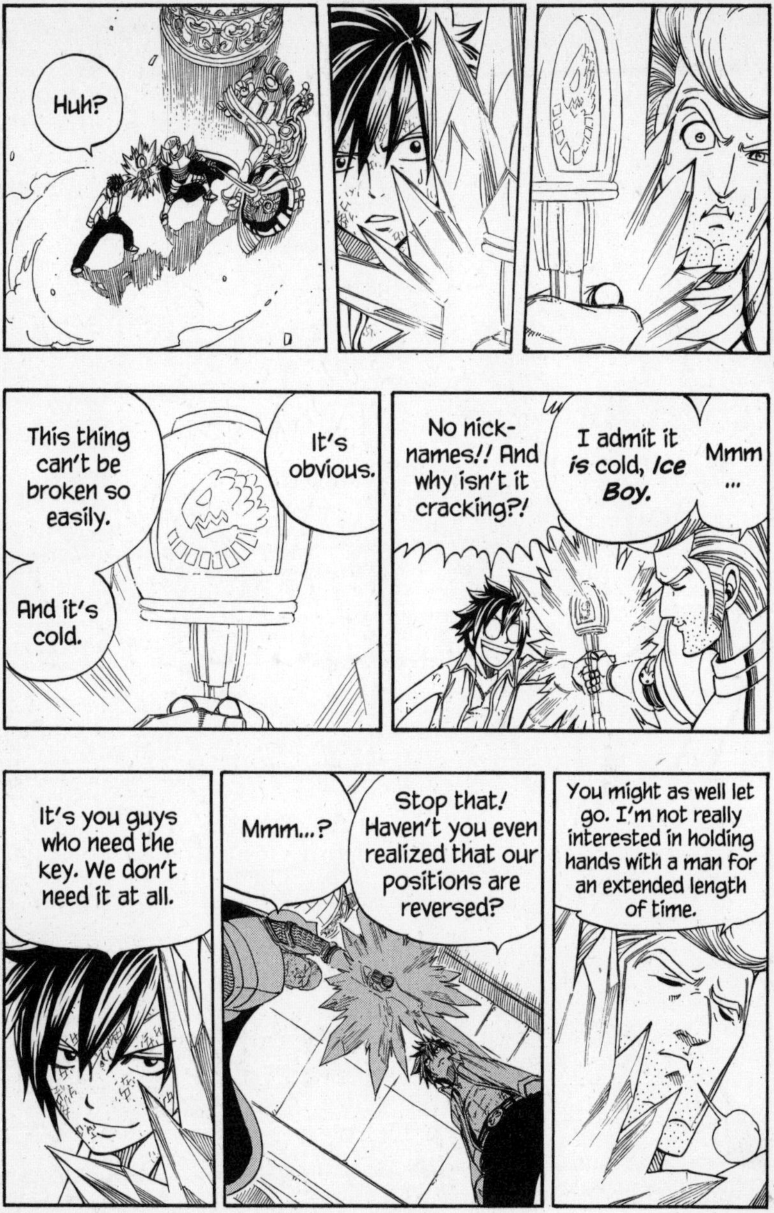
Huh?
Mmm ...
I admit it *is* cold, *Ice Boy.*
No nick-names!! And why isn't it cracking?!
It's obvious.
This thing can't be broken so easily.
And it's cold.
You might as well let go. I'm not really interested in holding hands with a man for an extended length of time.
Stop that! Haven't you even realized that our positions are reversed?
Mmm...?
It's you guys who need the key. We don't need it at all.

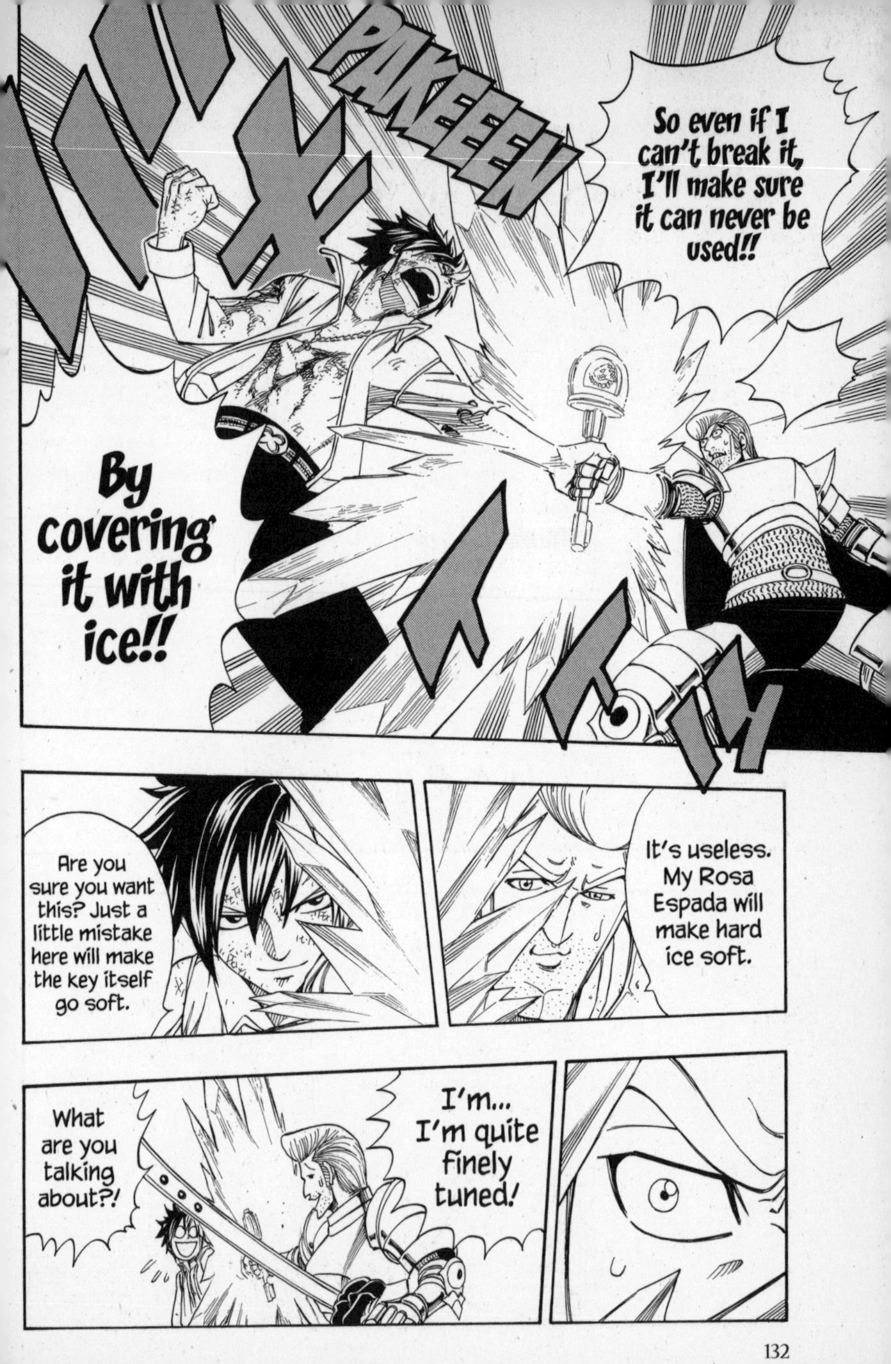
So even if I can't break it, I'll make sure it can never be used!!
PAKEEEN
By covering it with ice!!
It's useless. My Rosa Espada will make hard ice soft.
Are you sure you want this? Just a little mistake here will make the key itself go soft.
I'm... I'm quite finely tuned!
What are you talking about?!

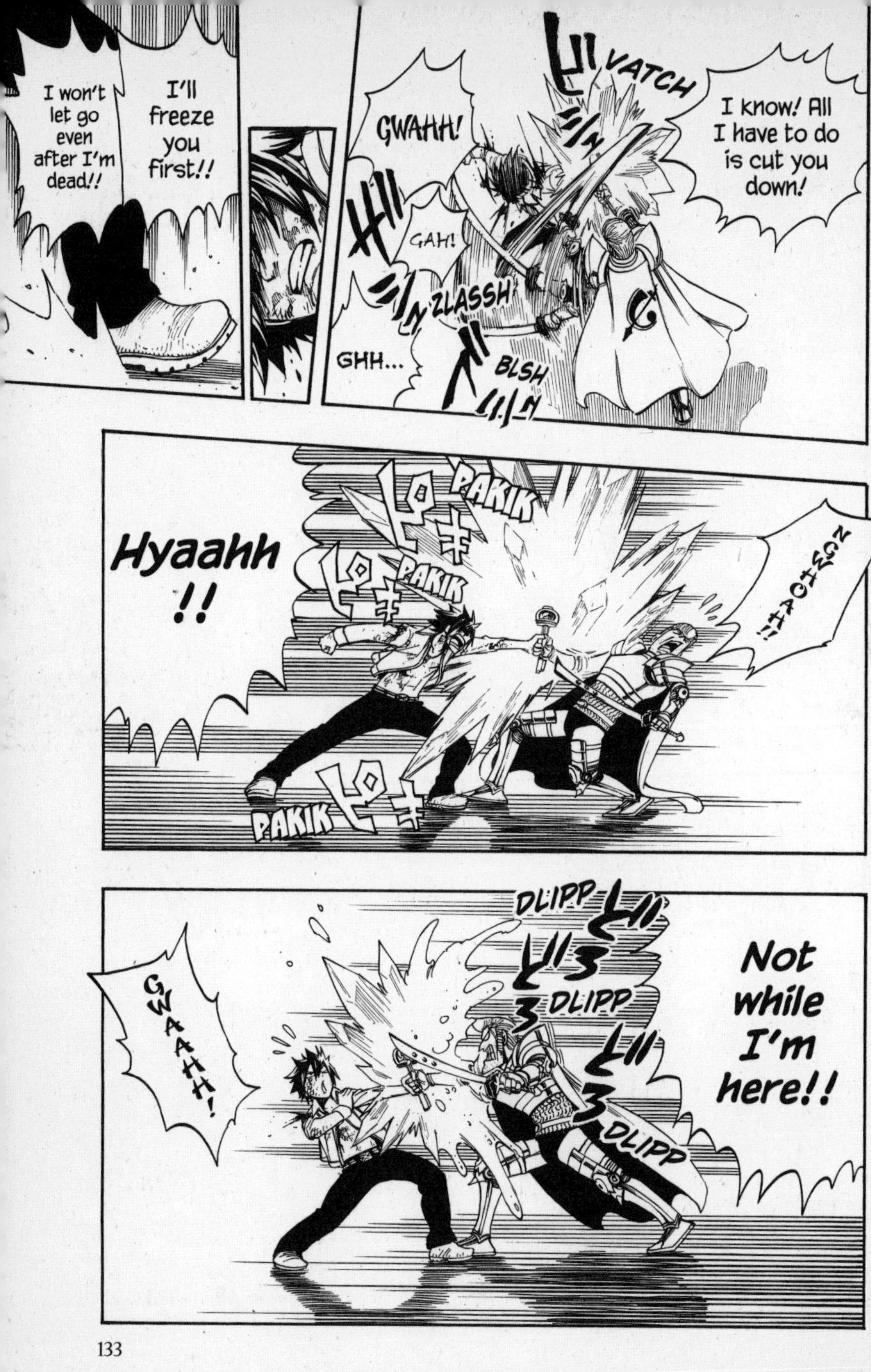
I know! All I have to do is cut you down!
VATCH
GWAHH!
GAH!
ZLASSH
GHH...
BLSH
I'll freeze you first!!
I won't let go even after I'm dead!!
ZNGOAAH!!
PAKIK
PAKIK
Hyaahh!!
PAKIK
Not while I'm here!!
DLIPP
DLIPP
DLIPP
GWAAHH!

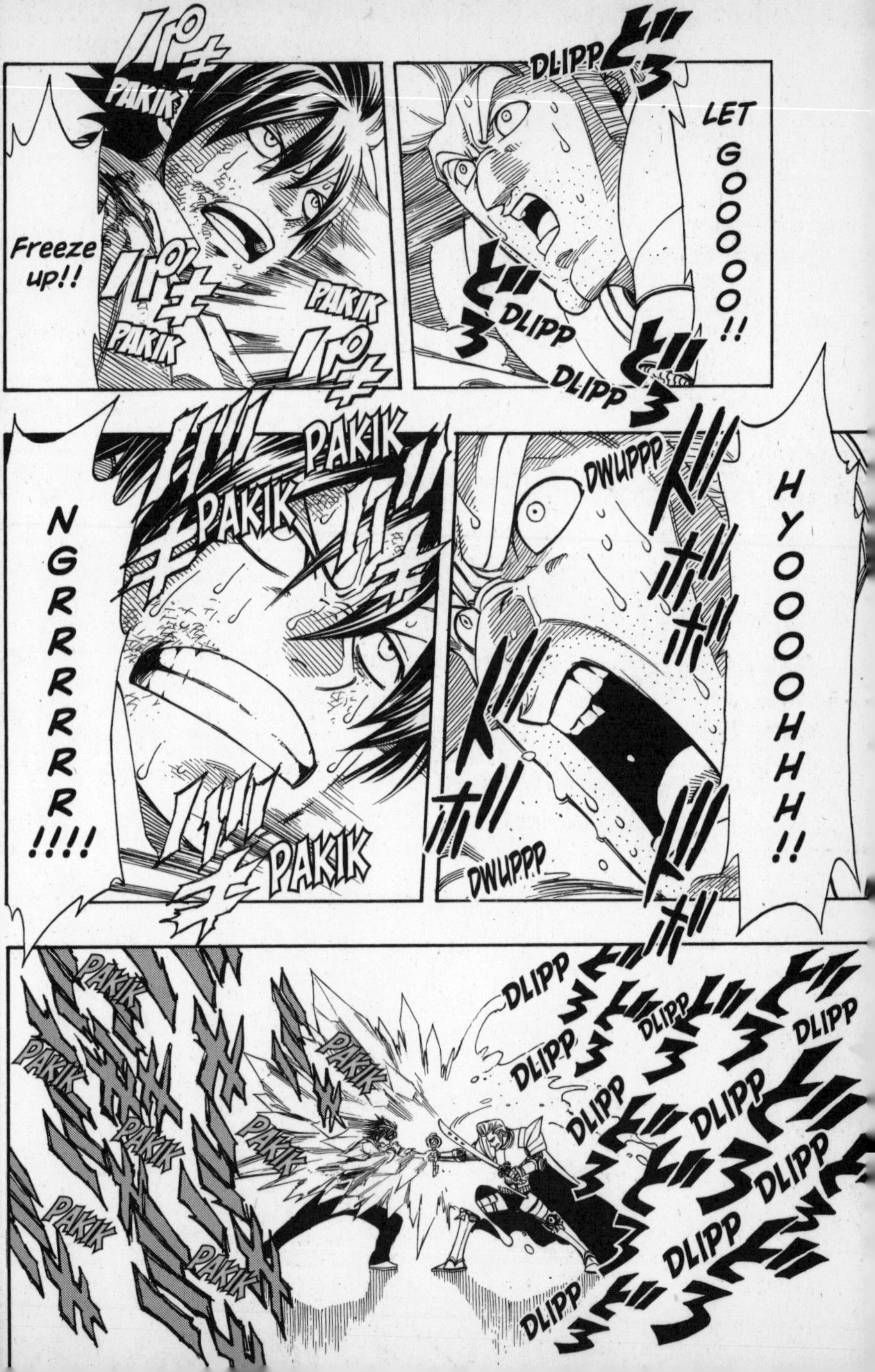
DLIPP
LET GOOOOOO!!
DLIPP
DLIPP
PAKIK
Freeze up!!
PAKIK
PAKIK
DWUPPP
HYOOOOOHHH!!
DWUPPP
PAKIK
PAKIK
NGRRRRRRR!!!!
PAKIK
DLIPP
DLIPP
DLIPP
DLIPP
DLIPP
DLIPP
DLIPP
DLIPP
DLIPP
DLIPP
PAKIK
PAKIK
PAKIK
PAKIK
PAKIK
PAKIK
PAKIK

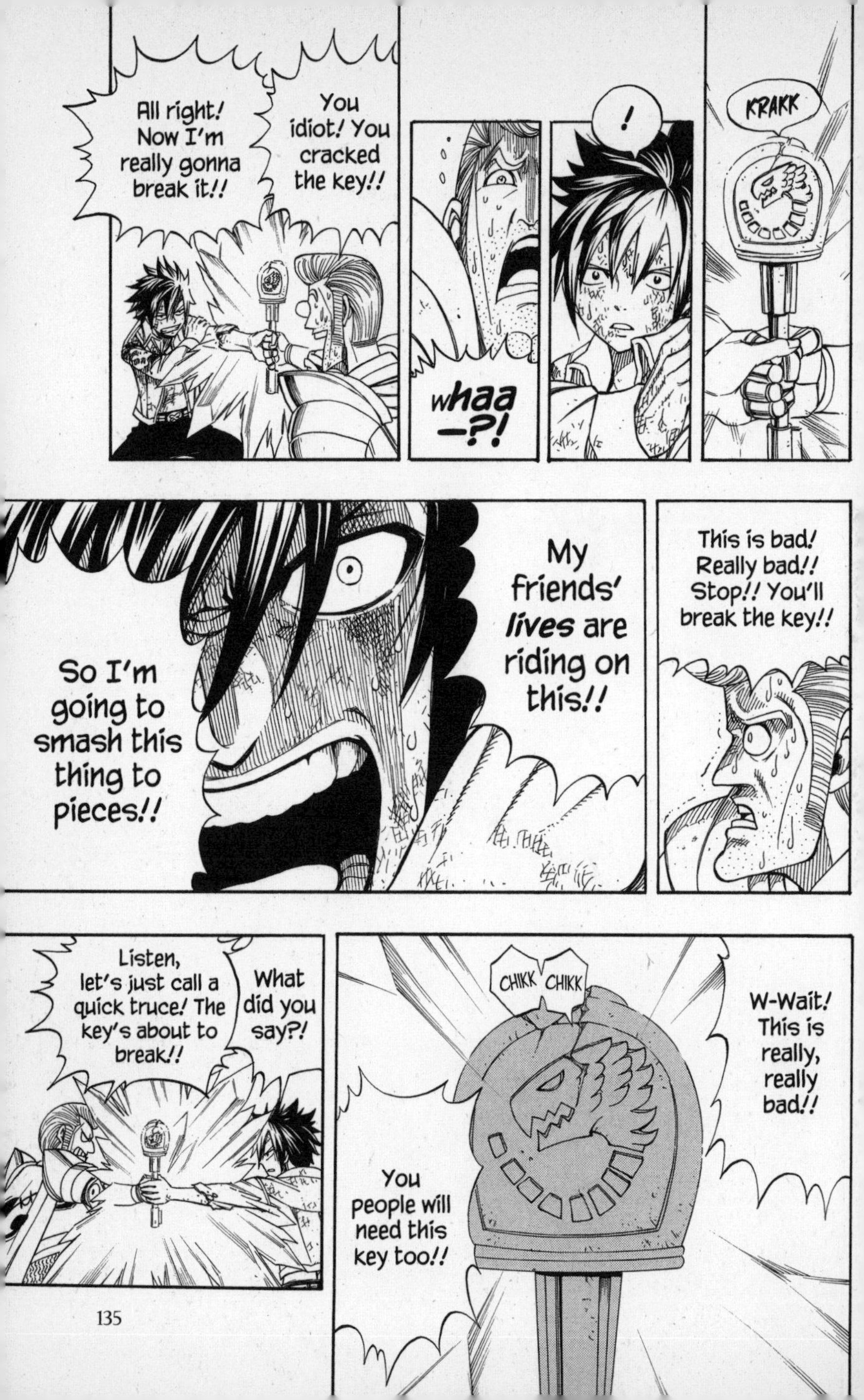
KRAKK
!
whaa—?!
You idiot! You cracked the key!!
All right! Now I'm really gonna break it!!
This is bad! Really bad!! Stop!! You'll break the key!!
My friends' *lives* are riding on this!!
So I'm going to smash this thing to pieces!!
W-Wait! This is really, really bad!!
CHIKK CHIKK
You people will need this key too!!
What did you say?!
Listen, let's just call a quick truce! The key's about to break!!

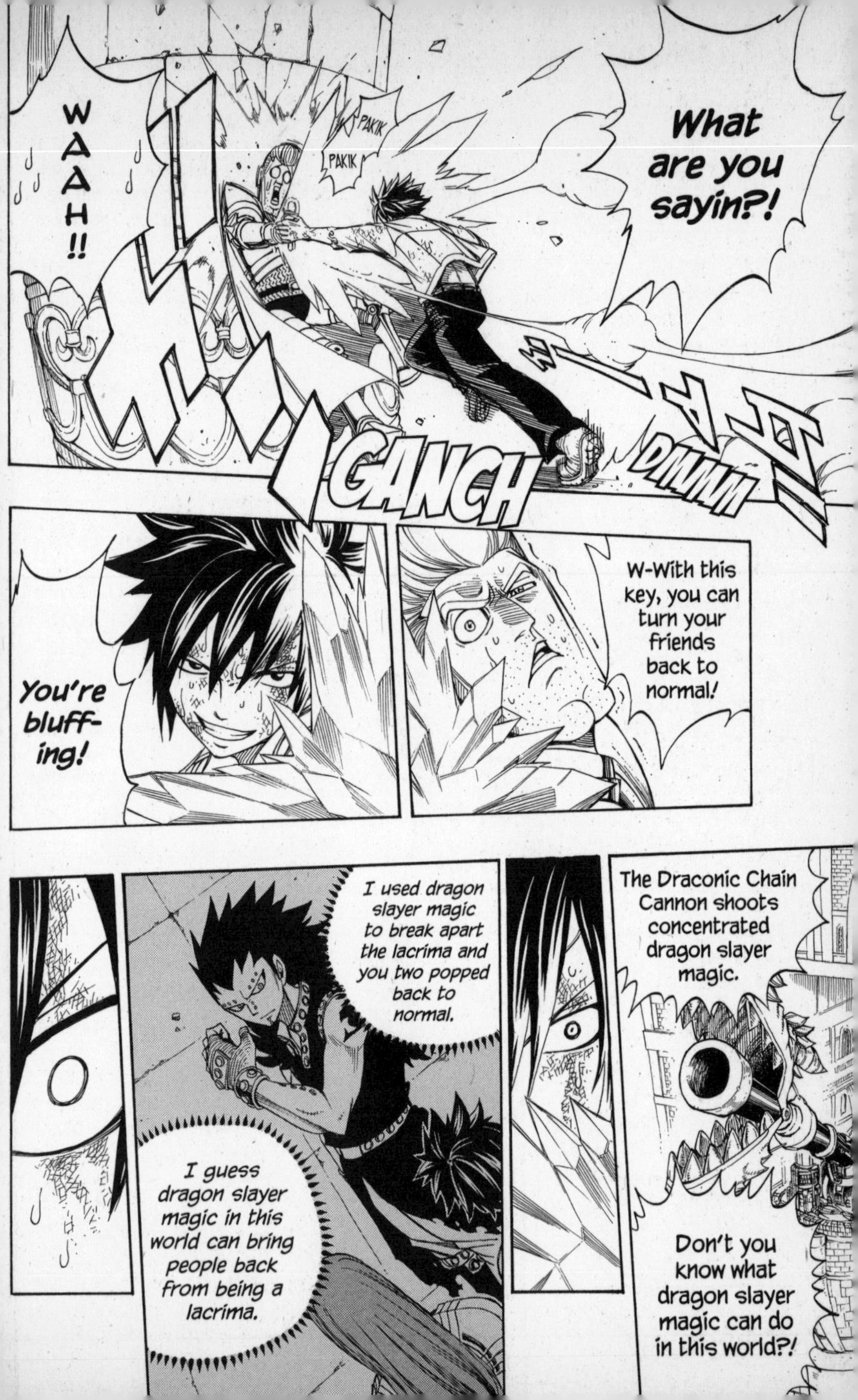
What are you sayin?!
PAKIK
PAKIK
WAAAH!!
GANCH
DWNNN
W-With this key, you can turn your friends back to normal!
You're bluff-ing!
The Draconic Chain Cannon shoots concentrated dragon slayer magic.
Don't you know what dragon slayer magic can do in this world?!
I used dragon slayer magic to break apart the lacrima and you two popped back to normal.
I guess dragon slayer magic in this world can bring people back from being a lacrima.

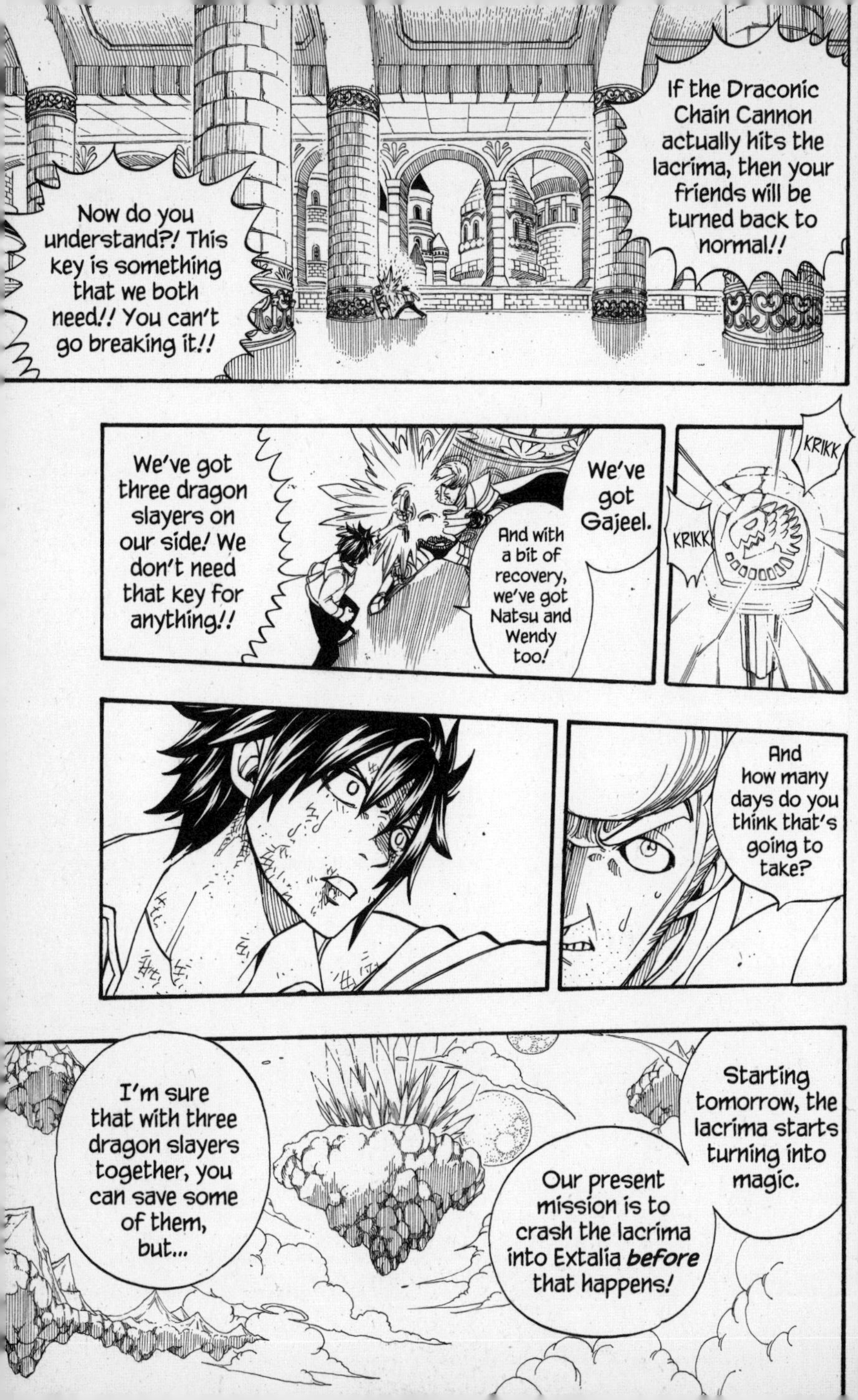
If the Draconic Chain Cannon actually hits the lacrima, then your friends will be turned back to normal!!
Now do you understand?! This key is something that we both need!! You can't go breaking it!!
KRIKK
KRIKK
We've got three dragon slayers on our side! We don't need that key for anything!!
We've got Gajeel.
And with a bit of recovery, we've got Natsu and Wendy too!
And how many days do you think that's going to take?
I'm sure that with three dragon slayers together, you can save some of them, but...
Starting tomorrow, the lacrima starts turning into magic.
Our present mission is to crash the lacrima into Extalia *before* that happens!

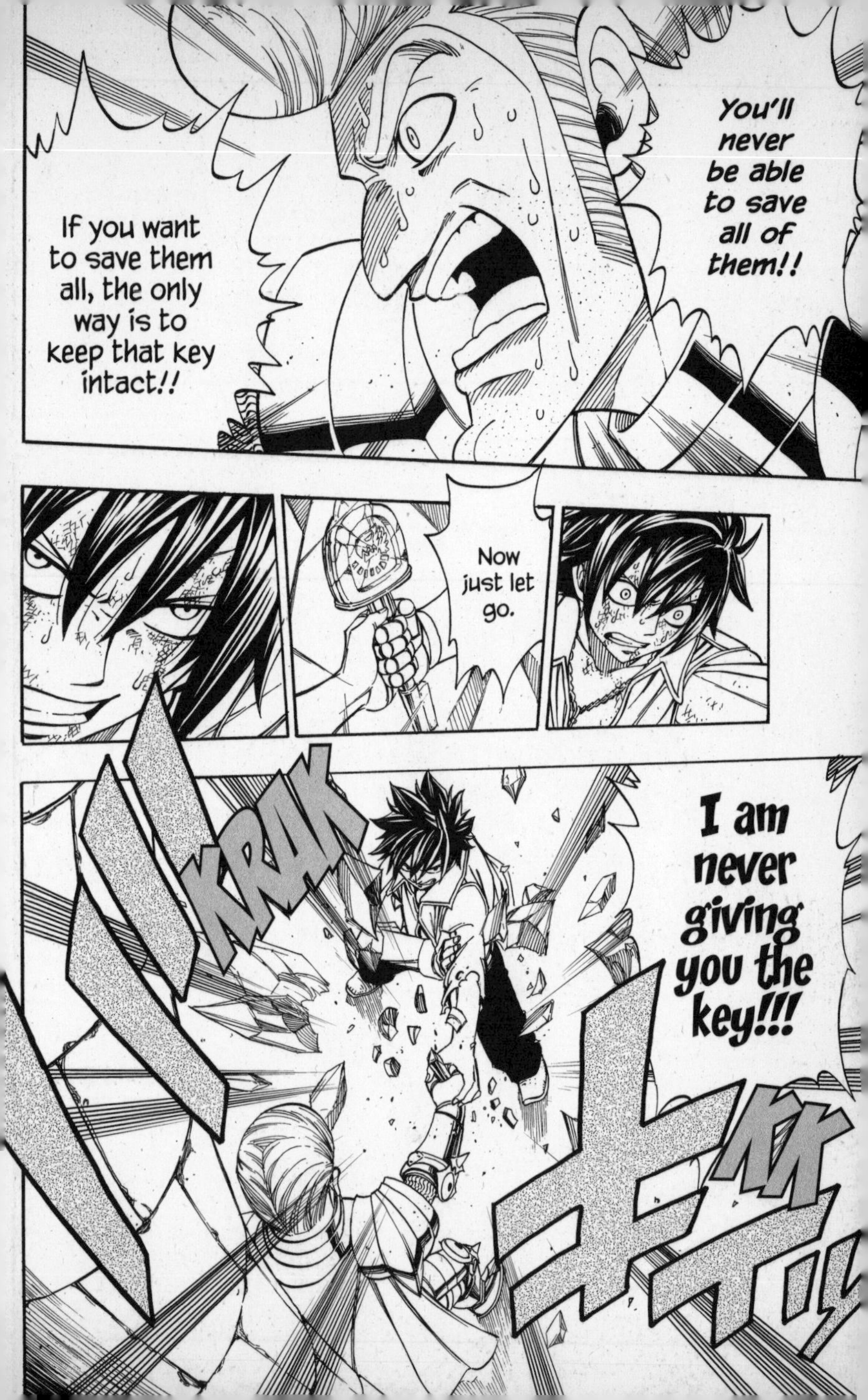
You'll never be able to save all of them!!
If you want to save them all, the only way is to keep that key intact!!
Now just let go.
I am never giving you the key!!!
KRAK

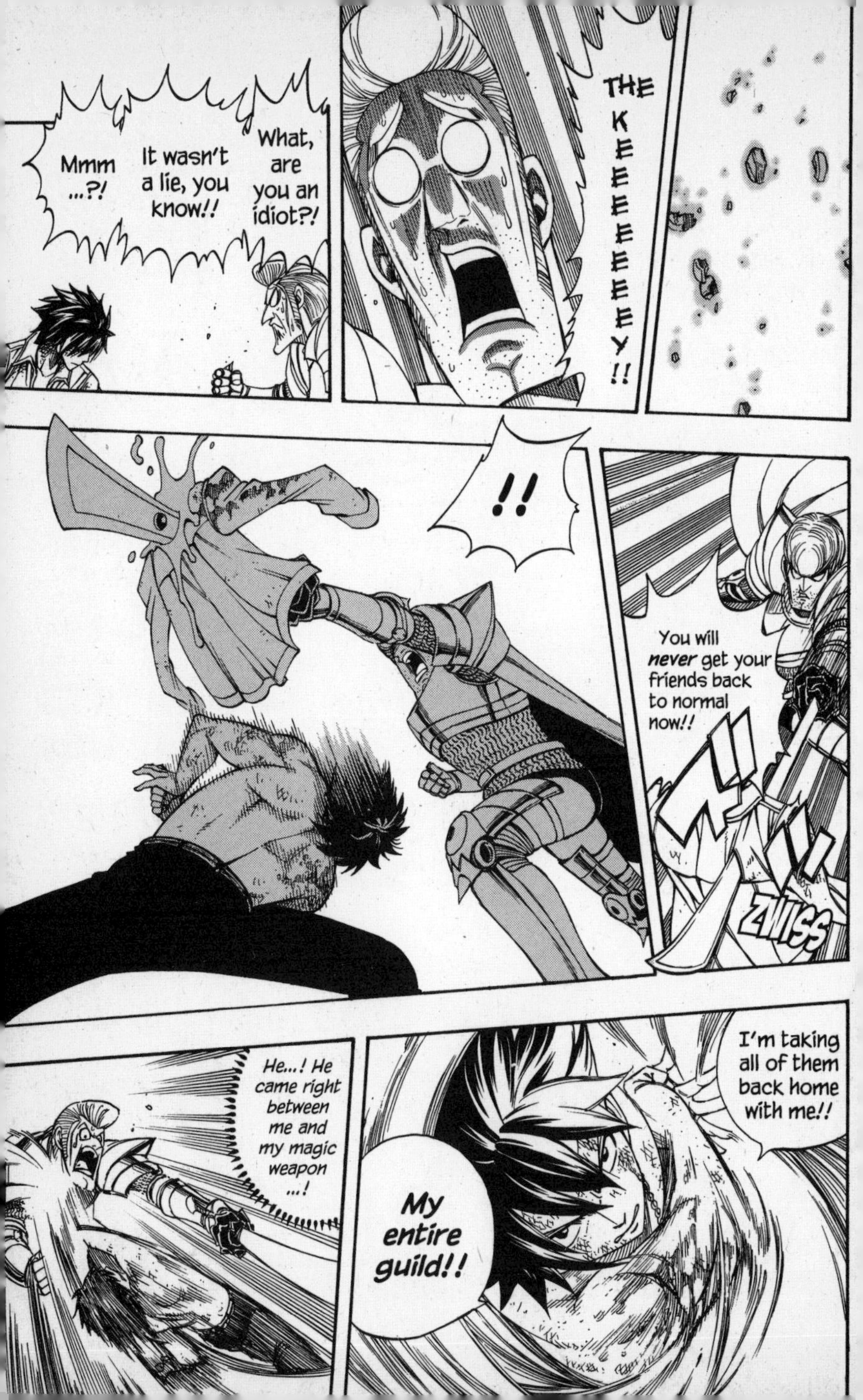
THE KEEEEEEEY!!
What, are you an idiot?!
It wasn't a lie, you know!!
Mmm ...?!
You will *never* get your friends back to normal now!!
ZWISS
!!
I'm taking all of them back home with me!!
My entire guild!!
He...! He came right between me and my magic weapon ...!

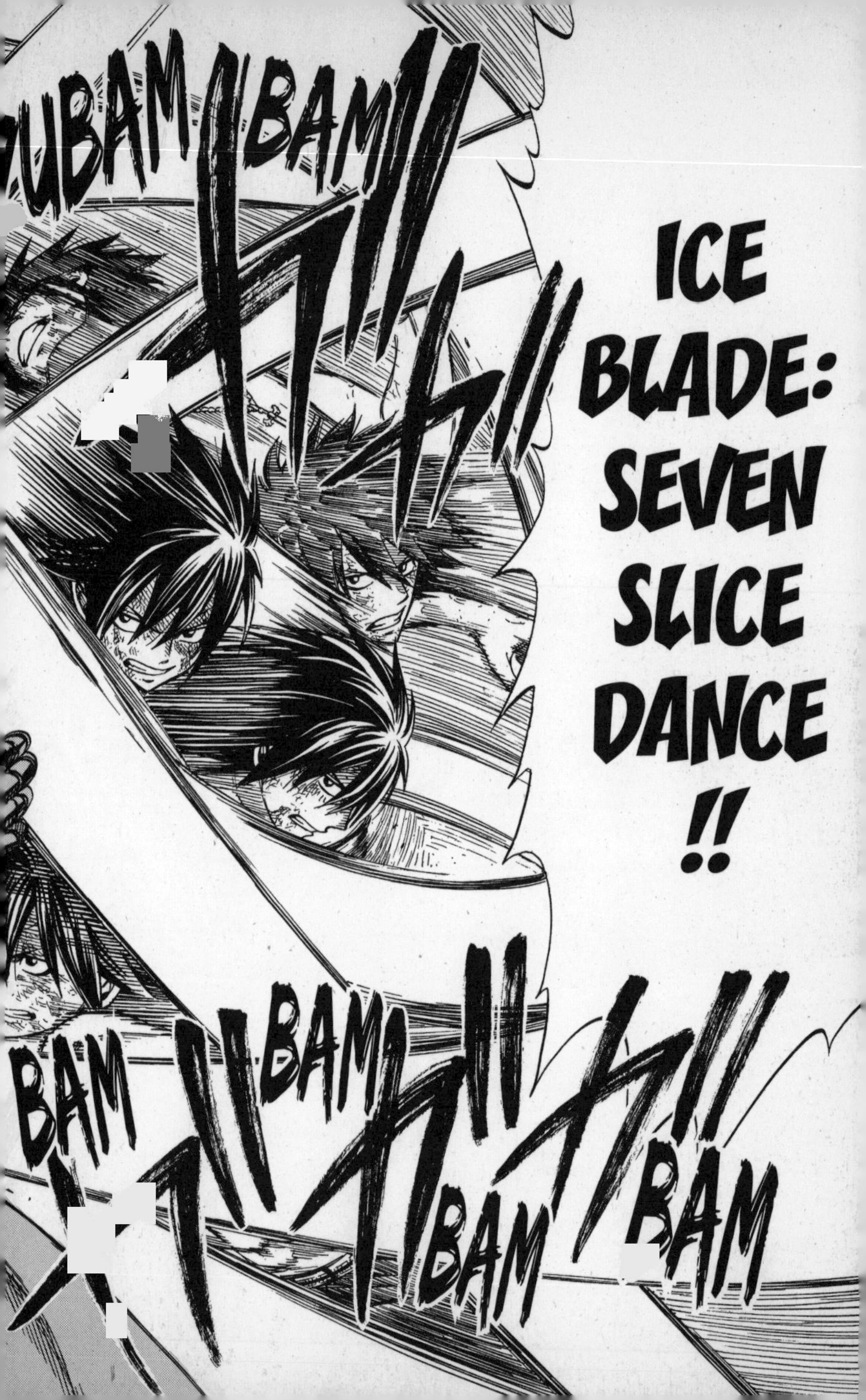
ICE BLADE: SEVEN SLICE DANCE!!
ZUBAM
BAM
BAM
BAM
BAM
BAM

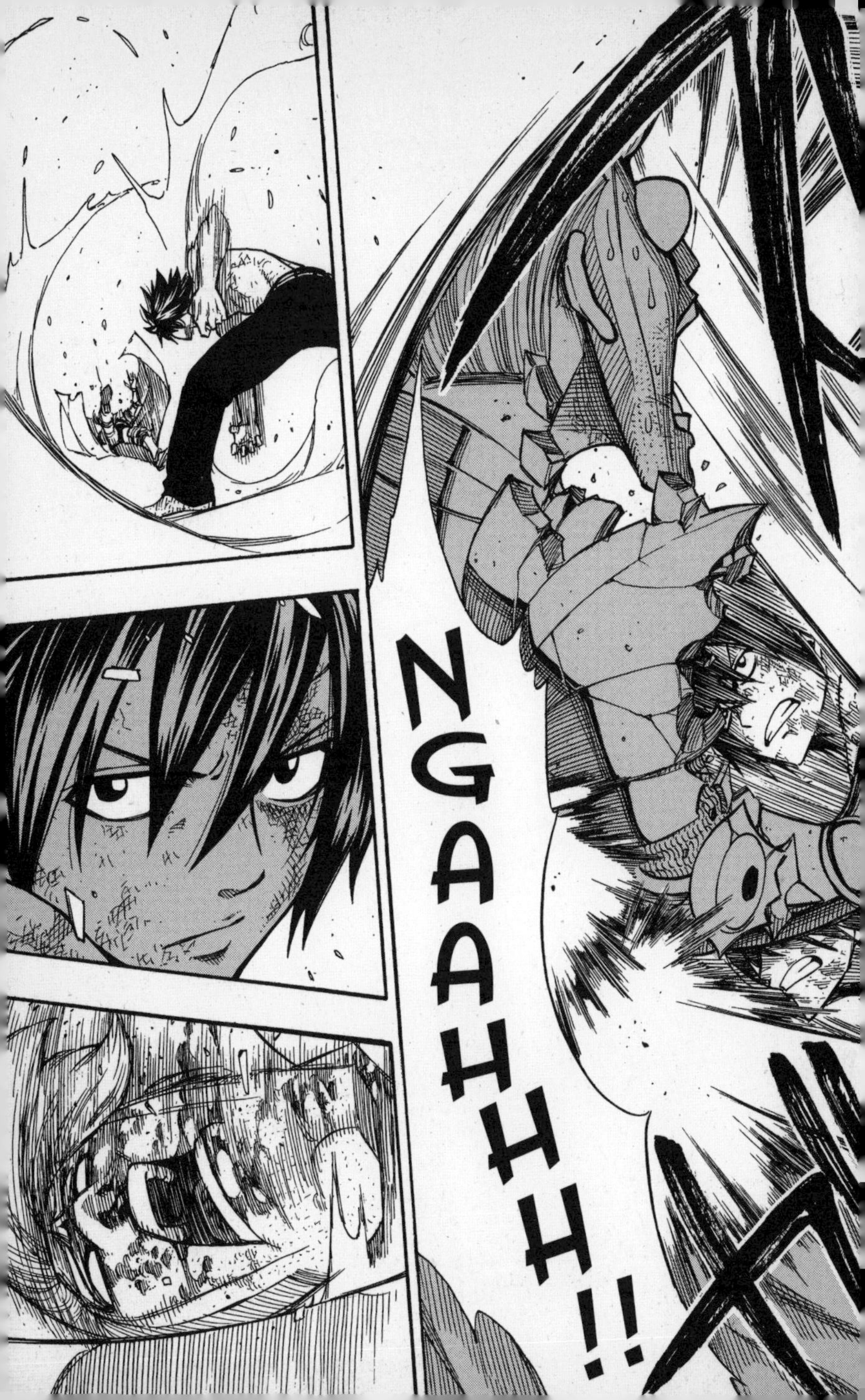
NGAAHHH!!

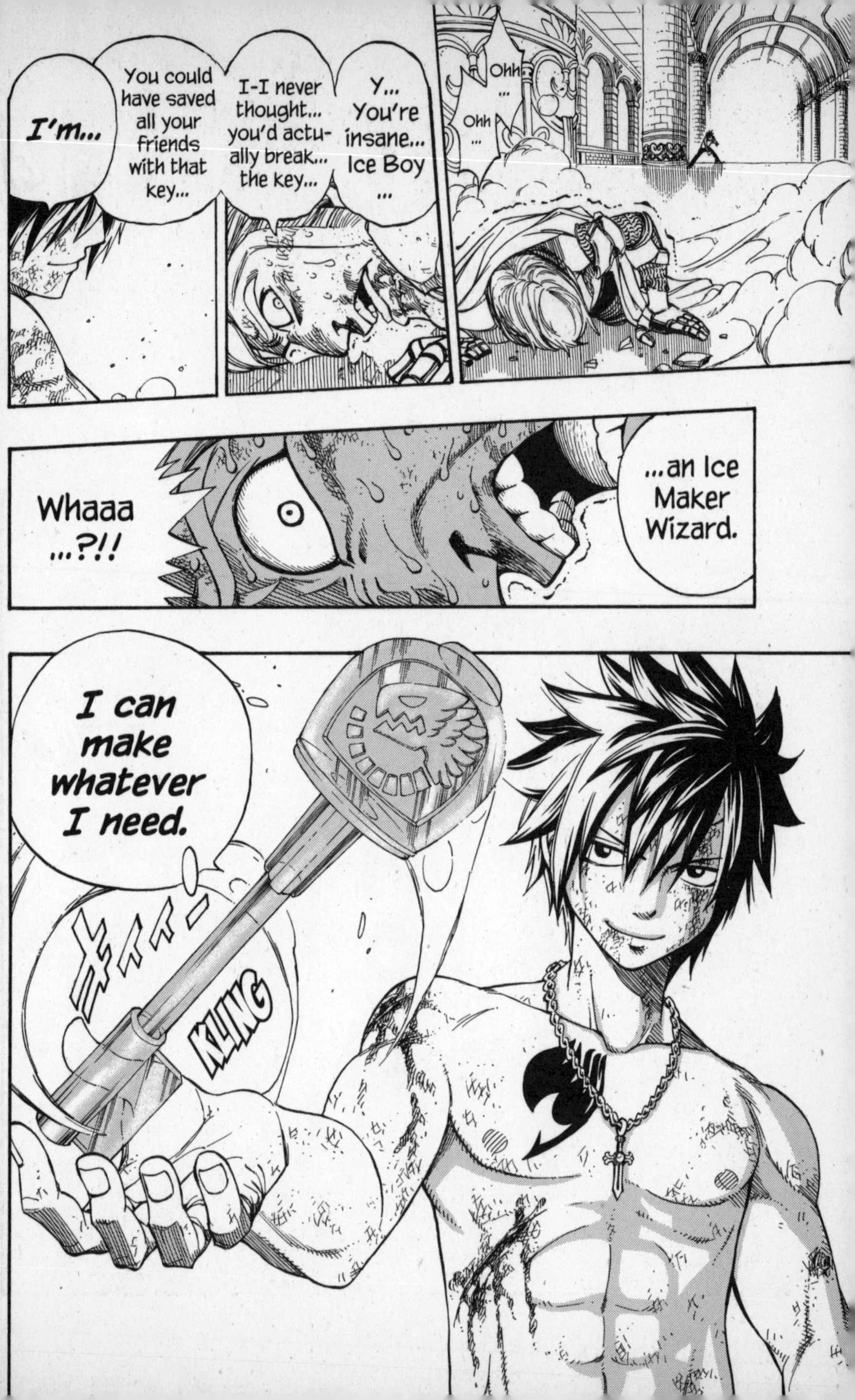

Ohh...
Ohh...
Y... You're insane... Ice Boy...
I-I never thought... you'd actually break... the key...
You could have saved all your friends with that key...
I'm...
...an Ice Maker Wizard.
Whaaa...?!!
I can make whatever I need.
KLING

FAIRY TAIL

フェアリーテイル

Chapter 186, My Cat

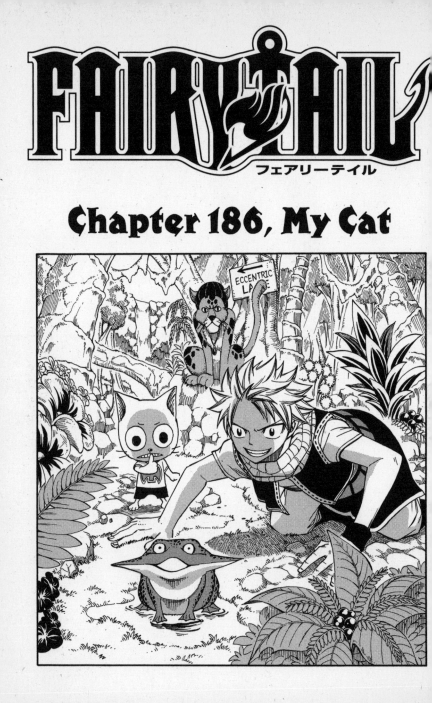

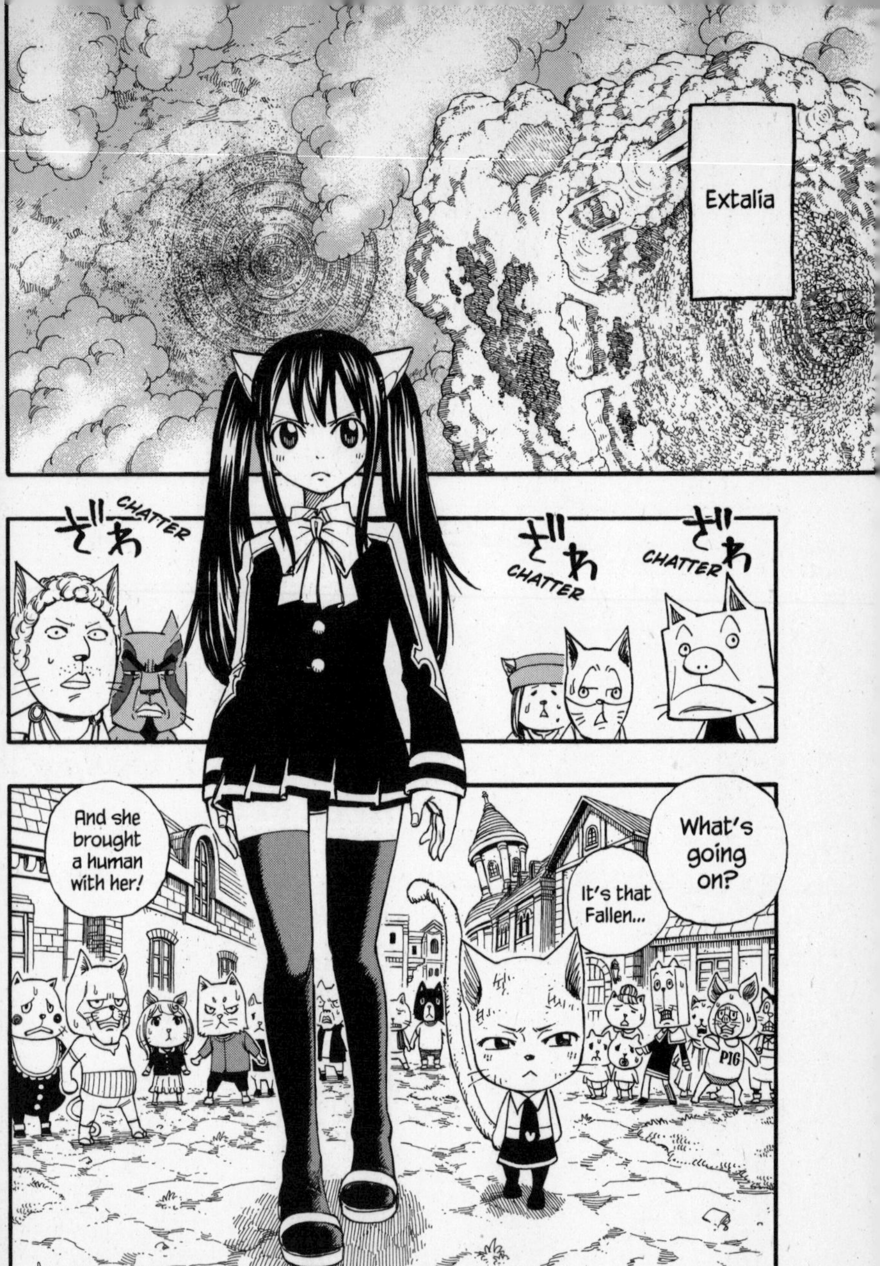
Extalia
ざわ
CHATTER
ざわ
CHATTER
ざわ
CHATTER
What's going on?
It's that Fallen...
And she brought a human with her!

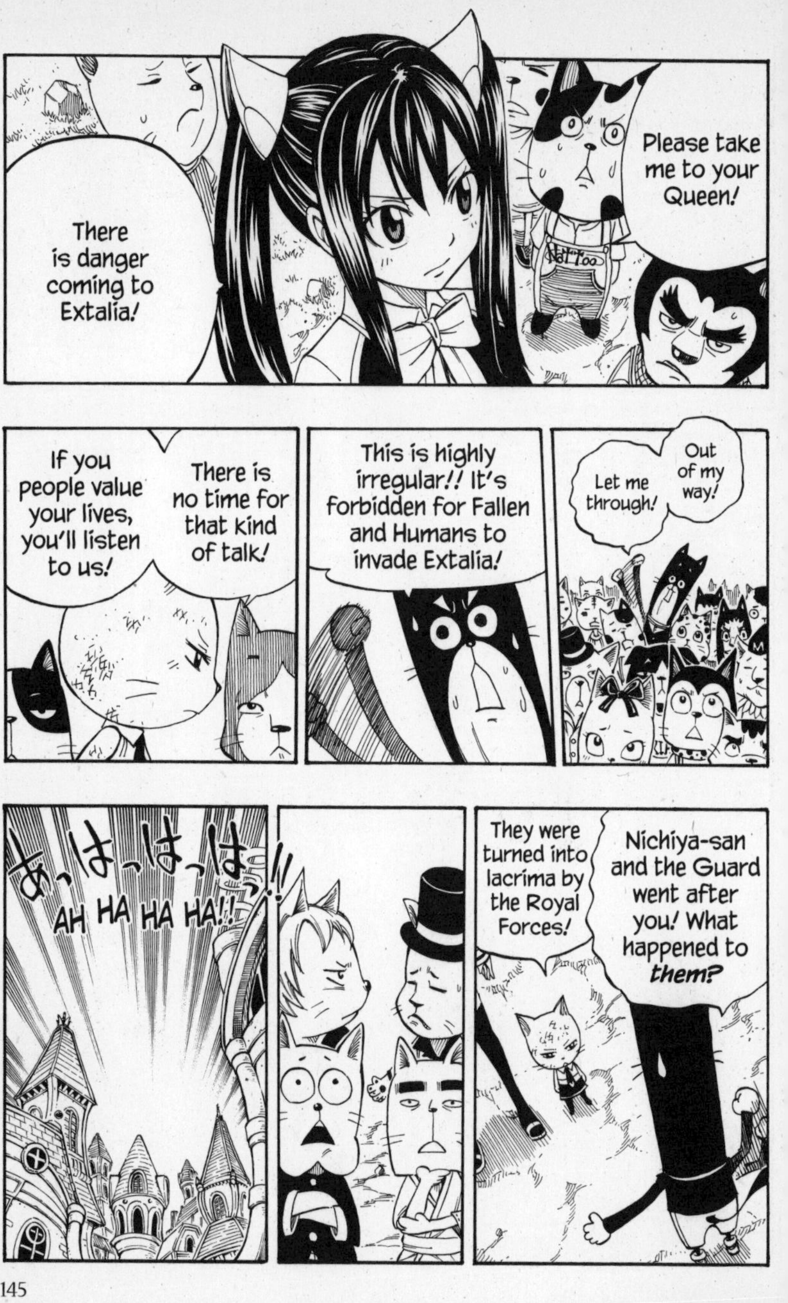

Please take me to your Queen!
There is danger coming to Extalia!
Out of my way!
Let me through!
This is highly irregular!! It's forbidden for Fallen and Humans to invade Extalia!
There is no time for that kind of talk!
If you people value your lives, you'll listen to us!
Nichiya-san and the Guard went after you! What happened to *them?*
They were turned into lacrima by the Royal Forces!
あっはっはっはっ!!!
AH HA HA HA!!

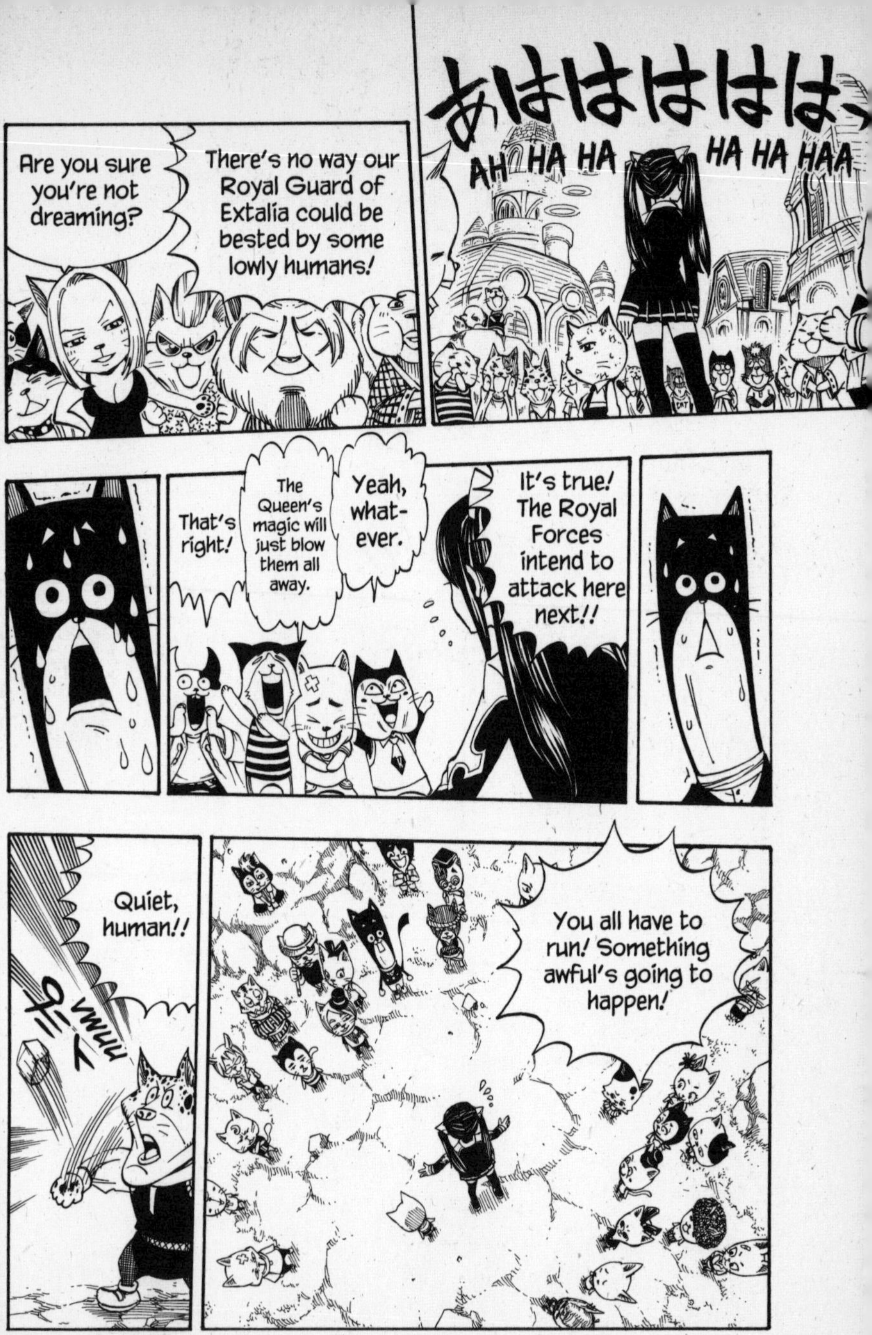
あははははは
AH HA HA HA HA HAA
There's no way our Royal Guard of Extalia could be bested by some lowly humans!
Are you sure you're not dreaming?
It's true! The Royal Forces intend to attack here next!!
Yeah, whatever.
The Queen's magic will just blow them all away.
That's right!
You all have to run! Something awful's going to happen!
Quiet, human!!
VWMM

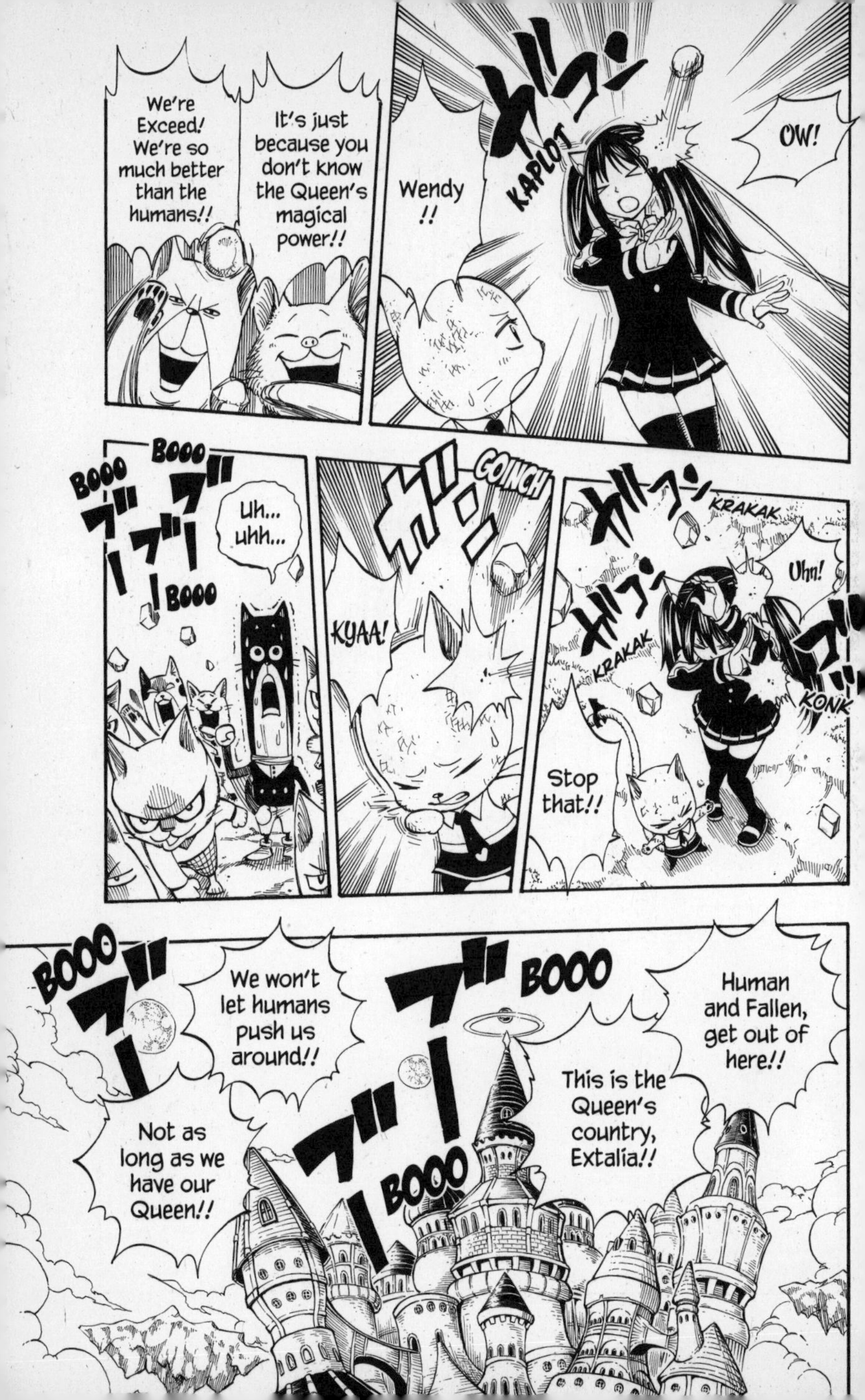
OW!
KAPLOT
Wendy !!
It's just because you don't know the Queen's magical power!!
We're Exceed! We're so much better than the humans!!
KRAKAK
Uhn!
KRAKAK
KONK
Stop that!!
GOINCH
KYAA!
BOOO
BOOO
Uh... uhh...
BOOO
Human and Fallen, get out of here!!
BOOO
This is the Queen's country, Extalia!!
We won't let humans push us around!!
BOOO
BOOO
Not as long as we have our Queen!!

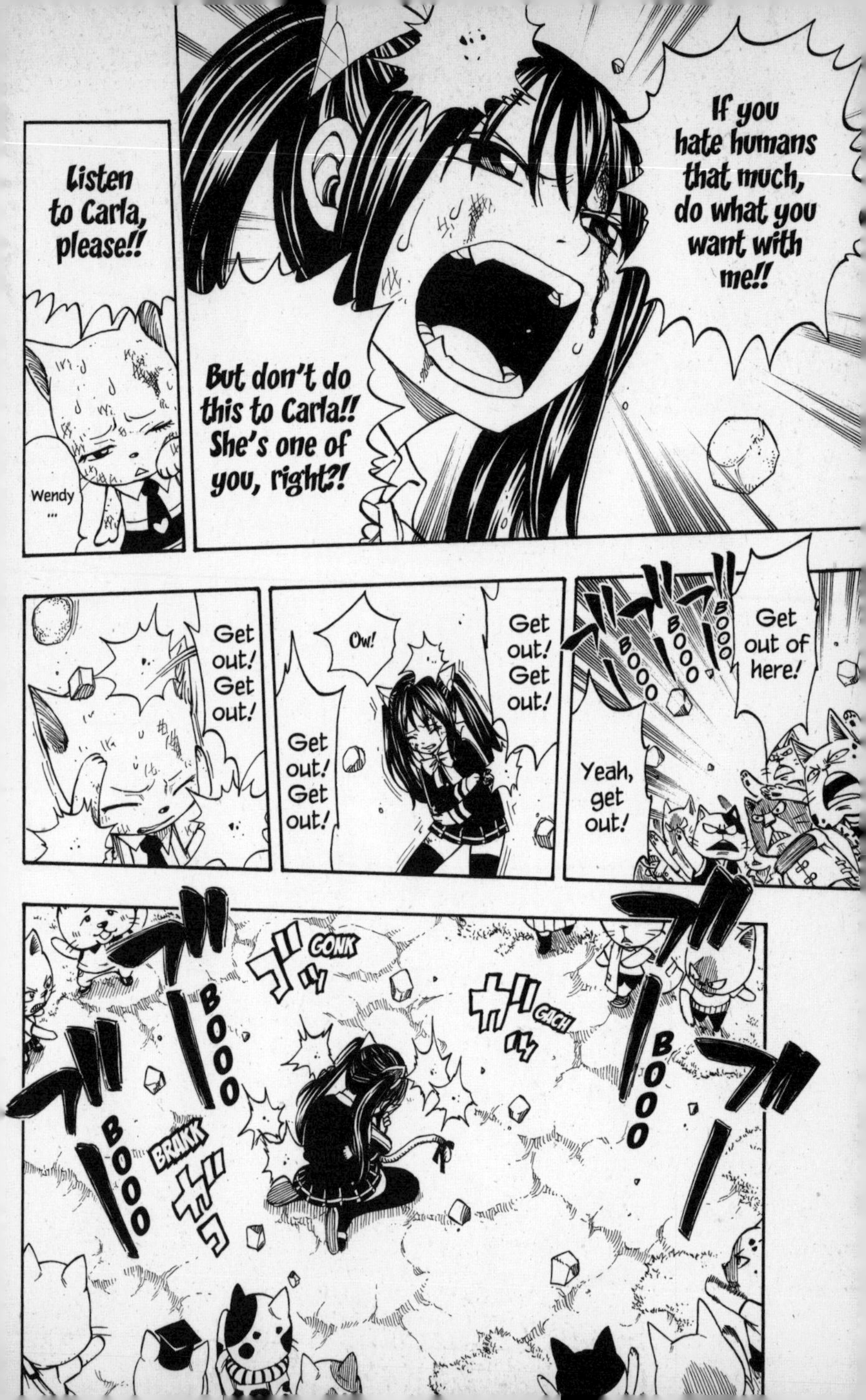

If you hate humans that much, do what you want with me!!
But don't do this to Carla!! She's one of you, right?!
Listen to Carla, please!!
Wendy...
Get out of here!
BOOO
BOOO
BOOO
Yeah, get out!
Get out! Get out!
Ow!
Get out! Get out!
Get out! Get out!
BOOO
GACH
GONK
BOOO
BOOO
BRAKK

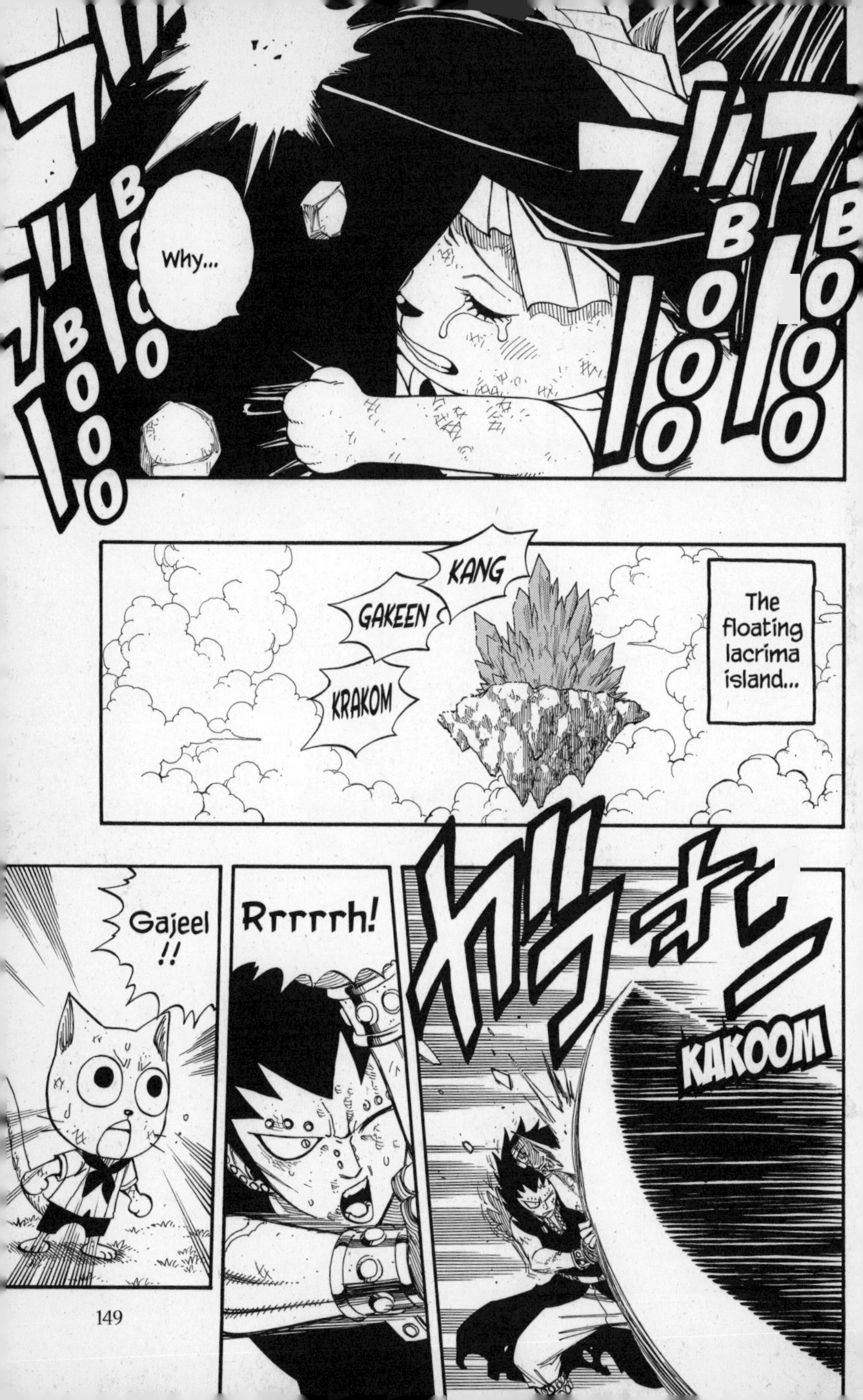
BOOOO
BOOOO
Why...
BOOOO
BOOOO
The floating lacrima island...
KANG
GAKEEN
KRAKOM
KAKOOM
Rrrrrh!
Gajeel!!

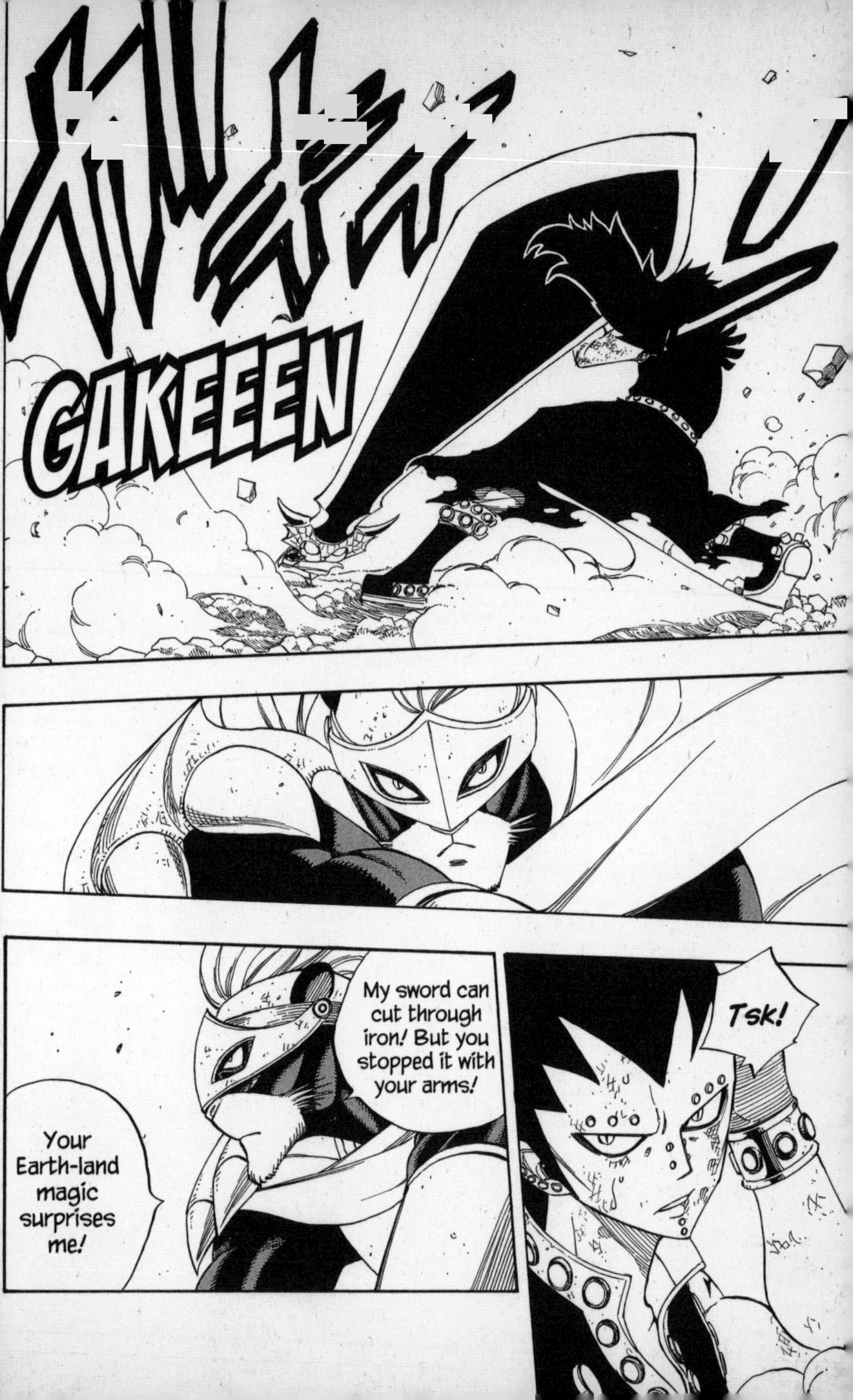
GAKEEEN
Tsk!
My sword can cut through iron! But you stopped it with your arms!
Your Earth-land magic surprises me!

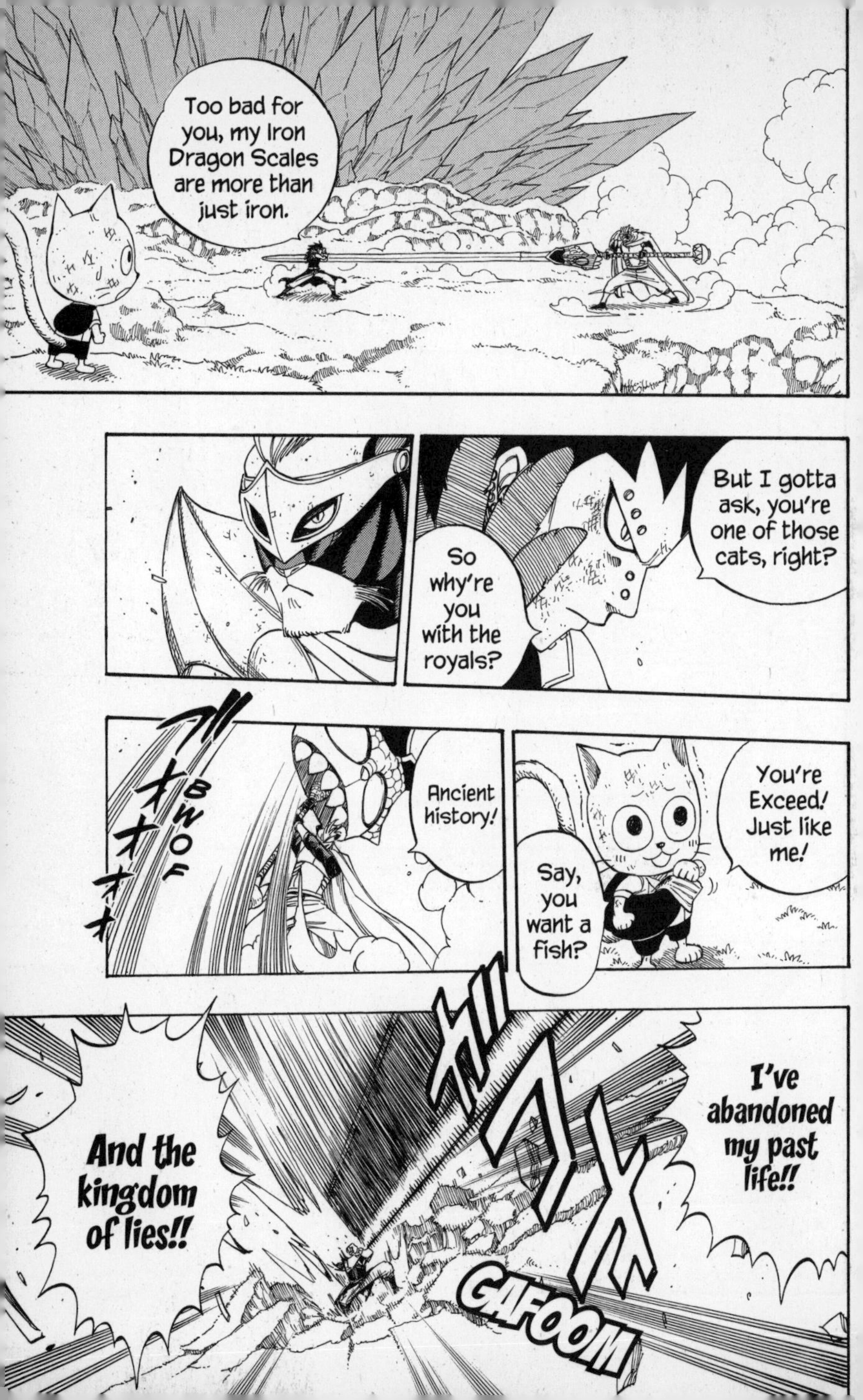
Too bad for you, my Iron Dragon Scales are more than just iron.
But I gotta ask, you're one of those cats, right?
So why're you with the royals?
You're Exceed! Just like me!
Say, you want a fish?
Ancient history!
BWOF
I've abandoned my past life!!
And the kingdom of lies!!
GAFOOM

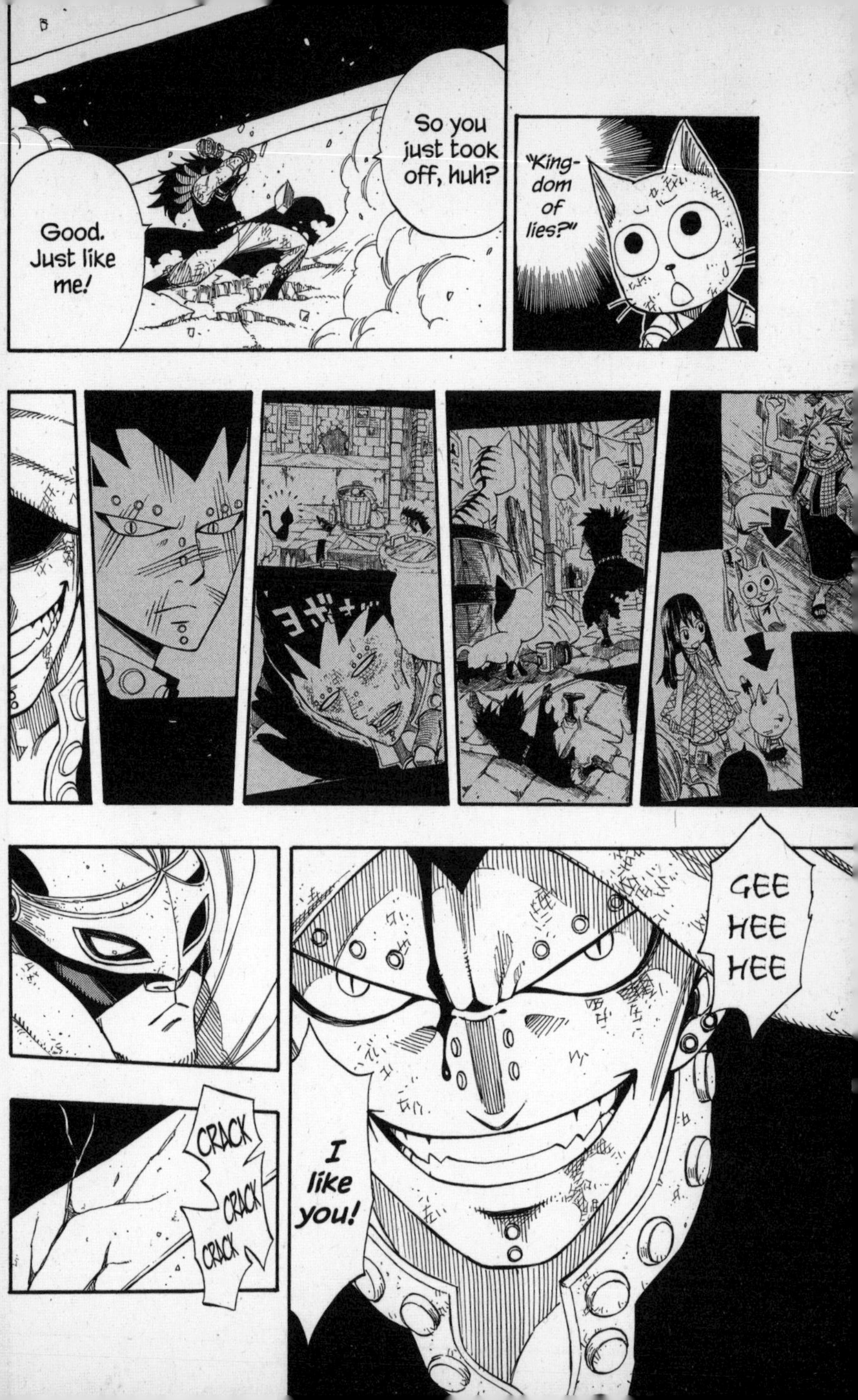
"King-dom of lies?"
So you just took off, huh?
Good. Just like me!
GEE HEE HEE
I like you!
CRACK
CRACK
CRACK

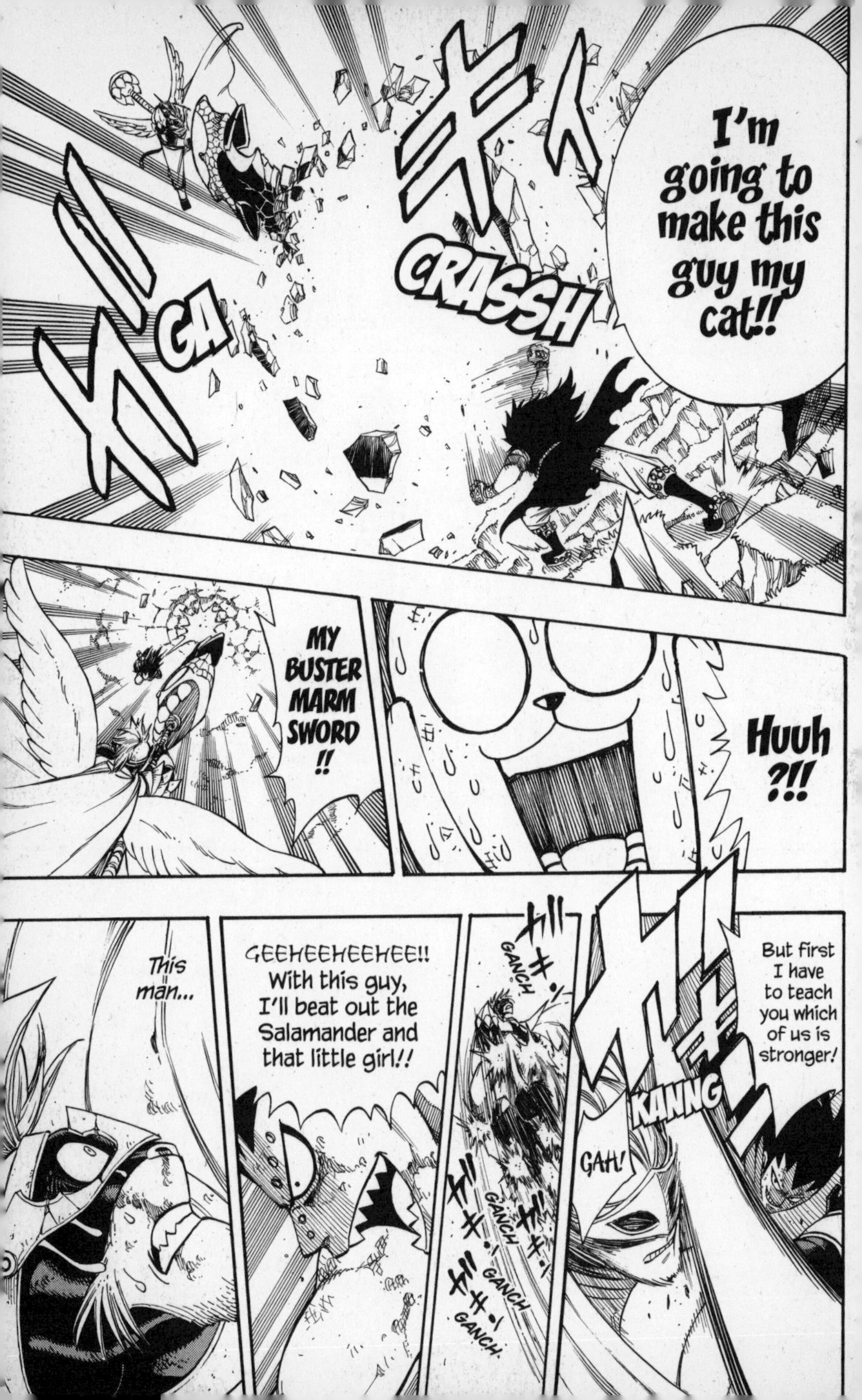
I'm going to make this guy my cat!!
CRASSH
GA
Huuh ?!!
MY BUSTER MARM SWORD !!
But first I have to teach you which of us is stronger!
KANNG
GAH!
GANCH
GANCH
GANCH
GANCH
GEEHEEHEEHEE!! With this guy, I'll beat out the Salamander and that little girl!!
This man...

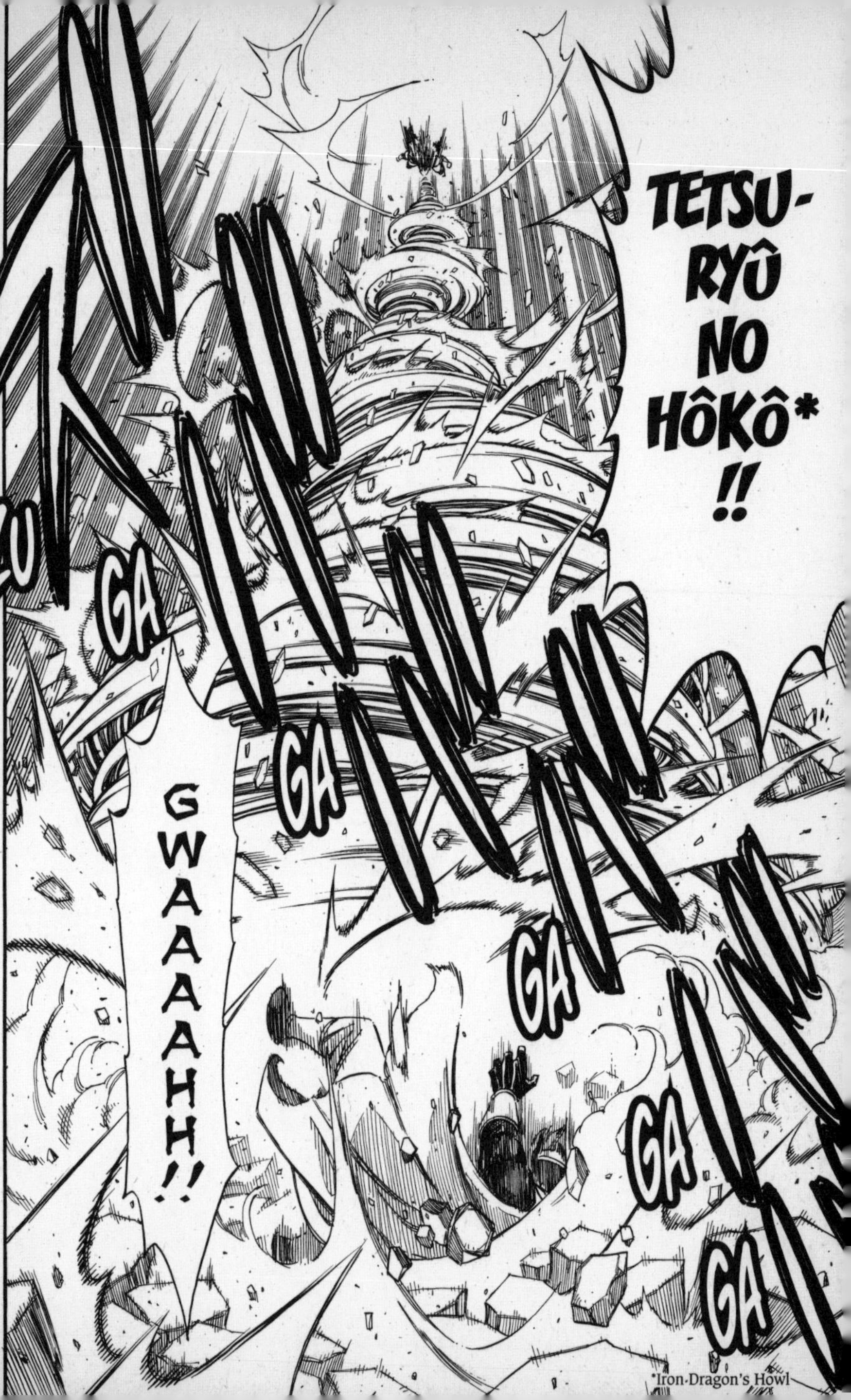
TETSU-RYÛ NO HÔKÔ* !!
ZU GA GA GA GA GA
GWAAAAAHH!!
*Iron-Dragon's Howl

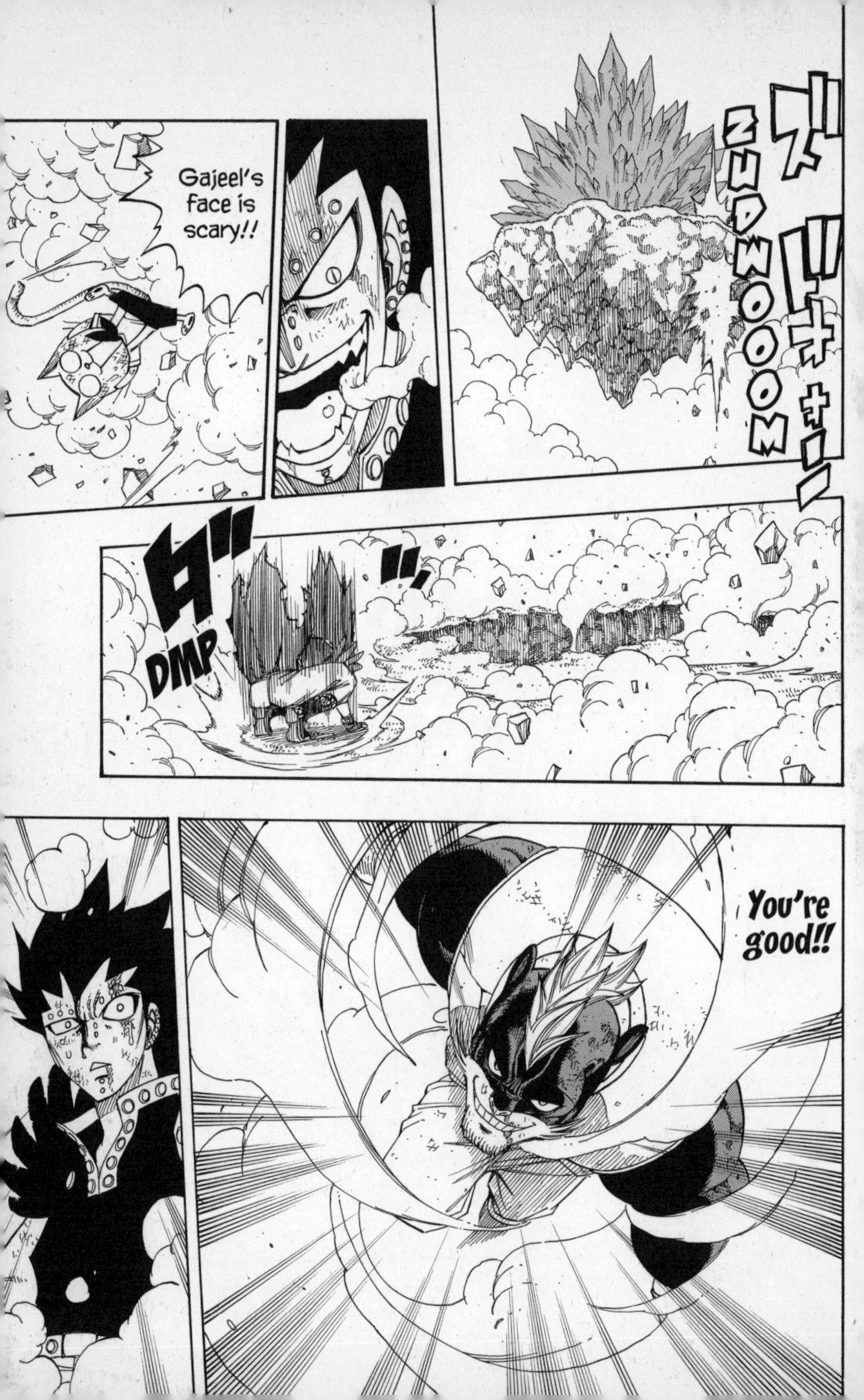
ZUDWOOOOM
Gajeel's face is scary!!
DMP
You're good!!

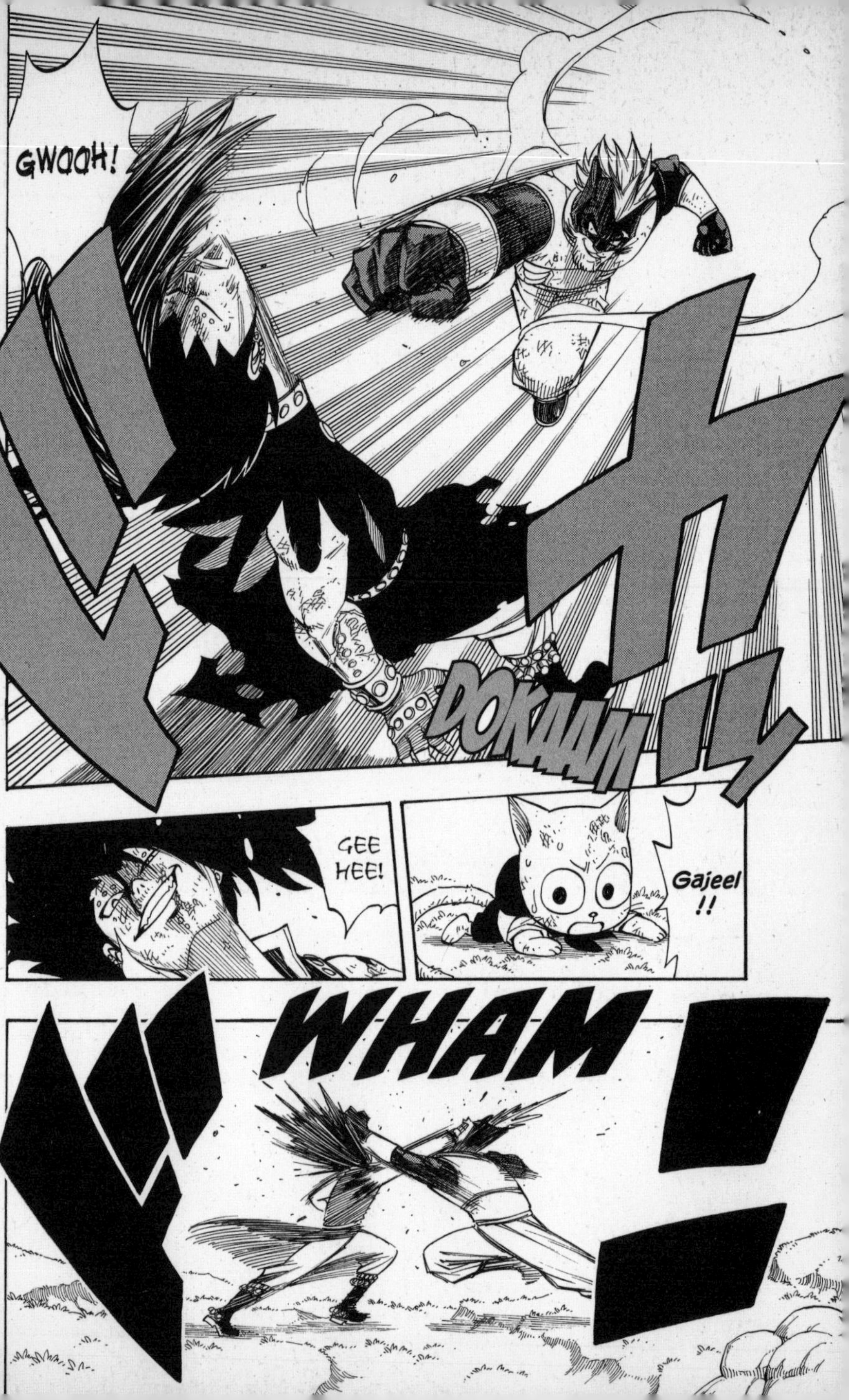
GWOOH!
DOKAAM!!
Gajeel!!
GEE HEE!
WHAM!!

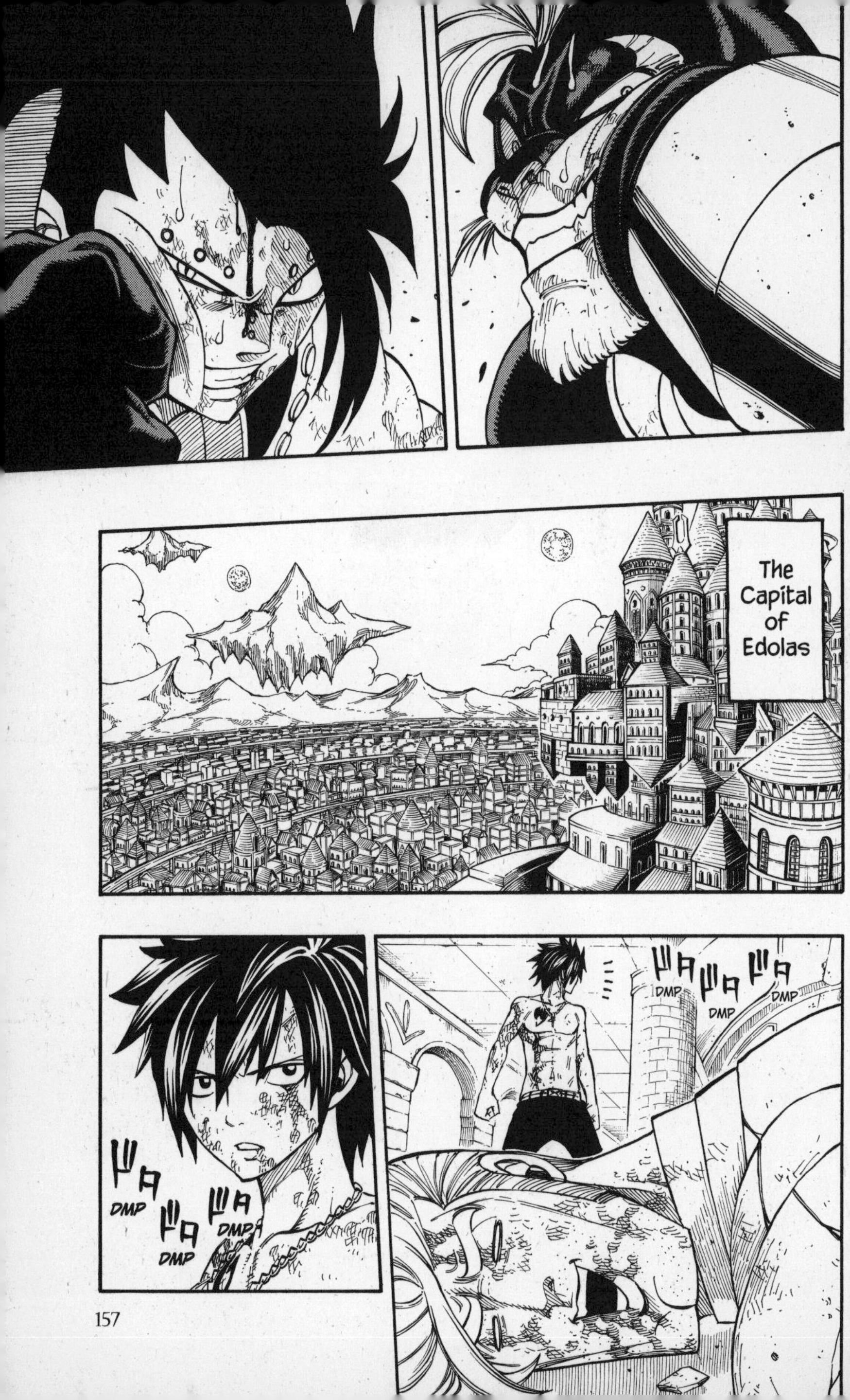
The Capital of Edolas
ドタ DMP
ドタ DMP
ドタ DMP
ドタ DMP
ドタ DMP
ドタ DMP

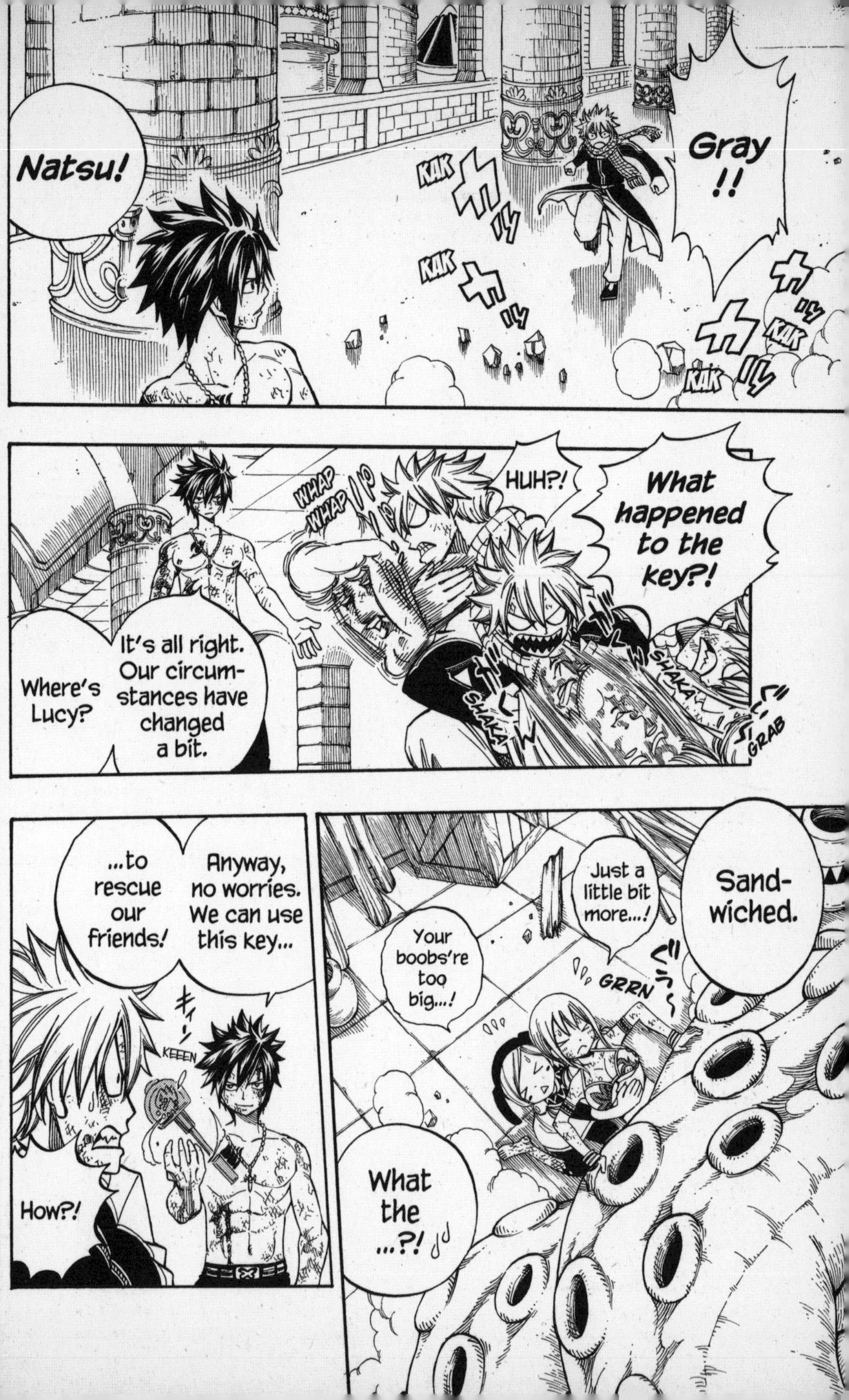
Gray !!
KAK
KAK
KAK
KAK
Natsu!
What happened to the key?!
HUH?!
WHAP WHAP
SHAKA
SHAKA
GRAB
It's all right. Our circumstances have changed a bit.
Where's Lucy?
Sandwiched.
Just a little bit more...!
GRRN
Your boobs're too big...!
What the ...?!
Anyway, no worries. We can use this key...
...to rescue our friends!
KEEEN
How?!

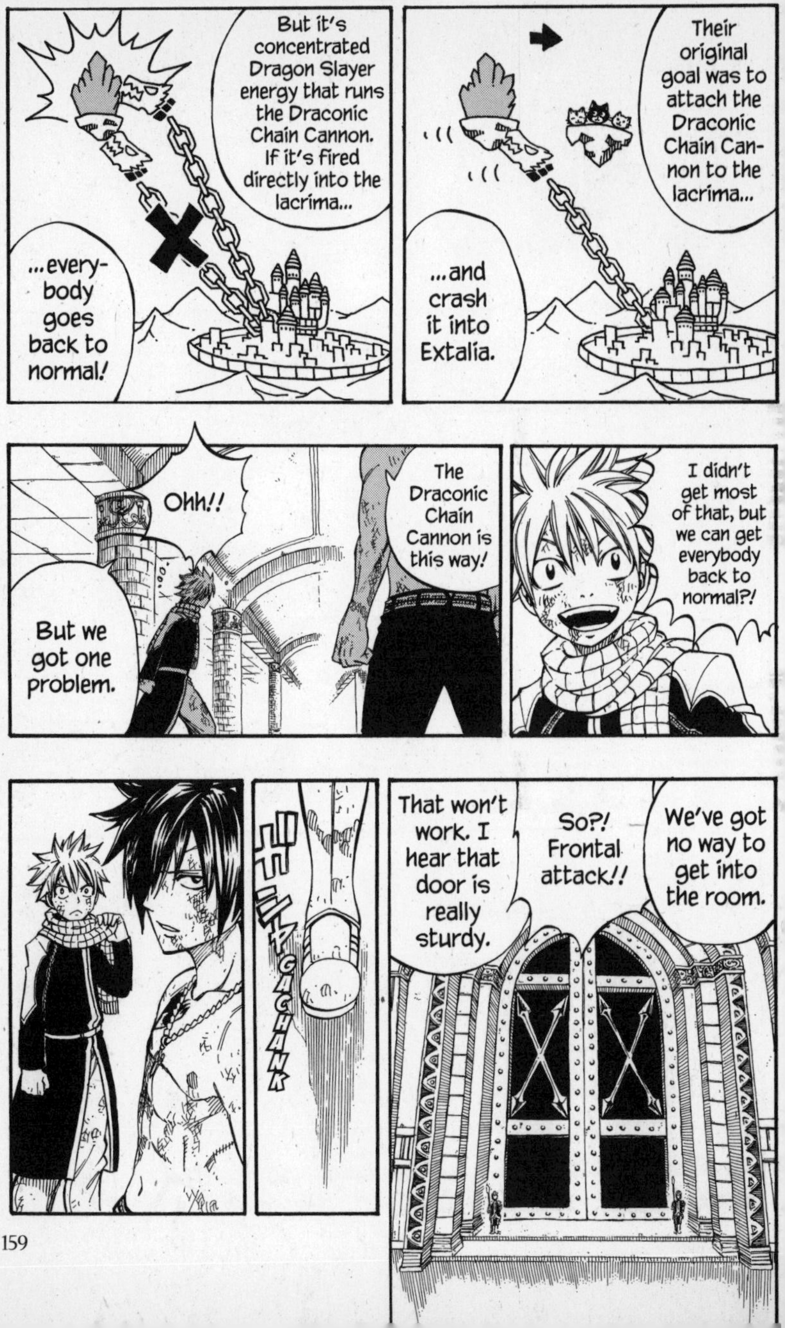
Their original goal was to attach the Draconic Chain Cannon to the lacrima...
...and crash it into Extalia.
But it's concentrated Dragon Slayer energy that runs the Draconic Chain Cannon. If it's fired directly into the lacrima...
...everybody goes back to normal!
I didn't get most of that, but we can get everybody back to normal?!
The Draconic Chain Cannon is this way!
Ohh!!
But we got one problem.
We've got no way to get into the room.
So?! Frontal attack!!
That won't work. I hear that door is really sturdy.
GACHANK

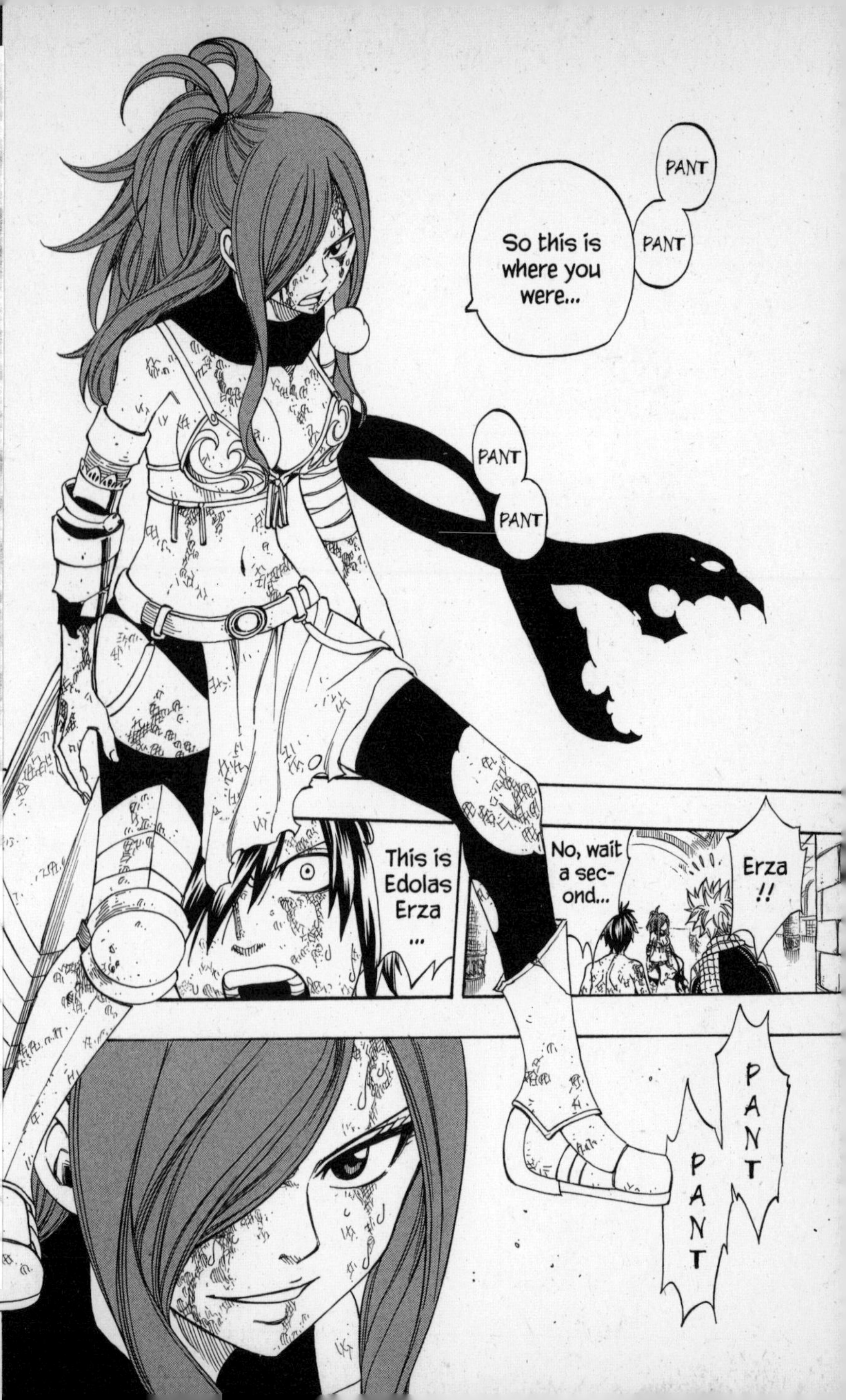
PANT
PANT
So this is where you were...
PANT
PANT
Erza!!
No, wait a sec-ond...
This is Edolas Erza...
PANT
PANT

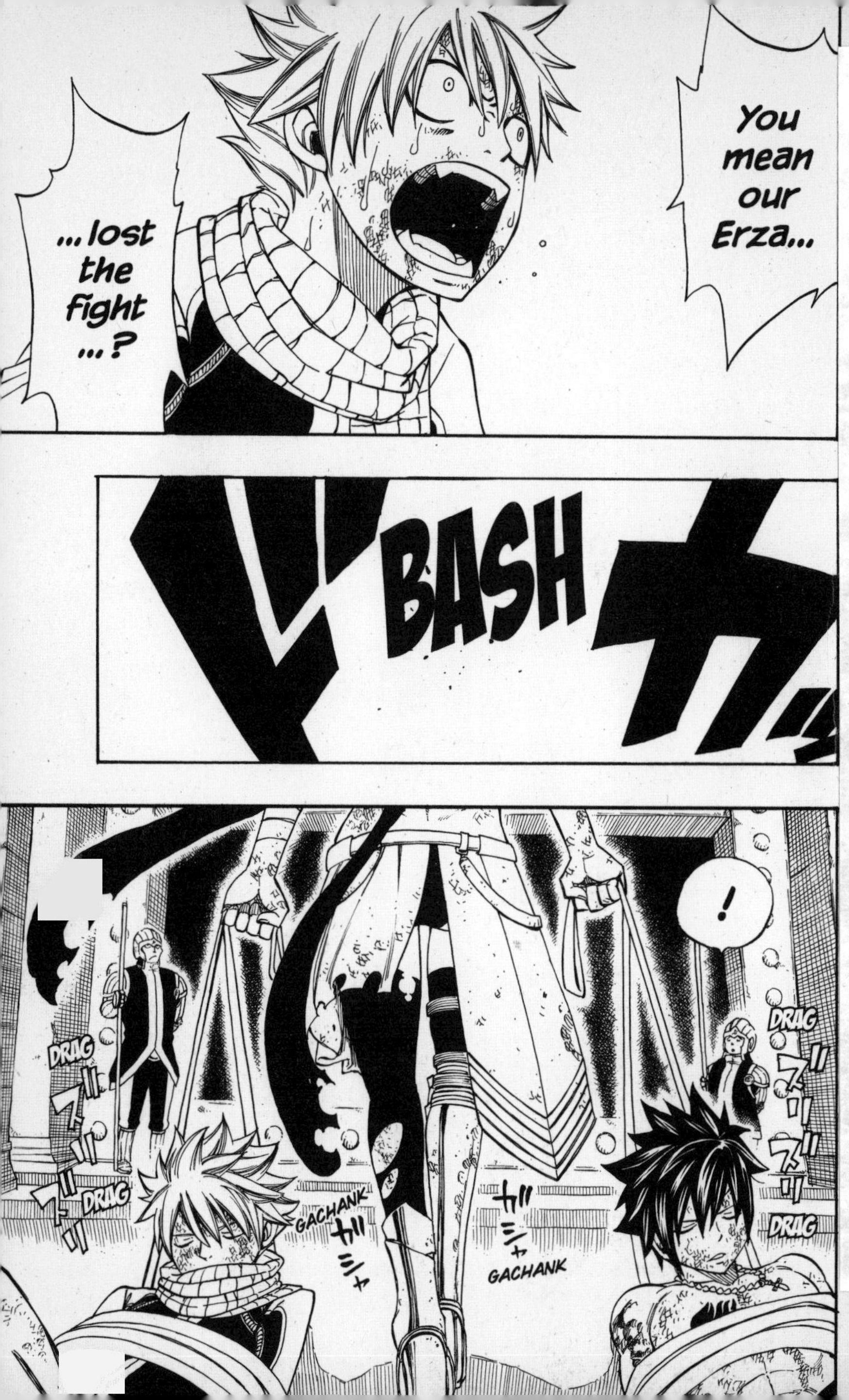
You mean our Erza...
...lost the fight...?
BASH
!
DRAG
DRAG
GACHANK
ガシャ
GACHANK
ガシャ
DRAG
DRAG

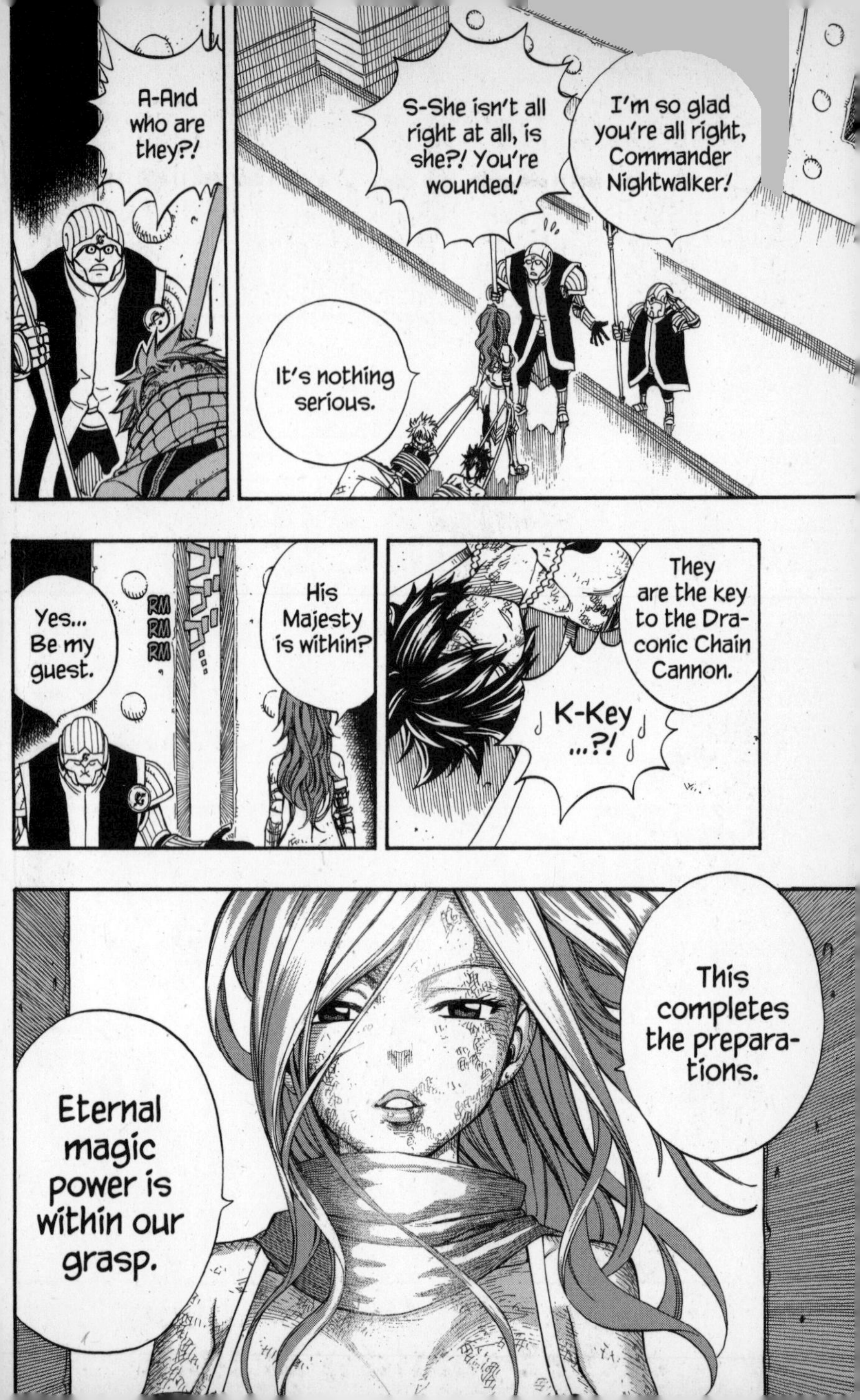
I'm so glad you're all right, Commander Nightwalker!
S-She isn't all right at all, is she?! You're wounded!
It's nothing serious.
A-And who are they?!
They are the key to the Draconic Chain Cannon.
K-Key ...?!
His Majesty is within?
RM RM RM
Yes... Be my guest.
This completes the preparations.
Eternal magic power is within our grasp.

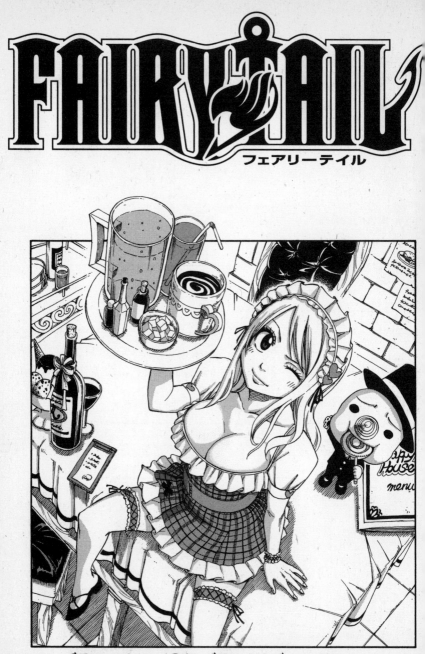

Chapter 187, Chain Cannon
of the Doomsday Dragon

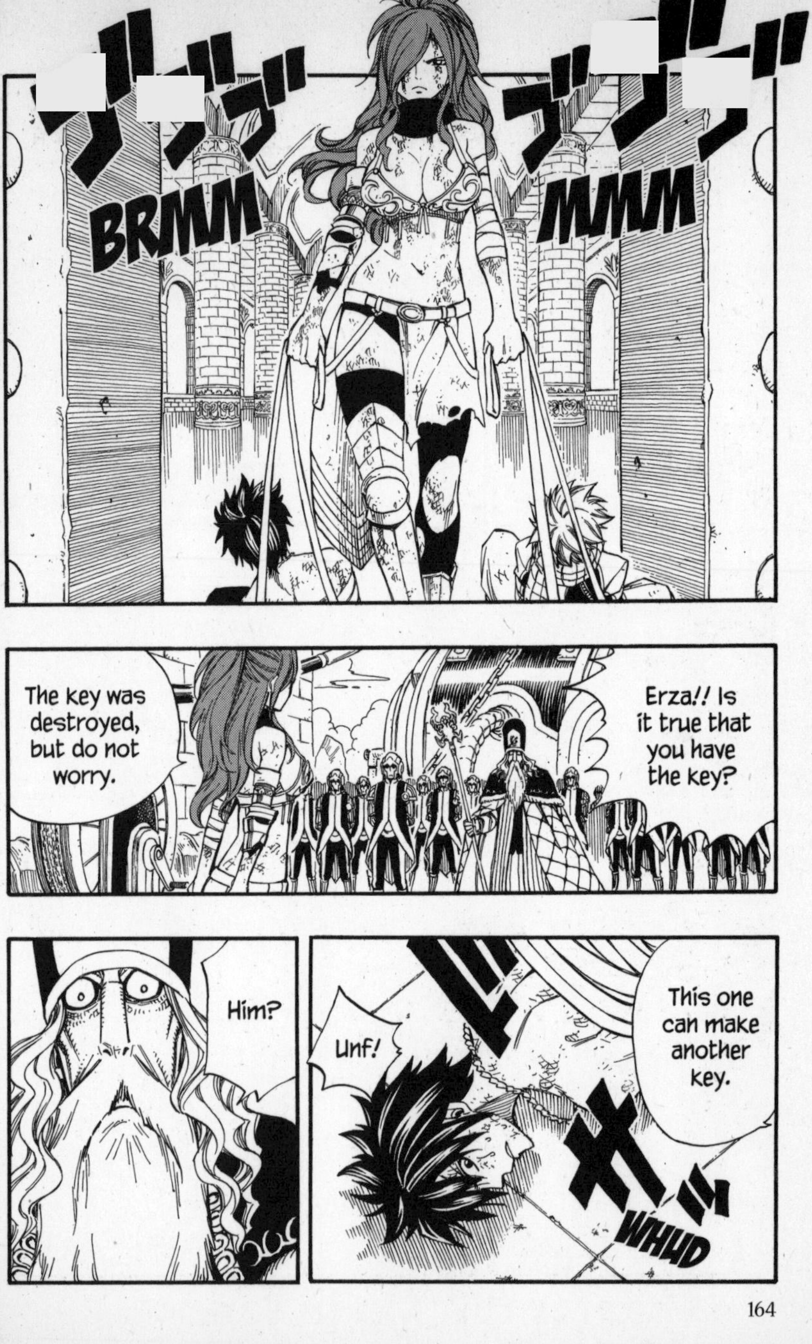
BRMMM
MMMM
Erza!! Is it true that you have the key?
The key was destroyed, but do not worry.
This one can make another key.
Unf!
WHUD
Him?

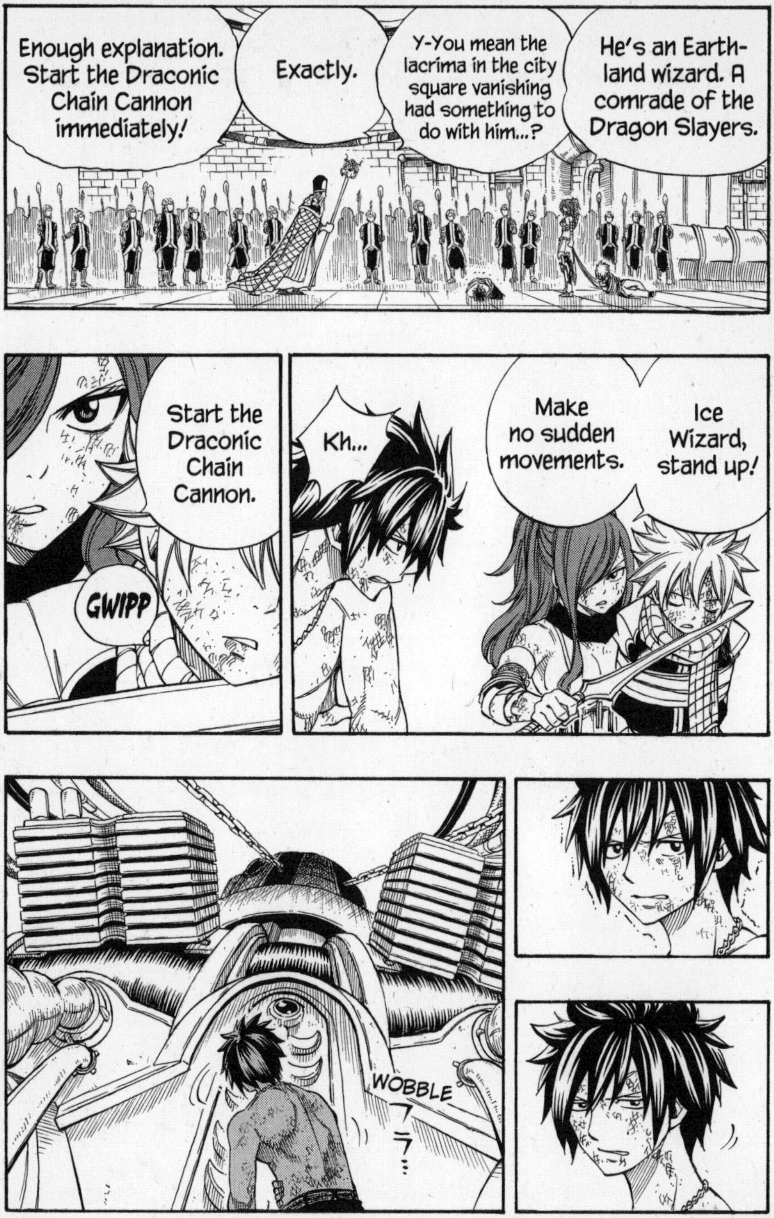
He's an Earth-land wizard. A comrade of the Dragon Slayers.
Y-You mean the lacrima in the city square vanishing had something to do with him...?
Exactly.
Enough explanation. Start the Draconic Chain Cannon immediately!
Ice Wizard, stand up!
Make no sudden movements.
Kh...
Start the Draconic Chain Cannon.
GWIPP
WOBBLE

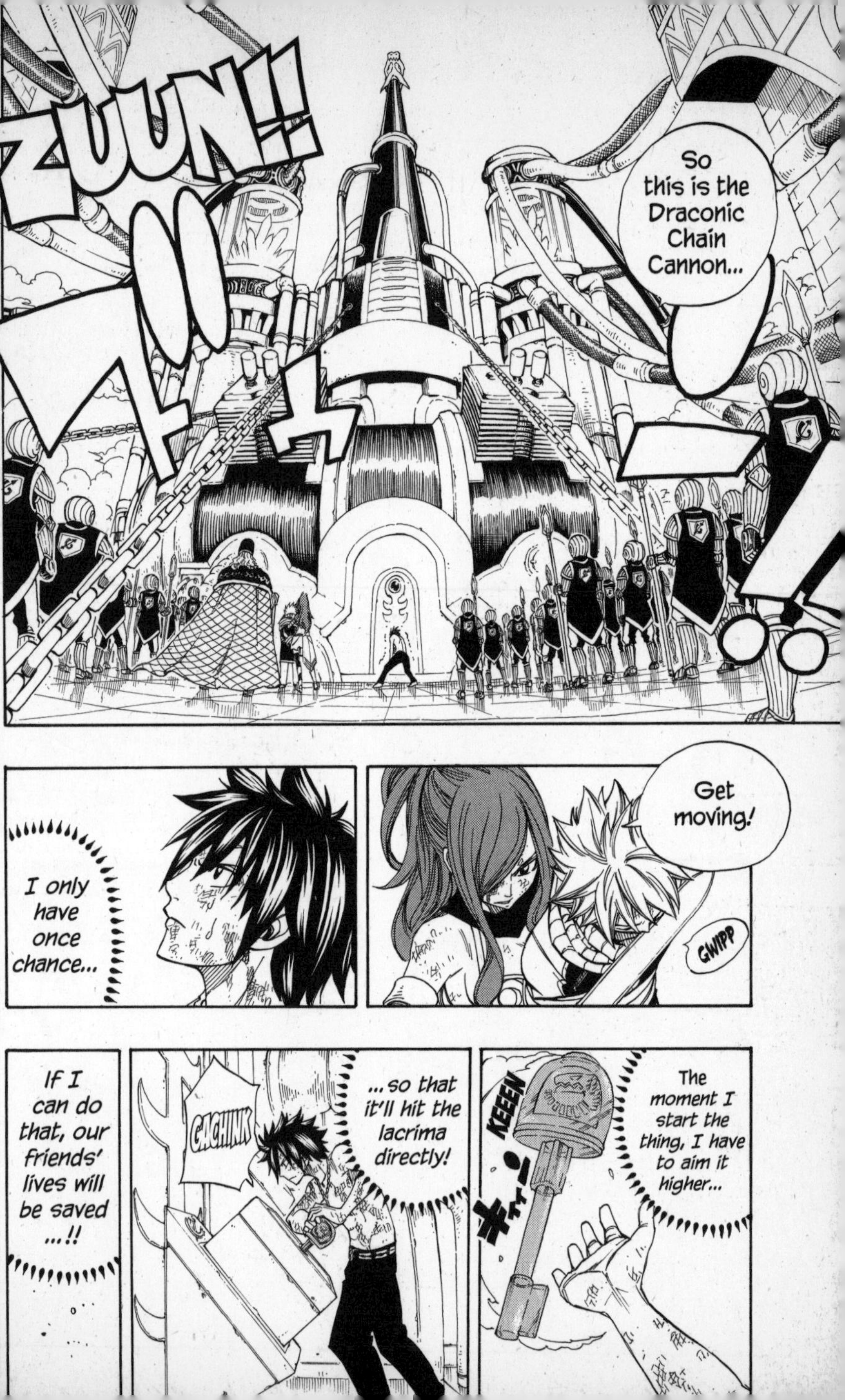
ZUUN!!
So this is the Draconic Chain Cannon...
Get moving!
GWIPP
I only have once chance...
The moment I start the thing, I have to aim it higher...
KEEEN
...so that it'll hit the lacrima directly!
GACHINK
If I can do that, our friends' lives will be saved ...!!

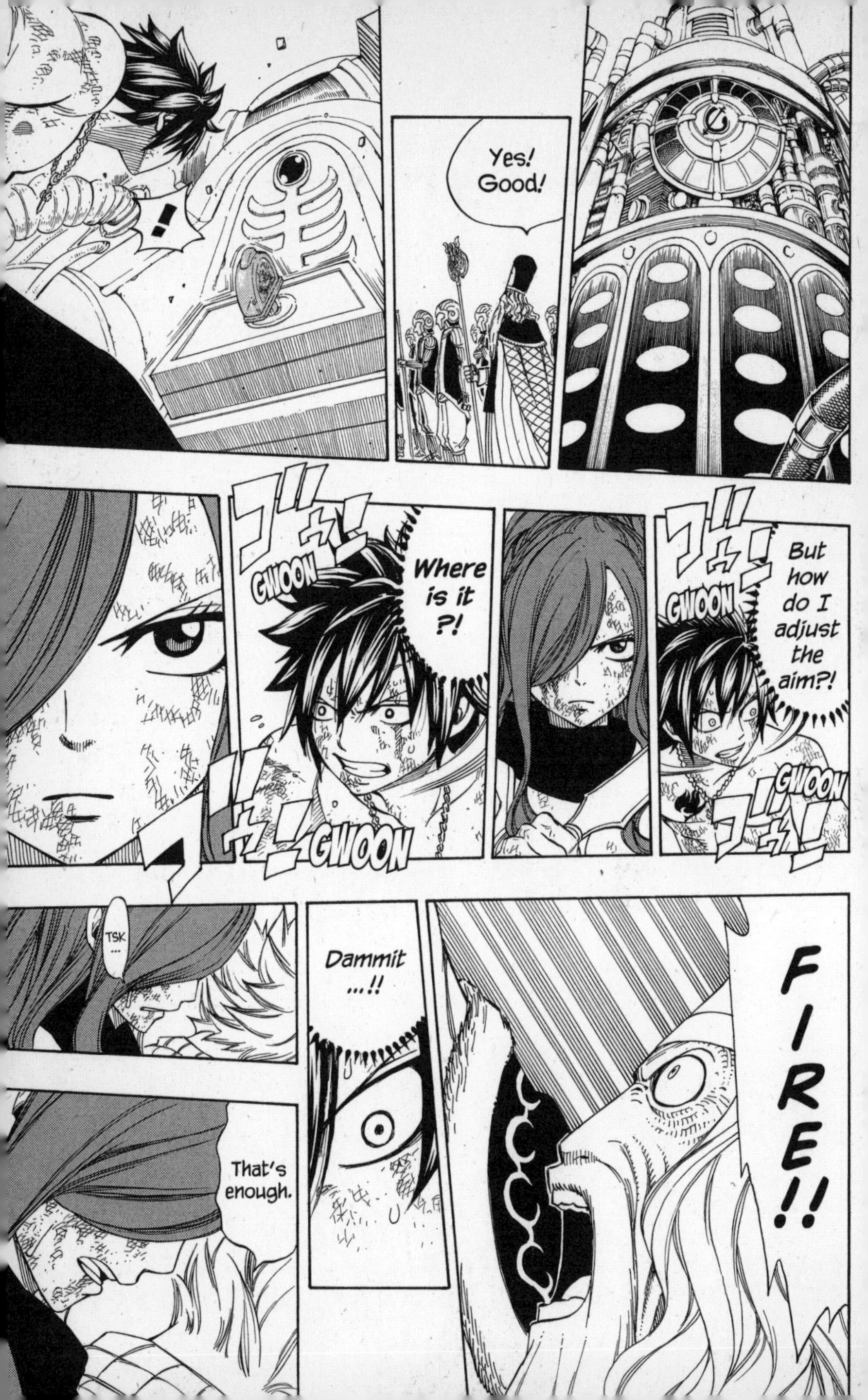
Yes! Good!
!
GWOON
But how do I adjust the aim?!
GWOON
GWOON
Where is it ?!
GWOON
FIRE!!
Dammit ...!!
TSK ...
That's enough.

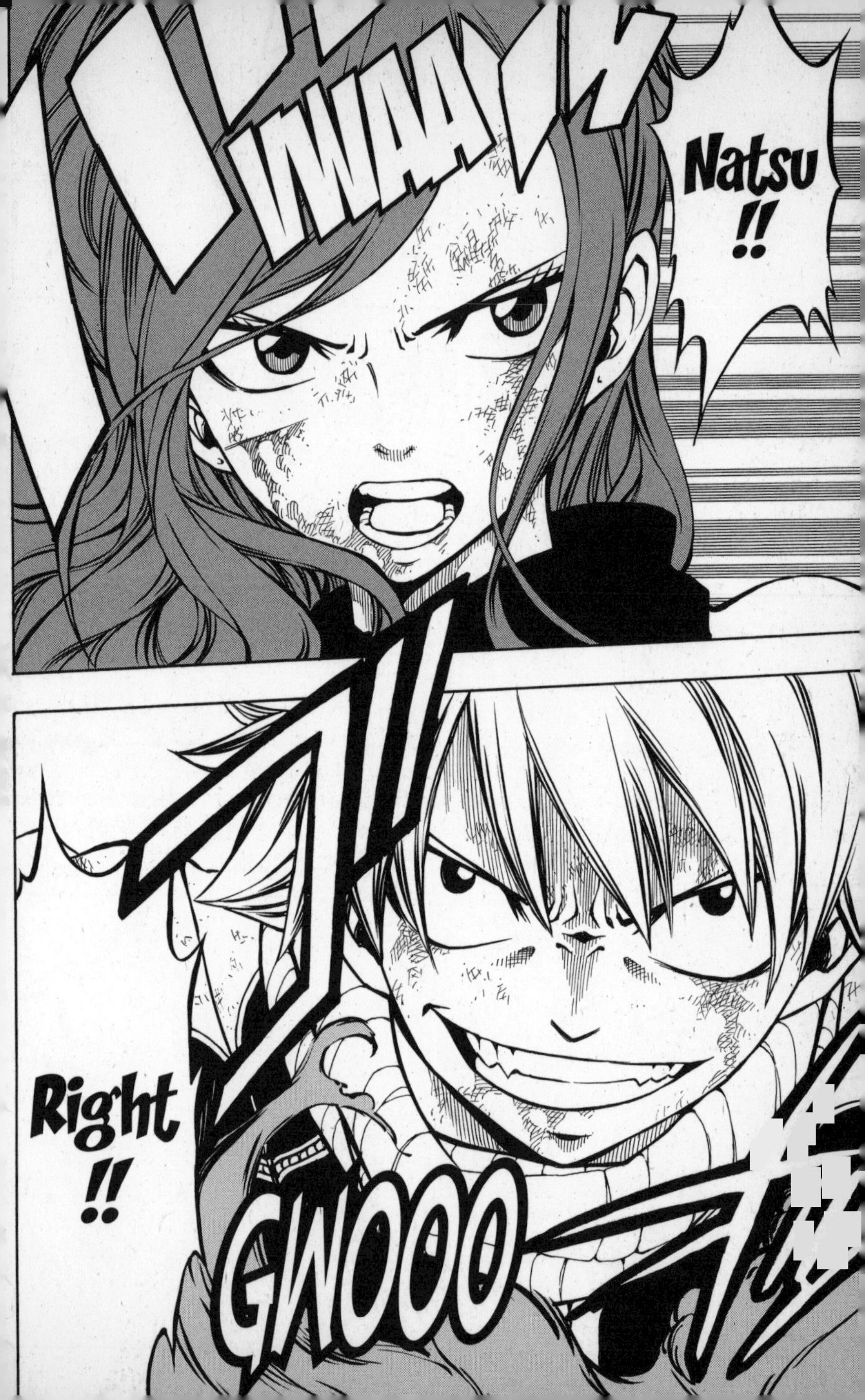
Natsu!!
Right!!
GWOOO

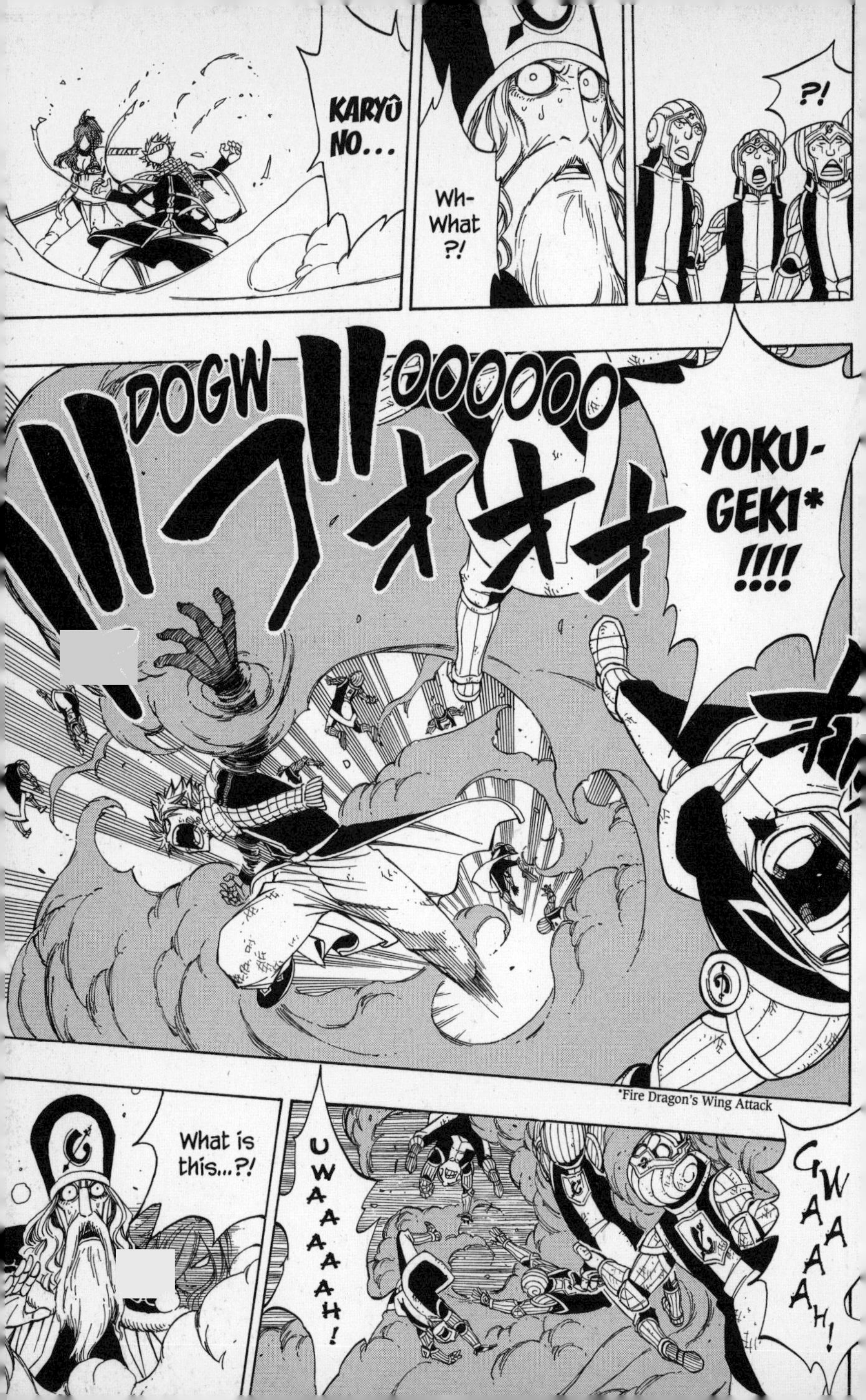
?!
Wh-What?!
KARYÛ NO...
YOKU-GEKI*!!!!
DOGWOOOOOO
*Fire Dragon's Wing Attack
GWAAAAAH!
UWAAAAAH!
What is this...?!

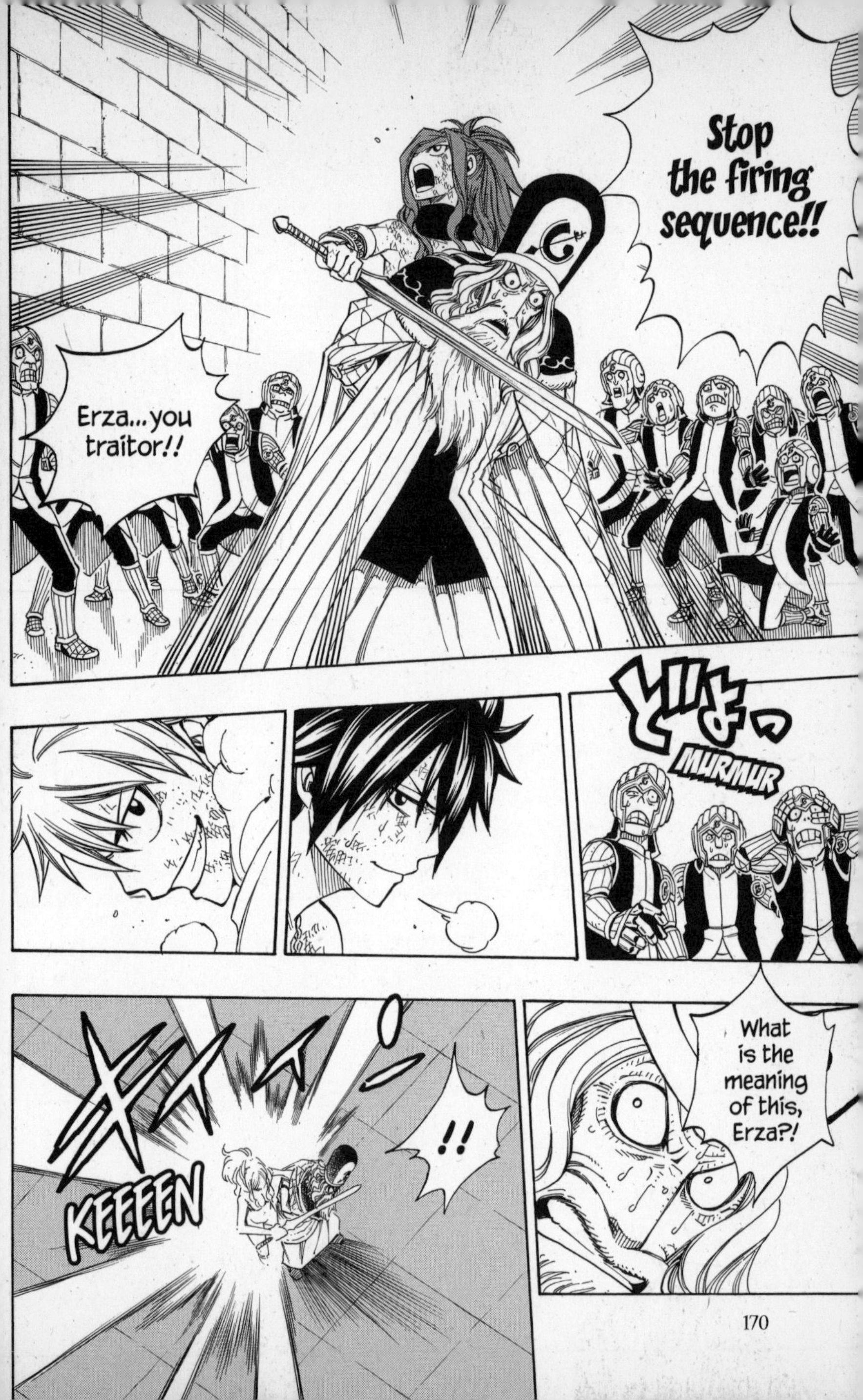
Stop the firing sequence!!
Erza...you traitor!!
MURMUR
What is the meaning of this, Erza?!
!!
KEEEEN

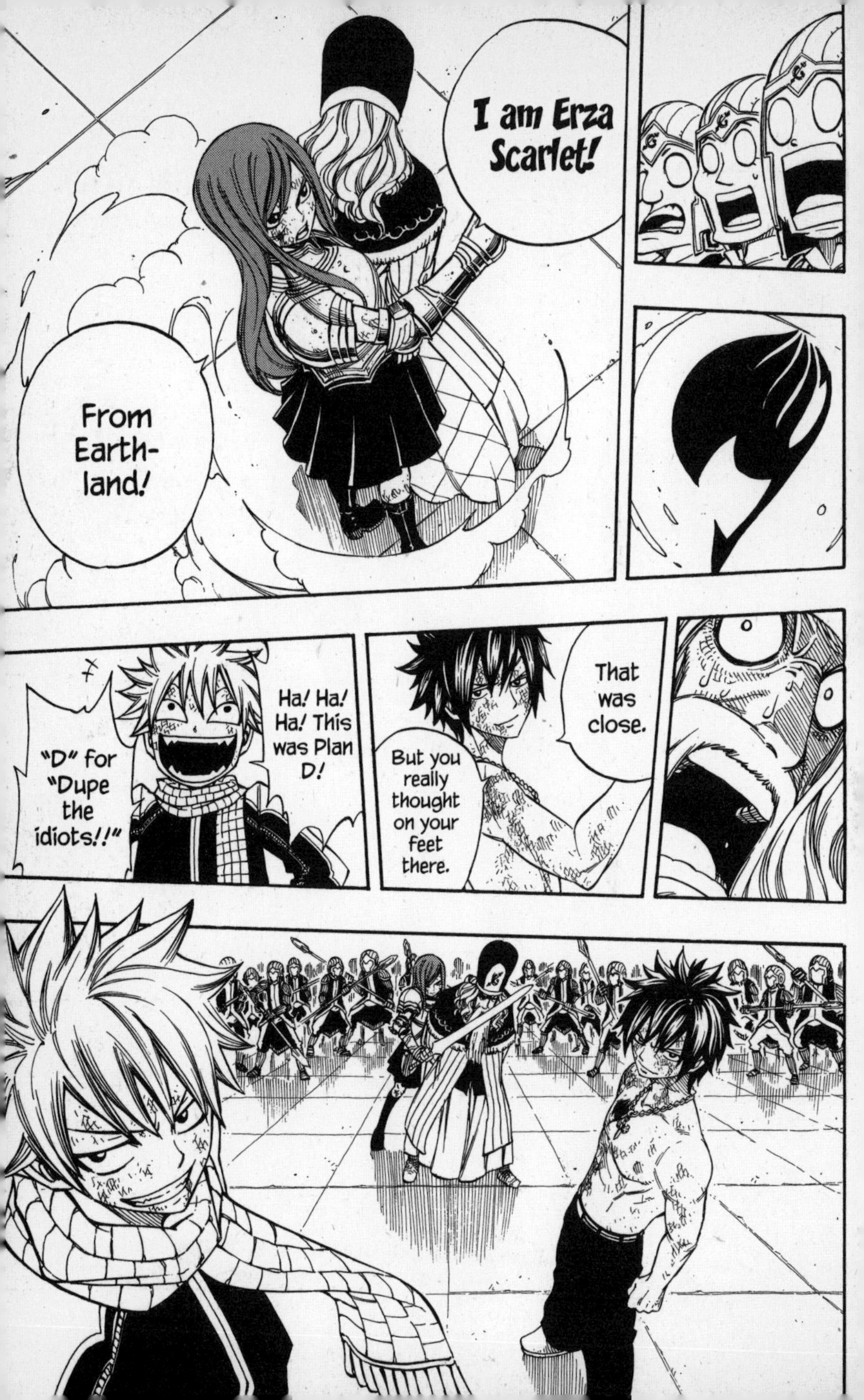
I am Erza Scarlet!
From Earth-land!
That was close.
But you really thought on your feet there.
Ha! Ha! Ha! This was Plan D!
"D" for "Dupe the idiots!!"

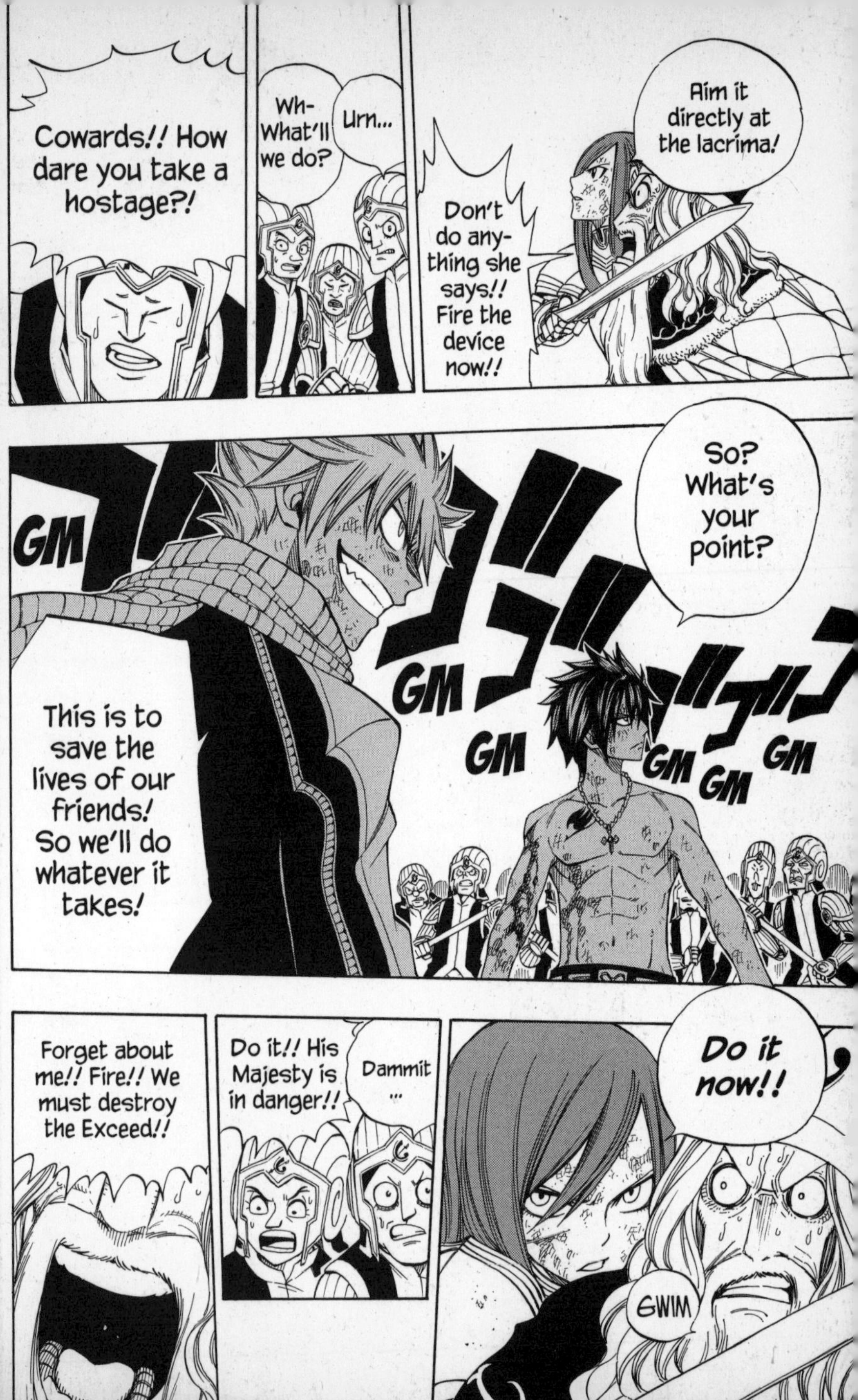
Aim it directly at the lacrima!
Don't do anything she says!! Fire the device now!!
Urn...
Wh- What'll we do?
Cowards!! How dare you take a hostage?!
So? What's your point?
GM
GM
GM
GM
GM
GM
This is to save the lives of our friends! So we'll do whatever it takes!
Do it now!!
GWIM
Dammit ...
Do it!! His Majesty is in danger!!
Forget about me!! Fire!! We must destroy the Exceed!!

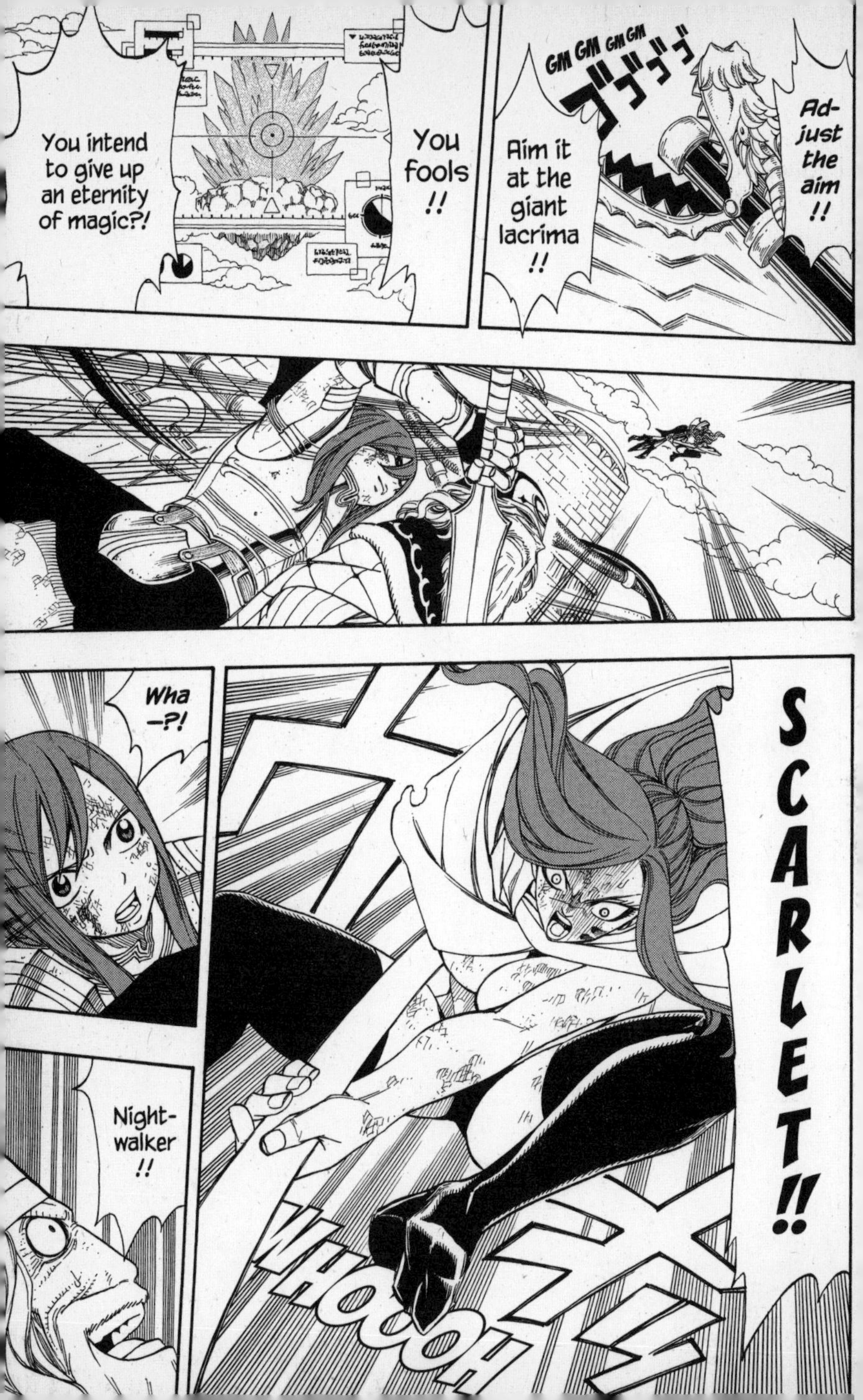
Ad-just the aim!!
GM GM GM GM
Aim it at the giant lacrima!!
You fools!!
You intend to give up an eternity of magic?!
SCARLET!!
WHOOOH
Wha-?!
Night-walker!!

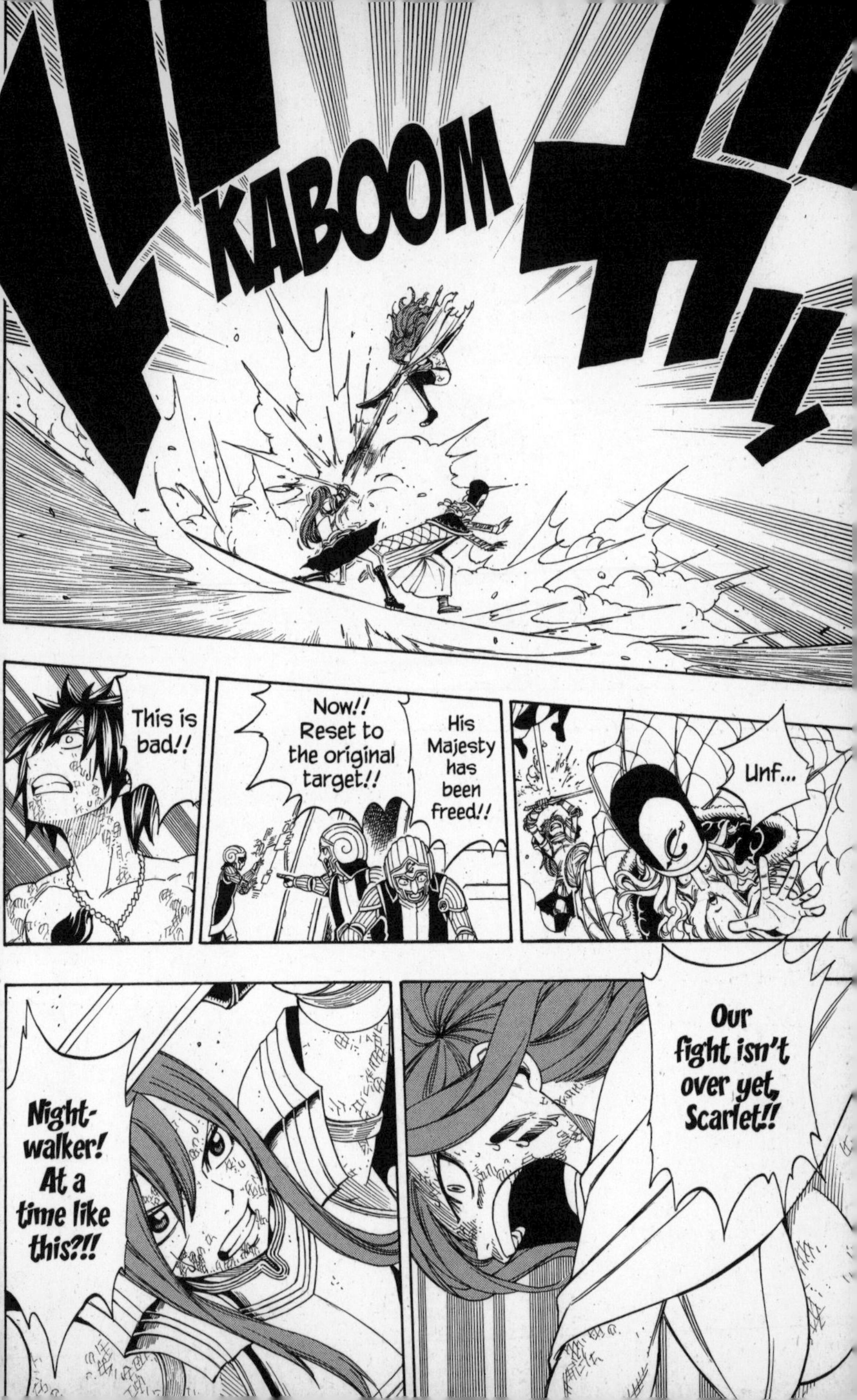
KABOOM
Unf...
His Majesty has been freed!!
Now!! Reset to the original target!!
This is bad!!
Our fight isn't over yet, Scarlet!!
Night-walker! At a time like this?!!

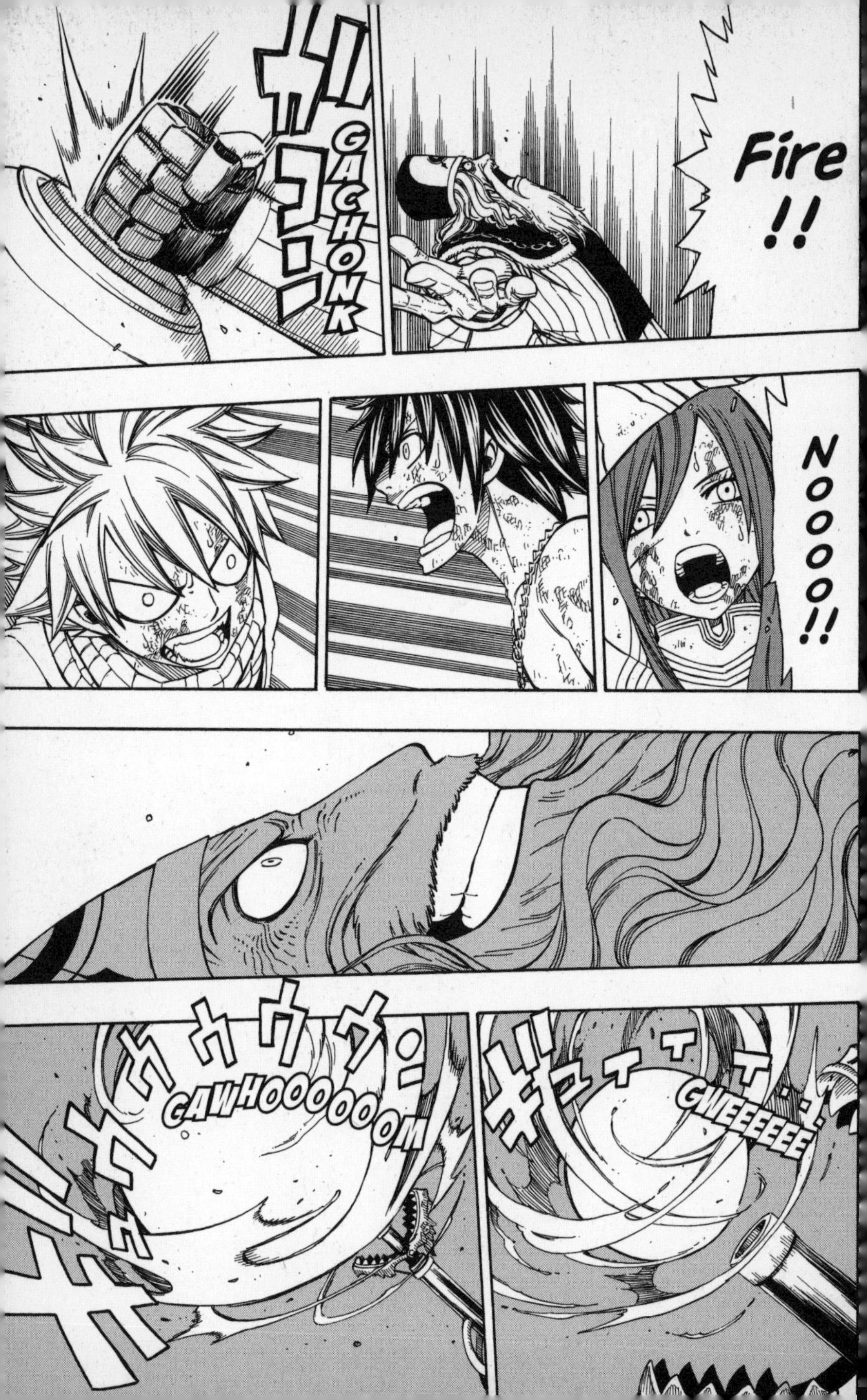
Fire!!
GACHONK
NOOOOO!!
GWEEEEEE
GAWHOOOOOOOM

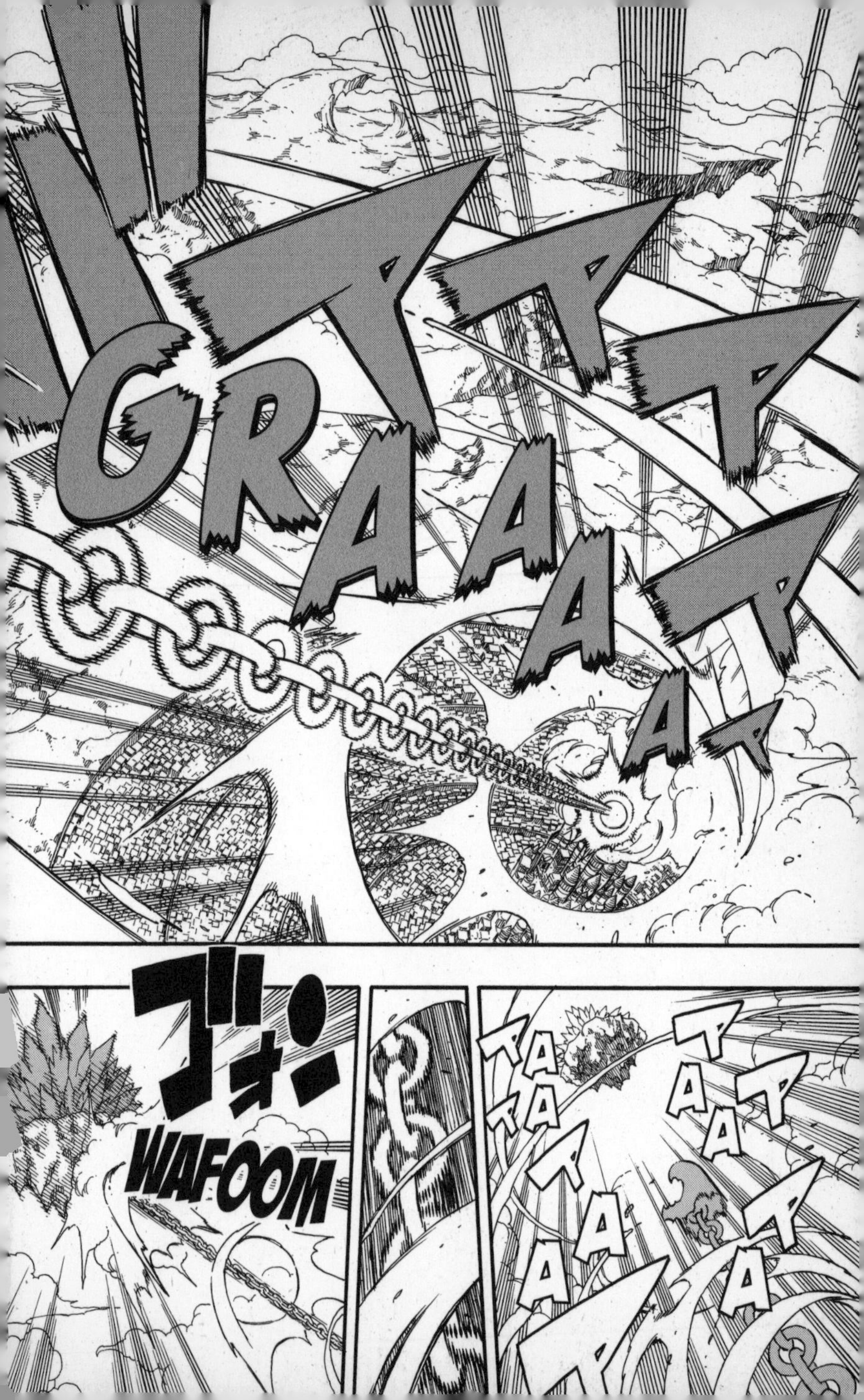
GRAAAAAAAAA
TATAAAAAA
TAATAAA
ゴォン
WAFOOM

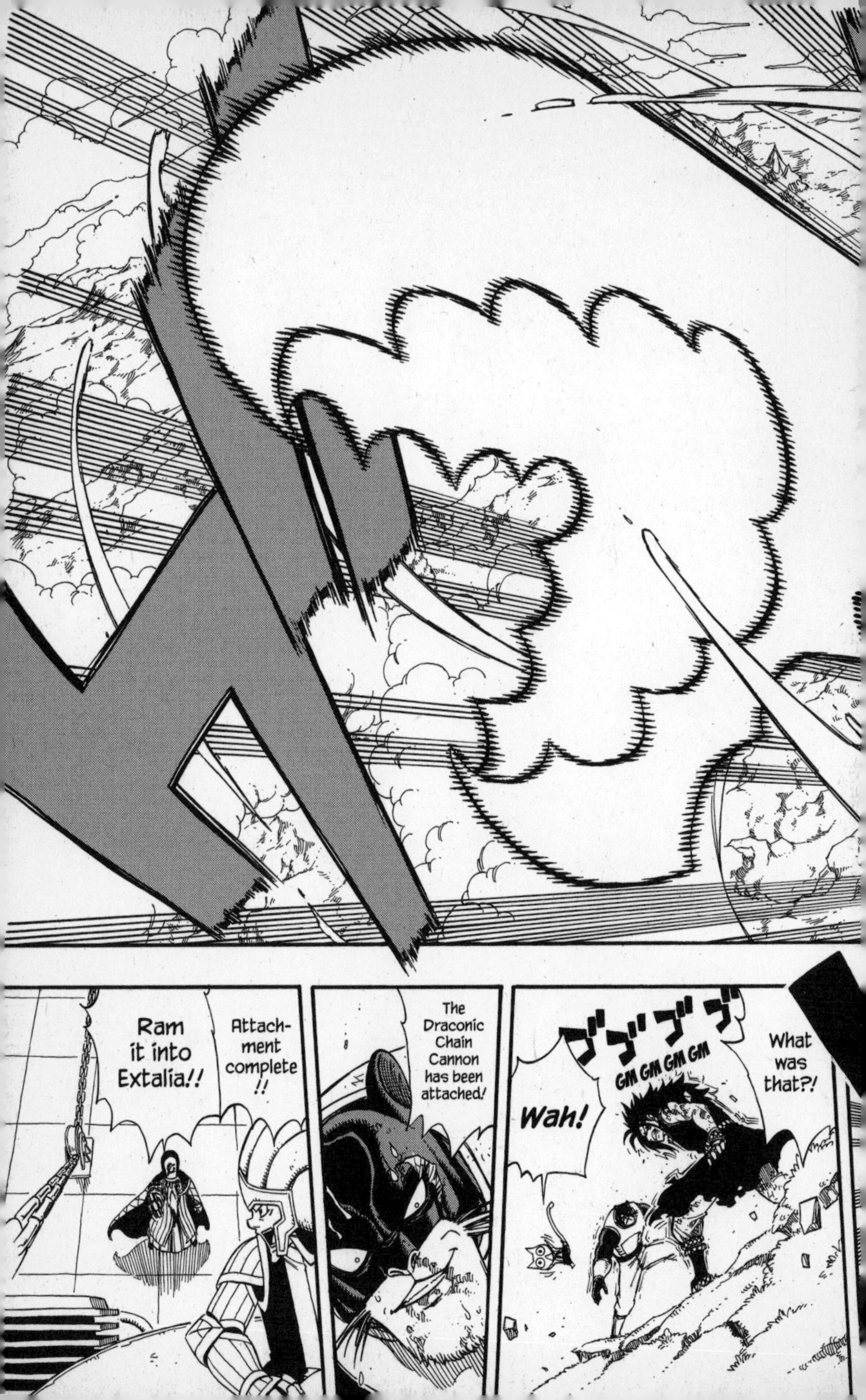
What was that?!
ゴゴゴゴ
GM GM GM GM
Wah!
The Draconic Chain Cannon has been attached!
Attach-ment complete!!
Ram it into Extalia!!

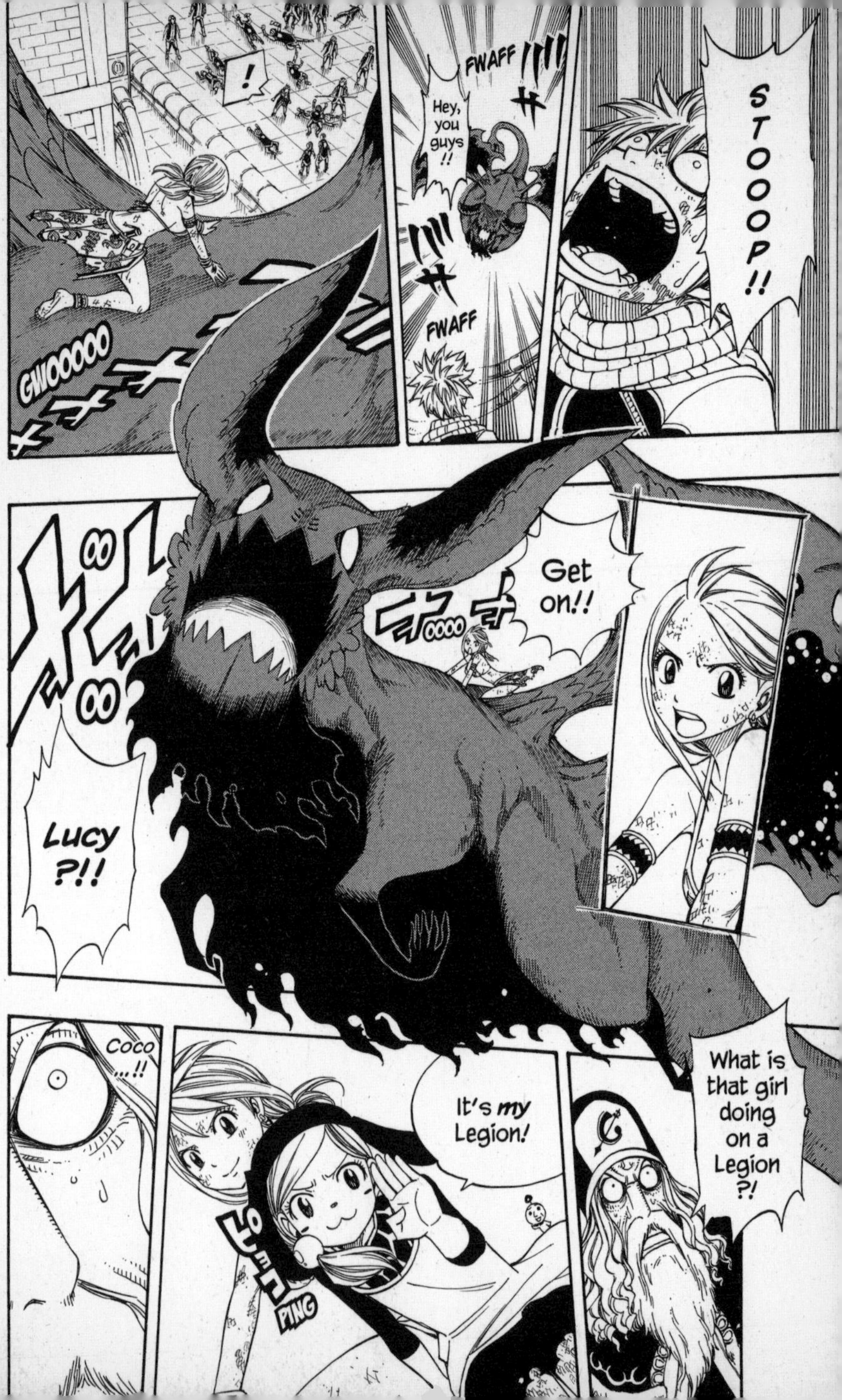
STOOOP!!
FWAFF
Hey, you guys!!
FWAFF
!
GWOOOOO
Get on!!
Lucy?!!
What is that girl doing on a Legion?!
It's *my* Legion!
PING
Coco...!!

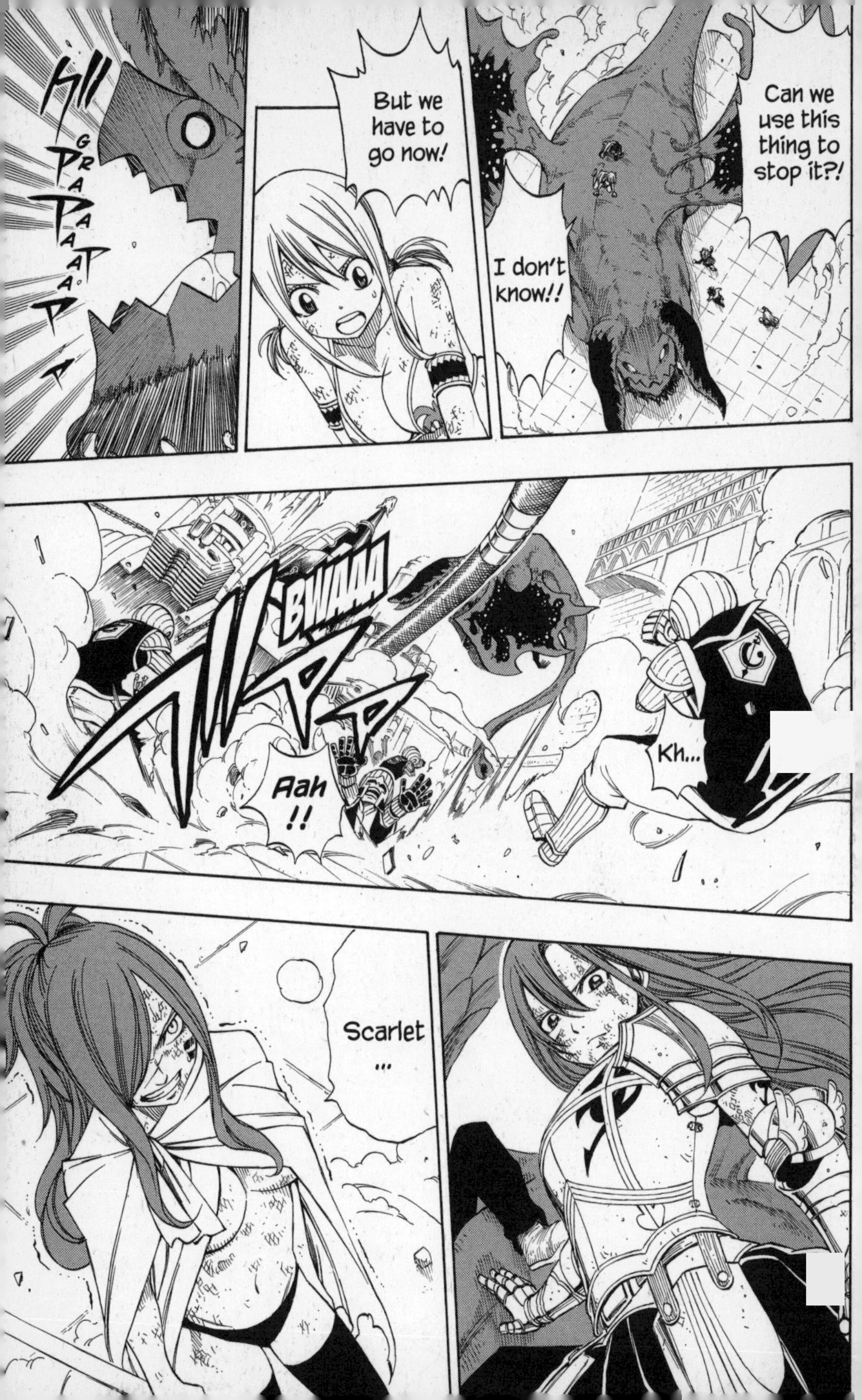
Can we use this thing to stop it?!
I don't know!!
But we have to go now!
Kh...
BWAAA
Aah !!
Scarlet ...

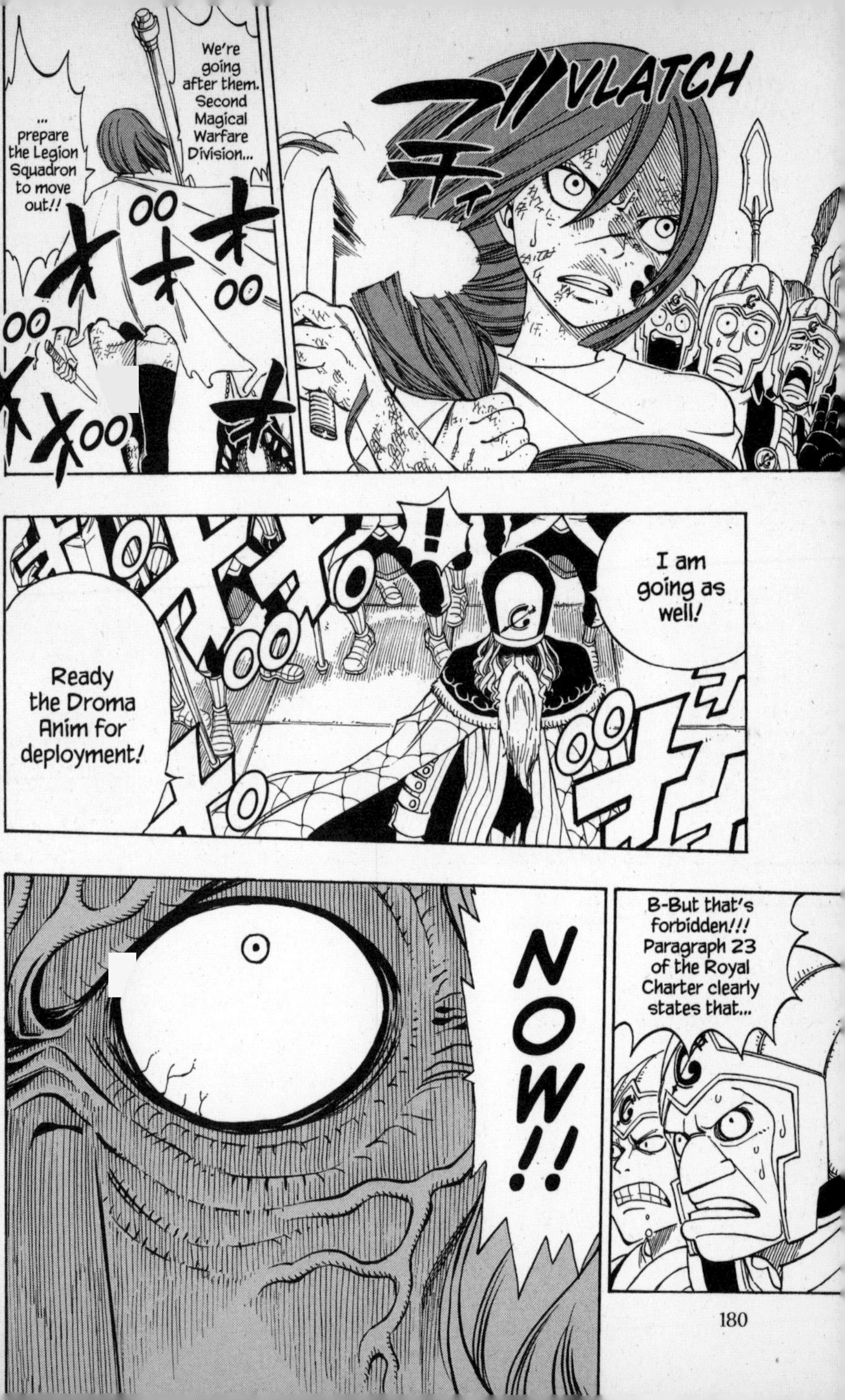
VLATCH
We're going after them. Second Magical Warfare Division...
... prepare the Legion Squadron to move out!!
OO
OO
OO
OO
I am going as well!
Ready the Droma Anim for deployment!
!!
B-But that's forbidden!!! Paragraph 23 of the Royal Charter clearly states that...
NOW!!

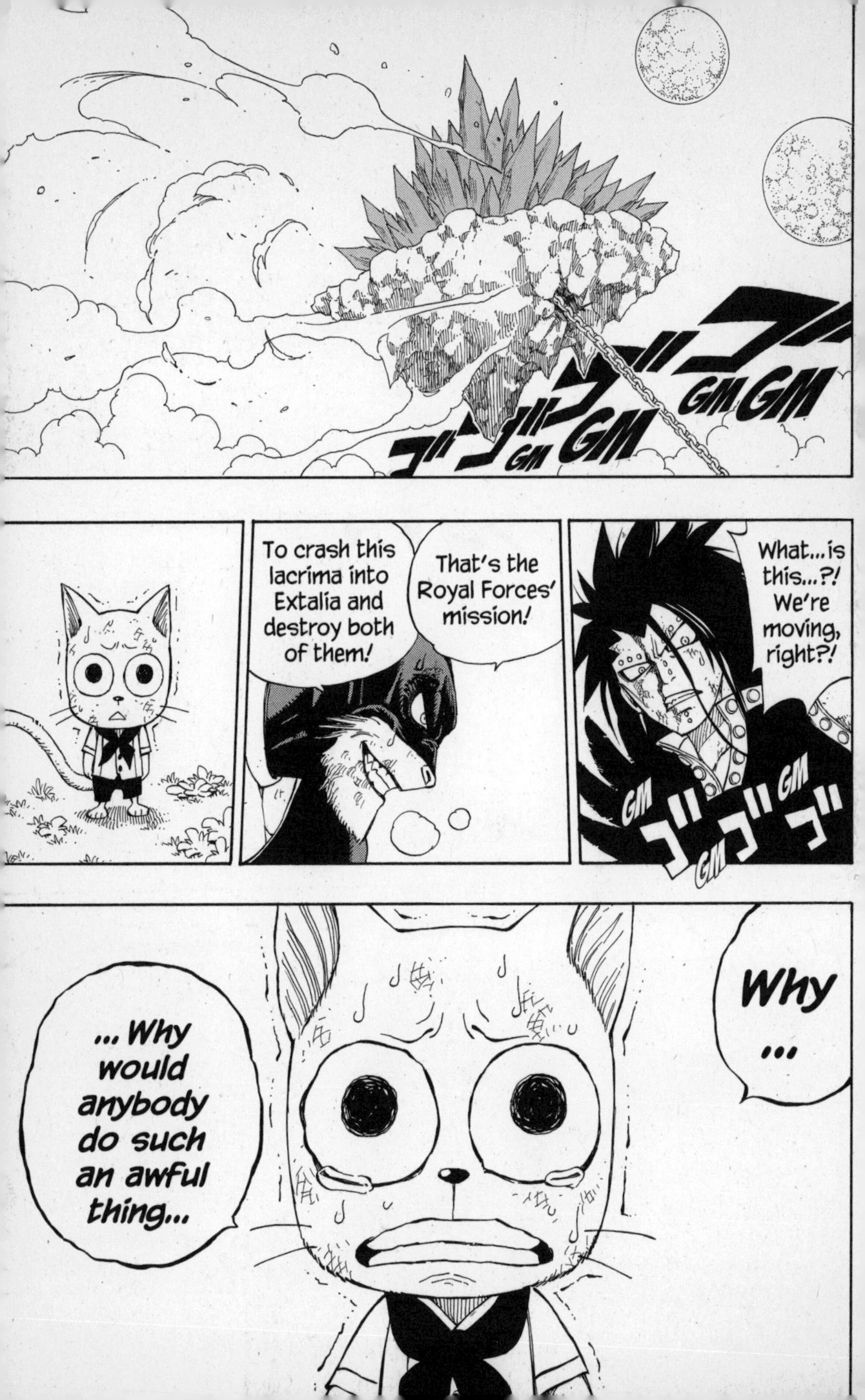
GM GM
GM GM
What...is this...?! We're moving, right?!
GM GM GM
That's the Royal Forces' mission!
To crash this lacrima into Extalia and destroy both of them!
Why...
...Why would anybody do such an awful thing...

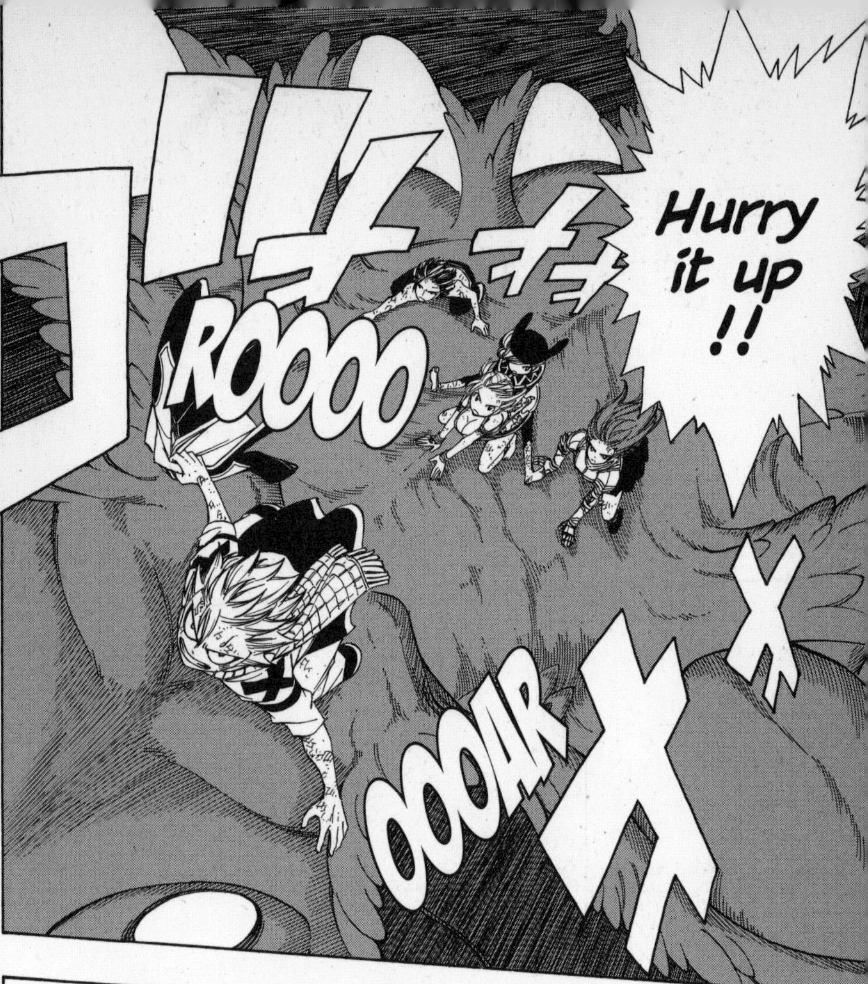
Hurry it up !!
ROOOO OOOAR
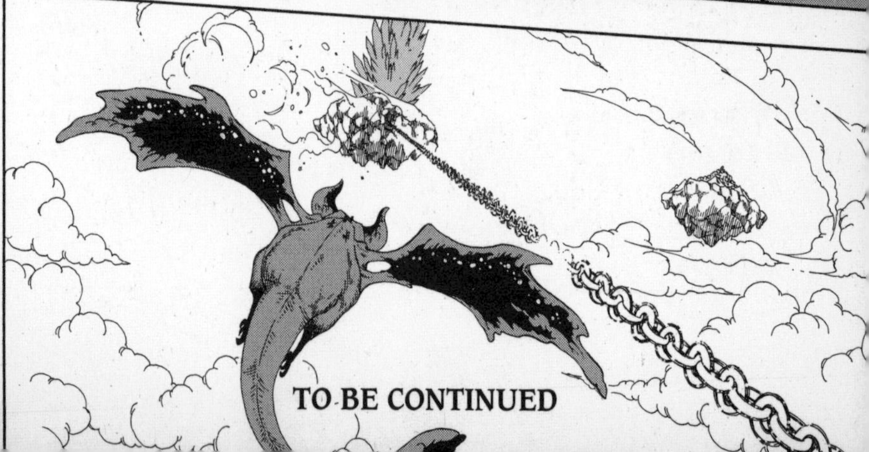
TO BE CONTINUED

FAIRY TAIL

フェアリーテイル

EXTRA

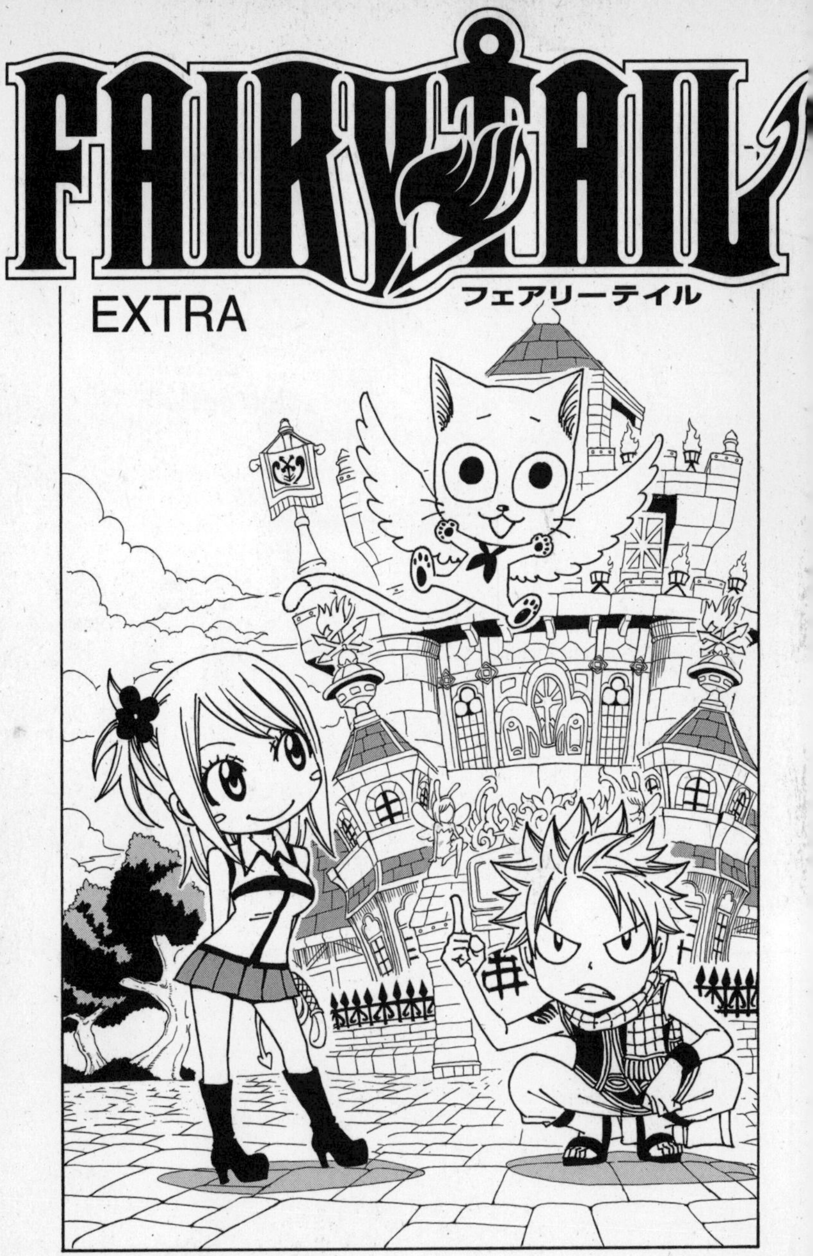

Continued from the left-hand page.

Lucy: So...her underwear, maybe?

Mira: Since it's Erza, it'd have to be the dead bodies of the monsters she's vanquished...

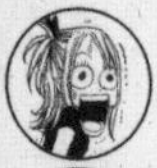: **Don't be scary!!**

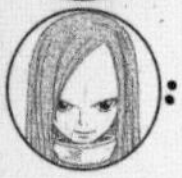: Heh! Shouldn't I be answering this question directly?

Lucy: Ah! Erza, it's been a while since you made an appearance in this corner!

Mira: All right, then what's in your luggage?

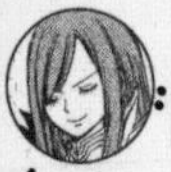: **FOOD.**

Lucy:
Mira: ...

Erza: Now, shall we proceed to the next question?

Lucy: Whoa! She just took over!

Strong Elfman had a weak Edolas counterpart. So by that logic, Strong Edolas Jet and Droy mean that the regular world guys are weak?

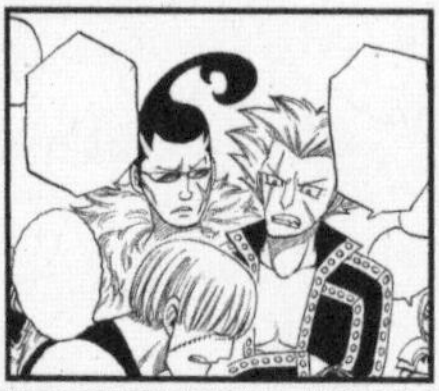

Erza: **Really weak.**

Lucy: Th-That's harsh...

Mira: Anybody would be compared to you, Erza...right?

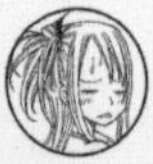: (You say that, Mira-san, but a long time ago, you were on par with Erza, right...?)

Erza: Now we read the final question.

Is this character actually necessary to the story?

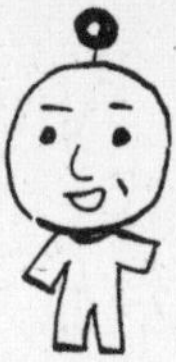

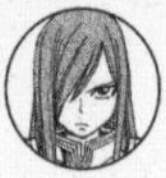: **Obviously!**

Mira: And wait, what is that anyway?

Erza: It is one of Mashima-sensei's doodles.

Lucy: It's one of those rarely seen characters that appears once in a great while in the manga.

Mira: Is it edible?

Lucy: What?! No way it'd be edible!

Erza: That is unfortunate.

Mira: It sure is! It looks especially delicious if it were spiced and deep fried.

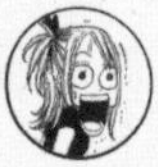: **No, it doesn't!!**

Erza: Putting that argument aside, that particular character makes an appearance in one frame of Volume 22. And it did not appear on the magazine version of the same scene. So it was added for the graphic novel volume especially.

Lucy: Added... But you said it was a doodle, right?

Mira: It must be rough on Mashima-sensei, being so busy and all.

Lucy: Don't go praising a guy for putting in a doodle!

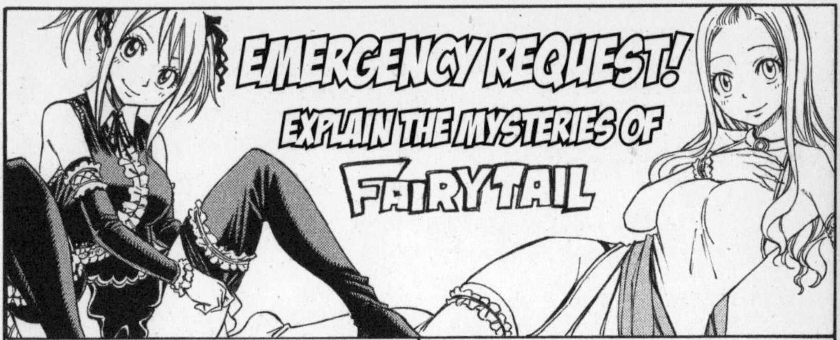

EMERGENCY REQUEST! EXPLAIN THE MYSTERIES OF FAIRY TAIL

At the Fairy Tail Counter...

: Sigh... What was with all that tedious chatter last time?

: Now, let's get started on our own tedious chatter this time!

Lucy: No! Tediousness is ***bad!!***

Mira: And the first question!

They said that the only member of Eisenwald that wasn't arrested was Erigor. What happened to him?

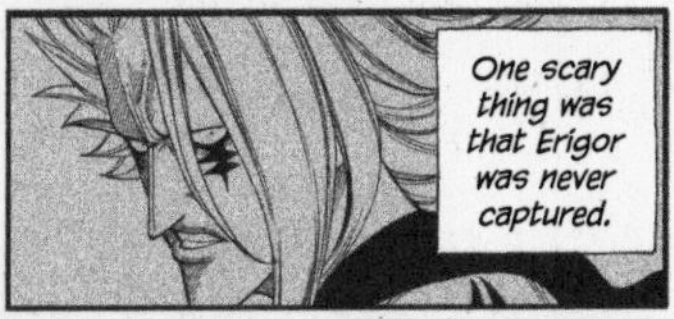
One scary thing was that Erigor was never captured.

Lucy: Oh, that. Actually there's a pretty sad story that goes along with that.

Mira: It's true that Erigor was never captured, and he was scheduled to appear in the Nirvana Arc.

: Well, it just didn't work out, so his part had to be cut. It made the author cry.

: He went and did all that work foreshadowing, but...

Volume 16, P. 117

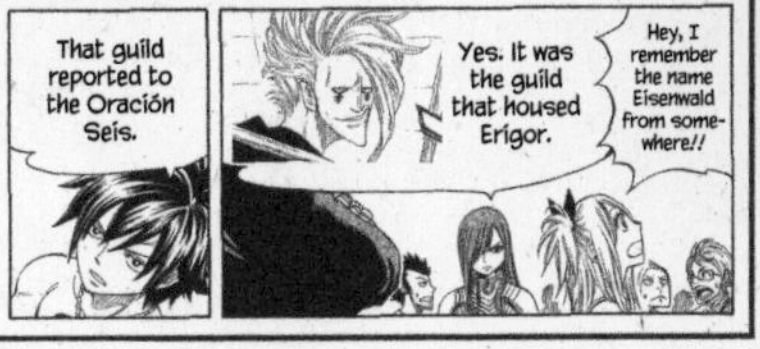
That guild reported to the Oración Seis.
Yes. It was the guild that housed Erigor.
Hey, I remember the name Eisenwald from some-where!!

Lucy: ...is how it turned out, but when the anime director was told about it, his **eyes just lit up,** so it's possible that when the episode comes to TV...

: Just possible...huh? ♡

Lucy: Now, on to the next question.

When Erza goes on a job, she always takes along a huge load of luggage. What's in it?

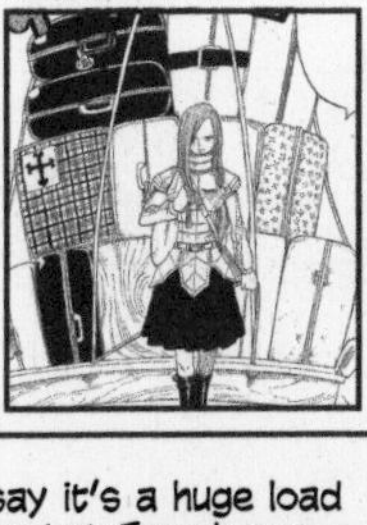

Mira: I want to say it's a huge load of her armor, but Erza keeps her stock of extra armor **in another dimension** so that can't be it.

Continued on the right-hand page.

The Fairy Tail Guild de Art is looking for illustrations! Please send in your art on a post card or at post-card size, and do it in black pen, okay? Those chosen to be published will get a signed mini poster! ♪ Make sure you write your real name and address on the back of your illustration!

TAIL de ART

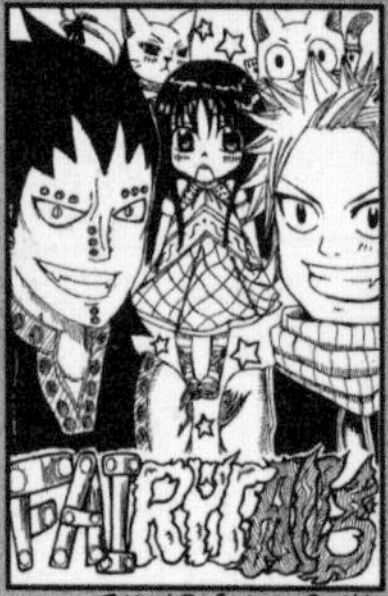
FAIRY TAIL

▼ The Three Dragon Slayers! A lot of work was put into the letters too!

Tottori Prefecture, Cynthia

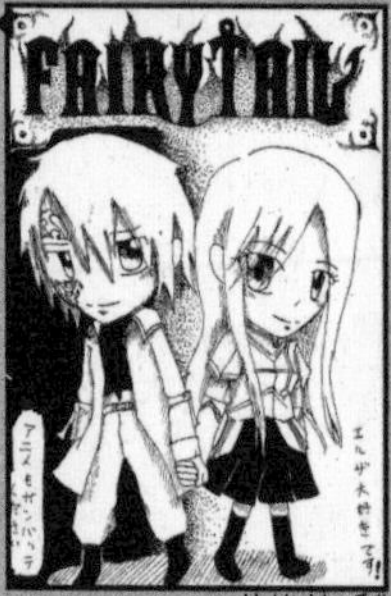
FAIRY TAIL

▼ The anime version of the Tower of Heaven arc made me cry...!

Hokkaido, Eri

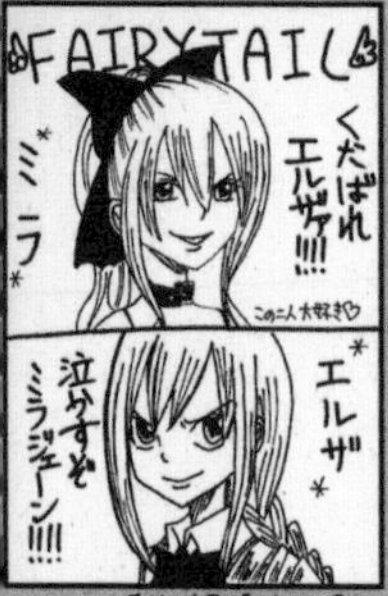
FAIRYTAIL
くたばれエルザァ!!!!
ミラ
エルザ
泣かすぞミラジェーン!!!!

▼ Erza and Mirajane of long ago. Which one of them was stronger?

Tottori Prefecture, Sora

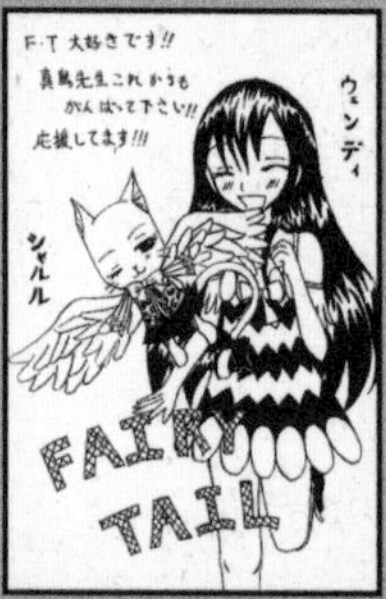
F・T 大好きです!!
真島先生これからもがんばって下さい!!
応援してます!!!
ウェンディ
シャルル
FAIRY TAIL

▼ The extremely popular Wendy and Carla. So popular, it even surprised the artist.

Chiba Prefecture, Yūya

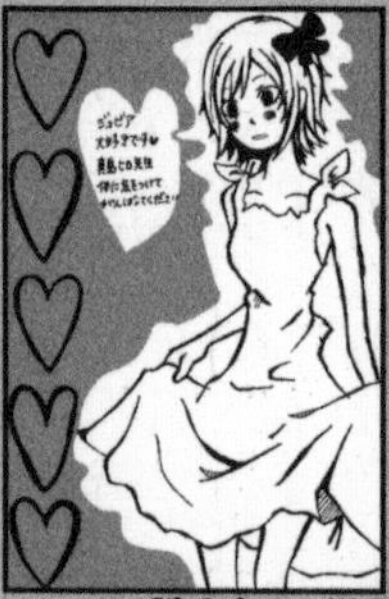

▼ Juvia looking very girlish. The one from Edolas is just scary!

Gifu Prefecture, Aki-P

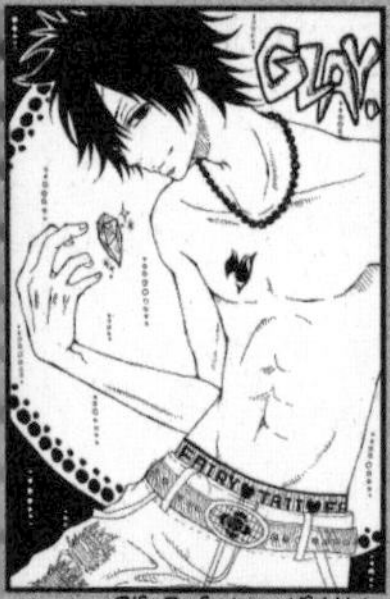
GRAY
FAIRY TAIL

▼ Ohh! Very cool!! And really well done!!

Gifu Prefecture, Yūri Hata

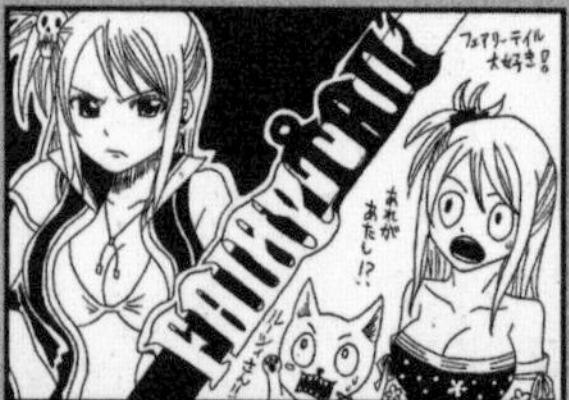
FAIRY TAIL
フェアリーテイル大好き♡
あれがあたし!?

▼ So-called "Doublucy." Which one do you like best?

Saitama Prefecture, Kazue Fujisawa

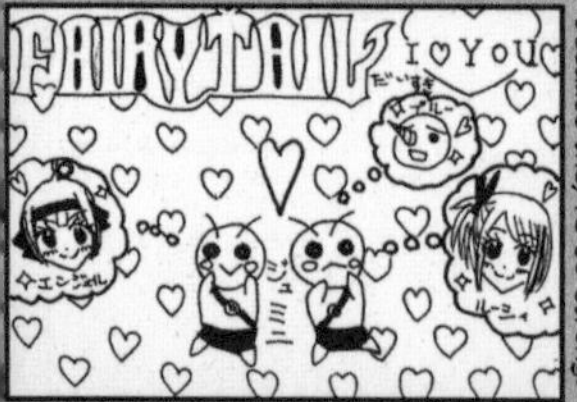
FAIRYTAIL
I ♡ YOU

▼ Gemini... They haven't appeared too much. It's because they're so strong.

Aichi Prefecture, FT Rocks!

Send to Hiro Mashima, Kodansha Comics
451 Park Ave. South, 7th Floor New York, NY 10016

FAIRY GUILD

▼ Half of each, the Earth-land and Edolas Natsus!

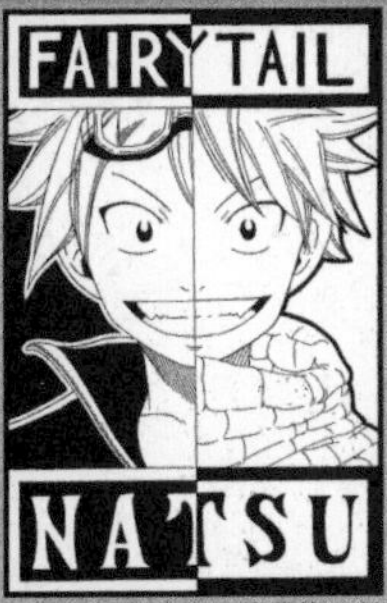
FAIRY TAIL
NATSU

Tochigi Prefecture, Reiji Katsuki

▼ Ohh! Cute clothes! ♡ I like it!

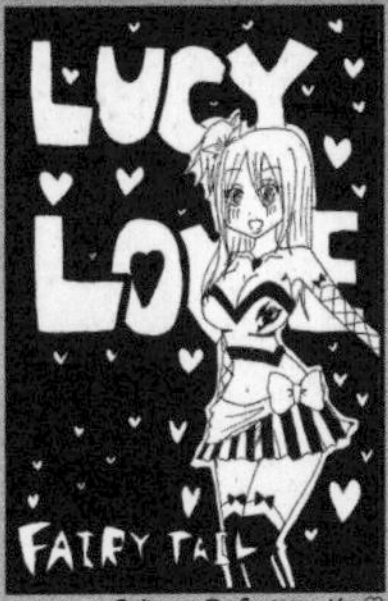
LUCY
LOVE
FAIRY TAIL

Saitama Prefecture, Yu-♡

▼ The three Fairy Tail ladies. They've all got great expressions!

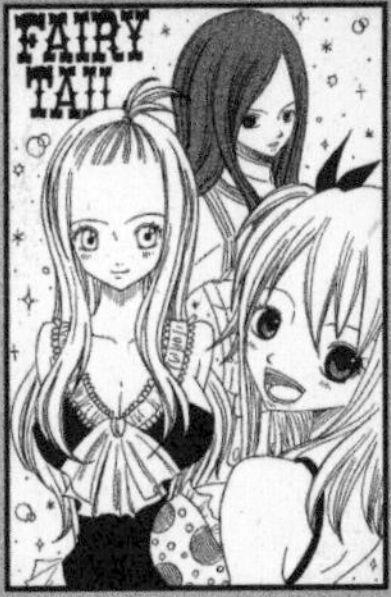
FAIRY TAIL

Mie Prefecture, Juriko Yonekawa

REJECTION CORNER

▼ Is that so...? A rejection... I-If you say so.

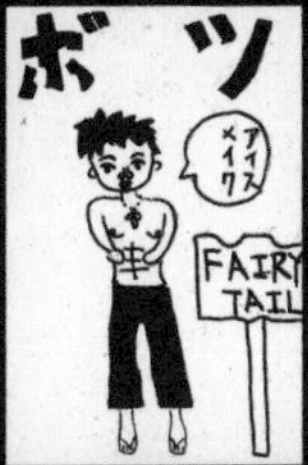
ボツ
アイスメイク
FAIRY TAIL

Kyoto, Akiho Yamamura

▼ Everyone coming together! Fight on!! This one gave me energy.

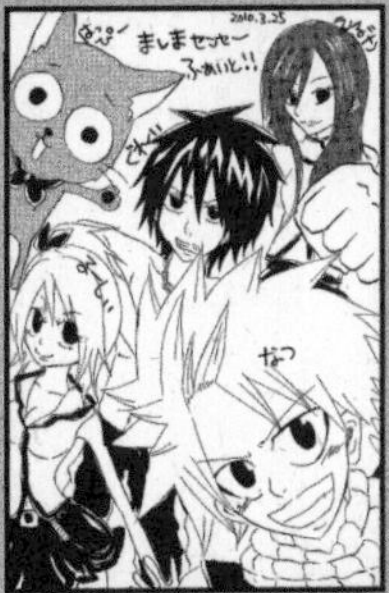

Aichi Prefecture, Rira

▼ Will these three ever meet again?

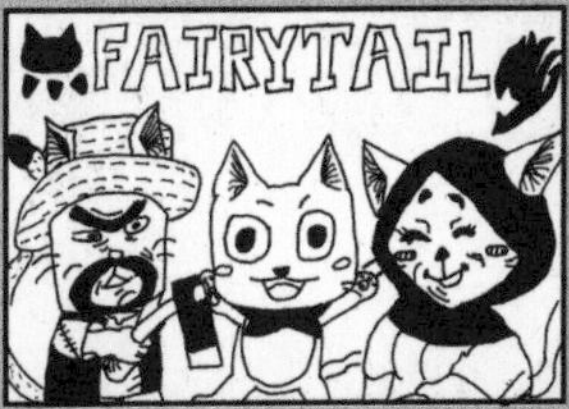
FAIRYTAIL

Tochigi Prefecture, Kenta Saito

▼ Everyone done up like dolls! They're all so cute!

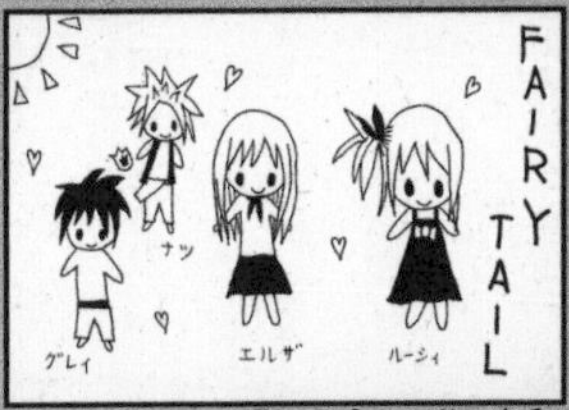
FAIRY TAIL
グレイ
ナツ
エルザ
ルーシィ

Chiba Prefecture: Happy's Egg

By sending in letters or postcards you give us permission to give your name, address, postal code and any other information you include to the author as is. Please keep that in mind.

Spot the Differences!

This image looks like the title page for Chapter 185 on page 123! But if you look very closely, you may spot differences... There are ten differences!! Can you find all of them?

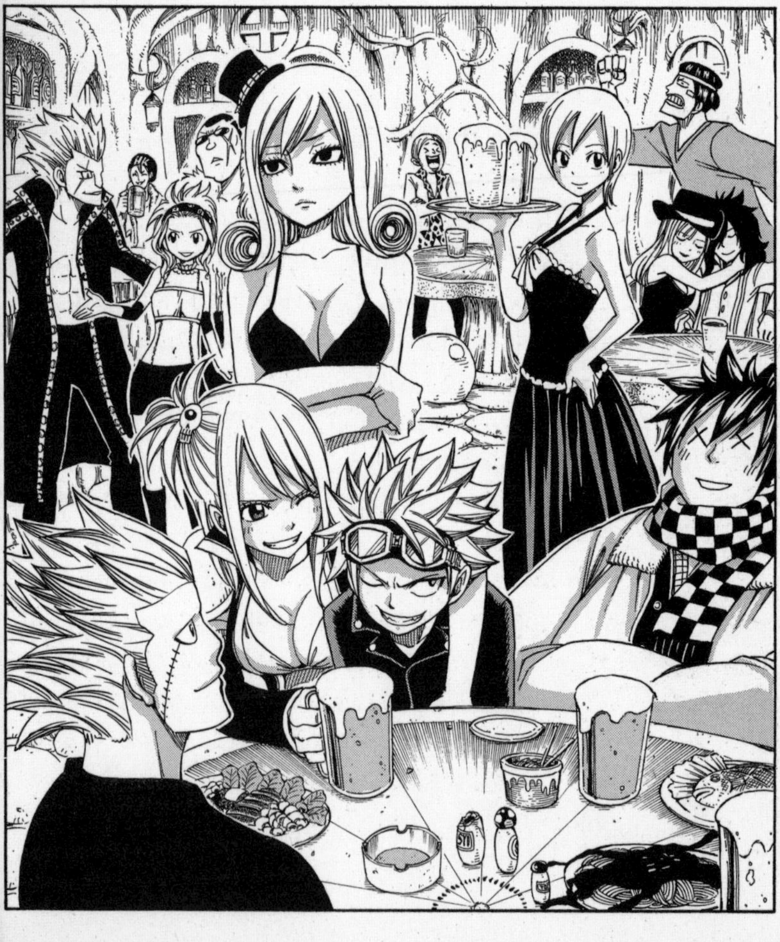

Afterword

あとがき

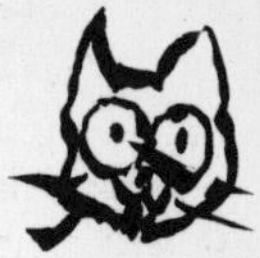

左手

(Left-handed)

I'm presently writing this afterword on June 29, 2010, one day before my scheduled trip to France. To put the time in perspective, tonight is the World Cup game between Japan and Paraguay, and after I watch that, I'm going to pack for my trip. Then, at 6 A.M. tomorrow, I take off. If you want to know why I'm going to France, there's an event held every year called the Japan Expo, and this year, I'm an invited guest! They're having a signing there! After going to Taiwan and America, this time it's on to France. Fairy Tail has gone worldwide! Actually I'm very grateful to France for awarding Fairy Tail two manga awards. It seems to be a country with quite a lot of fans. What with one thing and another, on the day before I was going off to France, I thought of having a signing here in Japan. Or to be more accurate, I really felt a desire to meet my Japanese fans. All the Japanese readers are always doing their best to cheer me on, and I want to express my thanks. That's true of all the other countries too. There are a lot of people in many countries around the world who I want to meet, and that includes everyone in Japan too.
So, next time in this space, my France Trip Diary…maybe?

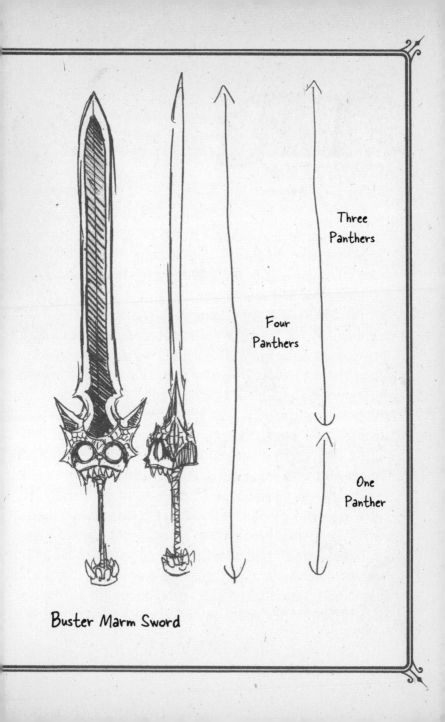

Three
Panthers

Four
Panthers

One
Panther

Buster Marm Sword

FAIRY TAIL 22

フェアリーテイル

Panther Lily's Weapon

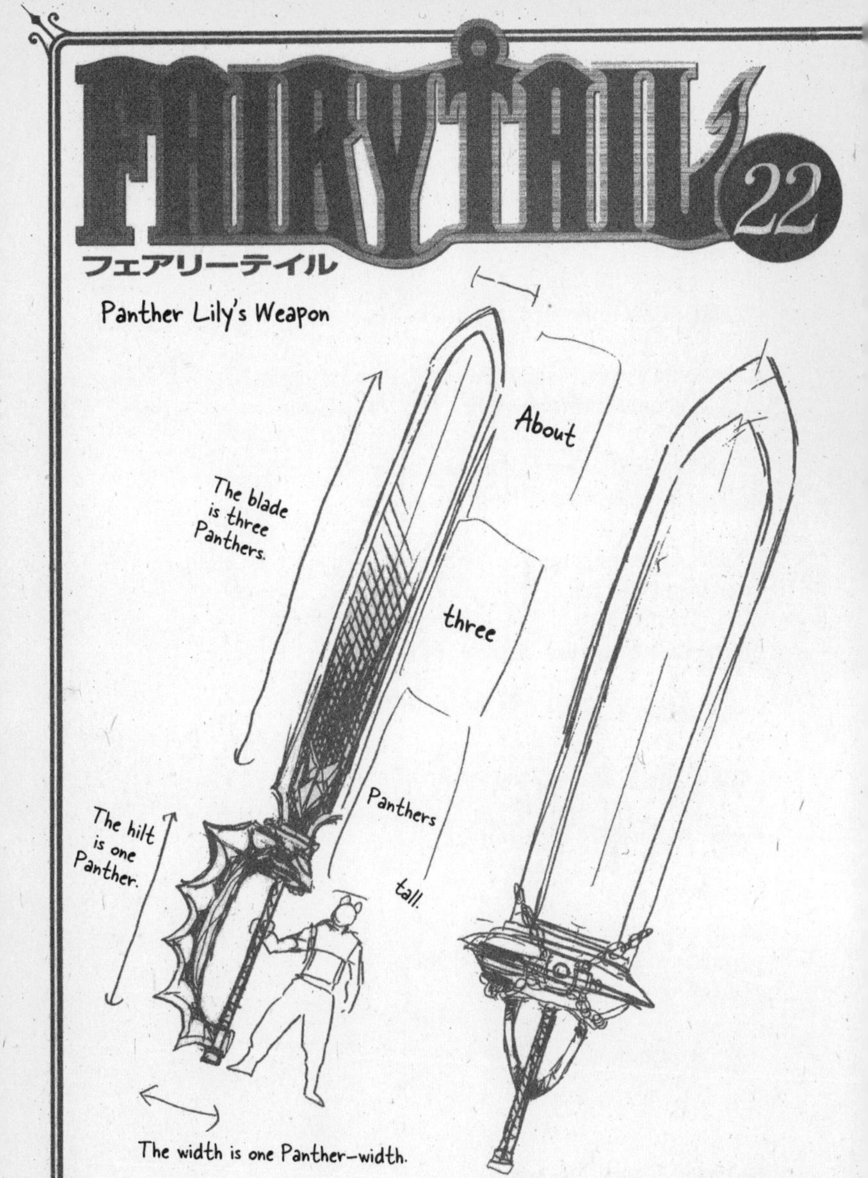
About
three
Panthers
tall.
The blade is three Panthers.
The hilt is one Panther.
The width is one Panther-width.

HIRO MASHIMA

Fairy Tail volume 22 is a work of fiction. Names, characters, places, and incidents are the products of the author's imagination or are used fictitiously. Any resemblance to actual events, locales, or persons, living or dead, is entirely coincidental.

A Kodansha Comics Trade Paperback Original

Published in the United States by Kodansha Comics, an imprint of Kodansha USA Publishing, LLC, New York.

Publication rights for this English edition arranged through Kodansha Ltd., Tokyo.

First published in Japan in 2010 by Kodansha Ltd., Tokyo

ISBN 978-1-61262-059-6

Printed in the United States of America

www.kodanshacomics.com

9 8 7 6 5 4 3 2 1

Translator/Adapter: William Flanagan
Lettering: AndWorld Design